Virginia 1619

Virginia 1619

Slavery and Freedom in the Making of English America

Edited by
PAUL MUSSELWHITE, PETER C. MANCALL,
and JAMES HORN

Published by the
OMOHUNDRO INSTITUTE OF
EARLY AMERICAN HISTORY AND CULTURE,
Williamsburg, Virginia,
and the
UNIVERSITY OF NORTH CAROLINA PRESS,
Chapel Hill

The editors and publishers gratefully acknowledge the generous support for this book from Dartmouth College and from American Evolution, the 2019 Commemoration.

The Omohundro Institute of Early American History and Culture is sponsored by the College of William and Mary. On November 15, 1996, the Institute adopted the present name in honor of a bequest from Malvern H. Omohundro, Jr.

© 2019 The Omohundro Institute of Early American History and Culture
All rights reserved
Manufactured in the United States of America

Cover illustration: Copper Alloy Finds from James Fort. Courtesy, Jamestown Rediscovery (Preservation Virginia)

Library of Congress Cataloging-in-Publication Data
Names: Musselwhite, Paul, editor. | Mancall, Peter C., editor. | Horn, James P. P., editor.
Title: Virginia 1619 : slavery and freedom in the making of English America / edited by Paul Musselwhite, Peter C. Mancall, and James Horn.
Description: Williamsburg, Virginia : Published by the Omohundro Institute of Early American History and Culture ; Chapel Hill : The University of North Carolina Press, [2019] | Includes bibliographical references and index. | "Although this volume centers on the events of a sweltering summer in the Chesapeake Tidewater, it began life in the mountains of northern New England. It grew out of a conference hosted at Dartmouth College in the spring of 2017 . . ." —Acknowledgments page.
Identifiers: LCCN 2018058603| ISBN 9781469652016 (cloth : alk. paper) | ISBN 9781469651798 (pbk : alk. paper) | ISBN 9781469651804 (ebook)
Subjects: LCSH: Virginia—History—Colonial period, ca. 1600-1775. | Virginia—Politics and government—To 1775. | African Americans—Virginia—History—17th century. | Indians of North America—Virginia—History—17th century. | Slavery—Virginia—History—17th century. | Democracy—United States—History.
Classification: LCC F229 .V835 2019 | DDC 975.5/01—dc23 LC record available at https://lccn.loc.gov/2018058603

The University of North Carolina Press has been a member of the Green Press Initiative since 2003.

Acknowledgments

Although this volume centers on the events of a sweltering summer in the Chesapeake tidewater, it began life in the mountains of northern New England. It grew out of a conference hosted at Dartmouth College in the spring of 2017. The conference was generously funded by the Dartmouth Conference Fund, which was established by the gift of Fannie and Alan Leslie. We are extremely grateful to all those at Dartmouth who helped to organize the conference, particularly Gail Patten and Courtney Hardy. The papers presented at the conference were honed and sharpened by the rich and collegial dialogue over two days in Hanover. We would particularly like to thank Warren Billings, Amy Turner Bushnell, Colin Calloway, John Coombs, Linda Heywood, Emily Rose, and James Walvin for their many critical contributions to the discussion.

Bringing this volume to press in such a speedy fashion has relied upon the generosity and efficiency of all the contributors, but also particularly the organization and flexibility of the staff at the Omohundro Institute of Early American History and Culture. Paul Mapp and Nadine Zimmerli offered extremely helpful feedback on the manuscript, and Nadine and Cathy Kelly have shepherded it through the production process, keeping us on schedule through each step. Becky Wrenn and Ginny Chew have edited the essays with an amazing combination of haste and thoroughness. Jonathan Chipman has dedicated many hours to drawing the wonderful maps of far-flung locales according to the different requirements of our authors. Cynthia Ingham has also provided invaluable assistance in organizing and indexing. The publication of this volume has also been supported by Jamestown Rediscovery and American Evolution, the 2019 Commemoration.

Contents

Acknowledgments v

Introduction
JAMES HORN *and* PAUL MUSSELWHITE
1

Before 1619
PETER C. MANCALL
22

"The Savages of Virginia Our Project"
The Powhatans in Jacobean Political Thought
LAUREN WORKING
42

Race, Conflict, and Exclusion in Ulster, Ireland, and Virginia
NICHOLAS CANNY
60

Virginia Slavery in Atlantic Context, 1550 to 1650
PHILIP D. MORGAN
85

Bermuda and the Beginnings of Black Anglo-America
MICHAEL J. JARVIS
108

"Poore Soules"
Migration, Labor, and Visions for Commonwealth in Virginia
MISHA EWEN
133

Private Plantation
The Political Economy of Land in Early Virginia
PAUL MUSSELWHITE
150

"A Part of That Commonwealth Hetherto
Too Much Neglected"
*Virginia's Contested "Publick" and the
Origins of the General Assembly*
ALEXANDER B. HASKELL
173

The Company-Commonwealth
ANDREW FITZMAURICE
193

"These Doubtfull Times, between Us and the Indians"
Indigenous Politics and the Jamestown Colony in 1619
JAMES D. RICE
215

Brase's Case
*Making Slave Law as Customary Law in
Virginia's General Court, 1619–1625*
PAUL D. HALLIDAY
236

Virginia and the Amazonian Alternative
MELISSA N. MORRIS
256

From John Smith to Adam Smith
*Virginia and the Founding Conventions of English
Long-Distance Settler Colonization*
JACK P. GREENE
282

Notes on the Contributors 309

Index 311

Virginia 1619

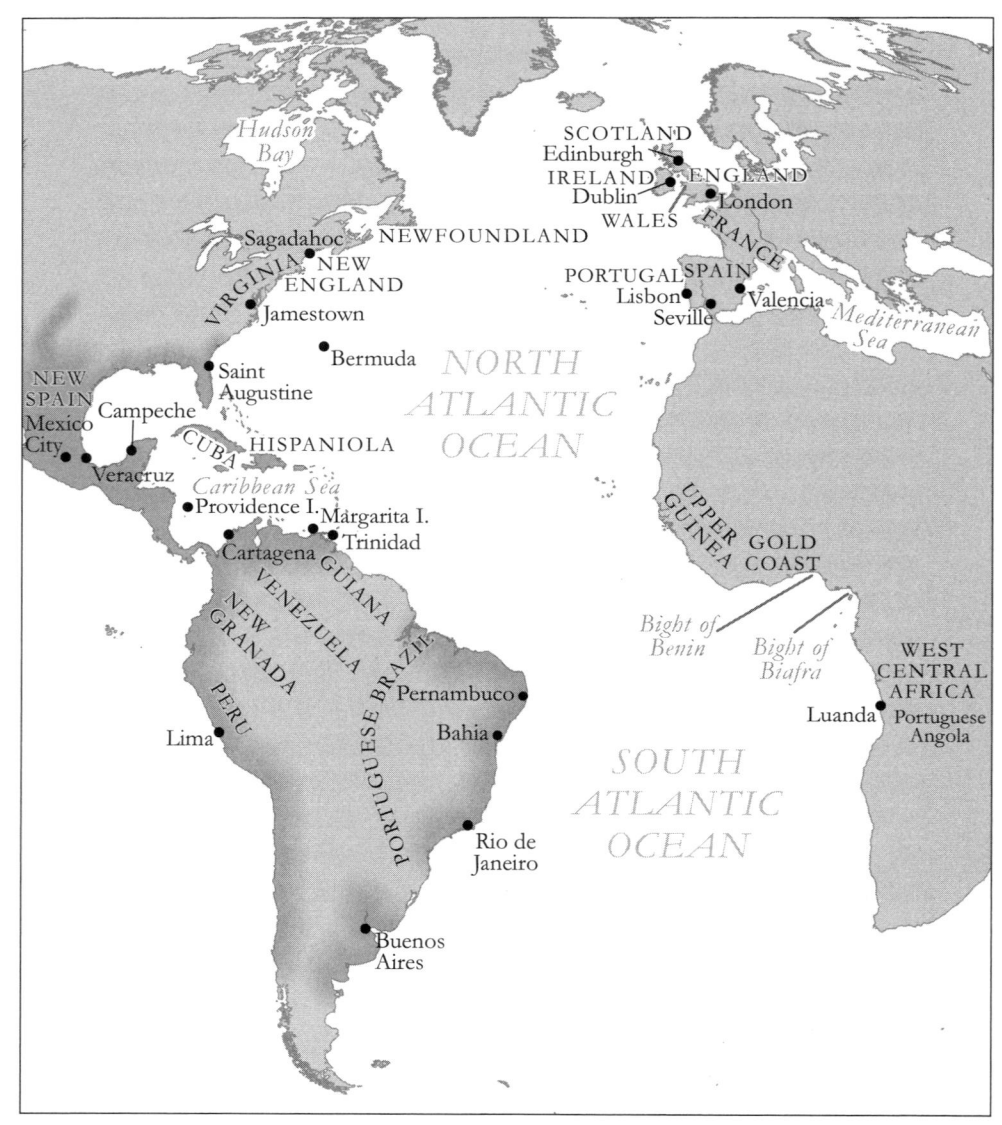

The Atlantic World in 1619. Drawn by Jonathan W. Chipman

Introduction

JAMES HORN *and* PAUL MUSSELWHITE

In the summer of 1616, John Rolfe sat down to write a brief description of Virginia. He had recently arrived in London accompanied by his wife, Rebecca, better known as the Indian "princess" Pocahontas (daughter of the great Powhatan chief Wahunsonacock), their baby son, Thomas, Pocahontas's sister Matachanna, and her husband, Uttamatomakkin, an adviser to Opechancanough, the Powhatan war chief and Wahunsonacock's de facto successor. Traveling with them were another half dozen or so Powhatans, young and old, including several women of marriageable age who the English hoped might be persuaded to convert to Christianity and wed suitable Englishmen; a Spanish spy, Don Diego de Molina, who spent five years in captivity at Jamestown; and the tough military commander and deputy governor of Virginia, Sir Thomas Dale. All had sailed from Jamestown on the warship *Treasurer,* captained by the experienced mariner Samuel Argall. The *Treasurer* would return to Jamestown the following year, bringing Argall back to begin a tempestuous tenure as deputy governor. It would come again to the shores of the Chesapeake in 1619, this time in consort with the *White Lion,* carrying a cargo of captive Africans. Those voyages lay in the future. But the future was a topic on the minds of all the *Treasurer*'s passengers in 1616.[1]

Besides being one of the strangest collections of travelers to cross the Atlantic in this period, the backgrounds of the voyagers, their reasons for going to England, and their political and commercial networks offer revealing insights into the complexity and variety of interactions that characterized the emergence and latency of English America. Dale, for example, had arrived in Virginia in 1611 in the midst of a devastating war against the Powhatans. Serving as high marshal responsible for prosecuting hostilities, he had been recommended for the position by Sir Robert Cecil, first earl of Salisbury, and Sir Henry Wriothesley, third

---

1. George Lord Carew to Sir Thomas Roe, June 1616, and John Chamberlain to Sir Dudley Carleton, June 22, 1616, both in Alexander Brown, *The Genesis of the United States* . . . , 2 vols. (Boston, Mass., 1890), II, 789–790; Susan Myra Kingsbury, ed., *The Records of the Virginia Company of London,* 4 vols. (Washington D.C., 1906–1935) (hereafter cited as *RVC*), III, 70, 243, 251.

earl of Southampton, politically powerful and immensely wealthy men who were leading figures in the Virginia Company of London, the financial sponsor and governing authority of the colony. Dale had expanded strict martial laws, enacted to control unruly settlers and enforce law and order; these laws would later prompt intense criticism of company leaders' treatment of settlers in these years. At an especially low ebb in the fortunes of the colony, he had succeeded in avoiding what would have been a disastrous defeat at the hands of the Powhatans, which might well have led to the end of the enterprise, and had eventually secured peace with the great chief, symbolized by the marriage of John Rolfe and Pocahontas in April 1614. Believing the English and Indians were now "firmly united together, and made one people," Dale and the company looked forward with confidence to the steady and "infinit" profits they had promised investors but that had so far proved elusive. "I have seen the best countries in Europe," he told Sir Thomas Smythe, treasurer of the Virginia Company, in his usual blunt manner, but "I protest unto you, before the Living God, put them all together, this country will be equivalent unto them if it be inhabitant with good people." He had introduced incentives for settlers to produce a range of crops and commodities that would increase productivity and encourage a diverse economy—industrial goods such as pitch, tar, and potash as well as crops such as sassafras, silk grass, hemp, and tobacco. Anyone could grow it, planter and secretary of the colony Ralph Hamor wrote of tobacco, and he assured his readers that it would provide sufficient profit for the planter's needs with little labor. On arriving back in Plymouth, England, in early June 1616, Dale reported with satisfaction that he had left the colony "in great prosperytye and pease [peace] contrarye to manye mens Exspectatyon." If his boast was somewhat inflated, there can be little doubt his influence on the fledgling colony had been huge and would have a highly significant bearing on what was shortly to come.[2]

---

2. Ralph Hamor, *A True Discourse of the Present State of Virginia*, introduction by A. L. Rowse (1615; rpt. Richmond, Va., 1957), 24, 41 ("firmely united"), 58 ("infinit"); Thomas Dale to Sir Thomas Smith, June 1613, and John Rolfe, "A True Relation of the State of Virginia," both in Edward Wright Haile, ed., *Jamestown Narratives: Eyewitness Accounts of the Virginia Colony: The First Decade, 1607–1617* (Champlain, Va., 1998), 757 ("best countries" and "protest"), 877; Sir Thomas Dale to Sir Thomas Smith, June 1613, Dale to Sir Ralph Winwood, June 3, 1616, both in Brown, *Genesis*, II, 639, 783 ("great prosperytye"); Kingsbury, ed., *RVC*, I, 267; John Smith, *The Generall Historie of Virginia, New-England, and the Summer Isles . . .* (1624), in Philip L. Barbour, ed., *The Complete Works of Captain John Smith (1580–1631)*, 3 vols. (Williamsburg, Va., and Chapel Hill, N.C., 1986), II, 239; Darrett B. Rutman, "The Historian and the Marshal: A Note on the Background of Sir Thomas Dale," *Virginia Magazine of History and Biography*, LXVIII (1960), 284–294; Rutman, "The Virginia Company and Its Military Regime," in Rutman, ed., *The Old Dominion: Essays for Thomas Perkins Abernethy* (Charlottesville, Va., 1964), 1–20; David H. Flaherty, ed., *For the Colony in Virginea Britannia; Lawes Divine, Morall, and Martiall, etc.*, comp. William Strachey (Charlottesville, Va., 1969); David Thomas Konig, "'Dale's Laws' and the Non-Common Law Origins of Criminal Justice in Virginia," *American*

Another passenger who harbored hopes for the colony's future was John Rolfe. Upon his return to England, Rolfe wrote *A True Relation of the State of Virginia* to memorialize Dale's achievements and to provide additional proof of Virginia's promise at what Virginia Company leaders clearly recognized as a critical moment. *A True Relation* was a candid assessment of Virginia in 1616 and consequently offered a reliable snapshot of the colony three years before the company's comprehensive reforms were launched and the first Africans arrived in the Chesapeake Bay.[3] Five English settlements were scattered along the James River and one across the Chesapeake Bay, where a saltworks was located. Several settlements were given over to raising corn and cattle; others specialized in the production of industrial goods, such as Bermuda Nether Hundred on the south bank of the James River, where fully a third of the colony's population lived, the majority of whom were company laborers contracted for three years to produce pitch, tar, potash, and charcoal. A few miles downriver, two dozen men were employed in cultivating tobacco. In all, 351 colonists, mostly young men, resided in Virginia, a small number, Rolfe admitted, "to advaunce so greate a *Worke*." Hence, the most pressing need was the recruitment of "good and sufficient men," the high ranking to command, soldiers to defend the colony from invasion and to make discoveries, and farmers, craftsmen, and laborers to promote profitable enterprises. With such men, Rolfe was confident Virginia would become self-reliant in corn and other supplies, valuable mines might be found inland, and towns, fortifications, and shipping promoted. Many things "might come with ease to establishe a firme and perfect Common-weale," he concluded.[4]

Journal of Legal History, XXVI (1982), 354–375; J. Frederick Fausz, "The Powhatan Uprising of 1622: A Historical Study of Ethnocentrism and Cultural Conflict" (Ph.D. diss., College of William and Mary, 1977), 267–285; Fausz, "An 'Abundance of Blood Shed on Both Sides': England's First Indian War, 1609–1614," *VMHB*, XCVIII (1990), 3–56.

3. John Rolfe, *A True Relation of the State of Virginia Lefte by Sir Thomas Dale Knight in May Last 1616* (1951; rpt. Charlottesville, Va., 1971), xvi–xxi, 12; Smith, *Generall Historie*, in Barbour, ed., *Complete Works*, II, 219; David B. Quinn, *Explorers and Colonies: America, 1500–1625* (London, 1990), 418; Lorri Glover and Daniel Blake Smith, *The Shipwreck That Saved Jamestown: The Sea Venture Castaways and the Fate of America* (New York, 2008), 90–95, 124–170, 186–189. Rolfe might plausibly be described as a truly Atlantic figure. After being caught in a hurricane only a few hundred miles from the American coast that led to the shipwreck of the passengers and crew of the *Sea Venture* on Bermuda for ten months, he had arrived in Jamestown with the other colonists in the spring of 1610 carrying with him the seeds of his and the colony's success. After a couple of years of experimentation, he perfected a type of tobacco from a blend of Bermuda and Virginia (and possibly West Indian) leaf that was the colony's commercial salvation and the basis of England's first transatlantic staple. He was also the first Englishman to marry a high-ranking Indian who had converted to the Church of England, a development he and the Virginia Company considered of the greatest consequence.

4. Rolfe, *True Relation*, 3 ("good and sufficient men" and "perfect Common-weale"), 5–11 ("so greate a *Worke*" on 11); Hamor, *True Discourse*, 17–20, 26, 29–33.

But as impressive as these accomplishments might have seemed to Rolfe, Dale, and other Virginia Company leaders, they did not impress investors or lead to a mass influx of settlers. For all those dreaming of the colony's future, others were doubting it. The commodities brought from Virginia in the hold of the *Treasurer* that were proudly touted by Dale were dismissed as "things of no great value" by the diligent letter writer John Chamberlain. Perhaps worse, the reputation of Virginia had fallen to such a degree that the entire venture was at risk. Rumors circulated of settlers who had been forced to labor seven or eight years as though they were "slaves" before they gained their freedom. It was said that many poor settlers wondered why the Spanish king had not come to rescue them from their wretchedness and that some had lived in such misery they had abandoned civility and fled to the Indians. Dale had sought to address these concerns by offering small private garden plots and other incentives to colonists, but he had failed to find a long-term solution. What it meant to labor in Virginia and how any spoils might be divided remained uncertain.[5]

Even the heavenly spoils remained contested. After the forging of peace with the Powhatans, did the arrival of Pocahontas presage a mass conversion to the Protestant faith and an Anglo-Indian alliance as the company hoped? For some skeptics of the company, the Powhatan delegation that accompanied Rolfe and Dale appeared little more than a publicity stunt orchestrated by company leaders. Chamberlain described Pocahontas in racially inflected language as "no fayre Lady" and then took a swipe at the company by continuing, "And yet with her tricking up and high stile and titles you might thincke her . . . to be somebody, if you do not know that the poore companie of Virginia out of theyre povertie are faine to allow her fowre pound a weeke for her maintenance." Chamberlain's dyspeptic comments likely had their origin in his resentment of the Virginia Company and the financial losses he had suffered, but not everyone was as disapproving of the Powhatans. Pocahontas's prestige as Wahunsonacock's daughter and her conversion and marriage to an Englishman captivated London society. She "did not onely accustome her selfe to civilitie, but still carried her selfe as the Daughter of a King," Samuel Purchas, clergyman and scholar, remarked. Consequently, she was "respected, not onely by the Company, . . . but of divers particular persons of Honor, in their hopefull zeale by her to advance Christianitie." The lord bishop of London, Purchas noted with satisfaction, afforded her "festivall state and pompe" well beyond the usual hospitality

---

5. Chamberlain to Carleton, June 22, 1616, in Brown, *Genesis*, II, 789 ("no great value"); Lyon Gardiner Tyler, ed., *Narratives of Early Virginia, 1606–1625* (1907; rpt. New York, 1966), 422–424 ("slaves" on 423); Don Diego de Molina to Don Alonso de Velasco, May 28, 1613, in Brown, *Genesis*, II, 648–649. For the allocation of garden plots, see Hamor, *True Discourse*, 16–18.

shown to ladies. The redemption of Pocahontas proved that Virginia's Indian peoples could be converted to Christianity, and therefore the happy prospect (from the English point of view) of the entire Powhatan paramount chiefdom in time being brought to Anglicanism and English manners appeared to be more than a distant hope. Thousands of "poore, wretched, and mysbeleiving people: on whose faces a good Christian cannot looke, without sorrow, pittie, and commyseracion," Rolfe believed, would be brought "to the knowledge and true worshipp of Jesus Christ."[6]

Pocahontas and Rolfe were ushered into the highest social circles amid "Plays, Balls, and other publick Entertainments." The high point of the visit came when the king and Queen Anne received Pocahontas, attired in her new finery, at the Banqueting House shortly after Christmas for a masque by Ben Jonson, written especially for the occasion. Placing her prominently on the royal dais, James I made clear his support for Pocahontas and desire for the Powhatan people to follow her example in converting to the Church of England. Prominent leaders of the company, including Lord De La Warr and Sir Edwin Sandys, were delighted. From the company's point of view, the visit had been highly successful in stimulating interest in the colony, and more particularly in encouraging some wealthy and pious supporters to contribute toward the cost of converting the Powhatan peoples in Virginia. The wave of church building in the colony that took place from 1617 was seen as a means to accommodate not only the thousands of English settlers the company planned to send over the next several years but also thousands of Indian converts. James I had already expressed his enthusiasm for the company's initiative to construct a college for Indian youth and ordered charitable collections to be taken throughout the country in 1616 and 1617 by the Church of England.[7]

---

6. Don Diego de Molina to conde de Gondomar, June 14, 1614, in Haile, ed., *Jamestown Narratives*, 789–790; Chamberlain to Careleton, Feb. 22, 1617, in Norman Egbert McClure, ed., *The Letters of John Chamberlain*, 2 vols. (Philadelphia, 1939), II, 50, 57 ("no fayre Lady" and "high stile"); Samuel Purchas, *Purchas His Pilgrimage; or, Relations of the World and the Religions Observed in All Ages and Places Discovered, from the Creation unto this Present . . .* (London, 1617), 954; Purchas, *Hakluytus Posthumus; or, Purchas His Pilgrimes: Contayning a History of the World in Sea Voyages and Lande Travells by Englishmen and Others* (1625; rpt. Glasgow, 1906), XIX, 118; Rolfe, *True Relation*, 12; Frances Mossiker, *Pocahontas: The Life and the Legend* (New York, 1976), 219–245; Camilla Townsend, *Pocahontas and the Powhatan Dilemma* (New York, 2004), 149.

7. Robert Beverley, *The History and Present State of Virginia*, new ed. (Williamsburg, Va., and Chapel Hill, N.C., 2013), 34; Purchas, *Hakluytus Posthumus*, XIX, 118; Townsend, *Pocahontas*, 139–152; Douglas Bradburn, "The Eschatological Origins of the English Empire," in Bradburn and John C. Coombs, eds., *Early Modern Virginia: Reconsidering the Old Dominion* (Charlottesville, Va., 2011), 36; James Horn, *1619: Jamestown and the Forging of American Democracy* (New York, 2018), 148–151; Kingsbury, ed., *RVC*, I, 538–541, III, 102, 128–129, 147, 165–166, 276–277.

Pocahontas's enthusiastic reception in London and her tragic death in .ng 1617 have overshadowed a different interpretation of the Powhatans' resence in England. Opechancanough was also planning for the future of the empire he was soon to inherit from Wahunsonacock. Uttamatomakkin, high priest and councillor, was dispatched to England to discover as much as possible about the English. The "King [Opechancanough] purposely sent him," Captain John Smith wrote, "to number the people here, and informe him well what wee were and our state." Seemingly also, Uttamatomakkin believed he was to play the role of an emissary to James's court, but in this expectation he was to be bitterly disappointed, and he was largely ignored by the king and his ministers. The English and the Virginia Company were committed to transforming a "barbarous Nation, and savage people" into a virtuous Christian commonwealth, which they perceived as a sacred duty laid upon them directly by God. More pragmatically, conversion would advance the task of absorbing Indian peoples into the English colony, thereby creating a large and naturally expanding population of Christians. Uttamatomakkin, however, had no intention of assuming English ways and did not accept Christianity as superior to Powhatan spiritual beliefs and religious rituals. He had expected to be received by the English with the respect befitting his rank but had been met instead with condescension. Unsurprisingly, on his return to Virginia he presented a scathing account of England and the English to Opechancanough, a portent of the calamitous breakdown in relations that would later overwhelm the colony.[8]

In spite of the high hopes of the Virginia Company and the colossal outlay in blood and treasure, then, the colony's prospects in 1616 were tenuous. Virginia had survived, which was remarkable when the challenges faced during its first decade are taken into account, but the future remained highly uncertain and the likelihood of any tangible returns equally so. Little profit was to be expected, Chamberlain wrote tersely, because no elaboration was needed. Most of the leaders who had steered the colony through its harrowing early years had departed or died. Investment in the company had evaporated; many investors transferred their interest to Bermuda, which was thriving, or to Newfoundland and Guiana, where dreams of fish, gold, and even tobacco seemed more attainable than in the Chesapeake. Finally, as Rolfe had openly acknowledged, only a few hundred settlers remained of the approximately eighteen hundred who had

---

8. Smith, *Generall Historie*, in Barbour, ed., *Complete Works*, II, 261; "A Brief Declaration," in Brown, *Genesis*, II, 774–779 ("barbarous Nation," 775); Kingsbury, ed., *RVC*, III, 73. Although Itoyatin was the next in line to inherit the chiefdom after Wahunsonacock, Opechancanough was the de facto ruler.

been dispatched to Virginia over the past decade, a desperately small number to carry forward a venture so freighted with aspirations and significance by its leaders.[9]

The Virginia Company stood at a threshold. Faced with imminent crisis, the company's leadership responded vigorously and devised a range of plans to completely overhaul the colony. The most noteworthy were those put forward by the grandees of the Virginia Company: Sir Thomas Smythe, one of the greatest London merchants and the leader of the company from its beginnings; Sir Robert Rich, the earl of Warwick, enormously wealthy and the owner of a fleet of privateers who preyed on Spanish shipping in the Spanish Caribbean; and Sandys, a leading parliamentarian, devout Anglican, and one of the most advanced political thinkers of the age. Their different visions for the future of Virginia and America gave primary emphasis to trade, plunder, or settlement, each representing a quite different approach to geopolitics, governance, religion, and political economy. Over the next few years, intensive debates among the three major groups and the associated struggle for mastery within the company raised searching questions about the long-term trajectory of the entire colonial project. Would English colonies be little more than "pirate nests," as feared by successive Spanish ambassadors in London, or perhaps small-scale fishing stations and trading posts, such as those already founded in the far north by different nations or along the Hudson River by the Dutch? Or would they evolve as prosperous settler societies ("New Britains," in what the English conceived as a New World) that would eventually expand across the North American continent and beyond? All three options were viable, and to some degree were already emerging, but which would prevail in Virginia?[10]

---

9. Irene W. D. Hecht, "The Virginia Colony, 1607–1640: A Study in Frontier Growth" (Ph.D. diss., University of Washington, 1969), 68–74; Wesley Frank Craven, *Dissolution of the Virginia Company: The Failure of a Colonial Experiment* (New York, 1932), 29–46; Edmund S. Morgan, *American Slavery, American Freedom: The Ordeal of Colonial Virginia* (New York, 1975), 71–91.

10. Kenneth R. Andrews, *Trade, Plunder, and Settlement: Maritime Enterprise and the Genesis of the British Empire, 1480–1630* (Cambridge, 1984); Philip III to the duke of Medina Sidonia, July 29, 1608, and June 11, 1609, MSS 2010.5, 2010.6, John D. Rockefeller Jr. Library, Special Collections, Colonial Williamsburg Foundation. The clergyman Richard Crakanthorpe and the influential alderman Robert Johnson both used the phrase "new BRITAINE" or "Nova Britannia"; see Crakanthorpe, *A Sermon at the Solemnizing of the Happie Inauguration of Our Most Gracious and Religious Soveraigne King James . . . Preached at Paules Crosse, the 24 of March Last, 1608* (London, 1609), D2v; and Johnson's *Nova Britannia: Offering Most Excellent Fruites by Planting in Virginia . . .* (London, 1609). Captain John Smith first used the name "New England" on his map of the region in 1616; see Barbour, ed., *Complete Works*, II, 394–395. For examples of Spanish ambassadors' concerns about Virginia's becoming a base for pirates, see Philip L. Barbour, ed., *The Jamestown Voyages under the First Charter, 1606–1609*, 2 vols. (Cambridge, 1969), I, 117–119, 163, II, 286.

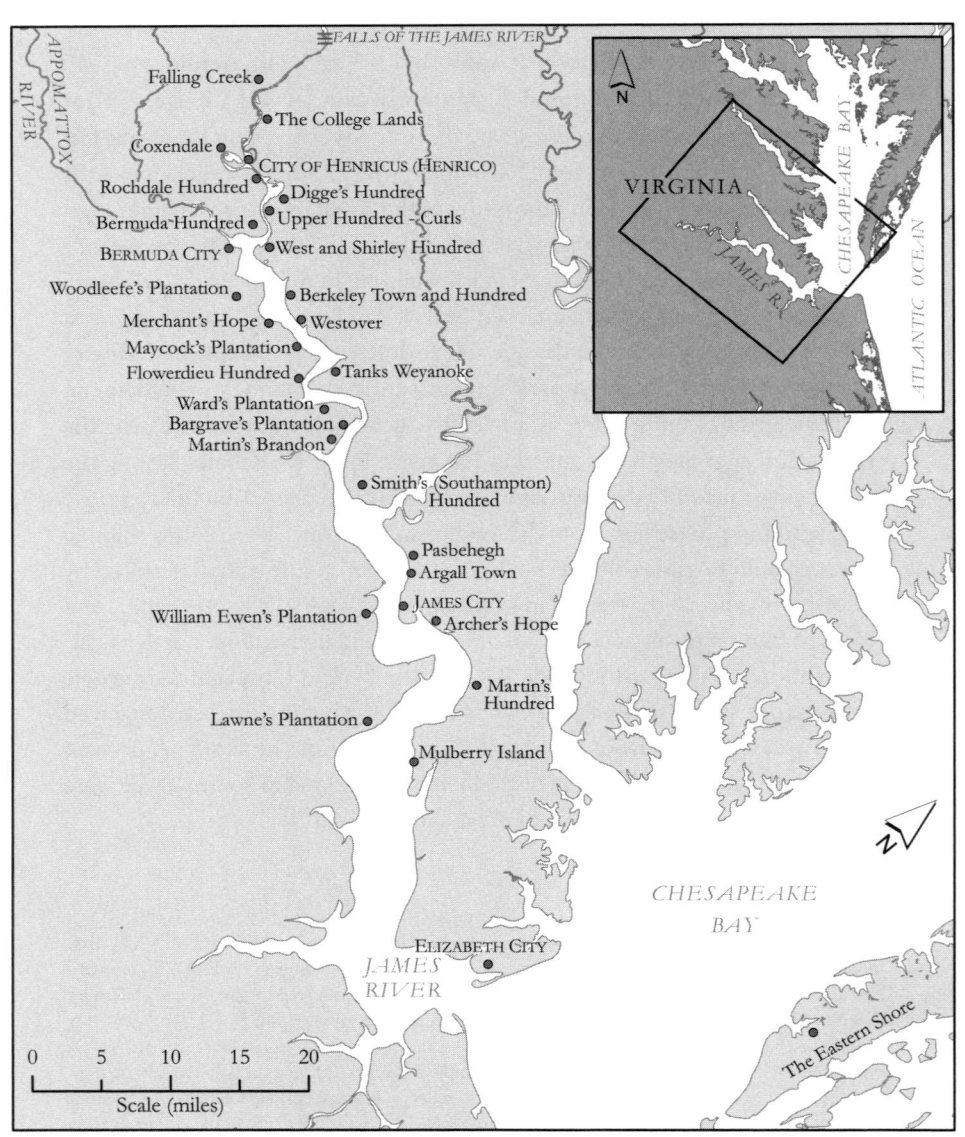

The Virginia Colony in 1619. Drawn by Jonathan W. Chipman

THE SIGNIFICANCE OF 1619, AND THE YEARS IMMEDIATELY BEFORE and after, lies in the extraordinary conjunction of events that ultimately gave definition to the English colonial project and shaped American society for centuries to come. These watershed events include the establishment of the rule of law (for the English); the first meeting of the General Assembly, the first representative self-governing body in English America or any part of the Americas; the arrival of the first enslaved Africans; a concerted effort to recruit reputable women of marriageable age to create a family-based society of independent householders; and the concomitant ratification of a system of private landholdings that would be the basis for a planter commonwealth. Insofar as these developments have attracted scholarly attention, however, they have been mainly considered as discrete topics—for example, studies of the "origins debate" and development of slavery, English interactions with Indian peoples, and the growth of tobacco cultivation and a plantation-based society—thereby largely obscuring the critical intersections among them and their combined impact. It is worth recalling that until very recently not a single monographic work or scholarly collection of essays has been devoted solely to 1619 and its wide-ranging significance. In fact, with the exception of studies associated with the four hundreth anniversary of the founding of Jamestown, detailed published work on the company period has been scarce over the past four decades.[11]

This collection offers a fresh approach that brings together the varied and far-reaching developments of 1619 into a single scholarly conversation. The essays consider the people directly involved in Atlantic colonization in these years and examine the array of ideas about governance, commerce, and race that would have profound implications for the expansion of English settlements in

11. Kingsbury, ed., *RVC*, III, 98–99. The classic study remains Craven's highly influential *Dissolution of the Virginia Company*. Surveys of scholarly works related to seventeenth-century Virginia generally can be found in Wesley Frank Craven, *The Southern Colonies in the Seventeenth Century, 1607–1689* (Baton Rouge, La., 1970), 417–452; Alden T. Vaughan, "The Evolution of Virginia History: Early Historians of the First Colony," in Vaughan and George Athan Billias, eds., *Perspectives on Early American History: Essays in Honor of Richard B. Morris* (New York, 1973), 9–39; Thad W. Tate, "The Seventeenth-Century Chesapeake and Its Modern Historians," in Tate and David L. Ammerman, eds., *The Chesapeake in the Seventeenth Century: Essays on Anglo-American Society* (Williamsburg, Va., and Chapel Hill, N.C., 1979), 3–50; Kathleen M. Brown, *Good Wives, Nasty Wenches, and Anxious Patriarchs: Gender, Race, and Power in Colonial Virginia* (Williamsburg, Va., and Chapel Hill, N.C., 1996); J. Frederick Fausz, "The Invasion of Virginia: Indians, Colonialism, and the Conquest of Cant—A Review Essay on Anglo-Indian Relations in the Chesapeake," *VMHB*, XCV (1987), 133–156; "Introduction," in Lois Green Carr, Philip D. Morgan, and Jean B. Russo, eds., *Colonial Chesapeake Society* (Williamsburg, Va., and Chapel Hill, N.C., 1988), 1–46; Morgan, *American Slavery, American Freedom*; Alden T. Vaughan, "The Origins Debate: Slavery and Racism in Seventeenth-Century Virginia," *VMHB*, XCVII (1989), 311–354; John C. Coombs, "Beyond the 'Origins Debate': Rethinking the Rise of Virginia Slavery," in Bradburn and Coombs, eds., *Early Modern Virginia*, 239–278; Lorena S. Walsh, "Introduction," ibid., 1–13; and Walsh's monumental

America and elsewhere. Viewed from different vantage points, the changes that took place reveal themselves as efforts by the Virginia Company, government officials, and others immersed in colonial activities to revitalize Virginia and in so doing to reassess the entire scope of English overseas enterprise. Far from a mere coincidence of seemingly contradictory impulses, the conjunction of freedom and slavery, of possession and dispossession, of kinship and bondage reflected a self-conscious debate about how English control over America could be asserted and maintained.

As in any debate, the ramifications of the events of 1619 contained elements of conflict and of consensus. On one level, the peculiar conjunction of events in 1619 was the product of growing divisions within the company. Warwick and his allies, whose focus was on challenging Spanish power in the Americas, had dispatched Samuel Argall back to Virginia in 1617 with plans to establish private estates modeled on those that had recently been laid out in the sister colony of Bermuda and with instructions to support sea raiders who were harrying the Spanish colonies in search of plunder in the form of precious metals, commodities, and enslaved people. The backlash against this scheme led to the takeover of the company by Sandys and his ally, the earl of Southampton. It was their radical new plan for the colony, laid out in their instructions to recently appointed governor Sir George Yeardley in 1618, that called for the distribution of small private land grants within a network of new corporate communities, the dispatch of large numbers of female colonists to establish families, the support for large-scale missionary efforts, and the gathering of a General Assembly.

Motives of Honor, Pleasure, and Profit: Plantation Management in the Colonial Chesapeake, 1607–1763 (Williamsburg, Va., and Chapel Hill, N.C., 2010). For religion, see Edward L. Bond, *Damned Souls in a Tobacco Colony: Religion in Seventeenth-Century Virginia* (Macon, Ga., 2000); and Rebecca Anne Goetz, *The Baptism of Early Virginia: How Christianity Created Race* (Baltimore, 2012). Studies that locate Virginia in an Atlantic setting are James Horn, *Adapting to a New World: English Society in the Seventeenth-Century Chesapeake* (Williamsburg, Va., and Chapel Hill, N.C., 1994); April Lee Hatfield, *Atlantic Virginia: Intercolonial Relations in the Seventeenth Century* (Philadelphia, 2004); Robert Appelbaum and John Wood Sweet, eds., *Envisioning an English Empire: Jamestown and the Making of the North Atlantic World* (Philadelphia, 2005); Peter C. Mancall, ed., *The Atlantic World and Virginia, 1550–1624* (Williamsburg, Va., and Chapel Hill, N.C., 2007); Karen Ordahl Kupperman, *The Jamestown Project* (Cambridge, Mass., 2007); and, generally, Malcolm Gaskill, *Between Two Worlds: How the English Became Americans* (New York, 2014). For Ireland and Virginia, see the voluminous work of Nicholas Canny, and also Audrey Horning's *Ireland in the Virginian Sea: Colonialism in the British Atlantic* (Williamsburg, Va., and Chapel Hill, N. C., 2013). Works dealing centrally with 1619 and its broad significance are Horn, *1619*, and the essays in this volume. See also Alexander B. Haskell's important intervention *For God, King, and People: Forging Commonwealth Bonds in Renaissance Virginia* (Williamsburg, Va., and Chapel Hill, N.C., 2017); Warren M. Billings, *A Little Parliament: The Virginia Assembly in the Seventeenth Century* (Richmond, Va., 2004); and Andrew Fitzmaurice's wide-ranging *Humanism and America: An Intellectual History of English Colonization, 1500–1625* (Cambridge, 2003) as well as his numerous essays.

These plans were not without their opponents in Virginia, particularly Captain John Martin, who believed the new plans restricted his ability to control his own estate (established under Argall's tenure) and limited his freedom to trade with the diverse indigenous peoples of the Chesapeake. Moreover, just as Yeardley was putting these reforms in place, with the gathering of the General Assembly in the summer of 1619, the *White Lion* and the *Treasurer*, dispatched to the Caribbean the previous year under the influence of Argall and Warwick, returned to Virginia with their cargo of enslaved Angolans, seized from a Portuguese vessel. Although the colony's leaders eagerly bartered supplies for the captive Africans, their arrival was a reminder of the rival visions and imperatives of the Warwick faction. Their presence did not fit with Sandys's vision for the colonial commonwealth. Even as the Angolans arrived off Point Comfort in late August 1619, however, merchants in London were getting ready to embark new ships for a far different voyage to Guiana, predicated on a strictly mercantile model of trading tobacco and searching for gold along the coast of South America. The promise of riches elsewhere in the Atlantic would sap the strength of investment in Virginia over the coming few years and encourage the pecuniary instincts of the crown as the king's agents came to see colonies as simply sources of customs revenue, thus posing a whole new series of questions for the Virginia Company. The events of 1619, then, were very visible manifestations of the conflicting motives of profit, conversion, glory, and commonwealth creation that had all uncomfortably coexisted behind English colonization up to that point.[12]

At the same time, the events of 1619 did point to a new consensus. Foremost was the need for labor and the challenge of its organization and regulation. Although the company's early leaders had famously lamented the laziness of colonists, the events of 1619 and the development of tobacco agriculture drove home to everyone that the task of planting a profitable commodity in America called for more than character and application; it simply needed more bodies, especially in the face of shockingly high mortality rates. The first General Assembly in 1619 identified this problem directly and encouraged the company to dispatch as many new colonists as possible. Any visions of commonwealth creation or crusade against Catholic Spain would rest upon controlling labor and upon a rationale that would support that control. The increasing shipment

12. W. Frank Craven, "The Earl of Warwick, a Speculator in Piracy," *Hispanic American Historical Review*, X (1930), 457–479; Mark G. Hanna, *Pirate Nests and the Rise of the British Empire, 1570–1740* (Williamsburg, Va., and Chapel Hill, N.C., 2015), 58–77; Tim Hashaw, *The Birth of Black America: The First African Americans and the Pursuit of Freedom at Jamestown* (New York, 2007), 86–91; Vernon A. Ives, ed., *The Rich Papers: Letters from Bermuda, 1615–1646: Eyewitness Accounts Sent by the Early Colonists to Sir Nathaniel Rich* (Toronto, 1984), 121–123, 148–157, 184–187; Horn, *1619*, 61–69, 91–92.

of paupers and indentured servants built upon civic commonwealth theory that emphasized the value of reformed laborers to the commonwealth. The ready acceptance of commodified African laborers, and the racial assumptions that lay behind it, reflected the well-established and carefully calculated trade of the Portuguese empire and its quick adaptation by English planters in Bermuda in the years immediately preceding 1619. Some Virginia leaders saw the colonies' future in terms of regulated and strictly reformed white labor, and others believed it required investing in enslaved Africans from the Iberian Atlantic, but all shared an understanding that the management of labor was critical to the future of English colonies.

Slavery and freedom, therefore, did not arrive simultaneously in Virginia by chance in 1619. They came, along with indigenous dispossession and the reinforcement of a gendered hierarchy, as part of an effort to wrestle with the question of how to make an English polity in America stable, profitable, and sustainable. Contemporaries understood the tensions between the visions that lay behind these events, but they were not able to resolve them, and neither have their descendants been able to for the subsequent four centuries.

Looking back at 1619, these essays encourage us to see, not a jumble of tragic coincidences, but the interweaving of ideology, pragmatic experience, and international rivalries. The contributors highlight how ideas fed into, and were shaped by, local contingencies in Virginia and elsewhere around the Atlantic rim. Through the importation of enslaved Africans, the construction of colonial political institutions, and the fostering of an exclusionary settler-colonial model of expansion, events in Virginia in this period served to sharpen and broaden English conceptions about their role in the Atlantic world. It made Virginia the center of debate over commonwealth, race, and empire, rather than merely a disorderly and dysfunctional periphery. By framing the events of 1619 in this way, the authors reshape our understanding of how England's first permanent beachhead ultimately became its model for a global settler empire.[13]

THE COLLECTION OPENS WITH PETER C. MANCALL'S EXPLORATION OF the circulation of knowledge about American commodities and natural resources and their crucial role in promoting colonization before 1614. He notes the declining interest in Virginia among colonial promoters such as Richard

---

13. Morgan, *American Slavery, American Freedom*; Bernard Bailyn, *The Barbarous Years: The Peopling of British North America: The Conflict of Civilizations, 1600–1675* (New York, 2012); Jack P. Greene, "The Exclusionary Legacy of Subjecthood in Making and Remaking the Atlantic World: English-Speaking America as a Case for Historical Reflection," Keynote address, Rice University, 2014, and his essay in this volume.

Hakluyt and his circle by the mid-1610s that reflected weariness with the recurrent failures of the English over the previous forty years to establish successful colonies in America. Masters of the sea they might have been, Mancall points out, but they had not mastered western lands. In drawing our attention to the waning of intellectual interest in America, its resources, and its peoples, Mancall reminds us also that the challenge for Virginia Company leaders at this critical juncture was not only financial. Lauren Working picks up on this theme from a different angle in tracing the ways English settlement in Virginia and the increasing knowledge of the "barbarous and savage people" who lived there influenced metropolitan politics. An outpouring of sermons sponsored by the company in the early years of Jamestown emphasized the holy mission of bringing the light of Christ to millions of souls who lived in blindness without the knowledge of scripture or God. Conversion was seen as a righteous work that would encourage the Powhatans to become a civilized people. It was a "noble Action for the planting of *Virginia,* with Christian Religion," as the English saw it, bringing tens of thousands of Indians to the Church of England. Although the effort stalled after 1610, the hope of converting the Indians did not perish and was taken up again in the reforms led by Sir Edwin Sandys in 1619. James I supported the company's pious efforts and expressed his "great zeal and affection" for spreading religion in Virginia. Converting the Powhatans was integral to the company's vision of a prosperous and moral community created for the good of the people, English and Powhatan alike.[14]

Similar themes emerge in Nicholas Canny's detailed comparison of Ireland and Virginia. If, as the lord deputy of Ireland Arthur Chichester grumbled in 1605, his countrymen were more committed to "the findinge out of Virgenia, Guiana and other remote and unknowen Countries" than to the "makinge Cyvell of Ireland," he need not have worried. As Canny comments, Ireland was much more attractive to English and Scots settlers than America throughout the seventeenth century. In both cases, however, the English, viewing themselves as conquerors, even compassionate conquerors, had no doubt they were entitled to appropriate the land of native peoples. They also conceived of their role as civilizing the Irish. In the early 1570s, Sir Thomas Smith described the many

14. Robert Gray, *A Good Speed to Virginia* (London, 1609), C2r ("barbarous"); Kingsbury, ed., *RVC*, I, 423, III, 307 ("noble Action"); "A Report of S[i]r George Yeardlyes[,] Going Governor to Virginia," Dec. 5, 1618, Ferrar Papers 93, Virginia Company Archives, http://www.virginiacompany archives.amdigital.co.uk ("great zeal"); Peter C. Mancall, *Hakluyt's Promise: An Elizabethan's Obsession for an English America* (New Haven, Conn., 2007); Mancall, *Nature and Culture in the Early Modern Atlantic* (Philadelphia, 2018); John Parker, "Religion and the Virginia Colony, 1609–10," in K. R. Andrews, N. P. Canny, and P. E. H. Hair, eds., *The Westward Enterprise: English Activities in Ireland, the Atlantic, and America, 1480–1650* (Liverpool, U.K., 1978), 245–270; Bond, *Damned Souls*, 1–35.

advantages of founding settlements in Ireland. English *coloni* (settlers) would cultivate a sparsely populated land, build towns, stimulate commerce, and establish "law, justice, and good order," which in turn would encourage the native Irish to become civil. In many respects, his proposals were strikingly similar to those of Sandys, and both suffered the same fate. Their plans for English society in colonial settings were violently rejected by the peoples they were supposed to benefit, in the form of the Powhatan "Massacre" of 1622 in Virginia and the Irish insurrection of 1641, justifying in English opinion the ruthless exclusionary strategies that subsequently followed.[15]

The next two essays investigate the Atlantic context of slavery and the slave trade. In reassessing the arrival of the "20. and odd Negroes" in Virginia, the authors emphasize the sheer scale of the slave trade to Spanish America and how state, company, and individual power were deployed and contested in the acquisition of African captives. Philip D. Morgan's comprehensive survey traces the broad forces shaping black experiences in the Atlantic world of this period. His essay makes three major arguments: first, more than half a million African slaves were forcibly transported to Spanish America before 1640, far more than previously estimated; second, the Portuguese dominated the shipment of captives from Africa to America and hence exerted a major influence on the development of racial attitudes and treatment of slaves in Virginia and Bermuda; and, third, the evidence pertaining to the status of the first Africans in Virginia suggests that from the outset they were regarded by the English as enslaved laborers, not servants. Of note is the huge increase in captives taken from West Central Africa in the first quarter of the seventeenth century, the "Angolan wave." The centrality of the slave trade from Portuguese Angola and the kingdoms of Kongo, Ndongo, and other African states and, more particularly, the local conditions that led to the mass transportation of slaves from the region are vital to understanding the experiences of the first Africans brought to Virginia by English privateers in 1619.[16]

---

15. Arthur Chichester to the earl of Salisbury, Oct. 2, 1605, SP 63/217, fol. 165v, The National Archives, Kew, U.K., cited in Lauren Working, "'The Savages of Virginia Our Project': The Powhatans in Jacobean Political Thought," in this volume; Nicholas P. Canny, "The Ideology of English Colonization: From Ireland to America," *WMQ*, 3d Ser., XXX (1973), 575–598; Canny, *Making Ireland British, 1580–1650* (Oxford, 2001). For Smith's venture in the Ards Peninsula, Ulster, see Horning, *Ireland in the Virginian Sea*, 65–68.

16. Kingsbury, ed., *RVC*, III, 243; Philip D. Morgan, "Virginia Slavery in Atlantic Context, 1550 to 1650," in this volume; John K. Thornton, *A Cultural History of the Atlantic World, 1250–1820* (Cambridge, 2012), 81–82; A. J. R. Russell-Wood, "The Portuguese Atlantic, 1415–1808," in Jack P. Greene and Philip D. Morgan, eds., *Atlantic History: A Critical Appraisal* (Oxford, 2009), 90–91; David Eltis and David Richardson, *Atlas of the Transatlantic Slave Trade* (New Haven, Conn., 2010), 136–137, maps 92 and 95.

Relations between the Portuguese and kingdoms of West Central Africa had been generally cordial for close to a century, based on reciprocal benefits and shared interests. But, in 1571, Sebastião I, king of Portugal, abruptly switched policy and commanded that a discrete Portuguese colony be carved out of the territories of former allies and ruled directly by the crown. Brutal fighting over the next twenty years gravely destabilized the region and paved the way for the ruinous warfare of the first half of the seventeenth century. In 1618–1619, armies led by Portuguese governor Luis Mendes de Vasconçelos, made up of colonial troops and enlisted companies of local mercenaries called the Imbangala, overwhelmed the forces of the kingdom of Ndongo and pushed through to the royal capital of Kabasa, which was summarily sacked. Such was the slaughter, a contemporary wrote, that rivers were spoiled by the huge numbers of dead livestock and people. Many of those captured, taken to the coast, and forcibly transported to America, John K. Thornton and Linda M. Heywood suggest, were from Kabasa and the towns and heavily populated agricultural lands between the Lukala and Lutete Rivers. In addition, Portuguese campaigns in areas near the principal slave port of Luanda and the Kongolese capital of São Salvador were nothing less than a state-sponsored regime of terror to promote the wholesale capture of victims for the lucrative slave trade and to further consolidate Portuguese control over the region. The colonization of America, as David Wheat has observed, was closely related to the colonization of West Central Africa.[17]

Since neither the Portuguese nor the Spanish recognized the legitimacy of English commerce with the Americas, any more than settlements, it was left to English privateers to obtain African slaves as best they could by plundering Portuguese slavers on the high seas. It is in this context that the Atlantic island of Bermuda took on great importance in the events surrounding 1619. Michael J. Jarvis shows how ideas for the future development of the island brought into focus three distinct and conflicting visions. Sir Robert Rich, earl of Warwick, energized by Protestant zeal and his hatred of the Spanish "Antechrist," advocated

---

17. Engel Sluiter, "New Light on the '20. and Odd Negroes' Arriving in Virginia, August 1619," *WMQ*, 3d Ser., LIV (1997), 395–398; John Thornton, "The African Experience of the '20. and Odd Negroes' Arriving in Virginia in 1619," ibid., LV (1998), 421–434; Horn, *1619*, 85–117; Linda M. Heywood and Thornton, *Central Africans, Atlantic Creoles, and the Foundation of the Americas, 1585–1660* (New York, 2007), 25–48, 109–145; Heywood, *Njinga of Angola: Africa's Warrior Queen* (Cambridge, Mass., 2017), 3–69; David Wheat, *Atlantic Africa and the Spanish Caribbean, 1570–1640* (Williamsburg, Va., and Chapel Hill, N.C., 2016), 68–103. The relations between Portugal and the kingdoms of West Central Africa are explored in more detail in Linda Heywood, "Reino de Angola / Kingdom of Angola: The Establishment and Consolidation of a Predatory State in Central Africa, 1575–1630," paper presented at the conference "Virginia in 1619: Legacies for Race, Commonwealth, and Empire," Apr. 27–29, 2017, Dartmouth College, Hanover, N.H. The editors of the volume extend their thanks to Dr. Heywood for her participation at the conference and for sharing her work.

using the island's harbors as a base for raiding Spanish shipping and possessions in the Caribbean. In contrast, Sir Edwin Sandys promoted a diversified economy and encouraged the cultivation of a range of profitable agricultural products. The third of the trio, Sir Thomas Smythe, supported generating income from shipping and the export of high-profit staples such as tobacco. Bermuda, as Jarvis remarks, was the first colony in the English Atlantic to develop a sizable population of Africans, at least one hundred by 1620 compared to thirty-two in Virginia. To the alarm of Sandys, the growth in the island's African population was largely the result of privateering. He characterized Bermuda before a meeting of the Virginia Company in May 1620 as "much frequented with men of Warr and Pirates" and went on to warn that "if ther be not a strict Course taken herin itt wilbe made an other Argier" (Algiers was a major base of the Barbary pirates). Such a development posed a direct threat to Virginia, he cautioned.[18]

Factional conflict within the company intensified as a consequence of the attack on a Portuguese slave ship in the Gulf of Mexico by Warwick's *Treasurer* accompanied by another English privateer, the *White Lion*. As Morgan and Jarvis observe, the pillaging of the slaver led directly to the first Africans' arrival in Virginia. The bitter arguments within the company that ensued were, as Sandys predicted, extremely damaging to the colony but ultimately even more so to the company. Warwick never forgave Sandys for his public criticism of the role he played in the privateers' attack on the slaver, which reached the ears of the king and his ministers and caused Warwick grave concern. The grievous rupture in their relations never healed and was one of the causes of the intensification of infighting among leaders that led to the dissolution of the company five years later.[19]

The arrival of the first Africans in Virginia took on greater significance for contemporary planters and company officials because it coincided with the ambitious attempt by Sandys and his followers to create a commonwealth in Virginia. Sandys's vision is explored in the next section from various perspectives by Misha Ewen, Paul Musselwhite, Alexander B. Haskell, and Andrew Fitzmaurice. Rolfe's phrase "a firme and perfect Common-weale," from his *True Relation*, carried freight and was not merely a rhetorical flourish; it meant a stable and reformed commonwealth, a society that greatly improved upon that of England. In the eyes of Sandys and his principals—Southampton, the brothers Nicholas and John Ferrar, and William Cavendish, son of the earl of Devonshire—Virginia

---

18. Kingsbury, ed., *RVC*, I, 367.
19. Ives, ed., *Rich Papers*, 121–143, 148–154, 155–157, 184–187; Michael J. Jarvis, *In the Eye of All Trade: Bermuda, Bermudians, and the Maritime Atlantic World, 1680–1783* (Williamsburg, Va., and Chapel Hill, N.C., 2010), 12–37; Michael Guasco, *Slaves and Englishmen: Human Bondage in the Early Modern Atlantic World* (Philadelphia, 2014), 119, 199–201.

offered an opportunity to construct a version of English society that would be founded on "a laudable form of Government by Majestracy and just Laws for the happy guiding and governing of the people." Such a society would be based on traditional English concepts of social hierarchy in which everyone had a place, an economy that offered everyone work and where land was widely available, and a church that embraced settlers and Powhatans under the capacious umbrella of Anglicanism. Most historians have failed to grasp the sheer boldness and originality of Sandys's vision. Adapting the ideas of leading European intellectuals of the second half of the sixteenth and early seventeenth century, he and other leaders of the company in London and at Jamestown sought to fashion a New World commonwealth.[20]

In the first place, Virginia's commonwealth required people. Misha Ewen considers the crucial importance of the transportation of large numbers of settlers to the colony, the largest movement of English people to America until these years. The commitment to a settler society necessarily demanded the organization of ships and provisions on a massive scale to accommodate what was effectively England's first mass migration to America. She investigates the ways in which the institutionalization of labor in the form of indentured servitude together with the increasing regulation of paupers, especially poor children in London, were responses to the Virginia Company's expanded vision for Virginia. Women and servants, she writes, were indispensable to the establishment of households and commonwealths. Paul Musselwhite argues that divergent English visions of landownership and patterns of commercial development, combined with local circumstances in the colony, fostered competing plans over individual versus corporate landownership and free enterprise in these years. Without question one of the most important developments of the period, the championing of private property by the company after 1616, essential to the imperative of attracting colonists and much-needed capital, was complicated by the potential for very different forms of landownership: baronial estates controlled by London merchants employing hundreds of indentured servants, townships and communal lands, and small farms or plantations.[21]

---

20. Kingsbury, ed., *RVC*, III, 98–99. For reassessments of Sandys's commonwealth, see Andrew Fitzmaurice, "The Commercial Ideology of Colonization in Jacobean England: Robert Johnson, Giovanni Botero, and the Pursuit of Greatness," *WMQ*, 3d Ser., LXIV (2007), 791–820; Haskell, *For God, King, and People*; and Horn, *1619*, 43–83, 119–152.

21. David R. Ransome, "'Shipt for Virginia': The Beginnings in 1619–1622 of the Great Migration to the Chesapeake," *VMHB*, CIII (1995), 443–458; Ransome, "Wives for Virginia, 1621," *WMQ*, 3d Ser., XLVIII (1991), 3–18; Christopher Tomlins, *Freedom Bound: Law, Labor, and Civic Identity in Colonizing English America, 1580–1865* (Cambridge, 2010); Steve Hindle and Ruth Wallis Herndon, "Recreating Proper Families in England and North America: Pauper Apprenticeship in Transatlantic

Alexander B. Haskell resituates the creation of Virginia's General Assembly in a late Renaissance intellectual and political context, foregrounding the ideals of the "publick" and commonwealth that animated Virginia Company leaders like Salisbury and Sandys. Two particular threats confronted the colony in this period. Sandys faced pressures from James I and his treasurer, Sir Lionel Cranfield, who had come to eye corporate bodies such as the Virginia Company as sources of wealth to which the king had a rightful claim. But a more immediate and greater threat came from the machinations of Warwick and his client in Jamestown, Deputy Governor Argall, who had similarly come to regard the public (company) stock of cattle, servants, and lands as fair game for their own benefit. In the context of the effort to protect the public store from plunder by the crown or unscrupulous grandees such as Warwick, the reforms of 1619 were devised, including the innovation of a General Assembly that gave the settlers themselves a voice in their collective affairs and well-being. In a similar vein, Andrew Fitzmaurice's essay argues that the Virginia Company's corporate structure created a unique space for leaders to explore radical new political and economic ideas that were not possible in the increasingly contentious domestic sphere of the later Jacobean period. He points out that the entangled discourses regarding popular government and reason of state in the creation of Virginia were closely tied to the political thought of necessity and self-preservation that flourished in the early seventeenth century. But both were regarded as potentially dangerous ways of thinking about politics, particularly about national politics in this period. Much adventurous thinking about both discourses accordingly occurred away from the national stage, and in particular in the semi-sovereign bodies politic that were created by corporations: notably, in chartered companies. Of these, the Virginia Company afforded not only an opportunity to explore such thinking but also a testing ground for their ideas in practice.[22]

A remarkable aspect of the company's understanding of the new Virginia commonwealth it was building was their leaders' opinion of the part the Powhat-

---

Context," in Herndon and John E. Murray, eds., *Children Bound to Labor: The Pauper Apprenticeship System in Early America* (Ithaca, N.Y., 2009), 19–36; W. Stitt Robinson, Jr., *Mother Earth: Land Grants in Virginia, 1607–1699* (Baltimore, 1957); Charles E. Hatch, Jr., *The First Seventeen Years—Virginia, 1607–1624* (Charlottesville, Va., 1957); Walsh, *Motives of Honor, Pleasure, and Profit*, 25–112.

22. Sir Edwin Sandys to Sir Lionel Cranfield, Sept. 9, 1619, in "Lord Sackville's Papers respecting Virginia, 1613–1631, I," *American Historical Review*, XXVII (1922), 498 ("publick"); Phil Withington, *The Politics of Commonwealth: Citizens and Freemen in Early Modern England* (Cambridge, 2005); Philip J. Stern, *The Company-State: Corporate Sovereignty and the Early Modern Foundations of the British Empire in India* (Oxford, 2011); Henry S. Turner, *The Corporate Commonwealth: Pluralism and Political Fictions in England, 1516–1651* (Chicago, 2016); Andrew Fitzmaurice, *Sovereignty, Property, and Empire, 1500–2000* (Cambridge, 2014); Paul Musselwhite, *Urban Dreams, Rural Commonwealth: The Rise of Plantation Society in the Chesapeake* (Chicago, 2018), chap. 1.

ans would play. Encouraged by Dale's felicitous assessment of English-Indian relations in 1616, Sandys and his supporters eagerly awaited the mass conversion of the Powhatans. A cautious approach was adopted to achieve this happy outcome in which settlers' own good example would "allure the Heathen people to submit themselves to the Scepter of Gods most righteous and blessed Kingdome, and so finally joyne with them in the true Christian profession." Company and colony leaders also placed their faith in first converting Indian children, who would then convert their parents, kin, and the larger population. But the godly work did not go smoothly. Governor George Yeardley wrote to Sandys in 1619 that Indian parents were very loath to part with their children "upon any tearmes." James D. Rice contends that the numerous measures in the General Assembly regulating settlers' behavior toward the Powhatans attest to the governor's anxieties about the Indians' "slippery desinges" and the uncertainty of the times. They were also doubtful times within Indian country, Rice points out. Wahunsonacock's successor, Itoyatin, and the de facto chief, Opechancanough, faced challenges internally and on the edges of their paramount chiefdom. Yeardley also glossed over significant differences among the colonists, centering on the degree and character of their involvement with local peoples and their competing visions of how Indians might fit into the colony's future. The simmering tensions of 1619, therefore, gave the lie to English dreams of a peaceful Anglo-Indian commonwealth and presaged the violent conflict that would accompany the later imposition of settler-colonial regimes throughout North America.[23]

Equally ominous for non-European peoples in the long run was elite English planters' use of their local authority, as implied in the reforms of 1619, to lay the foundations for almost boundless legal discretion and the establishment of a customary law tailored to enhancing their own interests. In reexamining the beginnings of slavery in Virginia, for example, Paul D. Halliday traces the ways magistrates exploited the judicial discretion that arose from the piecemeal establishment of English courts during the 1620s to reinforce their local authority, in sharp contrast with the increasingly careful parsing of jurisdiction in England itself. Virginia's General Court was created along with the General Assembly, and, despite its being at least as important (if not more so), has received considerably less attention. In 1625, an African named "Brase," captured by privateers in the Caribbean, came before the new court, which ordered that he become a servant to the governor, Sir Francis Wyatt. His case provides the earliest surviving record in any English colony of an African ordered to labor for reasons other than punishment. Judges with little or no legal training exercised an unusually

23. Kingsbury, ed., *RVC*, III, 102, 128–129 ("upon any tearmes" on 128), 161, 165–166, 175 ("slippery desinges"), 276 ("allure").

broad discretion at odds with the laws of England; they had an exalted sense of their authority, which they often used to serve their own interests, especially in their regulation of servant labor. In Brase's case, the first signs of a customary law of slavery emerged as the judges of the General Court began to invent it following the reforms of 1619. Their actions, Halliday asserts, set an important precedent for the construction of slavery in British law and for the discretionary basis of colonial law across the British empire.[24]

The volume concludes with two essays that offer broad perspectives on 1619, one geographical and the other temporal. Melissa Morris draws attention to the important parallel colonial enterprises that English merchants pursued in Guiana during these same years. The 1619 charter for the Amazon Company, she writes, suggests the appeal of contemporary alternatives. Along the South American littoral, merchants invested in short-term ventures for quick profits, embracing tobacco as a viable export commodity at a time when the Virginia Company was rebuking its colonists for growing it. In a strikingly similar turn of events, Guiana merchants and investors were subjected to the same political pressures from pro-Spanish interests at the English court as the Virginia Company. Finally, in a masterly wide-ranging analysis, Jack P. Greene reconsiders the long-term trajectory of English / British colonial expansion from the English Atlantic of Captain John Smith to the American settler empire praised effusively by the Scottish political economist Adam Smith. In 1624, when Captain Smith chronicled the progress of England's first overseas colony to achieve permanence, Virginia, the nascent English empire boasted only two other settlements, Bermuda and Plymouth. From these modest beginnings, over the next 150 years English America grew into a vibrant collection of prosperous and politically stable colonies. As England's first sustained experience with long-distance settler colonization, Greene argues, Virginia and the critical reforms of 1619 played a foundational role in modeling a global settler empire.[25]

AS THIS COLLECTION DEMONSTRATES, THE FERMENT OF IDEAS AND events surrounding 1619 were controversial and contested, even within the Virginia Company. Rather than simply being acted upon by the impersonal forces

---

24. A notable exception to the general lack of scholarship on the General Court is the extensive work of Warren M. Billings, in particular his *A Little Parliament*, 149–171. See Richard J. Ross and Philip J. Stern, "Reconstructing Early Modern Notions of Legal Pluralism," in Lauren Benton and Ross, eds., *Legal Pluralism and Empires, 1500–1850* (New York, 2013), 109–142; Benton and Lisa Ford, *Rage for Order: The British Empire and the Origins of International Law, 1800–1850* (Cambridge, Mass., 2016).

25. Joyce Lorimer, ed., *English and Irish Settlement on the River Amazon, 1554–1646* (London, 1989); Lorimer, "The Failure of the English Guiana Ventures 1595–1667 and James I's Foreign Policy,"

of the emerging Atlantic world, the people of Virginia in 1619 stood at a critical juncture. Many of the company leaders' proposals failed to materialize in ways they anticipated, but nevertheless their combined effect was dramatic. Within less than a decade from the arrival from Jamestown of Sir Thomas Dale, John Rolfe, Pocahontas, and their strange assortment of fellow passengers, the organization of the colony evolved and commercial prospects improved to such a degree that when the company's charter was rescinded by the King's Bench in 1624 no one in London or Virginia remotely considered abandoning the colony. Virginia had become the prototype for colonization, and in time new English colonies would spread across the northern continent and eventually stretch from Newfoundland to the Caribbean, a development that would have enormous and very different consequences for indigenous peoples, Africans, and Europeans. Although there were considerable variances from one place to another depending on local contingencies, all English settler colonies in the Americas were built to some extent on Virginia's experience and the events of 1619.

Journal of Imperial and Commonwealth History, XXI (1993), 1–30; Jack P. Greene, *Evaluating Empire and Confronting Colonialism in Eighteenth-Century Britain* (Cambridge, 2013), 20–49; Greene, "Negotiated Authorities: The Problem of Governance in the Extended Polities of the Early Modern Atlantic World," in Greene, *Negotiated Authorities: Essays in Colonial Political and Constitutional History* (Charlottesville, Va., 1994), 1–24; Christine Daniels and Michael V. Kennedy, eds., *Negotiated Empires: Centers and Peripheries in the Americas, 1500–1820* (New York, 2002); Craig Yirush, *Settlers, Liberty, and Empire: The Roots of Early American Political Theory, 1675–1775* (Cambridge, 2011); Thomas Y. Man, *English Colonization and the Formation of Anglo-American Polities, 1606–1664* (Beijing, China, 2016).

Before 1619

PETER C. MANCALL

Sometime around 1614, the English natural historian Edward Topsell began to write a book that he intended to call "Fowles of Heaven." He was by then perhaps the most famous naturalist in the realm as a result of two monumental works: *The Historie of Foure-Footed Beastes*, published in London in 1607, and the *Historie of Serpents*, which appeared the next year. Topsell, a trained minister who had written a series of religious tracts early in his career, came to see himself as the heir to the Swiss polymath Conrad Gesner, who in the mid-sixteenth century had produced his own grand natural history. Topsell's books brought Gesner's erudition to an English-reading public. With his bird book he hoped to bring the ornithological work of the Italian naturalist Ulysse Aldrovandi to the same audience and establish himself as the authority on the entire range of species on the planet.[1]

Fortunately for Topsell, one of his acquaintances was the younger Richard Hakluyt, who had been collecting details about the world beyond Europe since at least 1580. Hakluyt's major achievements, the two editions of the *Principal Navigations* (published in 1589 and then in a much-expanded version in three volumes from 1598 to 1600), did not contain many illustrations, but Hakluyt had long been interested in visual evidence of distant places. His concern for images could be seen in the efforts that he made in bringing out the 1590 illustrated edition of Thomas Harriot's *Briefe and True Report of the New Found Land of Virginia* and the English-language version of Jan Huygen van Linschoten's *Discours of Voyages into the Easte and West Indies*, published in London in 1598.[2]

---

1. Edward Topsell, "Fowles of Heaven," EL 1142, Huntington Library, San Marino, Calif.; Topsell, *The Historie of Foure-Footed Beastes* . . . (London, 1607); Topsell, *The Historie of Serpents; or, The Second Booke of Living Creatures* . . . (London, 1608); Conradi Gesneri, *Medici tigurini historiae animalium* . . . , 5 vols. (Frankfurt, 1565–1567); Topsell, *The Fowles of Heaven; or, History of Birdes*, ed. Thomas P. Harrison and F. David Hoeniger (Austin, Tex., 1972), xxix–xxxvi.

2. Richard Hakluyt, *The Principall Navigations, Voiages, and Discoveries of the English Nation* (London, 1589); Hakluyt, *The Principal Navigations, Voyages, Traffiques, and Discoveries of the English Nation*, 3 vols. (London, 1598–1600). For Hakluyt's understanding of the importance of images, see Peter C. Mancall, "Richard Hakluyt and the Visual World of Early Modern Travel Narratives," in Daniel Carey and Claire Jowitt, eds., *Richard Hakluyt and Travel Writing in Early Modern Europe*,

So, all things considered, it was perhaps not too surprising that Hakluyt sent Topsell a picture of a "virginia bird" that he called a "chuwhweeo," which is now known as a towhee (see Figure 1). Yet Hakluyt's attention to American birds did not represent one of his major fascinations. Indeed, had he been so concerned with the *naturalia* of the Western Hemisphere he might have tried to steer John White's watercolors of American creatures into print, but he never did, even though White was arguably a more precise painter of nature than of humans (see Figure 2), and it is likely that the image of this bird that he sent to Topsell had been created by White. (Topsell worked with illustrators to create new watercolors for his planned book.) Such pictures could have expanded the range of visual information about coastal North America that appeared in the 1590 illustrated edition of Harriot's study of the large region that the English then labeled "Virginia," which included modern Carolina as well as the lands around Chesapeake Bay. Instead, Hakluyt's gift to Topsell signaled that precise information about American birds had already begun to arrive in London and that Hakluyt wanted to ensure that it got into the right hands. In that sense, he was correct. Though Topsell never finished his manuscript—he became obsessed with cocks and never got beyond the letter *c*—he was nonetheless the obvious person to spread news about Virginia's natural endowments. Hakluyt would also likely benefit since integrating American birds into the catalog of natural history could only help his efforts, begun over three decades earlier, to encourage the permanent establishment of English colonies in North America.[3]

The gift of the picture was emblematic of the ways that information about the Western Hemisphere circulated in late Tudor and early Stuart England, and even well beyond. The picture was proof of something specific that existed in North America, one of the countless species of naturalia that Europeans were keen to understand and to explain, often because even a rather modest-looking animal or plant, like tobacco or sassafras, might come to have enormous value. Hence Hakluyt's gift to Topsell fit his and other English writers' generation-long obsession with trying to understand what the Western Hemisphere looked like and how its potential could be explained to policymakers who were unlikely to

---

Works Issued by the Hakluyt Society, Extra Ser., no. 47 (Farnham, Surrey, U.K., 2012), 87–101. For his role in bringing the work of other authors to the English public, see D. B. Quinn, C. E. Armstrong, and R. A. Skelton, "The Primary Hakluyt Bibliography," in Quinn, ed., *The Hakluyt Handbook*, 2 vols., Works Issued by the Hakluyt Society, 2d Ser., nos. 144–145 (London, 1974), II, 461–569.

3. For White as naturalist, see Paul W. Hulton and David B. Quinn, *The American Drawings of John White, 1577–1590*, 2 vols. (Chapel Hill, N.C., 1964), II, plates 4–30, 49–57, 69–70. For the likely source of Topsell's watercolor, see Thomas P. Harrison, ed., *The First Water Colors of North American Birds* (Austin, [1964]), 11–12; and David B. Quinn, ed., *The Roanoke Voyages, 1584–1590: Documents to Illustrate the English Voyages to North America under the Patent Granted to Walter Raleigh in 1584*,

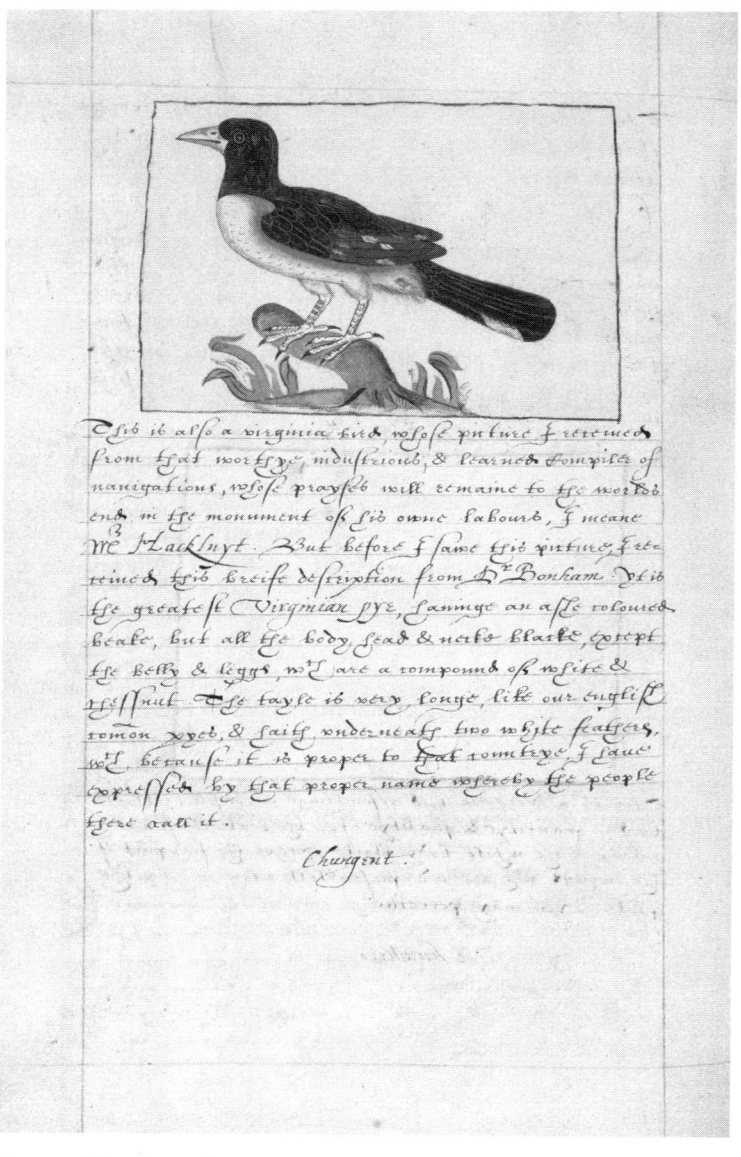

Figure 1. "Chuwhweeo." From Edward Topsell, "Fowles of Heaven," EL 1142, 35v. Courtesy, Huntington Library, San Marino, Calif.

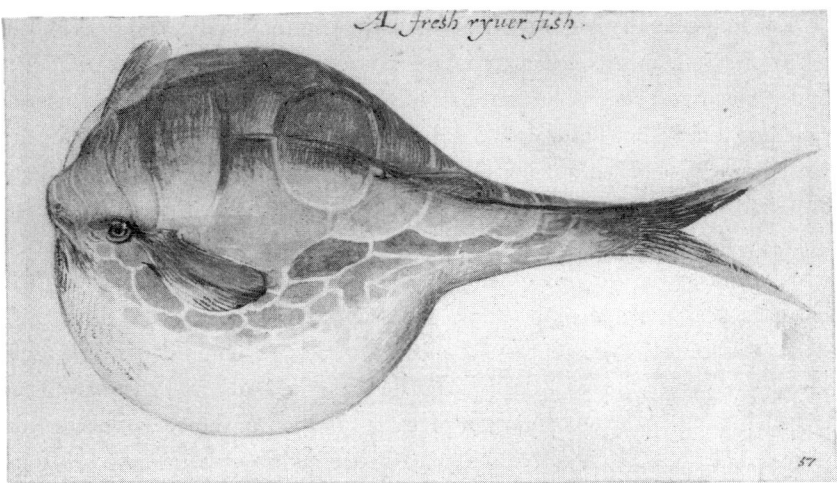

Figure 2. White Puffer Fish. By John White. © British Museum, London

see it with their own eyes. Hakluyt believed that the English had been slow to pursue the creation of overseas settlements and insufficiently attentive to the physical materials and images that other Europeans had been transporting east across the ocean. He must have been thrilled in 1583 when André Thevet, the royal cosmographer of the king of France, either gave or sold him the so-called Codex Mendoza, a manuscript written around 1540 in Mexico that described Aztec social practices, politics, history, and accounts of tribute. Hakluyt was living in Paris at the time, acquiring information about French overseas activities at the behest of Sir Francis Walsingham, a primary adviser to the queen. Eventually that manuscript would land in the hands of Samuel Purchas, who had much—but not all—of it engraved and printed in *Purchas His Pilgrimes* in 1625. These images were, Purchas told his readers, the most valuable thing that he had to offer—"the choisest of my Jewels," as he put it.[4]

Works Issued by the Hakluyt Society, 2d Ser., no. 104 (London, 1955), I, 452. For the larger context and modern identification of the towhee, see Bayard H. Christy, "Topsell's 'Fowles of Heavn,'" *Auk*, L (1933), 275–283. On Topsell's place in the history of American bird studies, see Elsa Guerdrum Allen, "The History of American Ornithology before Audubon," American Philosophical Society, *Transactions*, XLI (1951), 387–591 (Topsell appears on 447–448). For the history and context of the manuscript, see Topsell, *The Fowles of Heaven*, ed. Harrison and Hoeniger, xix–xxxvi.

4. J. H. Elliott, *The Old World and the New, 1492–1650* (Cambridge, 1970), 28–53; Henry Lowood, "The New World and the European Catalog of Nature," in Karen Ordahl Kupperman, ed., *America in European Consciousness, 1493–1750* (Williamsburg, Va., and Chapel Hill, N.C., 1995), 295–323; Samuel Purchas, *Purchas His Pilgrimes, in Five Books...* (London, 1625), III, 1065. On Hakluyt's living in Paris and his relationship with Thevet, see Peter C. Mancall, *Hakluyt's Promise: An Elizabethan's Obsession for an English America* (New Haven, Conn., 2007), 102–127. For the career of the codex from its

The English had been seeking accurate descriptions of the Americas before White first sailed westward in 1585. A memo from 1582 or 1583 that the politician and manuscript collector Sir Edward Hoby copied into his commonplace book reflected this desire. The detailed note was likely part of the directions for the voyage and possible colonizing venture of Sir Humphrey Gilbert and his allies, as historian David Beers Quinn argued. The surviving text reads like a how-to for explorers, with specific directions about everything they were to describe while on a voyage. The list of what to include anticipated, almost exactly, the entire genre of travel literature that began to appear in English at this time. Travelers were to note local geography, animals, birds, fish, shellfish (and possible sources of pearls), insects, soils, trees, flowers, minerals, and naval stores as well as human occupants and their practices. But words, however descriptive, were not enough. The memo noted that the expedition's artist, Thomas Blavin, should take along paper, quills, and inks "of all sortes of colours, to drawe all thinges to life."[5]

When Hakluyt shared the picture of the towhee with Topsell, it was not the first time that he had given information about the Americas to someone who could help him spread such knowledge. But, by 1614 or so, Hakluyt likely thought that English prospects for America were not as promising as they had seemed when he was in Paris thirty years earlier. It is possible that sending the gift to Topsell was among Hakluyt's final efforts to promote English activities in the Western Hemisphere. His last major publication, *Dialogues in the English and Malaian Languages,* a guide for English explorers eager to trade in the southwest Pacific, appeared the same year. Hakluyt arranged for the publication of the English-language version because he knew that the Spice Islands held great promise. Given that the Dutch legal theorist Hugo Grotius in 1609 had published a treatise arguing that no single European group could claim a monopoly of trade there, the region was open to English commerce and perhaps even colonization. No wonder that Hakluyt translated this text into English.[6]

Hakluyt knew better than most people in the early years of the seventeenth century that the English experience in the Americas could be summarized as one

---

creation through its experience with Thevet, Hakluyt, Purchas, and beyond, see Daniela Bleichmar, "History in Pictures: Translating the *Codex Mendoza*," *Art History*, XXXVIII (2015), 682–701.

5. Additional Manuscripts 38823, fols. 1–8, British Library, London, reproduced in David B. Quinn, ed., with the assistance of Alison M. Quinn and Susan Hillier, *New American World: A Documentary History of North America to 1612*, 5 vols. (New York, 1979), III, 239–245 (quotation on 242).

6. Gotardus Arthusius, *Dialogues in the English and Malaian Languages; or, Certaine Common Formes of Speech, First Written in Latin, Malaian, and Madagascar Tongues . . .*, trans. Augustine Spalding (London, 1614); Hugo Grotius, *The Free Sea*, ed. David Armitage, trans. Richard Hakluyt (Indianapolis, Ind., 2004).

failure after another. Lucky explorers came home empty-handed. The less fortunate died thousands of miles away. The English thought of themselves as masters of the sea, but colonization, except in Wales, Scotland, and Ireland, proved more elusive, and even the Celtic territories had proven to be far from ideal colonies. From this vantage point, the most remarkable thing about Virginia in 1619 is that there were still colonists there twelve years after its inauspicious founding.[7]

Virginia's survival until 1619 depended, then, on continued English interest and capital, both financial and human. But the story cannot be told from one side only. Earlier expansionary efforts had failed at least in part because the English proved incapable of understanding the indigenous peoples they encountered. And, more pressing still, they too often lacked any in-depth understanding of changes within Native communities that established the conditions the English experienced when they arrived. In Virginia, as in other parts of coastal North America, the English were not the first Europeans on the scene. Even before 1607, the indigenous peoples there had more experience with cross-cultural encounters and negotiations than the newcomers from the realm of James I.[8]

THE ENGLISH, AS HAKLUYT SAW IT, HAD LONG DEMONSTRATED AN interest in the Western Hemisphere, even if they did not always act on it in a particularly efficient manner. In the 1589 edition of *Principall Navigations,* he informed his readers that Christopher Columbus, fearful that the monarchs of Castile and Portugal would not support his mission, had sent his brother Bartholomew to seek funding from Henry VII in 1488. Alas, the poor man fell into the hands of pirates. Though he eventually made it to England, well, the rest is history. But Henry VII, not one to miss an opportunity, soon commissioned the Venetians John and Sebastian Cabot to seek new lands in the Western Hemisphere. Hakluyt believed this act gave the English a legitimate title to the mainland, as he argued in his "Discourse of Western Planting," an unpublished 1584 manuscript treatise that he provided to Queen Elizabeth and her advisers. Yet the Cabots' expeditions did not lead to any sustained colonization efforts, even though Sebastian brought home three Natives who were "clothed in beastes skinnes," as the chronicler Robert Fabian (in a report later used by Hakluyt) described, "and eate rawe flesh." When they arrived, no one in England could understand them, and they seemed, as Fabian wrote, "in their demeanor like to brute beasts." But a mere two years later, Fabian saw them at Westminster,

---

7. On those earlier colonizing ventures, see R. R. Davies, *Domination and Conquest: The Experience of Ireland, Scotland, and Wales, 1100–1300* (Cambridge, 1990).

8. See Daniel K. Richter, "Tsenacommacah and the Atlantic World," in Peter C. Mancall, ed., *The Atlantic World and Virginia, 1550–1624* (Williamsburg, Va., and Chapel Hill, N.C., 2007), 31–36.

"which that time I could not discerne [them] from Englishmen." He admitted, however, that he did not hear them speak.[9]

In the years that followed, the English proved less interested in American possibilities than other Europeans. A few books about America (and the world beyond Europe) appeared in English translations, including the first parts of Peter Martyr's *Decades,* which Richard Eden brought out in 1555, and Richard Willes's collection of accounts in 1577. But none could match in scale or depth the work of Giovanni Battista Ramusio, the Venetian civil servant and scholar whose third volume of travel narratives, devoted to travels to the Western Hemisphere, had appeared in 1556. Ramusio's volume included observations about the Americas by figures such as the Spanish natural historian Gonzalo Fernández de Oviedo y Valdés and the French explorer Jacques Cartier. These texts provided an Italian-reading audience with more details about the Western Hemisphere than even the most ambitious English reader could have found in the middle decades of the sixteenth century. Further, while some works of cosmography circulated in English, none contained the wealth of information—however inaccurate some of it might have been—found in works such as Sebastian Münster's *Cosmographiae Universalis,* published and then widely translated and reprinted during the middle decades of the century, or Thevet's *Cosmographie Universelle* of 1575. Except for the publishers of John Foxe's *Book of Martyrs,* which first appeared in print in 1563 and then in five more editions before the turn of the century, English printers tended to offer the public books less lavishly illustrated than those by Münster and Thevet. None offered nearly as much content about the Western Hemisphere as these Continental scholars. As a result, Continental audiences, or at least those who could read and purchase books, had easier access to images about the Western Hemisphere than virtually everyone in the queen's realm.[10]

---

9. Hakluyt, *Principall Navigations* (1589), 507–515 (quotations on 515); Richard Hakluyt, *Divers Voyages Touching the Discoverie of America, and the Ilands Adjacent* ... (London, 1582), sig A3r–v; Hakluyt, *A Particular Discourse concerninge the Greate Necessitie and Manifolde Commodyties That Are Like to Growe to This Realme of Englande by the Westerne Discoveries Lately Attempted ... Known as Discourse of Western Planting* (hereafter cited as *Discourse of Western Planting*), ed. David B. Quinn and Alison M. Quinn, Works Issued by the Hakluyt Society, Extra Ser., no. 45 (London, 1993), 92.

10. Richard Eden, trans., *The Decades of the Newe Worlde or West India ... by Peter Martyr of Angleria* (London, 1555); [Pietro Martire d'Anghiera], *The History of Travayle in the West and East Indies, and Other Countreys Lying Eyther Way, towards the Fruitfull and Ryche Moluccaes ... with a Discourse of the Northwest Passage ... Gathered in Parte, and Done into Englyshe by Richarde Eden,* ed. Richarde Willes (London, 1577); Giovanni Battista Ramusio, *Terzo volume delle navigationi et viaggi* ... (Venice, 1556); Sebastian Münster, *Cosmographiae Universalis* ... (Basel, 1552); André Thevet, *La cosmographie universelle* ..., 2 vols. (Paris, 1575). Thevet's *Cosmographie* was only one of his efforts to spread information about the Western Hemisphere; see also Thevet, *Les singularitez de la France Antarctique, autrement nommée Amérique: Et de plusieurs terres et isles decouvertes de nostre temps* (Paris, 1558). For the publishing history of Martyr's book, see John N. King, *Foxe's "Book of*

To be sure, there had been efforts to instruct Britons about distant places and how to get to them, notably Sir Humphrey Gilbert's 1576 pamphlet extolling the benefits of finding the Northwest Passage. But this publicity was not sufficient. Hakluyt, an assiduous scholar of travel accounts, recognized that, for a vigorous English colonization program to succeed, more information about the Western Hemisphere would have to be circulated. He approached the task both as an agent of the state, most notably in the manuscript now called the "Discourse of Western Planting" of 1584, and as a scholar, evident in the two editions of the *Principal Navigations*.[11]

Before he settled on the format of the folio-sized compendium of English travel narratives, Hakluyt had worked on a more intimate scale in *Divers Voyages Touching the Discoverie of America, and the Llands Adjacent,* which appeared in London in 1582. This slender book differed from other available accounts testifying to English travels abroad. The most notable of that genre at the time were the accounts generated by the expeditions of Martin Frobisher in 1576, 1577, and 1578. These books described the travails of sailing frigid waters and encountering Inuit and other northern American peoples who mystified English explorers, who presumed they were cannibals (as Fabian had reported about the three captives brought to London by Cabot) or possibly subhuman (as when the English pulled the shoes off an Inuk woman to see if she had cloven hooves). What had begun in planning rooms in London as a search for the Northwest Passage had evolved into a putative mining colony, which ultimately failed when the English realized that the two hundred tons of gold-flecked rocks shipped home from the third mission were best used for walls and roads. In other words, those first accounts of American encounters acknowledged the struggle, the loss of five sailors—the English presumed they had been eaten, though their fate was likely quite different—and what seemed at the time an enormous waste of money on an ill-fated get-rich-quick scheme.[12]

Martyrs" and Early Modern Print Culture (Cambridge, 2006), 92–139 (sixteenth-century editions), 162–242 (on the illustrations); and Elizabeth Evenden and Thomas S. Freeman, *Religion and the Book in Early Modern England: The Making of John Foxe's "Book of Martyrs"* (Cambridge, 2011).

11. Hum[ph]rey Gilbert, *A Discourse of a Discoverie for a New Passage to Cataia* (London, 1576); Hakluyt, *Discourse of Western Planting,* ed. Quinn and Quinn.

12. Dionyse Settle, *A True Reporte of the Last Voyage into the West and Northwest Regions* (London, 1577) (see [Bviiiv], Cv–Cijr for the story of the Inuk woman's feet); George Best, *A True Discourse of the Late Voyages of Discoverie, for the Finding of a Passage to Cathaya, by the Northweast, under the Conduct of Martin Frobisher* . . . (London, 1578); Thomas Churchyard, *A Prayse, and Reporte of Maister Martyne Forboishers Voyage to Meta Incognita* . . . (London, [1578]); Thomas Ellis, *A True Report of the Third and Last Voyage into Meta Incognita: Atchieved by the Worthie Capteine, M. Martine Frobisher Esquire* (London, 1578). For the saga and its documentation, see Peter C. Mancall, "The Raw and the Cold: Five English Sailors in Sixteenth-Century Nunavut," *William and Mary Quarterly,* 3d Ser., LXX (2013), 3–40.

In contrast, the texts in *Divers Voyages* did not testify to the vicissitudes suffered on any one journey. Instead, they offered a teasing glance at the profits to be found in North America. Hakluyt's collection made the argument that the English had every right to pursue territory there. The publication of these texts set the stage for the challenge that lay before Hakluyt from the early 1580s into the next century: persuading the English to sustain colonial efforts in the Western Hemisphere.

AT THE START OF HAKLUYT'S CAREER, FEW IN ENGLAND THOUGHT that colonies in North America made any sense. The scant available information suggested that other Europeans had already claimed much—or perhaps all—of the most valuable territory. Yet some accounts, such as the narratives of Cartier, did hint that there were resources to be extracted beyond minerals, notably furs. The European supply of beaver had collapsed by then, and the population of other fur-bearing mammals had dwindled. A continent filled with animals whose furs could be used to make hats and coats for European purchasers proved very tempting. (The possibility of those furs had earlier struck the imagination of French cartographers, who illustrated northeastern North America with large animals in the so-called Atlas Miller of 1519, now in the Bibliothèque Nationale, and, after Cartier, in 1547 in the Vallard Atlas, at the Huntington.) But neither the fur trade nor the seemingly endless schools of cod along the rich banks off Newfoundland provided sufficient motivation. Though it is possible that some Britons might have wondered about the legality of English possession of coastal North America and perhaps feared encounters with a powerful Spanish navy, Hakluyt had no doubts that they should proceed. He believed that Elizabeth I had a legitimate claim to the entire Western Hemisphere, especially to the territory between Florida and the Arctic Circle. In the "Discourse" he stated that her title was "more lawfull and righte then the Spaniardes or any other christian Princes." He dismissed the significance of Alexander VI's 1493 Bull of the Donation, noting that the pope was a Spaniard and hence never had the interests of other Europeans in mind, a situation that would have been more exasperating after the Reformation splintered European Christendom. Given the flimsy nature of the opposition, Hakluyt acted as though he believed that the English were not yet ready to commit because they lacked information that would convince them that colonization made sense.[13]

13. Hakluyt, *Discourse of Western Planting*, ed. Quinn and Quinn, 88–113 (quotation on 88). On the timing of the collapse of the European fur trade, see Eric Wolf, *Europe and the People without History* (Berkeley, Calif., 1982), 158–160. For cod, see Peter E. Pope, *Fish into Wine: The Newfoundland Plantation in the Seventeenth Century* (Williamsburg, Va., and Chapel Hill, N.C., 2004), 15–20.

Hakluyt understood that Britons lacked an ideology of colonization—a set of presumptions that would prompt English leaders to pursue new opportunities when confronted with novel evidence about America. Here the model employed by Bernard Bailyn, drawing on the structural anthropologist Clifford Geertz, is relevant. The contents of pamphlets about the American Revolutionary crisis constituted what Bailyn called "formal discourse," which contributed to politics but were not, in themselves, effective in the sense of defining "motives" or as "a form of weaponry." Instead, as Bailyn argued, such discourse "becomes politically powerful when it becomes ideology: when it articulates and fuses into effective formulations opinions and attitudes that are otherwise too scattered and vague to be acted upon; when it mobilizes a general mood, 'a set of disconnected, unrealized private emotions,' into 'a public possession, a social fact.'" In other words, as he wrote, this body of ideas shifts the direction of human action "when it crystallizes otherwise inchoate social and political discontent and thereby shapes what is otherwise instinctive and directs it to attainable goals; when it clarifies, symbolizes, and elevates to structured consciousness the mingled urges that stir within us." Such discourse lacks the capacity to create action on its own. Instead, it "can only formulate, reshape, and direct forward moods, attitudes, ideas, and aspirations that in some form, however crude or incomplete, already exist."[14]

No individual, no matter how talented, can change the way that an entire body politic thinks. Even Hakluyt, who understood more about the Americas than anyone in England in the latter decades of the sixteenth century (though he had never been anywhere farther than France), could only do so much. Yet he did create a "grammar of colonization." That is, his own writings and those he gathered for publication helped formulate arguments for English colonies in North America. The benefits were vast, as both he and his elder cousin, a lawyer who bore the same name and was thus well versed in the forms of legal argumentation, knew so well. In 1585, the older man had written a tract explaining the myriad gains to be had from establishing settlements in the place that the English were already calling "Virginia," specifically between forty and forty-two degrees north latitude. Such settlements, he argued, would spread Protestantism "among those infidels." They would also enlarge the realm and the glory of

---

14. Bernard Bailyn, "The Central Themes of the American Revolution: An Interpretation," in Stephen G. Kurtz and James H. Hutson, eds., *Essays on the American Revolution* (Chapel Hill, N.C., 1973), 3–31 (quotations on 11); see also Clifford Geertz, "Ideology as a Cultural System," first printed in David E. Apter, ed., *Ideology and Discontent* (New York, 1964), 47–76, and reprinted in Geertz, *The Interpretation of Cultures: Selected Essays* (New York, 1973), 193–233. Bailyn developed these ideas at length in *The Ideological Origins of the American Revolution* (Cambridge, Mass., 1967), esp. 1–21.

the queen; create markets for English manufactured goods; establish a base for finding the Northwest Passage; provide innumerable raw materials—wood for the building trades, naval stores, and furs, among others; provide additional protection to Ireland; and possibly establish mines. Perhaps most important, these outposts could provide working opportunities for young, displaced Englishmen. "Our people void of sufficient trades," as the lawyer put it, could there "be honestly imploied, that els may become hurtfull at home." In his simplest formulation, he wrote:

The ends of this voyage are these:
1. To plant Christian religion.
2. To trafficke.
3. To conquer.
Or, to doe all three.[15]

The same set of ideas animated the younger Hakluyt for the most fertile part of his career, from the early 1580s to around 1600, when the third volume of the expanded *Principal Navigations* appeared. His writings laid out a compelling argument for colonization. Time and again Hakluyt's works—and those of the individuals whose observations he included in his edited collections—described the natural wonders of North America and the potential for bringing English-style religion and culture to receptive Americans. These Natives lived, according to the 1584 report of the explorers Philip Amadas and Arthur Barlowe, in a veritable paradise. "Wee found the people most gentle, loving, and faithfull, void of all guile, and treason, and such as lived after the manner of the golden age," they wrote in the most famous passage of their account. "The earth bringeth foorth all things in aboundance, as in the first creation, without toile or labour."[16]

Taken together with his other projects, notably his participation in marrying engraved versions of the 1585 watercolors of the English artist John White to the text of Thomas Harriot's *Briefe and True Report of the New Found Land of Virginia* in the Frankfurt workshop of the Flemish engraver Theodor de Bry, Hakluyt laid out a plan that seemed ideal. While the de Bry engravings differed substantially from White's watercolors, the argument that Hakluyt and his allies intended to convey was clearest in the brief text introducing the fanciful images of the Picts at the end of the book. "The painter of whom I have had the first of the Inhabitants of Virginia," the text reads, with a reference to White, "give my

---

15. Mancall, *Hakluyt's Promise*, 128–155 ("grammar"); Quinn, ed., *New American World*, III, 64–69 (quotation on 66).
16. "The First Voyage Made to the Coastes of America," in Hakluyt, *Principall Navigations* (1589), 728–733 (quotation on 731).

allso thees 5. Figures fallowinge, fownd as hy did assured my in a oolld English cronicle." The author of this text wanted these images published along with the American images "for to showe how that the Inhabitants of the great Bretannie have bin in times past as sauvage as those of Virginia."[17]

Everything fit together, as Hakluyt saw it. But seeing it with a clear eye did not mean that others would agree, especially if there were competing ideas in circulation suggesting that colonization, although perhaps an aspirational ideal, was rather more difficult than Hakluyt and his allies suggested.

HARRIOT'S TEXT REVEALED THE POTENTIAL OF NORTH AMERICA TO an English reading audience—and also to readers who acquired the French, Latin, or German editions that emanated simultaneously from de Bry's workshop. But savvy English readers would have known that, by the time any copies of the newly printed book appeared in an English bookshop, the effort to settle "Virginia" had already failed. Rather than a newfound paradise, the attempt to colonize Roanoke Island led to more death and disappointment. Frobisher's three American voyages had produced no lasting changes in the north. The exertions to settle and then resupply Carolina fared no better. Those colonists who went there were lost, just like the five men Frobisher had left behind.

The next fifteen years were not much better. Hakluyt publicized details about Gilbert's exploration of Newfoundland, an expedition that produced another tragedy. The 1583 venture led to the deaths of the explorer and most of those who accompanied him, including the Hungarian poet Stephen Parmenius, a dear friend of Hakluyt's. Three ships went into those northeastern waters, but two of them sank before making it home. Still, fortunately for those seeking information about North America, the surviving ship's captain, Steven Hayes, brought back Parmenius's Latin treatise about the region, which Hakluyt translated and included in the *Principall Navigations*. The text survived, but not its author or the commander of the project.[18]

Other English travelers to North America fared little better. John Davis led three expeditions in search of the Northwest Passage in the mid-1580s. He survived, but, besides revealing more details about one corner of the northwest Atlantic, his journeys brought few rewards for the English. Scholars remained convinced that the Northwest Passage existed, but they were no closer to find-

17. Thomas Har[r]iot, *A Briefe and True Report of the New Found Land of Virginia* ... (Frankfort-am-Main, 1590), E (quotations). For Hakluyt's role in the 1590 edition, see Michiel van Groesen, *The Representations of the Overseas World in the De Bry Collection of Voyages (1590–1634)* (Leiden, 2008), 112–116.
18. Hakluyt, *Principall Navigations* (1589), 697–699.

ing it. Davis reported that he had encountered Inuit who paddled out to him in convoys with perhaps one hundred canoes—it is possible he meant kayaks—and offered him "fishes dryed, Salmon, Salmon peale, Cod, Caplin, Lumpe, Stonebase and such like, besides divers kinds of birds, as Partrige, Fesant, Guls, Sea birds and other kindes of flesh." Hoping to learn if these locals knew of the passage, he tried to communicate with them. "I still labored by signes to know from them what they knew of any sea toward the North," he wrote, "they still made signes of a great sea as we understood them." The conversations were just another classic "dialogue of the deaf" in which the participants could not understand one another. Davis went home unfulfilled. Hakluyt, ever the dutiful gatherer of information, printed the narratives relating to the journey in 1600.[19]

The 1600 volume of *Principal Navigations* also contained the narrative of Sir Walter Ralegh's meanderings along the Orinoco, in modern Venezuela, in 1595. The explorer had intended the journey to establish an English presence in Spanish-controlled territory and to curry favor with Queen Elizabeth. But even then, well before his subsequent voyage, imprisonment, and eventual execution, the journey did little to advance English interests in the region. At least the Arctic explorations of Frobisher and Davis had generated information about the North Atlantic that would be relevant for later explorers searching for the passage to the Pacific.[20]

News of these failed efforts did not dissuade other potential colonizers. An English expedition under George Waymouth landed along the modern coast of Maine in 1605 and returned to London with five Abenakis, who shared information with their captors. The following year, members of the Council of New England, who claimed the broad arc of land from forty to forty-eight degrees north latitude, sent Henry Challons to the region along with two of the captives, Mannido and Assacomoit. They went bearing what the veteran military leader and would-be colony builder Sir Ferdinando Gorges later called "credible informations" from the Abenakis who had lived with him. Despite their preparations, the voyage failed when the English explorers were taken prisoner by Spanish sailors, who seized the ships and stole the cargo. Even before news of the setback reached England, Sir John Popham, the lord chief justice, outfitted another vessel and sent it to the same region. But Challons did not appear at the

---

19. Hakluyt, *Principal Navigations* (1600), III, 98–120 (quotation on 120). For the concept of exchanging mutually unintelligible signs in another Atlantic encounter, see Wyatt MacGaffey, "Dialogues of the Deaf: Europeans on the Atlantic Coast of Africa," in Stuart B. Schwartz, ed., *Implicit Understandings: Observing, Reporting, and Reflecting on the Encounters between Europeans and Other Peoples in the Early Modern Era* (Cambridge, 1994), 249–267.

20. Hakluyt, *Principal Navigations* (1600), III, 627–662.

rendezvous site. The newly arriving English surveyed the coast, as the Council had hoped they would do, and set sail back for England.[21]

English supporters of the cause remained undaunted. In 1607, they sent two more ships with one hundred men on them under the leadership of George Popham, a relative of Sir John, and Rawley (or Ralegh) Gilbert, son of Sir Humphrey Gilbert. This time they shipped out with sufficient provisions and ordnance to defend themselves against potential foes. Before the ships returned, however, the elder Popham had died in England, as had Sir John Gilbert, Rawley's older brother. The Popham who had died in present-day Maine was, in Gorges's telling, the only English traveler who perished there that winter. But others suffered as well from an assault that Gorges did not describe, other than to mention that "their lodgings and stores were burnt, and they thereby wondrously distressed." No English accounts remain of an assault on the newcomers by locals, but a French Jesuit heard of just such an attack a few years later. He claimed that the Americans had used witchcraft to kill the English captain, and the English then turned on the Natives at Sagadahoc. "They drove the Savages away without ceremony," Pierre Biard wrote in 1612. In response, the Natives launched an attack on three English fishing vessels, which took eleven lives. The action prompted the English to flee the area. In his *Generall Historie of Virginia, New-England, and the Summer Isles,* published in 1624, Captain John Smith noted the venture's short life. All of the would-be colonizers "returned for England in the yeere 1608," he wrote, "and thus this Plantation was begunne and ended in one yeere, and the Country esteemed as cold, barren, mountainous, rocky Desart."[22]

The English barely had time to think about the implications of Sagadahoc's failure before the Virginia Company began its venture. Yet 1607 witnessed the start of another English effort to find the Northwest Passage, this time under

---

21. Ferdinando Gorges, *A Briefe Narration of the Originall Undertakings of the Advancement of Plantations into the Parts of America, Especially . . . New England* (London, 1658), 4–5, reprinted in James Phinney Baxter, ed., *Sir Ferdinando Gorges and His Province of Maine . . . ,* 2 vols. (Boston, 1890), II, 8–9; [Ferdinando Gorges], *A Briefe Relation of the Discovery and Plantation of New England . . .* (London, 1622), Bv. For details of what happened on that mission, which never reached New England, see the account of John Stoneman (the ship's pilot), "The Voyage of M. Henry Challons Intended for the North Plantation of Virginia, 1606," in Purchas, *Purchas His Pilgrimes,* IV, 1832–1837.

22. [Gorges], *A Briefe Relation,* Bv–B2r; Pierre Biard, "Relation for 1612," in Reuben Gold Thwaites, ed., *The Jesuit Relations and Allied Documents: Travels and Explorations of the Jesuit Missionaries in New France, 1610–1791,* 73 vols. (Cleveland, 1896–1901), II, 45–47; Philip L. Barbour, ed., *The Complete Works of Captain John Smith (1580–1631),* 3 vols. (Williamsburg, Va., and Chapel Hill, N.C., 1986), I, 299–300 (chronology of the colonial effort), II, 397–399 (quotation on 399). For a discussion of what happened at Sagadahoc, with analysis of Biard's claims, see Alfred A. Cave, "Why Was the Sagadahoc Colony Abandoned? An Evaluation of the Evidence," *New England Quarterly,* LXVIII (1995), 625–640.

the direction of Henry Hudson. Every spring from 1607 to 1610, Hudson set sail in search of a water route to the southwest Pacific. He plotted his first voyage through what scholars at the time believed would be a thawed Arctic sea. But Hudson turned back when he failed to sail through the ice fields of the north Atlantic. The next year he aimed for the Northeast Passage and again failed. In 1609, with a mixed Dutch and English crew, Hudson set sail once more for the Northeast Passage, but when ice blocked them again they decided to head west, relying on information that Hudson had learned from Captain John Smith about an interior waterway through North America. This time Hudson sailed up the river that now bears his name. When he got as far as modern Albany he realized the channel could not be a passage to the South Sea. Once again, he turned back.[23]

The following year, Hudson tried a more northerly route, which took him farther west than Davis had managed, through the strait that now bears his name and into what is now Hudson Bay. After a summer of searching and a winter hunkered down with his men in James Bay, Hudson's ship *Discovery* returned home to London, but without its captain, his son, and about a dozen others. Hudson and his closest allies, so the survivors reported, had been cast away after a mutiny led by four men. As it turned out, the alleged mutineers had succumbed afterward, mortally wounded, according to the extant accounts, by Inuit who had lured them into a trap. Subsequent efforts to find Hudson produced no trace. Eventually, four of the survivors faced charges of murdering Hudson and his allies, the only action that prosecutors could pursue, given the absence of their bodies and the belief that leaving them behind must have led to their deaths. But the trial in the High Court of Admiralty exonerated them in 1617, bringing to a close another sad chapter of English efforts to colonize North America.[24]

BY THE TIME THE BLOOD-STAINED *Discovery* REACHED ENGLAND IN 1611, news had also arrived of problems in Virginia. The reports were sufficiently alarming that the Virginia Company issued its own pamphlet, *A True Declaration of the Estate of the Colonie in Virginia, with a Confutation of Such Scandalous*

---

23. John K. Wright, "The Open Polar Sea," *Geographical Review*, XLIII (1953), 338–365. For the context of these voyages, see Helen Wallis, "England's Search for the Northern Passages in the Sixteenth and Early Seventeenth Centuries," *Arctic*, XXXVII (1984), 453–472. For details of Hudson's story, see Peter C. Mancall, *Fatal Journey: The Final Expedition of Henry Hudson—A Tale of Mutiny and Murder in the Arctic* (New York, 2009).

24. The trial records are High Court of Admiralty (HCA) 1/45, fols. 118–121, 127, 130, 135–136, HCA 1/6, fols. 88, 90, 133, HCA 1/7, fol. 2, all in The National Archives, Kew, U.K. The full story of the rebellion did not reach the English public until Purchas published the relevant narratives in 1625, especially the long account by Abacus Pricket; see *Purchas His Pilgrimes*, III, 598–608.

Reports as Have Tended to the Disgrace of So Worthy an Enterprice. In the vast body of literature generated by the arrival of Europeans in North America, this might be the only promotional tract that acknowledged that some Englishmen had engaged in cannibalism. Of course, such a venture would have its costs, the unknown author of the *True Declaration* asserted. "It is but a golden slumber," the pamphleteer noted, "that dreameth of any humane felicity, which is not sauced with some contingent miserie." After all, as the Latin saying had it, *"Dolor et voluptas, invicem cedunt,* Griefe and pleasure are the crosse sailes of the worlds ever-turning windmill."[25]

When that pamphlet circulated in England, Hakluyt had just about given up his own efforts to promote Virginia. He had recently provided a translation of a Spanish text that appeared in English as *Virginia Richly Valued.* The book extolled the great riches to be found in the region, notably from as-yet-undiscovered gold and copper mines, the pearl-filled oysters that crowded the shoreline, the buffalo to be hunted in the interior, and the perfect climate for mulberry trees to support the silk industry. Soon after that publication, Hakluyt appeared in the company's records as the owner of two shares of its stock. Then his interests turned away from the coasts of North America and toward the southwest Pacific.[26]

Hakluyt had played a central role in circulating information about English travelers abroad. He had helped lay the groundwork for policymakers who used evidence about Virginia's bounties to persuade investors to sustain their commitment. But there were limits to what Hakluyt knew. He did not anticipate either the rise of slavery in English America or the emergence of self-rule there. Both developments could have startled him. The idea that the English would import Africans violated his belief that colonies would provide work opportunities for chronically unemployed or underemployed young men. He understood, of course, that colonization would not be easy for the English. Although he hoped for the peaceful conversion of Natives to English-style civilization, he wanted the newcomers to bring military might to crush any local resistance. But that was a far cry from importing Africans. Similarly, while he would have known that some colonial plans—like those of Gilbert—called for the establishment of fiefs in North America that would be controlled by a patentee, he did not anticipate

---

25. Councell of Virginia, *A True Declaration of the Estate of the Colonie in Virginia* ... (London, 1610), 38–39, 60 (quotation).

26. Gentleman of Elvas, *Virginia Richly Valued, by the Description of the Maine Land of Florida, Her Next Neighbor* (London, 1609); Susan Myra Kingsbury, ed., *The Records of the Virginia Company of London,* 4 vols. (Washington, D.C., 1906–1935), III, 84, 326 (Hakluyt as stockholder). The hope for an English silk industry in or near Virginia survived for decades; see Edward Williams, *Virgo Triumphans; or, Virginia Richly and Truly Valued* ... (London, 1650), E3r–F3r.

that colonists in Virginia would someday manage to control their own affairs without direct guidance from the company.[27]

Although he did not imagine two of the defining developments in English America, Hakluyt's decision to circulate travel accounts contributed to—and in many ways inspired—an ideological shift toward colonization. *Divers Voyages,* the illustrated version of Harriot's *Briefe and True Report, Virginia Richly Valued,* and the two editions of the *Principal Navigations* provided a public intellectual apparatus for those hoping to establish colonies. The "Discourse," though not printed until the nineteenth century, provided policymakers with yet more evidence to convince them that the time had come to establish a permanent English presence in North America.

EVER SINCE THEIR ARRIVAL AT JAMESTOWN IN 1607, THE ENGLISH HAD off-and-on troubles with the Algonquians of Tsenacommacah, the territory the English called "Virginia." In some sense, that should not have been surprising given the earlier history of Europeans in the Chesapeake. In 1570, a group of Spanish Jesuits tried to establish a mission at a place they believed its Native residents called Ajacán, which modern scholars believe lay between the York and James Rivers. They took along a man named Paquiquineo, an Algonquian who had likely been kidnapped by the Spanish in 1561, traveled to Spain twice, became fluent in Spanish, and was baptized and took the name Don Luis de Velasco. Eventually, he managed to join the Jesuits' expedition and returned to his homeland. But, during the winter of 1570–1571, the friars, likely because they did not understand local protocols relating to trade, angered Paquiquineo. Although there remains some ambiguity about Paquiquineo's origins, what happened on the Chesapeake that winter was clear: Algonquians assaulted and murdered the Spanish clerics. Pedro Menéndez de Avilés, the *adelantado* of Florida, sought to avenge their deaths when he sailed up the bay in 1572, but, other than capturing some of the indigenous people there, the Spanish gave up on the idea of establishing a mission at Ajacán.[28]

Still, despite the problems that Europeans had already faced in the Chesa-

---

27. For Gilbert, see George Peckham, *A True Reporte of the Late Discoveries, and Possession . . . of the Newfound Landes . . . by . . . Sir Humfrey Gilbert,* reprinted in Quinn, ed., *New American World,* III, 34–60. For the rise of self-rule, see James Horn, *1619: Jamestown and the Forging of American Democracy* (New York, 2018).

28. Richter, "Tsenacommacah and the Atlantic World," in Mancall, ed., *Atlantic World and Virginia,* 36–43; "The Jesuit Mission on Chesapeake Bay, 1570–1571," in Quinn, ed, *New American World,* II, 556–566; Anna Brickhouse, *The Unsettlement of America: Translation, Interpretation, and the Story of Don Luis de Velasco, 1560–1945* (Oxford, 2015), 46–90.

peake, the contents and tone of the *True Declaration* of 1610 reveal that the English colonizers had arrived with certain expectations. Despite the views of some in England who believed that the Virginia Company lacked the authority to settle in the region, the anonymous author laid out a case. The writer emphasized the religious imperative of preaching "the Gospell to a nation conquered, and so set their souls at liberty, when we have brought their bodies to slaverie." (The phrasing here likely reflects the author's understanding of Galatians 5:1.) Further, the English believed that they had made a deal with the Powhatans: they had, through trade, purchased "the pearles of earth, and sell to them the pearles of heaven." They had not, so the author claimed, deprived the Natives of sufficient land to live, since the indigenous population stood at a mere two thousand in an (undefined) arc of territory that stretched more than one hundred miles. The only way to convert them was "by dailie conversation, where they may see the life, and learne the language each of other." But in the end what mattered most was that they had a deal. *"Pasepehay,* one of their Kings, sold unto us for copper, land to inherit and inhabite," the pamphleteer wrote. *"Powhatan,* their chiefe King, received voluntarilie a crowne and a scepter, with full acknowledgement of dutie and submission."[29]

Such statements reflected an ideology of conquest, like the attitude the English had developed toward Ireland, rather than a program for colonization and coexistence with the Powhatans. Had the English known more about the region and its peoples, they might have had different views. The first Europeans in the area were Spanish, not English, though there is no evidence that the Iberians enacted rituals of possession there as they did elsewhere. Instead, their presence in the region was fleeting, but perhaps long enough to introduce diseases that thinned the ranks of the Powhatans and other Chesapeake indigenous peoples before the arrival of the English, who likely added to the circulation of death-dealing pathogens. But that initial contact with Europeans altered indigenous material culture with the introduction of new goods. In a society where political power was based to some extent on the ability to distribute favors, including rare objects, the Powhatans, and especially their powerful chief Wahunsonacock, had mastered the art of solidifying alliances. The appearance of goods such as

---

29. Councell of Virginia, *True Declaration of the Estate of the Colonie in Virginia,* 8–11. Galatians 5:1 (in the 1599 Geneva Bible) reads: "Stand fast therefore in the liberty wherewith Christ hath made us free, and be not entangled again with the yoke of bondage." The English population estimation here was likely very low. As Helen C. Rountree has noted, there were perhaps fourteen thousand indigenous peoples in the region around 1607, and that number probably represented a population already reduced by European diseases; see Rountree, *Pocahontas's People: The Powhatan Indians of Virginia through Four Centuries* (Norman, Okla., 1990), 3.

glass beads, chalices, and copper enhanced the authority of the leader, which he used to create a confederation of smaller indigenous polities. In such a world, the English would not have been greeted as a superior power. But their arrival would instead provide an opportunity for Wahunsonacock to identify another subordinate group, which would need the Powhatans to survive.[30]

From the Natives' perspective, English who would not follow their guidance violated accepted practice. It did not take long for tensions to arise as a result of the newcomers' ignorance of prevailing customs and their inability to grasp that the Powhatans viewed them as subordinates. Further, the English—as in other colonial locales—lacked the resources they needed to establish settlements without the support of the local population. The newcomers suffered from diseases, including typhoid fever, dysentery, and possibly salt poisoning, that weakened their bodies and made them more irritable. They needed food, which they did not at first know how to produce for themselves. Unlike the Algonquians, the English on the shores of the James lacked a coherent political structure, and the imbalanced sex ratio of the immigrants made family formation more difficult, thereby depriving the colonists of necessary institutions for social cohesion. No wonder that an initial period of mutual amity collapsed into the first Anglo-Powhatan War in 1609, which lasted until the marriage of Pocahontas and John Rolfe in 1614.[31]

In other places, dire circumstances forced the English to abandon colonizing ventures. Virginia could have joined that list, which stretched back to Baffin Island and Newfoundland. But the recognition in 1613 that a particularly appealing kind of tobacco could be produced in large volume in the region set Virginia apart. Here was the solution to the English problem of colonization. Or at least it offered the possibility for success, though in the mid-1610s no one in England could have predicted that the importation of the crop would erase the public

---

30. For Ireland, see Nicholas P. Canny, "The Ideology of English Colonization: From Ireland to America," *WMQ*, 3d Ser., XXX (1973), 575–598. On Spanish claims, see Joseph Hall, "Between Old World and New: Oconee Valley Residents and the Spanish Southeast, 1540–1621," in Mancall, ed., *Atlantic World and Virginia*, 66–96. For possible epidemics, see Douglas H. Ubelaker, "Human Biology of Virginia Indians," in Helen C. Rountree, ed., *Powhatan Foreign Relations, 1500–1722* (Charlottesville, Va., 1993), 56–57. There is no evidence that the Spanish deployed the *requerimiento*, the policy enacted in 1513 that enabled these Iberians to justify the seizure of land. Instead, they relied on gift exchange, perhaps because they recognized that they lacked the human resources to conquer La Florida and the territory extending northward. For the ritual and its meaning, see Patricia Seed, *Ceremonies of Possession in Europe's Conquest of the New World, 1492–1640* (Cambridge, 1995), 69–99. For the power of gift exchange, see Richter, "Tsenacommacah and the Atlantic World," in Mancall, ed., *Atlantic World and Virginia*, 29–65; and Frederic W. Gleach, *Powhatan's World and Colonial Virginia: A Conflict of Cultures* (Lincoln, Nebr., 1997).

31. Martin H. Quitt, "Trade and Acculturation at Jamestown, 1607–1609: The Limits of Understanding," *WMQ*, 3d Ser., LII (1995), 227–258.

campaign against its use or create labor demands that soon enough would lead plantation owners to import Africans to the Chesapeake.[32]

HAKLUYT GAVE THAT PICTURE OF THE TOWHEE TO TOPSELL BECAUSE he was part of a network of scholars who understood that the knowledge of nature and distant places could fuel the drive toward overseas settlement. He no doubt believed that Topsell would eventually print the picture, adding to the store of natural history knowledge about Virginia. More important than the picture itself was the circulation of information about the Western Hemisphere within England. Details about America lay at the heart of a series of encounters: of American peoples with English explorers; of explorers telling their stories to chroniclers, including Hakluyt, who gathered news; of Hakluyt and similar chroniclers with printers, who decided what should be published and what had less of an opportunity on the market; and of printers with readers. If Hakluyt's plans worked, those who read his works would have learned one crucial thing before 1619: America might be a difficult place to settle for some English, but the investment was worth it.

Hakluyt sent the picture of the towhee to Topsell believing that the naturalist would integrate new evidence into the catalog of nature. Two years later, Hakluyt was dead, and Topsell was soon to give up on his bird book, as well as any other publishing ventures. But by then their efforts, along with those of others, had made America seem normal, acceptable, and worthy of continued support, despite the horrific toll that the earliest years of Virginia took on the English who went there.[33]

---

32. Daniel K. Richter, *Before the Revolution: America's Ancient Pasts* (Cambridge, Mass., 2011), 116–117; Peter C. Mancall, "Tales Tobacco Told in Sixteenth-Century Europe," *Environmental History*, IX (2004), 648–678.

33. There were various efforts after Topsell's death to publish his work on birds, but no book ever resulted; see Topsell, *Fowles of Heaven*, ed. Harrison and Hoeniger, xx–xxiii; and Harrison, ed., *First Water Colors of North American Birds*, 12–16. For the early difficulties in Jamestown, see Carville V. Earle, "Environment, Disease, and Mortality in Early Virginia," in Thad W. Tate and David L. Ammerman, eds., *The Chesapeake in the Seventeenth Century: Essays on Anglo-American Society* (Williamsburg, Va., and Chapel Hill, N.C., 1979), 96–125; James Horn, *A Land as God Made It: Jamestown and the Birth of America* (New York, 2005), 248, 255–278; Horn, "Imperfect Understandings: Rumor, Knowledge, and Uncertainty in Early Virginia," in Mancall, ed., *Atlantic World and Virginia*, 513–540.

"The Savages of Virginia Our Project"
The Powhatans in Jacobean Political Thought

LAUREN WORKING

When John Pory, widely traveled author and one-time member of Parliament, arrived in Virginia in 1619, he expressed a deep sense of disorientation by the Chesapeake and mourned the "solitary uncouthnes of this place, compared with those partes of Christendome, or Turky where I had bene." Troubled by the destabilizing effects of the voyage and the unfamiliar environment, Pory focused on the duties of his new role as secretary in Virginia, aware that he was the first to occupy the office. As speaker at the first General Assembly that met in Jamestown in 1619, Pory assisted other members of the House of Burgesses in drafting a set of laws based on instructions laid out by the colony's governing council in London. Many of these closely mirrored the concerns of statesmen in Jacobean England, addressing the fears of vagrancy, idleness, and nonconformity that characterized so many parliamentary rulings and royal proclamations of post-Reformation English society. Yet the first law, appearing before those against cards, dice, and excess in apparel and on trade regulations, concerned English relations with their Algonquian neighbors. "By this present General Assembly be it enacted that noe injury or oppression be wrought by the *English* ag[ain]st the Indians ... the *Chicohomini* are not to be excepted out of this Lawe, untill either that such order come out of *Englande,* or that they doe provoke us by some newe injury." Amid the expected language of conformity and duty, "the Indians" crucially influenced the way the English confronted the challenges of expanding the realm, where imperially minded gentlemen hoped to establish a polity bound by English laws and institutions that might incorporate the Powhatans "together with our English" in "a new BRITTAINE in another world."[1]

The author would like to thank the "Virginia in 1619: Legacies for Race, Commonwealth, and Empire" conference organizers and participants for their insights and support. This research was funded by Durham University's Arts and Humanities Doctoral Scholarship and a Jamestown Rediscovery Foundation–Omohundro Institute Short-Term Visiting Fellowship in 2016.

1. John Pory to Dudley Carleton, Sept. 30, 1619, in Lyon Gardiner, ed., *Narratives of Early Virginia, 1606–1625* (New York, 1907), 283, 286; "A Reporte of the Manner of Proceeding in the General As-

As the 1619 laws suggest, confronting the reality of Native Americans was a fundamental concern to both English policymakers in London and colonists. "It is everie mans dutie to travell both by sea and land, and to venture either with his person or with his purse, to bring the barbarous and savage people to a civill and Christian kinde of government," preached the minister Robert Gray in London in 1609. "The report goeth, that in *Virginia* the people are savage and incredibly rude, they worship the divell, offer their young children in sacrifice unto him, wander up and down like beasts, and in manners and conditions, differ very litle from beasts." Though Gray argued that Algonquians should first be persuaded to godliness by good example, he nonetheless concluded that "we might lawfully make warre upon the Savages of Virginia our proiect." By calling it "our project," Gray rendered Native Americans a collective responsibility.[2]

It was one thing for Gray to urge his English audience to venture person or purse, but how did gentlemen in London, beyond joint-stock investment or becoming colonists themselves, incorporate America within their understanding of political order? Historians have produced invaluable work on the life cycles and experiences of servants, slaves, laborers, lawmakers, and women who migrated to the seventeenth-century Chesapeake and on the alternatingly sociable and violent interactions between the English and Algonquians in this period.[3] The following discussion relates the experience of Jamestown to Jacobean politics, demonstrating how Anglo-Algonquian encounters in the Chesapeake contributed to the development of English political culture from the earliest decades of English expansion. In his prefatory verse to John Smith's *Generall Historie of Virginia* (1624), the Lincolnshire gentleman Thomas Macarnesse specifically addressed such gentlemen: he "*who loves to* live *at home, yet* looke *abroad, / And* know *both* passen, *and* vnpassen *road, /* [and seeks to

---

sembly," in H. R. McIlwaine, ed., *Journals of the House of Burgesses of Virginia, 1619–1658/59* (hereafter cited as *JHB*) (Richmond, Va., 1915), 9; Richard Crakanthorpe, *A Sermon at the Solemnizing of the Happie Inauguration* . . . (London, 1609), D2r–D2v, D3v.

2. Robert Gray, *A Good Speed to Virginia* (London, 1609), C2r, C2v, C4v.

3. James Horn, *A Land as God Made It: Jamestown and the Birth of America* (New York, 2005); James D. Rice, "Escape from Tsenacommacah: Chesapeake Algonquians and the Powhatan Menace, 1300–1624," in Peter C. Mancall, ed., *The Atlantic World and Virginia, 1550–1624* (Williamsburg, Va., and Chapel Hill, N.C., 2007), 97–140; Martin H. Quitt, "Trade and Acculturation at Jamestown, 1607–1609: The Limits of Understanding," *William and Mary Quarterly*, 3d Ser., LII (1995), 227–258; Karen Ordahl Kupperman, *Indians and English: Facing Off in Early America* (Ithaca, N.Y., 2000); J. Frederick Fausz, "An 'Abundance of Blood Shed on Both Sides': England's First Indian War, 1609–1614," *Virginia Magazine of History and Biography*, LCVIII (1990), 3–56; Edmund S. Morgan, *American Slavery, American Freedom: The Ordeal of Colonial Virginia* (New York, 1975); Bernard Bailyn, *The Barbarous Years: The Peopling of British North America: The Conflict of Civilizations, 1600–1675* (New York, 2012); Helen C. Rountree, *The Powhatan Indians of Virginia: Their Traditional Culture* (Norman, Okla., 1989).

know] *The prime Plantation of an vnknowne shore."* To neglect the conditions of the plantation, to fail to know "*the* men, *the* manners," was to "liv'st *the* lesse."[4]

Because Jamestown was the first English colony beyond Ireland to survive its first year, the particular concerns over "savage" behavior that emerged in the 1610s and 1620s, and the increasing conviction that assimilation was necessary to achieve political control, marked English discourse and ideas of sovereignty in specific ways. The intention here is not to downplay the richness and complexities of Algonquian societies; it is to examine the effect of language and assumptions about Algonquians, however misinformed or distorted, on metropolitan discourse at the time. The focus is on the Powhatans, not because other indigenous groups did not play active roles in shaping the Chesapeake, but because of the considerable familiarity of London policymakers with the groups under Wahunsonacock, or "*Powhatan* their greatest King," the "Emperor" whom the English acknowledged as the leading Algonquian figure in their reports about Virginia. The contrast between several sources and events from 1619 and the reflections on failed management following the 1622 Algonquian attack and the dissolution of the Virginia Company in 1624, highlights the distinct role that firsthand experience in Jamestown played in shaping concepts of authority and imperium in Jacobean London. Integrating colonial experiences in early Virginia with metropolitan discourse and policy making demonstrates that colonization and state formation informed one another and draws attention to the highly personal, often emotive nature of English colonial support in the early seventeenth century.[5]

The Politics of Virginia in Jacobean London

From their earliest attempts at colonizing America, English gentlemen situated Native Americans within their conceptions of political participation.[6] Colo-

---

4. "Thomas Macarnesse to His Worthy Friend and Countryman, Captain John Smith," in John Smith, *The Generall Historie of Virginia* ... (London, 1624), Av. English scholarship tends to focus on the importance of the colonies only once more coherent visions of empire emerge from the historical record, and it is rare to find Virginia integrated in any sustained discussions of James's English reign. See, for example, David Armitage, *The Ideological Origins of the British Empire* (Cambridge, 2000); Alison Games, "The English Atlantic World: A View from London," *Pennsylvania History,* LXIV (1997), 46–72.

5. Samuel Purchas, *Purchas His Pilgrimage* ... (London, 1613), 635; John Smith, *A True Relation of Such Occurrences and Accidents of Noate as Hath Hapned in Virginia* ... (London, 1608), C[1]v; Robert Johnson, *The New Life of Virginea* ... (London, 1612). On the agency of non-Powhatan groups, see Rice, "Escape from Tsenacommacah," in Mancall, ed., *Atlantic World and Virginia,* 97–140.

6. The shift from Atlantic to global history has impelled historians to situate Jamestown within a much larger framework of European travel and discovery, one that relates English colonization to broader intellectual, political, and socioeconomic activity. See Mancall, ed., *Atlantic World and*

nial promoters like Walter Ralegh or James I's secretary of state, Robert Cecil, pitched the colonization of Ireland and America as a political good, with the subordination of indigenous peoples becoming integral to the shared vision of authority articulated by courtiers, members of Parliament, and political theorists alike.[7] Although the aggressive expansion and development of the Tudor and Stuart state frequently employed the rhetoric of "savage" others dwelling on the fringes of society to describe those who resisted English authority—so that Native Americans were "othered" alongside many different faiths and ethnographic groups—such discourse should not imply a homogeneity of cultural difference. The task of colonizing the Chesapeake, and coming to terms with the reality of Algonquian peoples and their languages and customs, raised distinct and geographically specific questions about behavior, orthodoxy, and political control. Charters for the Muscovy Company (1555), the Levant Company (1581), and the East India Company (1600) heightened English interest in Eastern trade and diplomacy under Elizabeth I, but the relationships forged by merchants and ambassadors in the East, men who were bound by the laws and customs of the polities whose hospitality they enjoyed abroad, were fundamentally different from those exchanges in early Virginia. The trading posts and factories that the English established in Mughal India or the South Seas in this period did not depend on seizing large tracts of land from other peoples, nor grappling with the legitimation of such large-scale territorial possessions. Further, by James's ascension to the English throne in 1603, colonial promoters considered the subjugation of Ireland to be more securely under way, especially after the so-called flight of the Gaelic earls of Tyrone and Tyrconnell to the Continent in 1607, which left Ulster largely open to English and Scottish intervention. By 1620, the colonist and judge Luke Gernon believed that the Irish were exhibiting all "the simptomes of a conquered nation." "I knowe of some and heare of more of our nation who endeavoure the finding out of Virgenia, Guiana and other remote and vnknowen Countries," complained the lord deputy in Ireland,

---

Virginia; Jack P. Greene and Philip D. Morgan, eds., *Atlantic History: A Critical Appraisal* (Oxford, 2009); Audrey Horning, *Ireland in the Virginian Sea: Colonialism in the British Atlantic* (Williamsburg, Va., and Chapel Hill, N.C., 2013); L. H. Roper, *The English Empire in America, 1602–1658: Beyond Jamestown* (London, 2009); Alison Games, *The Web of Empire: English Cosmopolitans in an Age of Expansion, 1560–1660* (Oxford, 2008).

7. Ethan H. Shagan, *The Rule of Moderation: Violence, Religion, and the Politics of Restraint in Early Modern England* (Cambridge, 2011), 182, 212; Horning, *Ireland in the Virginian Sea*; Nicholas P. Canny, "The Ideology of English Colonization: From Ireland to America," *WMQ*, 3d Ser., XXX (1973), 575–598; Canny, *Making Ireland British, 1580–1650* (Oxford, 2001); D. B. Quinn, "Renaissance Influences in English Colonization: The Prothero Lecture," *Transactions of the Royal Historical Society*, XXVI (1976), 73–93; Michael J. Braddick, *State Formation in Early Modern England, c. 1550–1700* (Cambridge, 2000), 422.

Arthur Chichester, in 1605, at the expense of committing to the "makinge Cyvell of Ireland."[8]

Though colonists repeatedly protested that "restless discourse" in London damaged their survival, their concerns also indicate how pervasive interest in Virginia was perceived to be. Gentlemen invested money in colonial schemes, but also considerable time and energy. The merchant and member of Parliament John Ferrar's account of the life of his brother, Nicholas, is rife with comments on both brothers' involvement with the Virginia Company. When he returned to England after several years of travel through Europe, Nicholas "found his Brother John Ferrar in the great employments in the Virginia Plantations and Company" and again with "the Virginia business" in subsequent months.[9] Given the devastating death rates in early Jamestown, there were often more members sitting on Virginia councils in London than there were settlers alive in Jamestown. By the 1620s, the list of "adventurers" who supported the Virginia Company numbered more than six hundred people. Scholars have established at least forty-nine members of Parliament who were also members of the company, though John Ferrar claimed there were more than a hundred.[10] These numbers in and of themselves do not prove that much fervor or concerted colonial interest accompanied financial investment, but elsewhere gentlemen professed a deep conviction that they lived in a particular moment of opportunity. "No nation of Christendom is so fit for this action [of colonization]," celebrated an early traveler to New England, John Brereton, in 1602. "S[i]r Dudley Diggs is in consideration [for employment in Brussels], if this new discoverie of the northwest passage (wherein he is a great undertaker) will geve him leave to think of any thing else, for that possesseth him wholy," reported the London gossip John Chamberlain in 1611. Tracking the fluxes of colonial interest in North America in the 1610s, Chamberlain reported that, "when the busines of Virginia was at the

---

8. Arthur Chichester to the earl of Salisbury, Oct. 2, 1605, SP 63/217, fol. 165v, The National Archives, Kew, U.K. (TNA); Jonathan Eacott, *Selling Empire: India in the Making of Britain and America, 1600–1830* (Williamsburg, Va., and Chapel Hill, N.C., 2016), 22; Luke Gernon, "Discourse of Ireland, anno 1620," CELT: *The Corpus of Electronic Texts*, https://celt.ucc.ie//published/E620001.

9. Thomas Dale to the earl of Salisbury, Aug. 17, 1611, in Edward Wright Haile, ed., *Jamestown Narratives: Eyewitness Accounts of the Virginia Colony: The First Decade, 1607–1617* (Champlain, Va., 1998), 552; John Ferrar, "A Life of Nicholas Ferrar," in *The Ferrar Papers* . . ., ed. B. Blackstone (Cambridge, 1938), 20–21, 22. See also Wesley Frank Craven, *Dissolution of the Virginia Company: The Failure of a Colonial Experiment* (New York, 1932), 296.

10. Horn, *Land as God Made It*; Carville Earle, "Environment, Disease, and Mortality in Early Virginia," *Journal of Historical Geography*, V (1979), 365–390; Virginia Council, List of Lottery Participants, 1610, mssHM 961, Huntington Library, San Marino, Calif.; Council of Virginia, *A Declaration of the State of the Colonie and Affaires in Virginia with the Names of Adventurors* . . . (London, 1620); Alexander Brown, ed., *The Genesis of the United States; a Narrative of the Movement in England, 1605–1616* . . ., 2 vols. (London, 1890), II, 802.

highest, in that heat, many gentlemen and others were drawn by perswasion and importunity of frends to uder-write theyre names for adventurers."[11]

The English regularly related the allure of the American landscape and its commodities, from tobacco to the hope of mining precious metals, to perceptions of the Algonquians as gentle and hospitable. The polymath Thomas Harriot's widely read *Briefe and True Report of the New Found Land of Virginia* (1588) set the template. Harriot, a protégé of Walter Ralegh's, spent more than a year in Roanoke and provided the first protracted description of Algonquians, adding copperplate engravings as visual accompaniments in his 1590 version. Native Americans would "feare and love us, that shall inhabite with them," Harriot promised, for they desired "our friendships and love." By presenting the rich commodities of the soil alongside discussions of the generosity of coastal indigenous groups, Harriot appealed to the colonially minded gentlemen within his coterie of friends, men like Ralegh or Ralegh's friend Henry Percy, the "Wizard earl" of Northumberland. At the Inns of Court, gentlemen connected with Ralegh's circle and the court of James's son, the charismatic Prince Henry, wrote erotic verses and epic poetry about North and South America, offered their services as governors and secretaries, and incorporated tobacco smoking into their elaborate social rituals. These self-styled wits sought to survey, manage, and run their own estates while fostering an urbane intellectual culture that encouraged the fantasies of expansion and cultivation in North and South America.[12]

Appealing to friends and aspiring statesmen who had the interest—and the means—to colonize Virginia, Harriot's *Briefe and True Report* made the expected connection between civility and legitimate political order, but the tract also encouraged gentlemen to think about their own civility in relation to Algonquian societies. It was "not the nature of men, but the education of men," Robert Gray had summarized in his 1609 sermon, "which make them barbarous and uncivill." Harriot had chosen to include images of the ancient Picts in his 1590 edition in order to "to showe how that the Inhabitants of the great Bretannie have bin in times past as savage as those of Virginia." Such texts framed English

---

11. John Brereton, *A Briefe and True Relation of the Discoverie of the North Part of Virginia* . . . (London, 1602), C2r; John Chamberlain to Carleton, Dec. 4, 1611, SP 14/67, fol. 107v, Chamberlain to Carleton, Aug. 1, 1613, SP 14/74, fol. 101r, TNA.

12. Thomas Har[r]iot, *A Briefe and True Report of the New Found Land of Virginia* . . . (London, 1588), E[1]v, E2v; John Donne, "To His Mistress Going to Bed," in A. J. Smith, ed., *John Donne: The Complete English Poems* (London, 1996); Josuah Sylvester, "The Colonies," in *Du Bartas His Devine Weekes and Workes* . . . (London, 1611); William Strachey, "The Historie of Travaile into Virginia," circa early seventeenth century, Sloane MS 1622, British Library, London; [Richard Brathwaite, trans.], *A Solemne Joviall Disputation* . . . (London, 1617); T. Deckar [Thomas Dekker], *The Guls Horne-Booke* (London, 1609).

civility as the means to transform savagery to refinement, but they also envisaged long-term intervention in the Atlantic as integral to the future glory of the English as a nation. In *A Description of New England* (1616), the colonist John Smith specifically related "the greatest Princes of the earth" to their "planting of countries, and civilizing barbarous and inhumane Nations, to civilitie and humanitie." Understanding themselves as uniquely and providentially placed to participate in "civilizing Nations" and seeking to improve their own polity, gentlemen increasingly understood the two in relation to each other. Those who scoffed at, or railed against, colonization, wrote John Bonoeil, keeper of the king's silkworms, were "next a kinne, indeed, to these hateful Savages, enemies herein to God, their King, and Country."[13]

Discourses of Powhatan Savagery in the Metropolis

Beneath the English insistence on cultural superiority, concerns over the destabilizing power of savagery remained paramount. The mixture of uncertainty about, and confidence in, their own civil mores underpinned the way gentlemen defined their political responsibilities. The Roman historian Tacitus, often quoted in Jacobean discourse, had warned of the dangers of degeneration in the context of empire, a belief that seemed especially relevant with the renewed English experience of colonizing Ireland in the second half of the sixteenth century.[14] English reformers considered the "Old English" in Ireland, as Catholic descendants of twelfth-century settlers, to be religiously superstitious and politically unreliable, thereby undermining the Protestant cause that the English were pursuing with such difficulty. "The neglect of the Lawe," wrote the solicitor general in Ireland, John Davies, "made the English degenerate, and become Irish." "The veri English of birth," the chronicler Raphael Holinshed maintained, "conversant with the savage sort . . . become degenerat . . . [and] are quite altered." Hopes of making "a Virginian . . . thy Neighbor, as well as a Londoner" thus projected a vision of incorporation and inclusion between the Algonquians and the English, but the transformation must necessarily be one-way. When Englishmen debated government and their own behavior in

---

13. Gray, *Good Speed to Virginia*, C2r; Thomas Har[r]iot, *A Briefe and True Report of the New Found Land of Virginia* . . . (London, 1590), E[1]r; John Smith, *A Description of New England* . . . (London, 1616), I2v; John Bonoeil, *His Majesties Gracious Letter to the Earle of South-Hampton* . . . (London, 1622), M3v.

14. J. H. M. Salmon, "Seneca and Tacitus in Jacobean England," in Linda Levy Peck, ed., *The Mental World of the Jacobean Court* (Cambridge, 2005), 169–188; Graham Parry, *The Trophies of Time: English Antiquarians of the Seventeenth Century* (Oxford, 1995), 359; Andrew Fitzmaurice, *Humanism and America: An Intellectual History of Colonization, 1500–1625* (Oxford, 2007), 159–161.

political discourse, they drew on assumptions about Algonquian savagery and on contemporary experience to endorse the necessity of plantation abroad and conformity at home.[15]

Jacobean churchmen advocated the civilizing potential of English customs in sermons to members of the Virginia Company and their parishioners in London and were prime supporters of James's vision of imperium as a monarchical project that would advance English ambitions in America through effacing savagery. Robert Gray's sermon, quoted above, advocated the use of force in conversion and settlement, anticipating the more stringent governmental policies of the 1620s. "All Politicians doe with one consent," Gray maintained, "holde and maintaine, that a Christian king may lawfullie make warre uppon barbarous and Savage people, and such as live under no lawfull or warrantable gouernment, and may make a conquest of them." Gray also emphasized the dangers of lax authority in preserving English customs and government, "for by concord small things increase and growe . . . but by discord great things soone come to nothing." Londoners expressed skepticism in their belief that colonists were able to create an ordered society modeled on England. "If he desire to know what Civilizers of people Ghospellers are," wrote the Jesuit John Floyd in 1613, in a withering indictment of English Protestantism, "let him goe into *Virginia,* where he may find one of the two or three Ministers that went thither, become savage, not any Savages made Christians by their meanes." Floyd's attack on the colony went to the heart of English insecurities about their own political nation. The English failure to realize their hopes of converting Native Americans hardly came as a surprise, Floyd scoffed, when "the *Virginian* voyagers" were "tossed with a storme of sighes, raysed by their owne Church."[16]

It is within this context of confessional dispute, and the fears of savagery as a literal, physical embodiment of degeneration and political failure, that George Yeardley prepared to depart to Jamestown to become its governor in December 1618. On November 29, 1618, the king dined with Yeardley at the royal residence in Newmarket, outside Cambridge. In the company of the duke of Buckingham, Prince Charles, and other prominent members of James's court, Yeardley and the king conversed for an hour and a half about Virginia. A large part of the

---

15. [John Davies], *A Discoverie of the True Causes Why Ireland Was Never Entirely Subdued* . . . (London, 1612), Mm2v; Raphael Holinshed, *The Firste Volume of the Chronicles of England, Scotlande, and Irelande* . . . (London, 1577), D4v; John Donne, quoted in Thomas Festa, "The Metaphysics of Labor in John Donne's Sermon to the Virginia Company," *Studies in Philology,* CVI (2009), 76–99 (quotation on 92).

16. Gray, *Good Speed to Virginia,* C4r, D4r; John Floyd, *Purgatories Triumph over Hell* . . . (Saint-Omer, France, 1613), Bb3r; Floyd, *The Overthrow of the Protestants Pulpit-Babels* . . . (Saint-Omer, France, 1612), [M4]v.

conversation centered on how best to establish stability and social cohesion. James explicitly connected his concern that the Powhatans receive correct indoctrination with his desire to establish religious orthodoxy in England, with Jamestown reflecting the health, or sickness, of the domestic realm. The king wanted to know "what inclination the savages had to Christian religion" but also "the quality of our ministers in Virginia," who must "ever conforme themselves to the church of England" and "in no sorte (albeit soe farre from home) become authors of Novelty or singularity." Inquiring into the physical landscape of the English settlement, James asked for churches to be built like Protestant churches in England. Establishing political stability entailed razing what the English deemed to be illegitimate spaces of worship in Powhatan villages, supplanting them with structures that promoted an adherence to English forms. At the same time, English ministers themselves needed to be conforming members of the Church of England. By promising them preferment when they returned to England, James also perpetuated the idea that, for gentlemen, colonization in Virginia was a service to the state, rarely intended to be a permanent post.[17]

When Yeardley arrived in Virginia in 1619 to end martial law, his supporters hailed him as a hero who might finally achieve what the Virginia Company charters had promised: English law for English subjects. The London council hoped his arrival would initiate "a Magna Charta," with laws that would "not to be chested or hidden like a candle under a bushell" but available to all English subjects of the colony. The law was additionally meant to address the litany of other "abuses and oppressions now presently raigninge" by establishing stricter social hierarchies that would serve to settle and stabilize Virginia. Yet Yeardley's instigation of the common law, with its yearly general councils and its elected burgesses from the plantations, was as much an opportunity to enhance the civil lives of gentlemen in England as it was an attempt to ensure the rights and privileges of English colonists. It was in 1619 that the gentry faction of the Virginia Company, headed by Edwin Sandys and Henry Wriothesley, third earl of Southampton, wrested control from the merchant faction led by Sir Thomas Smythe and Robert Rich, second earl of Warwick.[18]

The Sandys-Southampton faction pursued a vision of plantation that involved industrious settlement and concerted efforts to establish traditional systems of English landholding. Patrons and supporters of Virginia projected a model of civility that specifically appealed to gentlemen and pandered to their

---

17. "A Report of S[i]r George Yeardlyes[,] Going Governor to Virginia," Dec. 5, 1618, Ferrar Papers (FP) 93, Virginia Company Archives, http://www.virginiacompanyarchives.amdigital.co.uk.

18. Ibid.; Fitzmaurice, *Humanism and America*, 61; see also Andrew Fitzmaurice's essay, "The Company-Commonwealth," in this volume.

tastes. James "layde a strict com[m]ande upon Sir George . . . in all p[ar]tes of Virginia to cherish up silkewormes, and to plant and preserve Mulberie trees for the increase of silke," a project that the earl of Southampton also endorsed. James's vision for the transformation of indigenous society was not merely one of industrious Protestant cultivation by laborers and servants tilling the land. Instead, and rather fancifully at this early stage, James and his councillors seemed to view the colony as a pleasure ground for more affluent members of society. The king endorsed planting vines, not merely for economic profit, but because "pretious liquour" would spur gentlemen to settle in Virginia. Following the king's discussion with Yeardley, members of the nobility began pitching their ideas to the king. The lord chancellor Francis Bacon promised the king he would find a means of granting the Virginia and Somers Island Companies a monopoly on tobacco, and the earl of Lincoln promised to send some of his best horses to set up a race track. Despite jabs at Yeardley's social status—the letter writer John Chamberlain mocked the pomp of Yeardley's new knighthood and departure to Virginia—others in the company subscribed to the belief that Yeardley's regime would renew the plantation and revive its reputation.[19]

From these early stages, then, English plans to "civilize" the Algonquians and advance their own civil society were interrelated. To policymakers in London, the willingness to exchange cultural habits, rather than impose them, seemed to indicate colonists' readiness to reject English authority and to question the stability and endurance of Englishness itself. Without obedience enforced by accountability to the law, colonists "would in shorte time grow so insolent, as they would shake off all governm[en]t, and there would be no living among them." Governors must cultivate "the better disposed of the Natives . . . thereby they may growe to a likeinge and love of Civility," but they must abstain from living among the Powhatans themselves. The council decided to change the names of indigenous towns to English ones, such as Kiccowtan to Elizabeth City, and to move their plantations closer together. The resolve to educate Powhatans in English schools reflected Protestant hopes of achieving conversion and social order through education, but the council's policies toward indigenous children remained cautious, with a view "neither utterly to rejecte them, nor yet to drawe them to come in."[20]

---

19. "A Report of S[i]r George Yeardlyes[,] Going Governor to Virginia," Dec. 5, 1618, FP 93, Virginia Company Archives; Bonoeil, *His Majesties Gracious Letter to the Earle of South-Hampton*; Chamberlain to Carleton, Nov. 28, 1618, SP 14/103, fol. 170v, TNA.

20. "A Reporte of the Manner of Proceeding in the General Assembly," in *JHB*, I, 10, 16; "Instructions to the Governor for the Time Beinge and Counsell of State in Virginia," July 24, 1621, FP 285, Virginia Company Archives; "To the Right Hono[ura]ble Our Very Good Lordes," in *JHB*, I, 35.

Events in 1619 demonstrate that company promoters in London celebrated English law largely for its capacity to bring civility and an enforceable political hierarchy to the colony. What happened on the ground was often far different, but gentlemen viewed the common law as one means, though not necessarily an exclusive one, of better subordinating Virginia to metropolitan control. During this time, councillors in London devised additional ways to establish hierarchical order in Virginia. The proposal to create a Virginian nobility, drafted in 1619, suggests that gentlemen debated other strategies to successfully settle the colony. The intention was, not to compete with English titles, but "the mor Earnestly for to Indeavover them sellves for to bring that plantatyon to p[er]fectyon" by better entrenching Virginia within the English governing system, with the Virginia earls, viscounts, barons, and baronets establishing "faythe and fidellyty to the Crowne of England." The proposal failed to lead to the creation of any new titles, but it offers a further glimpse into the efforts undertaken by English gentlemen to participate in the political life of the realm through their involvement with plantation schemes. From London, the failures to instill conformity in the colony did not just reflect poorly on the colonial effort but also on the lives and values of gentlemen who promoted the colony as a point of honor and as a political duty, and who used the notion of a superior English civility to justify their intervention in the first place.[21]

Civil London, Royal Virginia

In the early hours of March 22, 1622, between 500 and 600 Pamunkey, Appomattoc, Chickahominy, and Warrascoyak men launched an attack on the English plantations scattered along the James River. Several settlements were destroyed altogether, while others suffered human losses of up to 90 percent. A reported 347 colonists died, amounting to roughly one-third of the colony. Colonists nearest to Jamestown, warned of the attack by a converted Powhatan boy, fled to the fort for protection, preventing a much higher death toll. When news of the event reached London in June 1622, authorities urged Governor Francis Wyatt, who had taken over Yeardley's governorship in 1621, to pursue more violent tactics in subjugating the Algonquians. The colonist Edward Waterhouse, in a widely disseminated report on the attack, condemned the "base and bruitish triumph" by which the Algonquians celebrated the killings, but he found an advantage, too, in the freedom this act gave the English for retribution. The En-

---

21. "A Project from Mr Caswell for Creating Noblemen in Virginia," July 1619, FP 121, Virginia Company Archives. This may be the Richard Caswell listed in the Virginia Company investors in *A Declaration of the State of the Colonie* (London, 1620), who adventured a substantial £125.

glish were now able to counter "the treacherous violence of the Savages" using whatever means necessary, since the "right of Warre, and law of Nations" allowed them to "invade the Country, and destroy them who sought to destroy us."[22]

The attack irrevocably hardened English attitudes toward Algonquians, but it also challenged the colonial identity of the English themselves. In the aftermath, gentlemen in London reserved the harshest critiques for the colonists, using Algonquian violence to ask questions about the authority and preservation of English government in the context of its imperial aims. "Before the last Massacre," commented Sir Nathaniel Rich, "o[u]r Colonyes were almost made subiectes to the Savages." In August 1622, the council for Virginia in London wrote a letter to Francis Wyatt and the Council of State in Jamestown criticizing the sorry state of current affairs. "To fall by the handes of men so contemptible" reflected poorly on the English themselves; worse, the English had been "made in parte instrumentes of contriving it." The colonists now bore the brunt of "Allmightie God for the punishment of o[u]rs and yo[u]r transgressions." The council attributed colonial failures to the "neglect of the Devine worshipp" and the "enormous excesses of apparell and drinkeing" that had put Virginia in such "detestac[i]on of all good mindes, and scorne of others," and thus had "the Indians prevailed." By attributing the Algonquian victory to divine retribution for the sins of colonists, policymakers reprimanded Wyatt and his governing council for failing to establish a civil polity modeled on English hierarchical and spiritual order.[23]

Gentlemen in London formed new colonial strategies as a response to the attack. Greater measures of security and protection were needed, gentlemen iterated, for nothing less but "o[u]r intentions, and hopes, and the expectation of his Ma[ies]tie and the whole state" hung in the balance. In London, councillors promised to send more migrants to populate the devastated English plantations, but they also sought to "secure Virginia by settling private p[er]sons," an emphasis that, as argued above, was not antithetical to the establishment of common law and the General Assembly in 1619 but rather a crucial component of its success. The English failures to subdue the Algonquians meant there was "no way left to encrease the Plantation, but by abundance of private und[er]takers," since it was through "better Civill goverment" that "mutuall societies doth most conduce unto."[24]

---

22. Horn, *Land as God Made It*, 255–258; Edward Waterhouse, *A Declaration of the State of the Colony and Affaires in Virginia* ... (London, 1622), C3v, D3v–[D4]r.

23. Susan Myra Kingsbury, ed., *Records of the Virginia Company of London*, 4 vols. (Washington, D.C., 1906–1935) (hereafter cited as *RVC*), III, 666, IV, 118.

24. Ibid., III, 667, 669.

The outbreaks of violence on both sides also placed Anglo-Algonquian conflict into broader reflections of English statecraft. The council in London responded to the uprising by reflecting on what policies would be "most effectuall for the engageing of this State." In the months leading to the dissolution of the company, specific reactions against Powhatan actions featured in debates by colonists and councillors about political disintegration. In "A Breife Declaration of the Plantation of *Virginia* during the First Twelve Yeares," the Sandys-Southampton faction defended Yeardley's regime as one that had transformed the brutality of colonial life before 1619. Yeardley had arrived to find no defenses against "a forreign ennemie," whether Spanish or Algonquian, and "the natives he founde uppon doubtfull termes." The legitimacy of the monarch hinged on the subjugation of the Algonquians: "Neither did we ever perceive that at any time [the Powhatans] voluntarilie yealded themselves subjects or servants to our Gracious Soveraigne, neither that ever they tooke any pride in that title." Though the Sandys-Southampton faction highlighted that Yeardley's governorship had successfully brought peace between the English and Powhatans, the planters in Virginia were forced to admit that "beinge too secure in trustinge of a treacherous enimie, the Salvadges," had contributed to the political breakdown that ensued.[25]

Eventually, the disagreements and resentments grew so heated among factions within the company that its members appealed directly to the king to arbitrate. Events in Jamestown forced the king to bring "the whole case to his own hearing." A stronger monarchical involvement in colonization depended on the king's ability to eradicate savagery: "The wounds w[hi]ch since that great wound of the Massacre, it hath more lately receaved, from their handes whom it least beseemed, are still so wide and bleedinge, that unlesse his Ma[iest]ie, and yo[u]r Lo[rdship]ps as deputed from him, shall vouchsafe to apply a Soveraine hande for the healing of them, wee are resolute of opinion, that it is impossible, the Plantation ... should either prosper or long subsist." The deaths of hundreds of English men and women had caused nothing less than a crisis of order, and the struggle of James's subjects on new frontiers became a problem the king himself could no longer ignore. The royal investigation in 1623 brought Virginian affairs to the king's chambers and the Privy Council. The king, reported Chamberlain, had forbidden the House of Commons to intervene with "the thornie business touching Virginia." "There is a Commission of Privy Counsellors and others

---

25. Ibid., 669; "A Breife Declaration of the Plantation of *Virginia* during the First Twelve Yeares, When Sir *Thomas Smith* was Governor ... by the Ancient Planters Nowe Remaining Alive in *Virginia*," circa 1623, in *JHB*, I, 35, 36.

appoyned to advise upon a fit Patent to be given to the Company of Virginia ... [at] last being ouerthrowne," the diplomat Sir Francis Nethersole reported to the ambassador Dudley Carleton. "The Reformation intended as I heare is that there shall be a Company for trade, but not for Government of the Countrey of w[hi]ch his Ma[ies]ty will take care." James took the final measures necessary to assume clearer control of the colony in 1624, after pressuring the Virginia Company to surrender its patent. Colonization, "this worthie action reserved by the Devine providence," was "to bee perficted and Consumate, by his Royall hands," whereby the colony officially became affixed to the English crown.[26]

James's closer interest in colonization from 1619, following his dinner with Yeardley before the governor's departure to Virginia, and his decision to dissolve the bankrupt Virginia Company and declare Virginia a royal colony in 1624 suggest that events in Jamestown at this time were not incidental to Jacobean state politics more broadly. It was precisely because of the close political bonds and friendships between colonists like Francis Wyatt and George Sandys and their ties to Sandys's older brother in Parliament, Sir Edwin, that letters could be so candid about the difficulties and disappointments in Jamestown. Family ties and friendships between gentlemen in London and in the colony shaped how those in London offered political advice. When the colonist and former member of Parliament George Thorpe died in the attack, the lawyer Christopher Brooke wrote a vitriolic poem from London against the Powhatans. The lengthy poem advocated their violent destruction, with Brooke using tropes and figures from classical heroic verse combined with current news from Virginia to expound more widely on state strategies of governance. "Savage men," Brooke wrote, "thinke all things govern'd by chance," while Thorpe had been a great political actor, "used to negotiate / In matters of Religion, as of State." How shameful, Brooke urged, that those who were "ignorant" in knowledge of the art of government had bested the English. Following an epitaph to Thorpe in the poem, Brooke called for "Military judgements" and a more aggressive stance against the Powhatans, criticizing the "Children in Government, and in State-Learning" who had "Taxt [Thomas Dale] for cruell." Invoking the contemporary regime under Wyatt and his advisers as well as the governorship of Dale some ten years before, Brooke's poem indicates how well informed gentlemen could be on

---

26. The King to the Speaker of the House of Commons, Apr. 28, 1624, SP 14/163, fol. 106r, TNA; Chamberlain to Carleton, Apr. 30, 1624, SP 14/163, fol. 110r, TNA; Kingsbury, ed., *RVC*, IV, 530; Sir Francis Nethersole to Carleton, July 3, 1624, SP 14/169, fol. 19r, TNA; Lord President Mandeville to Secretary Conway, Oct. 17, 1623, SP 14/153, fol. 87, TNA; Governor Wyatt and Council of Virginia to the Privy Council, May 17, 1626, in Minnie G. Cook, cont., "Sir Thomas Wyatt, Governor: Documents, 1624–1626," *WMQ*, 2d Ser., VIII (1928), 157–167 (quotation on 166–167).

Virginian affairs and also suggests that personal relationships and losses were important components to hardening attitudes against Algonquians.[27]

Beyond the seventeenth-century enthusiasm for colonization, the letters, reports, and literature penned by affiliates of the company in London suggest that Jamestown shaped metropolitan ideas of government and imperium in an active way. Letters from Jamestown to members of Parliament and privy councillors offered advice, but they also called for a specific royal response. "We humbley refer unto your Princely conscideration," the assembly wrote to James in 1624, "invokinge . . . that divine and supreame hand to p[ro]tect us." Unlike circumstances with other trading companies of the time, the trial-and-error nature of early colonization and the dissolution of the Virginia Company opened intense debate about territorial expansion and government in London, and not just mercantilism and trade. The "Discourse of the Old Company," written in 1625, is perhaps the most blatant use of colonial experience to advise policy making and influence decision making on a state level. The discourse balanced the experience of failure with the importance of preserving English rights and privileges. Its authors maintained that the "third way" of government by "an absolute Comission, disprovided of other means, save what should be raysed from the Plantac[i]on[,] experience hath taught, that it cann worke no great effect." By appealing to kingly oversight but also to the importance of governing councils while drawing on actual colonial experience, the old planters proposed a strategy of state expansion that drew on the resources of the English state—for example, providing military support—while advocating legislation that protected subjects who sought to secure land and engage in trade and industry for their own private gains. The authors suggested that the king directly ordain and appoint a colonial council that was bound by oath to Charles I so that, "by his Ma[ies]ties Royall authoritie, w[i]th consent of Parliament, bothe Plantac[i]ons might be annexed to the Imperiall Crowne of this Realme, according unto the comendable pollicie of some other great Kingdoms." The members of the bankrupt company, aware of their inability to rely solely on private donors, pitched the sovereignty of the king over colonial endeavors as integral to establishing fairer commercial activity and greater territorial control. Affirming that he would maintain the plantation as he did the rest of his dominions, Charles voiced his belief that joint-stock companies might be good for business but they were unfit branches of state. Virginia would "immediately depend upon Our Selfe, and not be committed to any Company or Corporation," Charles proclaimed, "to whom it may be

---

27. C[hristopher] B[rooke], *A Poem on the Late Massacre in Virginia* . . . (London, 1622), A4v, B4r, C[1]r, C2r.

proper to trust matters of Trade and Commerce, but cannot bee fit or safe to communicate the ordering of State-affaires."[28]

In a 1622 sermon delivered at the popular public arena of Paul's Cross in London, the clergyman Samuel Purchas had praised the crown's attention to Virginia. A legitimate king, proclaimed Purchas, was not a king without a territory, "as the *American Caciques* and *Werowances*" were. Rather, the king was a man with the power to subdue those who "bordered on the confines of Humanitie," for "how great a part of wide and wilde *America,* is now-new-encompassed with *this,* with *His* Crowne?" The sermon pandered to James's belief in the monarch as a civilizing force. Kings, James had written in 1599, must always be "rooting out or transporting the barbarous and stubborne sort, and planting civilitie in their rooms." Even in 1622, Purchas's vaulting narrative of a Western world subordinating itself to monarchical authority seemed rather fanciful. By 1625, however, the English celebration of Virginia's place in the English commonwealth appeared somewhat more believable. *"Virginia* may performe as much with equall manuring as ever *Britannia* and *Ireland* could promise when first they became knowne to the then civiller World," Purchas wrote. Further, Virginia was important because it offered a key to English ascendancy over the rest of the Americas. The English were "growing and multiplying into Kingdomes . . . so *Virginia, New England, New found Land* in the [American] Continent already planted . . . and other Ilands may be the adopted and legall Daughters of England." Those years between 1619, when James first met with Yeardley, and his death in 1625 were some of the most troubled in Jamestown's history; they were also when James became more invested in the colony. His eventual decision to involve himself directly in "that worke w[hi]ch wee have begunne" is significant. The king was finally prepared to assume responsibility for matters in Virginia, and his interference was the direct result of the news and petitions that reached him and his Privy Council from Jamestown in the 1620s.[29]

IN THE CONTESTED POLITICAL CLIMATE OF THE 1620S, GENTLEMEN used colonization in the Chesapeake to convey fundamental, if at times competing, ideas about politics and reform. In their interactions with Powhatans, in

---

28. "The Answer of the General Assembly of Virginia to Captain Butler's Unmasking of Virginia," Feb. 16, 1624, FP 527, Virginia Company Archives; Kingsbury, ed., *RVC,* IV, 546, 547; Charles I, quoted in Horn, *Land as God Made It,* 279.

29. Samuel Purchas, *The Kings Towre* . . . (London, 1623), D4v–D5r; "Basilicon Doron," in *The Workes of the Most High and Mightie Prince, James* . . . (London, 1616), o2r; Samuel Purchas, "Virginias Verger . . . ," in *Hakluytus Posthumus; or, Purchas His Pilgrimes* . . . (London, 1625), 1816; "Commission to Sir Francis Wyatt," Aug. 26, 1624, in Cook, cont., "Sir Thomas Wyatt," *WMQ,* 2d Ser., VIII (1928), 160.

struggles to manage the behavior of colonists themselves, and in advancing the establishment of the common law in Virginia, councillors grappled with vital questions over what civil society was, who might successfully enjoy its benefits, and under whose authority and government it lay. "You wilbe contente to observe the very principle and rudiments of our Infant-Commonwealth," Pory reported to the ambassador Dudley Carleton from Jamestown in 1619, "which though nowe contemptible, your worship may live to see a flourishing Estate." Colonization in Virginia offered grounds for formative political experiments and exposed the promise, and catastrophes, that such models of government engendered.[30]

Gentlemanly hopes for "our Infant-Commonwealth" shaped colonial society, but it also placed Anglo-Algonquian relations in the heart of the political nation. Yeardley's and then Wyatt's failed attempts to foster peaceful relations with the Powhatans and other regional groups, and the ambiguity of colonial policies evident in the laws of the first General Assembly, contributed to points of tension and debate from which more aggressive views of imperium emerged. As a result, the geographically specific language of colonization infused metropolitan discourse. Amid fears of Catholic unorthodoxy and the Spanish threat, English Protestants began to voice their political ambitions through increasing familiarity with a region that had only recently entered the English imagination. Gentlemen learned of "Kiskaick somewhat short of Powhatans cheif Towne (called Worowocomaco ...) [where] should my second Plantation bee, for that would make good the inland, and assure us likewise of Pamunkie River." The member of Parliament and collector Walter Cope, seeking to acquire commodities for his cabinet of curiosities, wrote an enthusiastic letter about the shells and pearls that might be gained in Virginia from indigenous inhabitants, including "Pohatan, another of the kinges." From the alluring, if tentative, prospects of colonization in the Elizabethan era to Jacobean fantasies of visiting the "mighty Court of *Powhatan*," responses by metropolitan gentlemen toward colonization were often directly informed by specific events in the Chesapeake. The Jamestown-London connection shaped domestic political discourse, therefore, while helping to engender colonial support at a time when the survival of an English America was by no means secure.[31]

---

30. Paul Slack, *The Invention of Improvement: Information and Material Progress in Seventeenth-Century England* (Oxford, 2015), 54; Pory to Carleton, Sept. 30, 1619, in Gardiner, ed., *Narratives of Early Virginia*, 282.

31. "Sir Thomas Dale's Plan for Revitalizing the Colony, 1611," in Warren M. Billings, ed., *The Old Dominion in the Seventeenth Century: A Documentary History of Virginia, 1606–1700*, rev. ed.

For gentlemen in England, the imperatives of state were not forged merely through theory or abstract discourse but through real human interaction. "See here behold as in a Glasse," proclaimed the prefatory verses of John Smith's *Generall Historie* of 1624, "All that is, or is and was." This "Glasse" represented the hope of establishing a mirror realm on the banks of the James River, one that necessitated a knowledge of the indigenous inhabitants of the Chesapeake. The "was" offers a poignant reminder that the very presence of the Powhatans in Jacobean discourse was a result of a rising imperial-mindedness among English policy makers, one that altered, and ended, as much as it began.[32]

(Williamsburg, Va., and Chapel Hill, N.C., 2007), 42; Sir Walter Cope to the earl of Salisbury, August 1607, Cecil Papers, 124/18r, Hatfield House Library and Archives; John Taylor, *All the Workes of John Taylor the Water-Poet* . . . (London, 1630), 81.

32. T. T., "A Gentleman Desirous to Be Unknowne, Yet a Great Benefactor to Virginia, His Love to the Author, the Company, and History," in Smith, *Generall Historie of Virginia*.

Race, Conflict, and Exclusion in Ulster, Ireland, and Virginia

NICHOLAS CANNY

In the year 1619, which saw the first known arrival of Africans in Virginia, the first meeting of the Virginian General Assembly, and the introduction by the English colonists of a new land grant system in the colony, the lawyer and poet Sir John Davies made his final return to England from Ireland. He had been one of the prime architects for the plantation that had been under way in the province of Ulster since 1610 and had formulated the legal arguments to justify the lesser plantations that were also promoted in Ireland during the reign of James VI and I. In doing so, he explained how, under certain conditions, the indigenous Gaelic population might be incorporated into the civil society that the government was advancing. Davies's other achievement was modifying representation in the Irish Parliament, which had traditionally given voice only to the Old English Catholic population who dominated the more Anglicized parts of Ireland. His ostensible concern was to have members returned to Parliament from all the counties and boroughs throughout the country that had been recently designated by the government. His real purpose, however, was to ensure that the Parliament of 1613–1614, of which he became Speaker, would be controlled by its Protestant members, even though most Protestants in the country had only arrived in Ireland with the plantations. Besides acting for the government, Davies (as well as his father-in-law, Lord Audley) received significant Irish plantation estates, including in Ulster, and he also invested in the Virginia Company, indicating that his colonial vision was not confined to Ireland.[1]

Davies was but one of several English people who were involved in different capacities with the plantations being encouraged simultaneously in Ireland and

---

1. Hans S. Pawlisch, *Sir John Davies and the Conquest of Ireland: A Study of Legal Imperialism* (Cambridge, 1985). On Davies's father-in-law as a planter, see Rolf Loeber and Terence Reeves-Smyth, "Lord Audley's Grandiose Building Schemes in the Ulster Plantation," in Brian Mac Cuarta, ed., *Reshaping Ireland, 1550–1700: Colonization and Its Consequences: Essays Presented to Nicholas Canny* (Dublin, 2011), 82–100.

Virginia by the British monarchy. Some contemporaries recognized that the two endeavors were drawing on the same human and financial resources, but these observers usually concluded that plantation in Ireland was strategically the more important undertaking given the proximity of Ireland to Britain. Contemporaries also believed that those involved with Ireland stood a better chance of benefiting socially and economically than those who concentrated on Virginia.[2]

Research has shown that during the first half of the seventeenth century Ireland attracted a greater English (and also Scottish) investment than did British plantation in Virginia or in any other North American location. Plantations in Ireland also attracted a larger, more skilled, and more gender-balanced settler population from Britain than any other British plantations of that time. Irish plantations, at least until 1622, were also subjected to more regular monitoring than any colonization projects in the Americas because the government was concerned about the security of the kingdom as well as of the colonists. The unique aspect of the plantation in Ulster was that it was truly British in attracting Scottish, as well as English and Welsh, investment and settlers.[3]

In practice, plantations in Ireland proved more socially beneficial to those who persevered with them than proved to be the case in any American colony. Within two decades, several prominent planters in Ireland had purchased knighthoods and even noble titles; most of these were in the Irish peerage, but a few secured Scottish titles, and some in the second generation negotiated English titles. Despite, or perhaps because of, the conspicuous material and social success of planters in Ireland, critics suggested that this good fortune could only have been achieved fraudulently and because these planters had neglected their responsibility to reform, convert, and dominate the indigenous population. Thus, when plantation society in Ireland was overthrown by insurrection in 1641, many English commentators attributed its downfall to the planters' having placed profit before public duty. The surviving settlers in Ireland, like their counterparts in Virginia after 1622, eventually recovered from the insurrection, and they, as well as new arrivals from England and Scotland, promoted further plantations in the 1650s and again in the 1690s.[4]

2. For an appraisal of the interconnections with seventeenth-century Munster particularly in mind, see David Edwards, "Virginian Connections: The Wider Atlantic Setting of Boyle's Munster Estates and Clientele," in David Edwards and Colin Rynne, eds., *The Colonial World of Richard Boyle, First Earl of Cork* (Dublin, 2018), 74–88.

3. On the Irish side, see Nicholas Canny, *Making Ireland British, 1580–1650* (Oxford, 2001).

4. Charles R. Mayes, "The Early Stuarts and the Irish Peerage," *English Historical Review*, LXXIII (1958), 227–251; Nicholas Canny, *The Upstart Earl: A Study in the Social and Mental World of Richard Boyle, First Earl of Cork, 1566–1643* (Cambridge, 1982); Joseph M. McLaughlin, "The Making of the Irish Leviathan, 1603–25: Statebuilding in Ireland during the Reign of James VI and I" (Ph.D. diss., National University of Ireland, Galway, 1999); Jane Ohlmeyer, *Making Ireland English: The Irish*

From the 1580s until the 1690s, Ireland might have attracted more settlers from Britain than any single transatlantic destination, and in some decades it attracted more British settlers than all American locations combined. The nature of the surviving data means that only estimates can be offered, but these suggest that something like 180,000 British settlers were drawn to Ireland over this interlude. The Chesapeake colonies attracted an estimated 116,000 settlers over the same period, and the Irish figure was matched only by the West Indies, where all the British islands combined drew in an estimated 190,000 settlers from Britain. The difference was that Ireland drew on Scotland as well as from England and Wales, especially during the 1690s, the decade of the most rapid migration to Ireland. During the 1650s, however, the other decade of rapid population movement in the aftermath of the Cromwellian conquest of Ireland, the migrants to Ireland were almost all English.[5]

The obvious attractions of Ireland for prospective settlers were the proximity of Ireland to Britain, with the journey from Scotland to Ulster being especially easy to negotiate, and the invitations by English or Scottish proprietors for emigrants to occupy tenancies on the estates they had acquired in Irish plantations. Many were thus given the security they had been unable to attain in England or Scotland. Planters also extended invitations to artisans and traders to settle in plantation towns, where they might promote manufactures based on the natural resources of the country—resources the planters contended were being neglected by an inexpert Irish population. And, as the English launched each new plantation, the promoters of these schemes undertook the "discovery" of Ireland's resources, as though no English people had visited the country previously.[6]

Aristocracy in the Seventeenth Century (New Haven, Conn., 2012). After the 1690s, Ulster, and Ireland more generally, no longer provided opportunity for prospective British settlers. Instead of competing for British settlers with American colonies, therefore, Ireland had joined Scotland and England as a source of settlers for Britain's American colonies and would remain so through the eighteenth century and beyond; see Bernard Bailyn, with the assistance of Barbara DeWolfe, *Voyagers to the West: A Passage in the Peopling of America on the Eve of the Revolution* (New York, 1986).

5. Nicholas Canny, "English Migration into and across the Atlantic during the Seventeenth and Eighteenth Centuries," in Canny, ed., *Europeans on the Move: Studies on European Migration, 1500–1800* (Oxford, 1994), 39–75; Karen. J. Cullen, "Scottish Migration to Ulster during the 'Seven Ill Years of the 1690s,'" in Anders Ahlqvist and Pamela O'Neill, eds., *Celts and Their Cultures at Home and Abroad: A Festschrift for Malcolm Broun* (Sydney, 2013), 35–54; Cullen, *Famine in Scotland: The 'Ill Years' of the 1690s* (Edinburgh, 2010). Another estimate of Scottish migration to Ulster is that one hundred thousand people migrated and settled between 1610 and 1710; most of this movement was after the 1660s and especially in the 1690s.

6. Christopher Maginn and Steven G. Ellis, *The Tudor Discovery of Ireland* (Dublin, 2015), 187–190; T. C. Barnard, *Cromwellian Ireland: English Government and Reform in Ireland, 1649–1660* (Oxford, 1975).

The Nature of British Settlement in Ireland

Advertisements for plantation in Ireland implied that the places to be settled lay vacant, and the plantation scheme for Ulster stipulated that the key planters (described as "undertakers") should, after an appropriate interlude, have only "British Protestants" renting land from them, even though "natives" had been occupying those lands previously. Colonization in Ireland, then, necessarily involved the removal of some owners and occupiers of land. This practice was carried to the extreme in the Cromwellian settlement of the 1650s, which, in its idealistic phase, envisaged three of the four provinces of Ireland denuded of all native inhabitants. Those not killed or executed were either to be "transplanted" to smaller holdings in the province of Connacht or in County Clare or sent as servants to Barbados.[7]

Such clearance of people seemed feasible because three major Irish plantations—in the province of Munster in the 1580s, in Ulster in the years after 1609, and the Cromwellian settlement of the 1650s—occurred in the immediate aftermath of prolonged military conflict in which one of the weapons of war used by the government forces had been the deliberate induction of famine among the civilian population through the destruction of crops and livestock (on the grounds that the efforts of the farming population were making it possible for the opposing soldiers to hold out against the government). Therefore, the various sites for plantation in Ireland are likely to have borne the appearance of a blank sheet on which a fresh impression might be imposed more than did any location for plantation in mainland North America, including Virginia. Indeed, archaeologists and historians have established that indigenous habitation remained dense in the tidewater area down to the 1640s.[8]

English officials in Ireland found it difficult to reconcile the conditions laid down for the peopling of plantations with the government's general concern to render Ireland's diverse population indistinguishable from English people and equal with them under the law. Reconciling the two became more imponderable because, whenever the government was at war in Ireland (as it frequently was during the early modern centuries), its apologists denigrated all elements of Ireland's population as unreasonable people who, as one future governor of Ireland asserted, were but "beasts in the shape of men." Such categorization

---

7. John Cunningham, *Conquest and Land in Ireland: The Transplantation to Connacht, 1649–1680* (Woodbridge, Suffolk, U.K., 2011).

8. David Edwards, Pádraig Lenihan, and Clodagh Tait, eds., *Age of Atrocity: Violence and Political Conflict in Early Modern Ireland* (Dublin, 2007).

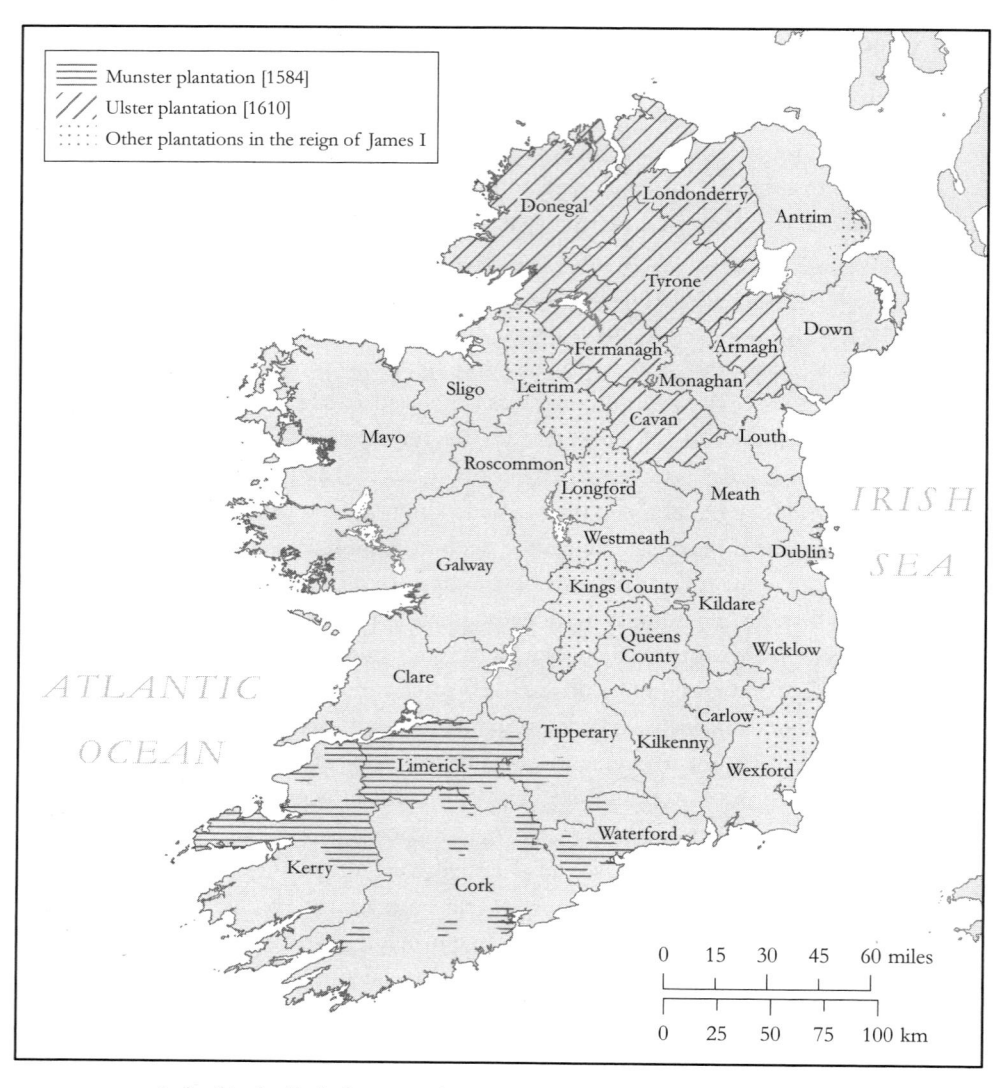

Ireland in the Early Seventeenth Century. Drawn by Jonathan W. Chipman

will be familiar to scholars of the early encounters between English settlers in Virginia and the indigenous population there.[9]

The problems that confronted Sir John Davies when he served first as solicitor general and then as attorney general for Ireland seemed soluble because he assumed office in the aftermath of a sequence of wars that had resulted in the death or exile of many of those most opposed to English rule. This sequencing made it possible for Davies to appear moderate, and he invoked as his reform model the so-called surrender and re-grant arrangements pursued by the government of Henry VIII in 1541/2, which had been occasionally attempted in modified form thereafter. Under this policy, clearly inspired by the medieval concept of vassalage, the monarch would recognize intransigent lords as subjects once they agreed to acknowledge the English monarch as their legitimate overlord. In return for their submissions, the monarch permitted these newly compliant lords to remain in control of their lordships provided they promoted English law and English land tenure within their lordships in place of Gaelic practice. Those in the sixteenth century who made such submissions, either personally to the English monarch in elaborate ceremonies at court or to the royal governor of Ireland in the field, were also admitted to the political community of Anglicized Ireland as knights or nobles or as members of the relevant Irish house of Parliament. The optimists who promoted the surrender and re-grant scheme were prepared to be patient with those who had surrendered "until they are somewhat trained and feel the commodity of a civil life." Ultimately their hopes rested on the designated heir to each surrendering lord agreeing to spend time in England, or in the English Pale in Ireland, to become familiar with English ways before being installed as successors to the initial grantees.[10]

It is unclear whether, under this scheme, all inhabitants within the former Gaelic lordships were to be recognized as crown subjects. If such was intended, there was a clear contradiction in the policy as it unfolded, because the inhabitants within each lordship were being made more subservient to their superiors than previously. Davies noted this anomaly, and, like his counterparts in Virginia, doubted if it was possible to reform society through the agency of lords who were themselves in the process of becoming civil. Instead of relying on lords to treat their dependents as subjects, Davies, in his capacity as attorney general, issued a decree in 1608 stating that the implication of the act passed by the Irish

---

9. Sir Arthur Chichester to Robert Cecil, Jan. 15, 1602, SP 63/210/24, the National Archives, Kew, cited in Canny, *Making Ireland British*, 167.

10. Lord Deputy St Leger and the Council of Ireland to King Henry VIII, Aug. 28, 1541, in Steven G. Ellis and James Murray, eds., *Calendar of State Papers: Ireland, Tudor Period, 1509–1547* (Dublin, 2017), 319–320; Christopher Maginn, "'Surrender and Regrant' in the Historiography of Sixteenth-Century Ireland," *Sixteenth Century Journal*, XXXVIII (2007), 955–974.

Parliament of 1541 declaring Henry VIII and his successors to be kings (rather than, as previously, lords) of Ireland was that "all the meer *Irish,*" regardless of rank, were "subjects and liege-men to the kings and queens of *England,*" which gave them "the benefit and protection of the law of *England,* when they would use or demand it." This ruling clarified what Davies had in mind in 1606 when he had issued a proclamation in the name of King James declaring that all denizens in Ireland regardless of rank were crown subjects with equal access to the law. Despite such an apparently definitive ruling, the position of native Irish (especially those of lower rank) before the law remained ambiguous because of the frequency with which their rights continued to be curtailed, even in peacetime, by the issuance of commissions of martial law.[11]

Davies maintained his apparently benevolent attitude toward all Irish people regardless of rank or ethnic origin in the many pronouncements he issued during his time in Ireland, 1603–1619. While appearing magnanimous toward the weak and defenseless, however, he remained consistently critical of landed proprietors, most of whom, he contended, had no legal title to the land they occupied. He became more strident in making such assertions after 1608, when, again as attorney general, he pleaded a case before the Court of King's Bench in Ireland that led to that court's pronouncing the inheritance followed in Gaelic Ireland—which the court dubbed the "custom of tanistry"—"contrary to the publick good ... [and] repugnant to the law of reason." Sustained by this finding, and aware also that Ireland had experienced a recent comprehensive conquest, the judges of the King's Bench, on the urging of Davies, decreed that King James enjoyed "the lordship paramount of all the lands within such realm," which, following the precedent established by ancient Rome, he might distribute either as a reward to those servants and warriors who had enabled the conquest "or to such colonies as he will plant immediately upon the conquest." King James, according to Davies and the judges of the Court of King's Bench, had, out of clemency, foregone his just entitlement and had instead established a Commission for the Remedy of Defective Titles to provide all the "natives or ancient inhabitants" who wished to enjoy the king's protection and become "his subjects" "to continue their possessions," on which they were but trespassers under common law, until such time as the Commission would regularize their position. Regularization permitted the Commission to restore whichever proprietors it favored to some of the land they occupied with "good title ... according to the

---

11. John Davies, *A Report of Cases and Matters in Law Resolved in the King's Courts in Ireland* (Dublin, 1762), 102, 107. The expression "mere Irish" when used here and elsewhere was always intended to designate "pure Irish" to distinguish between Irish-born people of Gaelic descent and Irish-born people of English ancestry.

rules of the law which the conqueror hath allowed or established, if they will submit themselves to it."[12]

Ireland and Virginia

The legal tenor to the discussion concerning Irish affairs in the years before 1619 renders it superficially different from anything being said of Virginia because Virginia did not have an established common law court system such as Davies was extending from the English Pale into the Gaelic parts of Ireland. Yet what the authorities had in mind for the indigenous populations in the two places of settlement was considerably similar. Thus, despite Davies's rhetoric, the native Irish in Ulster (and in Ireland more generally) had, in practice, little opportunity to benefit from the processes of English common law (other than when it served the purposes of officials to champion their causes whenever they wished to undermine their lords), not least because, as one acute English observer remarked, "in Ulster, all the gentlemen and common people (excepting only the judges' train) and the very jurymen put upon life and death and all trials in law, commonly speak Irish, many Spanish, and few or none could or would speak English." Similarly, those English officials in Virginia who contemplated how Native peoples might secure title to property that would be recognized under English common law went through the motions of identifying a means by which they might improve their position even when they knew these means could have little positive consequence for those with whom they dealt.[13]

Officials in both cases assumed that, where the ownership of land was concerned, everything belonged to the crown by right of conquest and that those of the native population who might be given title to land would acquire it by favor rather than by right. This is best illustrated in Virginia by the invitation extended by Captain Christopher Newport, purportedly on behalf of King James, to Wahunsonacock, the Native American ruler of the tidewater region of Virginia, known to the English as Powhatan, to undergo a ceremony where his head would be adorned with a copper crown. The immediate purpose behind the

12. "The Case of Tanistry," in Davies, *Report of Cases*, 86, 89, 111, 112; Pawlisch, *Sir John Davies*, 55–83. Tanistry, strictly speaking, related to political succession whereby a successor to a ruling lord was chosen from an extensive kin group while the lord was still in office. When the actual succession took place, it was followed by a redistribution of property within the lordship to take account of the new political configuration. Davies considered this practice of redistributing land, which he dubbed "gavelkind" after what he considered an analogous practice once followed in Kent, as especially unreasonable.

13. Fynes Moryson, "The Commonwealth of Ireland," in C. L. Falkiner ed., *Illustrations of Irish History and Topography*... (London, 1904), 262; Patricia Palmer, *Language and Conquest in Early Modern Ireland: English Renaissance Literature and Elizabethan Imperial Expansion* (Cambridge, 2001).

enactment was to persuade Wahunsonacock and his followers to supply food to the English in time of need. The similarity between what transpired in Virginia and the surrender and re-grant ceremonies played out with Gaelic Irish lords in the sixteenth century, however, suggests that it also was designed to signify that the English would permit a Native lord, in this case Wahunsonacock, to continue to govern his traditional followers as a vassal of King James and that the followers of the lord were being assured that this was a first step toward their also becoming crown subjects. That such was in the mind of Newport is suggested by another pageant, encouraged this time by Governor Sir Thomas Dale in 1614, when some of the Chickahominy tribe petitioned to become subjects of King James, agreeing to relinquish their tribal name and to become known instead as "Tassantessus," by which they seemingly meant crown subjects. Some other English colonists in Virginia, including William Strachey and Alexander Whitaker, also considered how the Native population, or at least their leaders, might be made crown subjects, and Governor Dale in 1614 wished to promote intermarriage between settler men and Native women to make the indigenous population in Virginia as "one people" with the English settlers there.[14]

We know from hindsight that such assimilationist views had little impact, and, among historians who have commented on the Dale episode, Bernard Bailyn attaches no importance to it because the actions of Governor Dale indicated that his real ambition was to gain English control over the tidewater. Bailyn also insists that Dale's apparently conciliatory overtures should be regarded skeptically since he made it clear that the only alternative for Natives unwilling to become subordinates to the English was to seek refuge in a "straunger Countrie." Under these circumstances, it is unsurprising that, by 1619, it was already clear that an English assimilationist policy was making little progress in Virginia. Even the possibility of the English accepting Native lords as subordinate subjects was abandoned after the insurgency of 1622, when it was evident that the Native population would never become reconciled to subservience to the English in their own country.[15]

---

14. "Letter of Sir Thomas Dale, 1614," in Samuel Purchase, *Hakluytus Posthumus; or, Purchas His Pilgrimes* . . . (1625; rpt. Glasgow, 1906), XIX, 102–108; "The Government Returned Againe to Sir Thomas Gates, 1611," in John Smith, *The Generall Historie of Virginia, New-England, and the Summer Isles* . . . (1624), in Philip L. Barbour, ed., *The Complete Works of Captain John Smith (1580–1631)*, 3 vols. (Williamsburg, Va., and Chapel Hill, N.C., 1986), II, 245–246. For more on these various experiments, see Nicholas Canny, "England's New World and the Old, 1480s–1630s," in Canny, ed., *The Origins of Empire: British Overseas Enterprise to the Close of the Seventeenth Century*, vol. I of *The Oxford History of the British Empire* (Oxford, 1998), 148–169.

15. Bernard Bailyn, *The Barbarous Years: The Peopling of British North America: The Conflict of Civilizations, 1600–1675* (New York, 2012), 73–74; "Sir Thomas Dale's Plan for Revitalizing the Colony,

By 1619, it was becoming apparent also in Ireland that those natives wishing to become subjects of the crown had to settle for being ruled by British settlers in areas in which they and their ancestors had been dominant for centuries. Those in the previously Gaelic parts of the country who sought to get title to some of their property began to realize that the Commission for Defective Titles was a legal instrument designed to assist officials in restructuring Gaelic society as these officials considered appropriate. This became all the more evident during the interlude 1610–1622, when officials embarked on an aggressive policy of "plantation" and required occupiers of land in designated Gaelic areas to submit whatever title they could present for the properties they occupied and have them subjected to legal scrutiny. In return for their cooperation, proprietors were assured that, if the Commission identified some equitable reason why they should be established as titleholders, they would receive a patent for a significant proportion (usually two-thirds) of what they had previously occupied. Such forced regularization also gave officials the opportunity to oblige Gaelic grantees to concede the status of freeholders to some of those who had customarily held land from them. Once this restructuring was complete, officials could assign estates to incoming planters (usually English Protestant officials or officers in the army who also would have been English) from the one-third of the area retained by the crown. Then, once these "planters" had taken up residency on their newly granted estates, they, rather than the native proprietors, would be selected by the assize judges to act as jurors and serve as sheriffs. Thus, those who survived as native proprietors were answerable to British Protestant settlers in areas where previously they had been dominant. And the new reality became all the more apparent when some of the incoming British proprietors were given commissions for the exercise of martial law over the lowly elements of the native population who would previously have been retainers of the native lords. Plantations of this nature were proceeded with on a limited scale previous to 1622. Nonetheless, proprietors throughout the country felt threatened by them, and when Thomas, Viscount Wentworth (later earl of Strafford), became governor of Ireland in 1632 he made clear his intention of extending the scheme countrywide, including into areas where land had been possessed by Irish proprietors of English ancestry for centuries.[16]

Although the similarities are striking between the rituals followed by the agents of the crown who sought to induce lords in Virginia to become subjects

---

1611," in Warren M. Billings, ed., *The Old Dominion in the Seventeenth Century: A Documentary History of Virginia, 1606–1700*, rev. ed. (Williamsburg, Va., and Chapel Hill, N.C., 2007), 41 (quotation).
16. Canny, *Making Ireland British*, 165–187.

and those that had been enacted in Ireland in the previous century, there is nothing to suggest that the English in Virginia ever contemplated that Native lords would be given title under English law to one-third of the land that English settlers coveted for themselves. Nor, for that matter, is there anything to suggest that Native Americans in Virginia could conceive of land as a resource from which its owners might generate an income by charging rents to tenants who would harvest crops or raise livestock on demarcated farms. Indeed, insofar as we can discern why the Native Americans were at all interested in interacting with the English, it had nothing to do with the ownership of land but rather it was because they cherished foreign commodities, notably tools, fish hooks, copper, colored beads, and even guns, which they were prepared to exchange for foodstuffs or animal skins. As such commercial interactions developed, and as the English also sought to produce commodities that would sustain the colony, they expanded outward from their original place of settlement on the James River. This growth led inevitably to conflict that might be regarded as analogous to tensions over the ownership of land that were developing in Ireland. Suggesting such similarities might be to stretch comparison beyond the point of usefulness, especially because the only comparison that was meaningful for landowners in Ireland or their legal representatives was that with their counterparts in England and Scotland. Landowners in those other two jurisdictions in what was a tripartite composite monarchy had been given assurances by their respective Parliaments that proprietors who could demonstrate that their families had enjoyed undisputed occupancy of their lands for sixty years could be certain that their titles would not be open to legal challenge.[17]

Plantation in Ulster

Landowners throughout Ireland had good reason to be concerned over the prying by officials into the titles they held to their estates as a preliminary to their being dispossessed of a portion of what they had customarily held. Their cause of grievance, however, was minor compared with that of native occupiers of land in the six of the nine counties of the province of Ulster that the government had decided in 1609 would become the site of a comprehensive plantation.

The opportunity to proceed with plantation in Ulster arose unexpectedly in 1607 when the principal native lords in the central and western sectors of the province, together with their families, suddenly abandoned Ireland, in an episode known in Irish historiography as the Flight of the Earls. They had left

---

17. Bailyn, *The Barbarous Years*, 16–116.

in the hope of being given refuge, or perhaps further military aid, by the king of Spain. Officials in Ireland were surprised by this development because they considered that those who had departed, including the prime opponents of Queen Elizabeth during the war years, 1594–1603, had been treated with excessive generosity when King James had restored them to their estates.[18]

Because they resented the clemency extended to former rebels, officials, led by Davies, had been championing the claims of subsidiary lords in Ulster. They hoped to force the great lords to establish their subordinates as freeholders on the estates they had received from King James. Such concern for the lesser lords faded once the principals had fled Ireland in 1607, and the government accepted the legal and strategic advice of Davies that the entire land surface of the six counties where the departed lords had held their estates belonged rightfully to the crown. Davies therefore recommended that the crown should proceed with a plantation that would create a stable, prosperous, and exemplary society in Ulster, previously the most unruly province in Ireland.

Some of the best minds in the governments of England, Ireland, and Scotland, including that of Sir Francis Bacon, contributed to the fashioning of a plantation program for Ulster. The scheme hinged on the undertakers, who would be wealthy Protestants of high social standing from England and Scotland. Collectively, these men were assigned one-third of the area designated for planting, and all undertakers were obliged to construct defensible buildings on the property at their expense. Then, after an appropriate interlude, undertakers were required to remove all natives from their lands and to replace them with British Protestants. The justification for this plan was the belief that British settlers would promote advanced agricultural, artisanal, and trading practices as well as Protestantism, and would, on these exemplary estates, provide a practical example of how the resources of a previously backward region might be developed for everybody's benefit.[19]

A second allocation of property was assigned to those who had served the crown in Ireland in civil or military capacities, and land was provided also for the endowment of the Protestant church. The "servitors" and the clergy who would become the proprietors of these estates were at liberty to choose tenants of any nationality, but the planners anticipated that the many former army officers who would become servitors would grant tenancies to soldiers previously under their

18. The circumstances that led up to plantation in Ulster and the formulation of the plantation scheme have been summarized in Canny, *Making Ireland British*, 165–205. For a general account, see Jonathan Bardon, *The Plantation of Ulster: The British Colonisation of the North of Ireland in the Seventeenth Century* (Dublin, 2011); and, for specific aspects, see Éamonn Ó Ciardha and Mícheál Ó Siochrú, eds., *The Plantation of Ulster: Ideology and Practice* (Manchester, U.K., 2012).

19. Canny, *Making Ireland British*, 187–295.

command. The servitors, like the undertakers, were obliged to build defensible buildings, and the government expected, given the military background of many servitors, that they would prove useful in keeping native disruption in check.[20]

The third allocation of land in the plantation (again, approximately one-third of the whole) was assigned for distribution among natives. It was expected that those who had previously cooperated with officials in challenging the great lords would be favored for grants. Some such were indeed granted estates, but others were ignored, and a few were even incarcerated without charge and died in the Tower of London. Then, surprisingly, some who had been persistent opponents of crown government were granted estates in the plantation. Given such inconsistency, the only logic that Gerard Farrell has been able to discern in the allocation of estates to native proprietors is that the government hoped to "neutralize" those who had the greatest capacity to disrupt the settlement by including them as grantees. However, not even these, claims Farrell, were assigned as much land as they had previously occupied.[21]

Natives, no less than undertakers and servitors, were required to build defensible buildings and were theoretically as entitled as their English and Scottish counterparts to serve on juries and become sheriffs. In practice, few of the native grantees had the resources necessary to erect defenses, besides earthen works, and few were appointed to civil positions of trust in the ensuing decades. More often, as Farrell has found, the native grantees experienced difficulty in adjusting to individual ownership of land while they also considered themselves bound by customary obligations to support a wider kin group. Many native grantees thus incurred debts to cover the costs of adjusting to a new style of proprietorship. Some looked to Dublin merchants for financial support to cover their indebtedness, but they frequently also negotiated loans from their British Protestant neighbors to whom they offered mortgages on their estates as security against default. These practices led to many foreclosures and the loss of property. The story that Farrell has narrated is a relentless erosion of the position of the "deserving Irish," who, as Farrell has stated, "were suddenly competing in a market economy with English and Scottish settlers already familiar with this economic system."[22]

Reference to the widespread failure of native grantees to become successful plantation proprietors does not imply that all undertakers and servitors proved

---

20. Ibid., 200–203.

21. Gerard Farrell, *The "Mere Irish" and the Colonisation of Ulster, 1570–1641* (New York, 2017), esp. 170–214.

22. Farrell, *The "Mere Irish,"* 247. The buildup of Irish indebtedness can be tracked in Jane Ohlmeyer and Éamonn Ó Ciardha, eds., *The Irish Statute Staple Books, 1596–1687* (Dublin, 1998).

exemplary managers. Many of them also lacked the means or the ability to meet with plantation conditions, and others withdrew silently from the scheme when they discovered that they had been allocated land of poor quality or in inaccessible locations. Those British grantees who did not persist frequently sold their allocations to their more enterprising British neighbors, many of whom extended their holdings well in excess of what had been intended under the plantation scheme because, as was noted, they were also expanding their estates at the expense of unsuccessful natives. Ownership never shifted in the other direction, however, because Irish people were explicitly forbidden under the plantation conditions from acquiring Ulster plantation land through purchase. Within decades, the proportion of land held by natives within the plantation scheme shrank, and those natives who remained landowners tended to occupy poor-quality land remote from seaports.[23]

Thus, notwithstanding the stated ambition of Davies to promote the position of the lesser lords in Gaelic Ulster, they, no less than the Native elite in Virginia, were quickly marginalized in an economy and society they could hardly comprehend. Some became tenants to British proprietors on land that had once been theirs, while others reacted as it was expected their Virginian counterparts would do by seeking refuge in distant places. The preferred destination for Ulster natives of high status was in Catholic countries in western Europe. There they could enter seminaries in Spain, France, or Flanders, become junior officers in the Spanish army based in Flanders, or, in the case of women, enter convents as nuns or marry those Irish who had received military commissions. Of the men who withdrew, like their counterparts in Virginia, they did so in the hope of returning in more propitious times to recover what they had lost and to take revenge on those who had dispossessed them.[24]

Matters in Virginia were somewhat different because the Powhatan chiefdom was still powerful. The Native population had lost control of some prime land along the James River, however, and there can be little doubt that hostility and resentment toward the English was on the rise among the Indian peoples. The combination of these factors made it possible for them to mobilize quickly in 1622 and to launch an attack that, but for accidental factors, might have delivered a fatal blow to a rapidly expanding colony. No such attack was possible at this stage in Ulster, where, besides the ability of many planters to defend themselves, they could rely on strategically placed garrisons of English soldiers to protect them. It was not until 1641, when the British authorities were distracted by the

23. Farrell, *The "Mere Irish,"* 214–276.
24. Nicholas Canny, "Ireland and Continental Europe, c. 1600–c. 1750," in Alvin Jackson, ed., *The Oxford Handbook of Modern Irish History* (Oxford, 2014), 333–355.

recent conflict between the crown government and the Scottish Covenanters and by the widening rift between king and Parliament in England, that the discontented natives in Ulster, and in Ireland more generally, could mobilize an attack aimed at canceling the reverses they had suffered since the beginning of the plantation process.[25]

What is known of events in Ulster, and throughout Ireland, in 1641 reveals that native grantees in the Ulster plantation were the first to challenge the British presence in the province. The actions of these discontented landowners were bolstered in 1642 by the return to Ireland of some of their kin who had served in the Spanish army. There is also evidence to suggest that the landowners were forced to take action by disgruntled subordinates, who, in turn, shifted the insurrection in more radical directions. This knowledge allows us to speculate on how people of modest circumstances interacted with settlers in Ulster, which, in turn, makes it possible to consider how these relationships compare with those that developed between Native Americans and ordinary English settlers in Virginia.[26]

This comparison has been pursued by Audrey Horning in her book *Ireland in the Virginian Sea*. Horning, an archaeologist by training, has drawn on the evidence assembled by William Kelso and the Jamestown Rediscovery Team of archaeologists to show that the area in which the English chose to create towns had been previously used intensively by Native Americans, who remained a significant and conspicuous presence in these places until the 1640s. Moreover, she explains how the archaeological archive points to close "intercultural sharing of residences and settlements" between Natives and newcomers, including sexual relations between English men and Native American women, that persisted until the 1622 "massacre." Interracial relations therefore extended far beyond "economic exchange" and included some Native Americans who lived both within James Fort and in the houses of artisans in the area surrounding Jamestown.[27]

Given this evidence that English people of modest circumstances commingled in Virginia with Native Americans who were at an enormous "cultural distance" from themselves, Horning thinks it is safe to assume that relations between natives and nonelite newcomers in Ulster would have been even more relaxed since English and Irish peoples were not that culturally distant from each

---

25. M. Perceval-Maxwell, *The Outbreak of the Irish Rebellion of 1641* (Montreal, 1994), 162–178, 213–239.

26. Farrell, *The "Mere Irish,"* 258.

27. Audrey Horning, *Ireland in the Virginian Sea: Colonialism in the British Atlantic* (Williamsburg, Va., and Chapel Hill, N.C., 2013), 164–165, 305, 309; William M. Kelso, *Jamestown: The Buried Truth* (Charlottesville, Va., 2006); Kelso, *Jamestown: The Truth Revealed* (Charlottesville, Va., 2017).

other. And she does find evidence in both "archaeological and documentary records" suggesting that, at what she sometimes calls the subaltern level, "the Irish and the incoming planters were able to at least tolerate one another." The archaeological evidence (and also contemporary maps) certainly demonstrates that "Irish-style dwellings" persisted in areas that were intended to be under firm British control, and she is impressed that "intercultural imbibing" occurred throughout plantation Ulster. As she compares the two experiences, therefore, Horning concludes that settlers in Ulster, as in Virginia, found themselves in a world occupied and used by an existing population, which meant that in Ulster, as in Virginia, the "survival" of the settlers "depended upon accommodation and adaptation."[28]

Horning's arguments are welcome because, although the harsh aspects of the plantation in Ulster are seldom ignored, insufficient attention has been given to those planters who aspired to integrate some of the indigenous population within the plantation society and economy. Both the planners of the scheme and the principal planters recognized that settlers would be in a numerically inferior position relative to natives at the outset, which explains why, as Gerard Farrell has described it, they sought either to expel or conciliate those of the natives who seemed most threatening. On the other side, many existing tenants sought to establish a relationship with the incoming proprietors in the hope of being retained on the lands they had customarily farmed. Some new proprietors welcomed such apparent compliance and granted leases to native farmers, anticipating that they might receive an immediate income from their estates before introducing tenants from England and Scotland.

In the early stages, then, plantation in Ulster might have lived up to the hypothesis of the advocates of plantation that the indigenous farming population would be more prosperous and secure than when they had been answerable to Gaelic lords. The surviving evidence suggests that, in many instances, good working relations were established between native tenants and British proprietors to the point where some tenants began to assume an English appearance, attend Protestant service, and even intermarry with incoming British settlers. Some British proprietors who had accepted land as undertakers in the plantation wished to continue with such arrangements and pleaded with the authorities for permission to retain as tenants those Irish who conformed in religion. This request was, however, not entertained, and undertakers were reminded

28. Horning, *Ireland in the Virginian Sea*, 234–235, 261–262, 294–296. For all the plantation maps, see Annaleigh Margey, ed., *Mapping Ireland, c. 1550–1636: A Catalogue of Manuscript Maps of Ireland* (Dublin, 2019); see also Margey, "Representing Colonial Landscapes: Early English Maps of Ulster and Virginia, 1580–1612," in Mac Cuarta, ed., *Reshaping Ireland*, 61–81.

repeatedly that they could be fined or have their grants canceled if they failed to meet the condition that they retain only "British Protestants" as tenants. When successive surveys showed that many undertakers were falling short of this requirement, officials began to enforce the regulation more rigorously with the result that, by the 1630s, when the native population was recovering demographically from the devastation of war, many native tenants who had seemed secure on plantation land were forced onto marginal holdings to make way for English and Scottish tenants.[29]

We can assume that the more rigid enforcement of the policy of excluding natives from the estates of undertakers contributed to the popular resentment that manifested itself in the insurrection of 1641. Another source of native disquiet was that, as Ulster assumed a more settled appearance, the province became a more attractive place for potential British settlers, and not only on the estates of undertakers. Proprietors of plantation lands, including native proprietors, welcomed overtures from such tenants if they were ready to pay large entry fines for extensive holdings on which they would be designated tenants-in-chief, on the understanding that they would be liable to pay modest annual rents thereafter.[30]

Attention to such processes will explain why the native farming population in Ulster became increasingly alienated from plantation society as they were being progressively marginalized within it. Some people of poorer circumstances continued to be employed by the incomers as laborers, servants, and wet-nurses, but those who previously had been employed as fighting men were identified from the outset as implacable opponents of civil society. Some lurked in the woods, which explains the trope of settlers in the early years that they could proceed with plantation work only with an axe in one hand and a sword in the other.[31]

The threat represented by such irreconcilables diminished over time as many former soldiers followed their social betters into exile on the European continent, where they found employment in the ranks of the Spanish army. Officials welcomed the departure of such dissidents even though they were enlisting as soldiers with a potential foreign enemy. They became more concerned, however, over the number of young people attending at seminaries, convents, and other educational institutions in Catholic Europe, because a steady trickle of these had begun to return to Ireland after they had been trained as missionaries for the Counter-Reformation. Most returnees settled in the towns of the south and east of Ireland, where they received support and protection from the Catholic

29. Canny, *Making Ireland British*, 219.
30. Farrell, *The "Mere Irish,"* 245.
31. [Thomas Blennerhasset], *A Direction for the Plantation of Ulster* . . . (London, 1610), A4–B.

merchant elite. Brian Mac Cuarta has shown, however, that some priests who were Ulster natives returned to what was a more challenging and hazardous mission where patronage was necessarily meager because few Catholic landowners had survived there and where many of the British Protestants who dominated the province were prepared to invoke the law to be rid of a priestly presence. Mac Cuarta has also established that some missionaries from the Pale traveled occasionally into Ulster to bolster the efforts of the Catholic clergy already ministering there. There was a political consequence to this development because, as zealous priests set about their missionary task, they also made their congregations more aware of how unfairly they were being treated in the secular as well as the spiritual domain.[32]

The differences between the enterprises sponsored by the British government in Ulster and in Virginia are so numerous that enumerating them seems superfluous. In alluding to what they shared in common, Audrey Horning has highlighted that there were more British people who had an interest in both enterprises than was the case with any previous pair of Irish and American colonization ventures. Another commonality was that the British were, in each instance, determined to take possession of whatever land they considered necessary for a successful plantation, contending that they would put it to better use than the native populations had ever done. The planters always intended to use the land to raise the livestock and food crops necessary to sustain the quality of life to which settlers would have been accustomed, but they also planned in each instance to produce commodities—silk, flax, hemp, rape, woad, hides, and wool come to mind—that could be manufactured and sold. The colonists in both Ireland and Virginia were also intent on seizing and exploiting natural commodities of which they believed the natives were either unaware or incapable of exploiting. These, in both instances, included natural forests, fish from both fresh- and salt water, and coal and iron, and some colonists experimented with glass production in each location.[33]

The promoters of colonization in both Ireland and Virginia, like all European colonists in all Atlantic locations, were interested in gaining control of compliant workforces to support the various enterprises that interested them, although each also accepted that they would have to attract some skilled artisans from outside. In the case of Virginia, the English experienced difficulty in persuading the Native population to become involved with the agricultural

32. Brian Mac Cuarta, *Catholic Revival in the North of Ireland, 1603–41* (Dublin, 2007).
33. Horning, *Ireland in the Virginian Sea*, 275; Audrey Horning, "Shapeshifters and Mimics: Exploring Elite Strategies in the Early Modern British Atlantic," in Edwards and Rynne, eds., *The Colonial World of Richard Boyle*, 27–42.

and manufacturing pursuits being promoted by the English, at which point the English looked to alternative sources of labor. Even when the English realized that Native Americans in Virginia would not work for them, however, they continued to trade with them and relied on Native Americans to guide them into the interior. This mutual interest in trade explains the interdependency between the two populations that prevailed for several decades.[34]

It seems reasonable to expect that colonists in Ulster would have experienced less difficulty in persuading the local population to work for them and with them given that the economy of the province was primarily agrarian and, notwithstanding the rhetoric to the contrary, was not fundamentally different from the rural economies of Scotland or the north of England. One obstacle in the way of mobilizing a labor force was that the population of Ulster had been depleted during the closing stages of the Nine Years' War (1594–1603), and another was that one cohort of grantees—those described as undertakers—were prohibited from having any Irish as tenants on their estates. Many undertakers, as was mentioned, chose to ignore this exclusion clause until the government began to enforce it, so many of the indigenous population were initially absorbed into plantation society. Also, many of lowly status secured menial employment from incoming planters. Even then, and despite the sparseness of the native population, many were denied a place in the emerging planter-dominated society of Ulster. Moreover, there were particular categories of people within Gaelic society—notably former soldiers and members of learned families—whom the planters considered threatening. Some of these adversaries made intermittent attacks upon the settlers until they made life easier for the plantation, at least in the short term, by abandoning Ulster to make careers in Catholic Europe. Their retreat may be likened to the withdrawal southward and westward of many Native Americans in Virginia, since, like the departing American Indians, the Irish who traveled to continental Europe went in the hope of returning either to encourage their kin to remain true to the cultural values of their ancestors or to take revenge upon those who had displaced them. In the case of Virginia, the opportunity to take revenge came as early as 1622, but the discontented of Ulster had no chance, before 1641, to launch a concerted attack. Some of those in exile never ceased conspiring to have Spain break the peace with Britain, however, claiming that another Spanish military expedition to Ireland would trigger widespread revolt within the country. Even without such disruption, as was noted, many of those who had become clerics had been returning surrepti-

---

34. April Lee Hatfield, *Atlantic Virginia: Intercolonial Relations in the Seventeenth Century* (Philadelphia, 2004), esp. 8–38.

tiously to Ireland and encouraging the native population to spurn the lures of the planters and remain loyal to their native culture as well as to Catholicism.[35]

British officials and settlers were, in both instances, fearful of religious practices that were alien to the Protestant experience, and they were especially suspicious of priests, whom they considered to be responsible for encouraging their followers to resist the lures offered to them by newcomers. In the case of Ulster, the Catholic clergy, many of whom had spent time on the European continent, certainly encouraged their congregations to retain their identity at the same time that the government was seeking to have Irish tenants removed from the estates of undertakers. Also in the 1630s, the native population was experiencing a natural demographic recovery at the very time when more British, and particularly more Scots people, were at hand to take up tenancies in Ulster. Also, the authorities in Dublin, London, and Edinburgh were distracted first by conflict between the royal army and that of the Scottish Covenanters and then by the mounting tensions between the government of King Charles and his critics in the English Parliament, explaining in part Opechancanough's decision to attack the English settlers in Virginia for a second time in 1644. In the case of Ireland, this conjuncture of events explains why dissidents in Ulster, and soon thereafter throughout Ireland, considered 1641 an opportune year to attempt the overthrow of the plantation. It also explains the ferocity of the onslaught that the native population unleashed upon settlers in Ulster and almost everywhere in Ireland where there was a significant settler presence.[36]

Revenge

Given that the Irish conflagration of 1641 was, in part, a native response to colonial exploitation, it seems appropriate to compare what happened there with the onslaught that the Native population in Virginia launched in 1622, and again in 1644, upon the settlement in Virginia. Such a parallel study seems pertinent, not because the two indigenous populations shared much in common besides their humanity, and not because any British observers of the time had explicitly likened the two peoples to each other, as English authors of the sixteenth century had frequently done. And the two insurrections also differed greatly in scale. Despite such differences, a parallel study seems relevant because the two contemporary English authors, Edward Waterhouse and John Temple, who composed the best-remembered accounts of these two insurrections, structured

35. Phillippo Osullauano Bearro Iberno [Philip O'Sullivan Beare], *Historiae Catholicae Iberniae compendium* (Lisbon, 1621).
36. Farrell, *The "Mere Irish,"* 277–301; Canny, *Making Ireland British*, 460–550.

their narratives along almost identical lines. Thus, when the authors explained and described the insurrections that had been enacted, each employed the format, themes, and tropes that one associates with colonial discourses. Each were then led to the conclusion that the future stability of the respective colonies would be assured only when all indigenes had been removed from their midst.[37]

Each narrative proceeded from the proposition that the English who had become involved respectively in Ireland and Virginia had been benevolently disposed toward the "beastly" and "barbarous" people among whom they had settled. Each population, they contended, had been given practical demonstrations by the settlers of how extra wealth could be generated by adding value to primary produce, which satisfied them that the colonization ventures they described and defended were to the benefit of natives as well as newcomers. The natives, according to each narration, seemed impressed by these demonstrations and took to living, trading, and engaging socially with the English. This positive reaction had convinced the English that their respective natives were on the point of embracing civil and Christian living, but each author then explained how subsequent events demonstrated that apparent compliance was but "treacherous dissimulation" aimed at putting the English off their guard. The settlers, despite their technological superiority, were unprepared for the barbarous assault that was the product of a carefully hatched conspiracy. The conspirators, it was alleged in each case, had planned to attack the settlers in several locations at precisely the same time to achieve their total extermination. As the two authors detailed the horrific events that were enacted in their respective settlements, each remained convinced that the plantations would have been totally destroyed had not some of the natives who had received the Christian message raised the alarm in sufficient time to prevent everybody from being slaughtered. In the case of Ireland, the intelligencer was one Owen O'Connolly, "a gentleman of a meere *Irish* Family, but one that had long lived among the *English,* and had been trained up in the true *Protestant* Religion," while in Virginia some of the instruments of God who had preempted the intended "universall" "slaughter" were "converted to Christianity."[38]

37. Nicholas Canny, "1641 in a Colonial Context," in Mícheál Ó Siochrú and Jane Ohlmeyer, eds., *Ireland 1641: Contexts and Reactions* (Manchester, U.K., 2013), 52–70; David Beers Quinn, *The Elizabethans and the Irish* (Ithaca, N.Y., 1966), 106–123; Edward Waterhouse, *A Declaration of the State of the Colony and Affaires in Virginia* ... (London, 1622); John Temple, *The Irish Rebellion; or, An History of the Beginnings and First Progress of the Generall Rebellion Raised within the Kingdome of Ireland, upon the Three and Twentieth Day of October, in the Year, 1641* ... (London, 1646). Quotations from Temple's work are from the 1746 edition: *The Irish Rebellion; or, An History of the Attempts of the Irish Papists to Extirpate the Protestants in the Kingdom of Ireland* ... (London, 1746).

38. Temple, *The Irish Rebellion,* 30; Waterhouse, *Declaration,* 20. Temple usually described the settlers as English but occasionally described them as British, taking account of the presence of Scots.

Having thus discussed how, in each instance, a total calamity had been averted, the two authors explained that the acts of treachery had exposed the natives as a "false-hearted people, that know not God nor faith," absolving the English from any moral restraint in future dealings with them. In the case of Waterhouse, he concluded that, after the events of 1622, the English were, "by right of Warre, and law of Nations," entitled to "invade the Country, and destroy them who sought to destroy us." Temple, after 1641 in Ireland, was satisfied that the English were liberated from their previous obligation to convert the Irish to civility and Protestantism and instead to have "such a Wall of Separation set up betwixt the *Irish* and *British,* as it shall not be in their [the Irish] Power to rise up . . . to destroy and root them [the British] out in a Moment."[39]

Race, Conflict, and Exclusion in Virginia and in Ulster

This parallel study of the plantation processes in Ulster and Virginia reveals each to have been a colonizing project. As such, the first objective of the planters was to take possession of the principal resources of their respective colonies and to deploy them for the benefit of themselves, of the indigenous peoples who had previously monopolized them, of the people of Britain, and of humanity at large. The theorists of colonization contended that the more efficient management of resources would, in itself, become an instrument to draw some of the indigenous population to embrace civility. The optimists believed that those who participated in such a brief educational program would soon embrace Protestantism and become crown subjects.

There is evidence that some colonists in both locations were persuaded by such arguments and that their reform efforts achieved some positive responses from the native populations. It was never clear, however, what precise benefits would accrue to natives who proved willing to take the path to civility, and neither was there agreement on how long it would take them to be accepted as equals. When Sir John Davies took stock of the reaction of some natives in Ulster to what he represented as the opportunities being offered them, he pronounced himself confident "that the next generation will in tongue and heart, and every way else, become English; so as there will bee no difference or distinction, but the Irish Sea betwixt us." Even as he contemplated this idyllic future, Davies acknowledged that whatever progress he and his associates had made had been achieved only because the current generation in Ulster had been subjected to "an entire, perfect and finall Conquest of Ireland" that had left them with no

---

39. Waterhouse, *Declaration*, A3v, 23; Temple, *The Irish Rebellion*, viii.

option but to shift their allegiance from their former lords to "the Crowne of England," which was "brai'd [braided] (as it were) in a Morter with the *Sword, Famine, and Pestilence*."[40]

For Davies, therefore, a once-barbaric people could be drawn into civil society only in the aftermath of a comprehensive conquest such as had been completed in Ireland. Even then, he and his associates (and certainly those who succeeded them) proved reluctant to consider Irish people who were supposedly on the path to reform as equals with themselves. The way colonists behaved in Virginia suggests that, independently of Davies, they had reached much the same conclusion on how barbaric natives might be made civil, and a succession of governors at Jamestown tried to bully the Native population there to comply with their wishes. The Virginia colonists, though, unlike their counterparts in Ireland, never commanded the resources necessary to promote a comprehensive conquest, and, whenever they did employ heavy-handed tactics, the Native population either resisted immediately or retreated to the west and the south with a view to returning to recover what had been taken from them at an opportune moment.

Experiences in Ulster and Virginia made it clear to the colonists in each location that it would be necessary to apply force as a first step to promoting reform. Both groups anticipated that this would provoke conflict between natives and newcomers, but each remained satisfied that they could withstand any retaliatory action from natives who they no longer considered potent. This contemptuous attitude explains the astonishment of each group when local insurgencies came close to obliterating their settlements. Once the colonists had regained the upper hand, authors in each case (again, independently of the other) wanted to exclude from plantation society those who had sought to destroy them.

Such calls for exclusion were justified on the grounds that their recent assailants were irredeemable barbarians, lacking in reason. These arguments were tantamount to contending that their opponents were racially different from themselves, and at the close of the Elizabethan era one English author had even devised an unpublished genealogical stemma for the Gaelic Irish to demonstrate that they, like the American Indians, were descended from Satan. In Ireland, however, such extreme pronouncements were put to the side once the crisis had passed, and authorities again contemplated how to secure the allegiance of at least some of the Gaelic Irish by conciliatory methods—this time backed by the power of the state. The stratagem favored in the seventeenth century

---

40. Sir John Davies, *A Discoverie of the True Causes Why Ireland Was Never Entirely Subdued . . . until the Beginning of His Majesties Happy Raigne* (London, 1612), 73–74, 272.

was that of arranging marriages between Irish male heirs and the daughters of British Protestant officials or planters. These alliances were usually enabled by the state's declaring Irish heirs to be wards of the court, which entitled officials to assign these heirs to reputable Protestant families in Britain or Ireland who would raise them in their households and choose wives for them.[41]

Such arrangements, which were a variation on the surrender and re-grant provisions of the previous century, frequently achieved a change in the political, cultural, and religious allegiance of the heads of Irish noble houses. That officials promoted these conversions shows that they no longer considered the Irish to be racially different from British or other European peoples. Many British men of lowly social position in plantation Ulster married Irish wives, suggesting that settlers of modest circumstances shared this opinion. We learn of such alliances principally because, after 1641, some of the surviving settlers identified many of the wives, who had reverted to their traditional loyalties at the onset of revolt, as persecutors of the British with whom they had previously been neighbors and co-religionists. The experience of 1641 may explain why there were fewer subaltern intermarriages later in the seventeenth century even when intermarriage at the upper social levels was officially encouraged as a means of Protestantizing and Anglicizing the prospective heads of those Irish noble families who were still in possession of their estates. Although marriages between Catholic natives and Protestant settlers at the lower social levels seem to have become more infrequent than previously, landowners of British descent continued to grant leases to native Irish tenants and to employ Irish servants, including domestic servants. When objections were raised against such practices, they had nothing to do with race but were made on the grounds of religion. Protestants who retained papists in their houses or in proximity to them were sometimes warned that they were exposing themselves to such dangers as poisoning or assassination, which, it was alleged, were encouraged by priests. Despite these alarms, the total segregation of natives from newcomers that Sir John Temple had advocated, and that became official policy for an interlude during the Cromwellian era, was never achieved.[42]

We find also in the seventeenth century that the idea cultivated by many pamphleteers in Elizabethan times—that the Gaelic Irish were a racially distinct people who shared much in common with the recently discovered populations of America—fell from favor. The racial argument lost currency for a variety of

---

41. Gervase Markham, "The New Metamorphosis," Additional Manuscripts 14824, British Library, London.

42. For such a transformation, this time in the case of the ancient O'Brien family of Thomond, see Brendan Kane, *The Politics and Culture of Honour in Britain and Ireland, 1541–1641* (Cambridge, 2010), 158–180.

reasons, not least because it had become implausible given that more English people had now had direct dealings with Irish people than in the sixteenth century. And, however much Protestant zealots wished to create exclusive Protestant communities in Ireland, those who owned estates recognized that they would always require Irish tenants and servants because they could never hope to attract sufficient Protestant settlers from outside to meet their needs.

In colonial Virginia, there were some promoters of colonization who encouraged intermarriage between English men and Native American women of high social standing as a means of attracting more of the Native population to Christian and civil living. Here the moralizing of John Rolfe as he contemplated marriage to Pocahontas comes to mind, since his scruple concerned a biblical injunction against interracial mixing. Rolfe overcame his scruples and satisfied himself that he was following God's will by marrying Pocahontas. This, however, proved to be an exceptional alliance, and it appears that consensual sexual mixing between Natives and newcomers in Virginia at the subaltern level was discouraged after 1622. Thereafter, cross-cultural marriages in Virginia were few, and the notion of racial incompatibility between the two peoples became fixed in the minds of English settlers. The Native Americans might have had no objection to the two populations in Virginia living at a remove from each other because they had no interest in becoming workers in a colony that was increasingly preoccupied with crop production, particularly tobacco. As with Ireland, however, the two populations never became absolutely separate because, in this case, some individuals in each community retained an interest in fostering trade across the cultural divide.[43]

We find in the case of Virginia as with Ireland that further incidents of conflict between natives and newcomers did occur in subsequent decades. Leaders of the settler population blamed such disturbances, in each instance, on external interference—in the case of Ireland, possible invasion by Britain's Continental enemies, and, in the case of Virginia, invasion by Indian tribes from beyond the frontier that lay to the west of them. In both cases, the settlers (who by now were the descendants of settlers) had become ever more confident of their ability to manage the working relations they had established with the natives within their direct sphere of influence even when these people differed from themselves either racially or in religion.

---

43. John Rolfe to Sir Thomas Dale, in "John Rolfe Requests Permission to Marry Pocahontas, 1614," in Warren M. Billings, ed., *The Old Dominion in the Seventeenth Century: A Documentary History of Virginia, 1606–1700*, rev. ed. (Williamsburg, Va., and Chapel Hill, N.C., 2007), 270–274.

Virginia Slavery in Atlantic Context, 1550 to 1650

PHILIP D. MORGAN

In the history of Virginia, the year 1619 is often said to be pivotal, decisive, transformative. It was a watershed moment, a crucial turning point, heralding, in journalist Tim Hashaw's extravagant phrasing, the "birth of Black America" or marking, in historian Lorena Walsh's more measured terms, "the first step toward the development of a slave society in the colonial Chesapeake." Admittedly, it was not a planned, but rather a contingent, event. In late August of that year, the *White Lion,* an English privateer operating under a Dutch letter of marque and captained by John Colyn Jope, limped into Point Comfort, at the mouth of the James River, supposedly short of food and water. In the words of tobacco planter (and widower of Pocahontas) John Rolfe, the ship carried "not any thing but 20. and odd Negroes." Jope had acted in concert with another English privateer, the *Treasurer,* commanded by Captain Daniel Elfrith. In mid-July, they had seized about 60 slaves from the *São João Bautista*—a Portuguese slaver en route to Veracruz in Spanish America—whose captain, Manoel Mendes da Cunha, had embarked 350 Africans in Luanda, the coastal capital of the Portuguese colony of Angola. The two privateers made their way northward from the site of their heist—the Bay of Campeche—until they reached the Chesapeake Bay. Once there, Jope bartered his captives for provisions. Elfrith arrived a few days after Jope. He had about 30 captives to sell but, perhaps because his letter of marque was no longer valid, decided to make for Bermuda, though not before off-loading "two or three of negroes" at Point Comfort. The sale of the *White Lion*'s human cargo was, therefore, the first documented arrival of African captives in Virginia, but the *Treasurer* added a few more. The story of Chesapeake slavery begins at this point.[1]

I thank John Coombs, David Eltis, Jack Greene, James Horn, and David Wheat for their helpful suggestions. Jack's encouragement was especially meaningful.
   1. Tim Hashaw, *The Birth of Black America: The First African Americans and the Pursuit of Freedom at Jamestown* (New York, 2007); Lorena S. Walsh, *Motives of Honor, Pleasure, and Profit: Plantation*

The fate of some of the *White Lion* Africans—and their descendants—strongly suggests that, from the outset, they were considered slaves, not servants. Not long after acquiring his share, Governor George Yeardley sent five women and three men—none of whom he named—from the ship to work at Flowerdew Hundred. When he made his will eight years later, in 1627, Yeardley differentiated between servants and "negars"—long after the latter would have been freed had they been considered equivalent to servants. A decade later, in 1637, his son Argoll Yeardley still owned two of the original *White Lion* Africans, known by their first names only—Andolo and Maria—another indication of their enslaved status. And, finally, in 1653 Argoll sold two girls, ten-year-old Doll and twelve-year-old Denise, daughters of Andolo and Maria, again pointing to the enslaved condition of the first arrivals. Rarely were the ages and arrival dates of Africans recorded in early Virginia, suggesting that they were intended to serve for life, not for a specified length of time. The other major owner of *White Lion* Africans, cape merchant Abraham Piersey, also retained possession of them until his death—in 1627—implying that he, like Yeardley, regarded his black laborers as permanent chattel, not as servants (who would have merited an earlier release).[2]

The number of Africans in early Virginia grew slowly. In 1620, the first census listed 32 unnamed "negroes"—17 women and 15 men—representing the 29 from the *White Lion* and the 2 or 3 from the *Treasurer*. Significantly, these 32 were listed in the 1620 muster in a separate category of labor, as "not Christians," unlike servants. Deaths exceeded births, so that, five years later, only 22 Africans (10 men, 10 women, and 2 children) survived. Occasional shipments brought in small groups of additional slaves. Yet the parasitic character of English "slaving" in the 1620s and 1630s, based as it was on incidental seizures from Iberian vessels, was simply insufficient to meet Virginia's expanding demand for labor. Furthermore, Virginia faced stiff competition for labor with the founding of five

---

Management in the Colonial Chesapeake, 1607–1763 (Williamsburg, Va., and Chapel Hill, N.C., 2010), 113; Susan Myra Kingsbury, ed., *The Records of the Virginia Company of London*, 4 vols. (Washington, D.C., 1906–1935) (hereafter cited as *RVC*), III, 243; Engel Sluiter, "New Light on the '20. and Odd Negroes' Arriving in Virginia, August 1619," *William and Mary Quarterly*, 3d Ser., LIV (1997), 395–398; John Thornton, "The African Experience of the '20. and Odd Negroes' Arriving in Virginia in 1619," *WMQ*, 3d Ser., LV (1998), 421–434; Deposition of John Wood, High Court of Admiralty, 13/44, fols. 131–132, The National Archives, Kew, U.K. (my thanks to James Horn). For other useful accounts, see Linda M. Heywood and Thornton, *Central Africans, Atlantic Creoles, and the Foundation of the Americas, 1585–1660* (New York, 2007), 5–8; and Michael Guasco, *Slaves and Englishmen: Human Bondage in the Early Modern Atlantic World* (Philadelphia, 2014), 1, 201–202. For the voyage of the *São João Bautista*, see *Voyages: The Trans-Atlantic Slave Trade Database*, http://www.slavevoyages.org, voyage no. 29252. For the political implications, see John C. Coombs, "Building the Machine: The Development of Plantation Slavery in Colonial Virginia, 1630–1730" (unpublished manuscript), chap. 1.

2. Hashaw, *The Birth of Black America*, 103–112; Walsh, *Motives of Honor*, 114–119.

British colonies in the Caribbean between 1625 and 1632. For whatever reason, most Chesapeake settlers do not seem to have conceived of African slaves as the solution to their labor scarcity. After all, in 1640 Virginia contained no more than about 150 blacks in a population of more than 8,000. Still, beginning in the 1630s and 1640s, the richest Virginia planters—elite officeholders for the most part—began buying slaves, more as a matter of choice than of chance. Apparently, these planters reckoned that enslaved workers were more profitable than servants. They probably would have echoed the prescient claim made by Bermuda Governor Nathaniel Butler in 1621 that "slaves are the most proper and cheape instruments for this plantation." In the late 1640s, councillor Samuel Mathews acted on Butler's advice and was probably the largest slaveowner in Virginia: he possessed 40. As a result, by 1650 at least 300 (and perhaps as many as 500) blacks resided in the colony, but they still constituted only a small fraction—about 2 to 4 percent—of the total population.[3]

The aim of this essay is to contextualize the arrival of Africans in Virginia and the colony's early commitment to slavery. To do so means looking backward and forward, searching in part for origins and in part for consequences. If the temporal boundaries of the subject are elastic, the same goes for the spatial parameters. At the very least, Virginia must be situated in its Atlantic world setting, connected to Europe, Africa, and other parts of the Americas. At the beginning of English settlement in Virginia, no one had in mind to establish slavery; there was no institutional blueprint. Nevertheless, in fairly short order, the institutional foundations were set in place, even though African slaves fully replaced indentured servants as the primary form of bound labor only in the late seventeenth century.

The following discussion addresses two sets of questions. First, what did the English know about slavery and why did they revive the institution when it was dying out in northwestern Europe? The second query concerns the nature of the Atlantic slave trade in its early phases. What were its dimensions, its patterns, and its ensuing implications? Spain and its empire played a key role in both.

3. William Thorndale, "The Virginia Census of 1619," *Magazine of Virginia Genealogy*, XXXIII (1995), 155–170; Martha W. McCartney, "An Early Virginia Census Reprised," *Quarterly Bulletin of the Archaeological Society of Virginia*, LIV (1999), 178–196; Walsh, *Motives of Honor*, 112, 114, 137; John C. Coombs, "Beyond the 'Origins Debate': Rethinking the Rise of Virginia Slavery," in Douglas Bradburn and Coombs, eds., *Early Modern Virginia: Reconsidering the Old Dominion* (Charlottesville, Va., 2011), 239–278, esp. 247; Coombs, "The Phases of Conversion: A New Chronology for the Rise of Slavery in Early Virginia," *WMQ*, 3d Ser., LXVIII (2011), 332–360; John J. McCusker and Russell R. Menard, *The Economy of British America, 1607–1789* (Williamsburg, Va., and Chapel Hill, N.C., 1985), 136; Governor Nathaniel Butler to Sir Nathaniel Rich, Jan. 21, 1620/21, in Vernon A. Ives, ed., *The Rich Papers: Letters from Bermuda, 1615–1646: Eyewitness Accounts Sent by the Early Colonists to Sir Nathaniel Rich* (Toronto, 1984), 229.

Before 1641, more than half a million Africans arrived in the Spanish Americas, almost 60 percent more than was previously thought. The slave trade to the early Spanish Americas, it is now clear, was formidable. Much as the Spanish dominated the early transatlantic slave trade, so, too, did Chesapeake slavery owe much to Spanish and Portuguese inspiration. The late Winthrop Jordan, the distinguished historian of race, will be quoted a number of times in the following pages because his insights are still worth recalling. Yet his claim that, "of all the important early English settlements, Virginia had the least contact with the Spanish, Portuguese, Dutch, and other English colonies," seems farfetched, if not just plain wrong. If Jordan had the benefit of reading recent scholarship, he might well have changed his mind. He famously argued that slavery and prejudice were "equally cause and effect, continuously reacting upon each other, dynamically joining hands to hustle the Negro down the road to complete degradation." Then, again, he also asserted, "Much more than with the other English colonies, where the enslavement of Negroes was to some extent a borrowed practice, the available evidence for Maryland and Virginia points to less borrowing and to this kind of process: a mutually interactive growth of slavery and unfavorable assessment." The mutual interaction is persuasive; the relative lack of borrowing is unconvincing—as even Jordan concedes at one point.[4]

ONE CONUNDRUM IS WHY AND HOW EUROPEANS REVIVED SLAVERY when it had largely died out in northwestern Europe. Sixteenth-century Englishmen prided themselves on being free. They developed, in Jordan's words, a "preening consciousness of the peculiar glories of English liberties." The cleric William Harrison was most emphatic in 1577 when he declared, "As for slaves and bondmen we have none." But, although slaves in England were rare or nonexistent, the language of slavery was a dense, rich living tradition, "a memory trace of long standing," in Jordan's apt phrase. The most widely read text, the Bible, was suffused with ideas of liberty and bondage. The notion of slavery as the product of sin was commonplace. Villeinage or manorial bondage was extinct, but it survived in legal discourse. Galley slavery was not a practical punishment on the English high seas, but it was a subject of lively discussion. For many Englishmen, the defining features of slavery were evident: a complete loss of freedom; a perpetual, open-ended, inheritable condition; a loss of humanity, a

---

4. Alex Borucki, David Eltis, and David Wheat, "Atlantic History and the Slave Trade to Spanish America," *American Historical Review*, CXX (2015), 433–461, esp. 440; Winthrop D. Jordan, *White over Black: American Attitudes toward the Negro, 1550–1812* (Williamsburg, Va., and Chapel Hill, N.C., 1968), 61, 72, 80. Jordan would have benefited from April Lee Hatfield, *Atlantic Virginia: Intercolonial Relations in the Seventeenth Century* (Philadelphia, 2004), esp. 7, 8, 63–69, 80–82, 137–168.

descent into bestiality; an association with captivity and warfare; and a tendency for slaves to be infidels or heathens, meriting God's punishment for evil, for sin, for Ham's disobedience. Slavery did not exist in sixteenth-century England, but Englishmen possessed a well-defined understanding of it. They did not have to invent the institution out of whole cloth. Furthermore, most Englishmen daily experienced forms of dependency and the denial of various rights. The conditions of labor endured by dependent workers and slaves may appear to be more matters of degree than of kind; and yet serfs, convicts, servants, apprentices, and so on always had more protection against the power of a social superior or an employer than did slaves. Finally, if slavery had almost no place in early modern England, it was impossible to deny its widespread presence elsewhere. Thus, in 1596, when the English Privy Council ordered the expulsion of all blacks (who were hardly numerous), they were to be taken to Portugal and Spain and sold.[5]

Wherever early modern Englishmen ventured—not just Spain and Portugal—they encountered slavery, or its near equivalents, in its many varied forms. In Italy, where household slavery predominated, European slaves from the Black Sea and Baltic regions were common. In one decade in the early fifteenth century, no fewer than ten thousand slaves—mostly white females—were sold in Venice alone. A majority of Muscovite slaves were natives who sold themselves into slavery; one increasingly popular variant has been dubbed "limited service contract slavery." Elite slaves, ranging from government ministers to cavalrymen, were part of the Russian system. In seventeenth-century Scottish mines, a system of life-binding arose (and was occasionally imposed even on unborn children), and some miners were forced to wear brass collars, a form of discipline frequently used on slaves. Scottish colliers were regularly termed "slaves," and they, in turn, invoked their slavery to challenge their masters. Historians now consider their lot a form of life bondage or serfdom. Debt bondage—a version of servitude based on an initial agreement to borrow funds and that continued until (if ever) the debt was repaid—was widely practiced in Southeast Asia, Latin America, Africa, and China. In the early modern era, the Ottoman Empire was a remarkably diverse polity, but one unifying feature was enslavement. The kaleidoscope of types—ranging from powerful military slaves, or Janizaries, to

5. Jordan, *White over Black*, 49, 52 (quotations); [William Harrison], *An Historicall Description of the Iland of Britaine* . . . (1577), in Raphaell Holinshed, *Holinshed's Chronicles of England, Scotland, and Ireland* (London, 1807), I, 275; Guasco, *Slaves and Englishmen*, 11–40, 115–118; David Eltis, *The Rise of African Slavery in the Americas* (New York, 2000), 3–7, 77; Simon P. Newman, *A New World of Labor: The Development of Plantation Slavery in the British Atlantic* (Philadelphia, 2013), 3, 17–35; David Eltis and Stanley L. Engerman, "Dependence, Servility, and Coerced Labor in Time and Space," in Eltis and Engerman, eds., *The Cambridge World History of Slavery*, III, *AD 1420–AD 1804* (New York, 2011), 1–21.

menial domestics—made Ottoman slavery particularly notable. Exposure to many kinds of slavery made it clear that there was no single model, but rather various types: an incorporative system designed to sustain a group; a state-run form that sought to achieve communal goals; and a variant aimed at making profits for private individuals. Slavery was no monolith.[6]

Africa appeared exotic and mysterious to most Europeans. Slavery was present in various forms—a kin-based, household institution; a form of tribute mechanism; and a labor-intensive, sometimes plantation-centered system—but Europeans were initially more interested in trading for gold, pepper, ivory, and other tropical commodities than for slaves. To Europeans, sub-Saharan Africans seemed radically different from themselves in appearance and culture. Jordan emphasized the contrasting perceptions of skin color, religion, savagery, and sexuality. The unfortunate coincidence of simultaneously encountering manlike beasts (apes) and allegedly beast-like men in proximity to one another led to wild speculations about relationships between the two. The distinguished historian David Brion Davis has broadened the context, singling out medieval Arabs and their Muslim converts as crucial transmitters of the negative symbolism of African blackness. The Arabic word for slave, *abd*, in time connoted only a black slave. The stereotypes of medieval Muslim writers, for whom the blackness of Africans evoked associations of filth, evil, ugliness, and sin, were passed along to Spaniards, the Portuguese, and later to other Europeans.[7]

6. Steven A. Epstein, *Speaking of Slavery: Color, Ethnicity, and Human Bondage in Italy* (Ithaca, N.Y., 2001), 132–139; David Brion Davis, *Slavery and Human Progress* (New York, 1984), 55; William D. Phillips, Jr., *Slavery from Roman Times to the Early Transatlantic Trade* (Minneapolis, Minn., 1985), 154–170; Charles Verlinden, *The Beginnings of Modern Colonization: Eleven Essays with an Introduction*, trans. Yvonne Freccero (Ithaca, N.Y., 1970), 33–40, 79–97; T. F. Earle and K. J. P. Lowe, eds., *Black Africans in Renaissance Europe* (New York, 2005), esp. 1–47, 213–224; Richard Hellie, *Slavery in Russia, 1450–1725* (Chicago, 1982), esp. xvii–xviii, 33–71; Christopher A. Whatley, "Scottish 'Collier Serfs,' British Coal Workers? Aspects of Scottish Collier Society in the Eighteenth Century," *Labour History Review*, LX, no. 2 (Autumn 1995), 66–79; P. E. H. Hair, "Slavery and Liberty: The Case of the Scottish Colliers," *Slavery and Abolition*, XXI (2000), 136–151; Eltis and Engerman, eds., *Cambridge World History of Slavery*, III, esp. 5, 11–12, 173; Ehud R. Toledano, *Slavery and Abolition in the Ottoman Middle East* (Seattle, 1998); Toledano, *As If Silent and Absent: Bonds of Enslavement in the Islamic Middle East* (New Haven, Conn., 2007).

7. David Eltis, "The Relative Importance of Slaves and Commodities in the Atlantic Trade of Seventeenth-Century Africa," *Journal of African History*, XXXV (1994), 237–249; Jordan, *White over Black*, 3–43; Guasco, *Slaves and Englishmen*, 60–77; David Brion Davis, *Inhuman Bondage: The Rise and Fall of Slavery in the New World* (New York, 2006), esp. 48–79. The development of racial thinking is a huge topic: for examples, see the articles in *Constructing Race*, special issue of *WMQ*, 3d Ser., LIV (1997), 1–252; David M. Goldenberg, *The Curse of Ham: Race and Slavery in Early Judaism, Christianity, and Islam* (Princeton, N.J., 2003); Rebecca Anne Goetz, *The Baptism of Early Virginia: How Christianity Created Race* (Baltimore, 2012), esp. 9–10; Francisco Bethencourt, *Racisms: From the Crusades to the Twentieth Century* (Princeton, N.J., 2013); and Steven A. Epstein, "Attitudes toward Blackness," in Craig Perry, David Eltis, Stanley L. Engerman, and David R. Richardson, eds., *The Cambridge World History of Slavery*, II, *AD 500–AD 1420* (forthcoming).

In the early seventeenth century, there were far more white slaves in the Old World than slaves of African descent in the Americas. As Jamestown was being founded, about a quarter-million white slaves inhabited the Eastern Hemisphere, based in two main areas: the Mediterranean region—including the Islamic Middle East and North Africa—and Russia. In the latter, about one in ten persons were enslaved. The English were particularly interested in the Mediterranean, where the capture and enslavement of thousands of their mariners became increasingly commonplace. No other experience influenced the way most English folk thought about slavery in the early modern era more than the enslavement of their countrymen in the Mediterranean world. The practice of ransoming captives meant that some ex-slaves returned to England to tell their stories. The harsh reality of galley slavery, forced conversions, "turning Turk," and sexual violence became real in the constant retelling. Englishmen learned of the horrors of slavery most directly in Mediterranean lands, as public celebrations cast the liberated captives as symbols of Christian freedom. In the early modern era, servitude was not a black preserve.[8]

From a purely economic perspective, western Europeans should have revived (or expanded) white slavery, historian David Eltis has argued, since it would have been much cheaper to enslave and transport white vagrants, criminals, and prisoners of war to the New World than to sail all the way to West, Central, or even Southeast Africa and purchase increasingly expensive African slaves at roughly three times the cost. Transatlantic shipments of northern Europeans would have been quicker to arrive and cheaper to deliver because voyages were shorter. Because of different epidemiological factors, crew and passenger mortality would have been much lower than in the African trade. The reason this policy did not materialize has less to do with logistics (although historian Seymour Drescher has made a strong case for institutional and political hurdles to European enslavement) and more to do with "an almost intangible barrier," a cultural force that brought a sense of unity to Christians of western Europe, blocking the possibility of any significant revival of white slavery. Europeans could kill other Europeans in battle (as they did on a large scale in the Thirty Years' War from 1618 to 1648), burn them as witches, dispatch them to galleys, ship them overseas as convicts, and impress them into the navy, but never transport

8. Robert C. Davis, *Christian Slaves, Muslim Masters: White Slavery in the Mediterranean, the Barbary Coast, and Italy, 1500–1800* (New York, 2003); Davis, *Holy War and Human Bondage: Tales of Christian-Muslim Slavery in the Early-Modern Mediterranean* (Santa Barbara, Calif., 2009); Guasco, *Slaves and Englishmen*, 121–154; Linda Colley, *Captives: Britain, Empire, and the World, 1600–1850* (New York, 2002); Nabil Matar, *Turks, Moors, and Englishmen in the Age of Discovery* (New York, 1999); William G. Clarence-Smith and David Eltis, "White Servitude," in Eltis and Engerman, eds., *Cambridge World History of Slavery*, III, 132–159.

them to chattel slavery. Christian whites essentially became non-enslaveable. James Thompson's famous lyrics to "Rule Britannia" declared triumphantly that "Britons never will be slaves."[9]

In the American colonies, supposedly free Englishmen, even if temporarily bound by contract to serve a master for a specified number of years or until age twenty-one, sometimes complained of slave-like conditions. After the Powhatan Uprising of 1622, a white servant begged to be "freed out of this Egipt" and released from "this bondage." In the following year, another servant excoriated his master for selling him "like a damnd slave." In 1657, seventy royalist sympathizers claimed that they were "freeborn people of this nation" who had been sold "as the goods and chattels" in Barbados and continued to be "bought and sold still from one planter to another, or attached as horses and beasts for the debts of their masters." In a shrewd reference to Mediterranean slavery, the petitioners noted that not even the "cruel Turks" enslaved their own countrymen. Tellingly, the petitioners neglected to mention African slaves, even as the island was in the throes of becoming a full-fledged slave society. Accusations of being treated like slaves—while exaggerated—had great rhetorical power. After all, slavery was a legitimate threat as a punishment, even if rarely deployed. Servants (technically, their contracts or their labor, not their persons) were bought and sold, and they often experienced harrowing material conditions. Servitude and slavery had much in common, even though, as Jordan notes, "servitude, no matter how long, brutal, and involuntary, was not the same thing as perpetual slavery" or hereditary, lifetime service.[10]

From an English perspective, Indians were legitimate candidates for slavery—never more so than when they rose up, as in 1622 and 1644, revealing, in Virginia Company secretary Edward Waterhouse's words, their "unnaturall bruitishnesse," so that they "may now most justly be compelled to servitude

---

9. Eltis, *Rise of African Slavery*, 1–84; Seymour Drescher, "White Atlantic? The Choice for African Slave Labor in the Plantation Americas," in David Eltis, Frank D. Lewis, and Kenneth L. Sokoloff, eds., *Slavery in the Development of the Americas* (New York, 2004), 31–69; Drescher, *Abolition: A History of Slavery and Antislavery* (New York, 2009), 11–15, 21–24, 45–59.

10. Kingsbury, ed., *RVC*, IV, 41, 58, 61, 235, 473; Emily Rose, "The Politics of Pathos: Richard Frethorne's Letters Home," in Robert Appelbaum and John Wood Sweet, *Envisioning an English Empire: Jamestown and the Making of the North Atlantic World* (Philadelphia, 2005), 92–108; Thomas Burton, *Diary of Thomas Burton, Esq., Member in the Parliaments of Oliver and Richard Cromwell from 1656 to 1659 . . .*, 4 vols. (London, 1828), IV, 255–258, 260–262, 268, 301–308; Marcellus Rivers and Oxenbridge Foyle, *Englands Slavery; or, Barbados Merchandize: Represented in a Petition to the High and Honourable Court of Parliament, . . . on the Behalf of Themselves and Three-Score and Ten More Free-Born Englishmen Sold (Uncondemned) into Slavery . . .* (London, 1659), esp. 5, 6, 8; Jordan, *White over Black*, 62–63. For commentary, see Guasco, *Slaves and Englishmen*, 2–4, 167–171; Eltis, *Rise of African Slavery*, 78; and Newman, *A New World of Labor*, 80–81.

and drudgery"—yet Indian slavery never became an important institution in Virginia. The first mention of an Indian slave, a guide named Kempes, dates to the earliest years of colonization. In 1622, an Indian slave known as Chauco warned of an impending attack by Opechancanough. But Indian slaves became a notable presence in white households only about midcentury, mostly among ordinary, nonelite planters and confined to the colony's southwestern counties. Part of the reason for Indian slavery's marginality was epidemiological. Native Americans simply did not survive in sufficient numbers to become a reliable source of labor. White settlers also thought that Indians were less easily enslaveable than Africans and believed that they ran away more often and were less effective laborers, all of which was reflected in lower valuations. In addition, from their first interactions with the Powhatan chiefdom, English colonists sought to create Native tributaries, akin to Spanish precedents (in turn, Wahunsonacock, the paramount chief, hoped to incorporate the English through fictive kinship). The original goal of incorporation, even when it degenerated into military campaigns of extermination, remained and is evident in attempts to protect Indians—as in the mid-seventeenth-century law that banned settlers from using Indian children placed in English care "as slaves" and mandated "bring[ing] them up in Christianity, civility, and the knowledge of necessary trades." Indians were valuable trading partners and useful military allies. They retained their nationhood, a quality Englishmen admired.[11]

Virginians developed their slave system alongside other English colonies. Bermuda is notable for a number of firsts: the first English colony to import an African, in 1616; by 1619, historian Michael J. Jarvis observes, it was the first English colony to boast about one hundred slaves; it was the first to cultivate Spanish tobacco; and, in 1623, the first to pass a racially discriminatory law in English America. Although slavery was not fully codified in early Bermuda or in Virginia, Jarvis states that blacks' "servile status was assumed from the outset." Similarly, English settlers on Providence Island, which they established in 1630,

---

11. [Edward Waterhouse], *A Declaration of the State of the Colony and Affaires in Virginia* ... (London, 1622), 25, as cited in Alexander B. Haskell, *For God, King, and People: Forging Commonwealth Bonds in Renaissance Virginia* (Williamsburg, Va., and Chapel Hill, N.C., 2017), 215; Kristalyn Marie Shefveland, *Anglo-Native Virginia: Trade, Conversion, and Indian Slavery in the Old Dominion, 1646–1722* (Athens, Ga., 2016), 9, 11, 32–33, 35; Guasco, *Slaves and Englishmen*, 181–192; Coombs, "Beyond the 'Origins Debate,'" in Bradburn and Coombs, eds., *Early Modern Virginia*, 253; Jordan, *White over Black*, 89–90; Davis, *Inhuman Bondage*, 73, 98–99; William Waller Hening, ed., *The Statutes at Large; Being a Collection of All the Laws of Virginia* ..., 13 vols. (Richmond, Va., 1809), I, 396. See also Owen Stanwood, "Captives and Slaves: Indian Labor, Cultural Conversion, and the Plantation Revolution in Virginia," *Virginia Magazine of History and Biography*, CXIV (2006), 434–463; and C. S. Everett, "'They Shalbe Slaves for Their Lives': Indian Slavery in Colonial Virginia," in Alan Gallay, ed., *Indian Slavery in Colonial America* (Lincoln, Nebr., 2009), 67–108.

routinely acquired Africans, taking it for granted that they were necessary to thrive. By the late 1630s, several hundred slaves, forming a slight majority of the total population, lived on the island, making the colony Anglo-America's first true slave society. As the numbers rose, concerns for whites' safety mounted, culminating in a 1638 slave rebellion, which historian Karen Kupperman notes was "the first in any English colony." New England's history was shaped by slavery. In 1614, before there was any large-scale English settlement in New England, an English ship captain kidnapped "foure and twenty" Native Americans (including a Patuxet Indian man named Squanto) and sold them as slaves in Spain. Twenty-four years later, the first documented shipment of enslaved Africans arrived in Massachusetts, eighteen years after the *Mayflower's* journey and nineteen years after the *White Lion* had sold its slaves at Jamestown. The *Desire* brought cotton, tobacco, salt, and "negroes" in return for captive Indians that it had sold in the West Indies. In the same year, 1638, Massachusetts colonist Samuel Maverick ordered one of his slaves to rape another in hopes of breeding them. Here was another precedent-setting event: "the first known attempt in North America to 'breed' African slaves." In 1636, less than a decade after settlement, the governor and council in Barbados announced that *"Negroes* and *Indians"* arriving on the islands "should serve for Life." Two years later, the Providence Island Company referred to its "Negroes" as "perpetually servants." In 1645, Massachusetts's "paradoxically named Body of Liberties" proved to be "the first legal codification of chattel slavery in North America."[12]

Barbados was the British colony that was most influential, however, because in Eltis's words it became a "global economic giant," a powerhouse of the preindustrial era. Furthermore, as historian Simon Newman reminds us, the island "played a foundational role in defining how plantation labor developed throughout British America." It "attracted more bound laborers, white and black, than any other seventeenth-century English colony." Within a decade of its settlement in 1627, the supply of voluntary white servants failed to keep pace with demand, and soon thereafter a majority of the white servants shipped to Barbados were involuntary migrants—vagrants, convicts, rebels, and prisoners of war—who were systematically and brutally exploited. Treating white bound laborers as if

---

12. See Michael J. Jarvis's essay, "Bermuda and the Beginnings of Black Anglo-America," in this volume; Karen Ordahl Kupperman, *Providence Island, 1630–1641: The Other Puritan Colony* (Cambridge, 1993), 170, 172; Alison Games, "'The Sanctuarye of Our Rebell Negroes': The Atlantic Context of Local Resistance on Providence Island, 1630–41," *Slavery and Abolition*, XIX (1998), 3; Wendy Warren, *New England Bound: Slavery and Colonization in Early America* (New York, 2016), 3–4, 7–8, 12, 34–35; Guasco, *Slaves and Englishmen*, 2, 187–188, 206–208, 213–217. For the first inklings of a customary law of slavery in Virginia, see Paul D. Halliday's essay, "Brase's Case: Making Slave Law as Customary Law in Virginia's General Court, 1619–1625," in this volume.

they lacked almost all human rights eased the transition to slavery on Barbados. As economic historian Russell Menard notes, "The 1640s was a crucial decade in the history of Barbados, and in the history of all of British America, for it was in that decade that large-scale plantation agriculture and African slavery became central to the island's economy." Once established on the island, those institutions spread to other parts of British North America. Barbados set an example and informed the development of racial slavery elsewhere.[13]

While British colonists learned about slavery from one another, their primary teachers were the Spanish and Portuguese. In Iberian towns, black slaves were a routine presence, and they constituted 10 percent of the population of Lisbon as early as the middle of the fifteenth century. In 1535, a visitor claimed that "in Lisbon there are more men and women slaves than free Portuguese." By the end of the fifteenth century, black Africans made up as much as 40 percent of the remarkably diverse slave population of Valencia, which also included captive Moors and penally enslaved Mudejars, Greeks, Tartars, Russians, and Circassians. English merchants cultivated extensive commercial networks in the coastal cities of the Iberian Peninsula, where slaves constituted 5 to 15 percent of the population. In the late fifteenth and early sixteenth century, some prominent English merchants resident in Andalusia—men such as Thomas Malliard and Robert Thorne—were slaveholders, actively engaged in the transatlantic slave trade. Black slaves toted water jugs, sold goods on the streets and in markets, rowed in the galleys, and served as personal servants. They demonstrated that they were versatile and effective workers. In fact, many male slaves, particularly black Africans, engaged in agricultural production. At the same time, the news that Africans and people of African descent were being carried off to forced labor in America was hardly a secret. The Portuguese and Spanish had set an example that could be followed. As Jordan cautions: "It would be surprising if there had been a clear-cut line of influence from Latin to English slavery. Elizabethans were not in the business of modeling themselves after Spaniards." Yet, he continues, "from about 1550, Englishmen were in such continual contact

13. Eltis, *Rise of African Slavery*, 193–223, esp. 196, 198; Newman, *A New World of Labor*, 6, 7, 71–107, 189; Russell R. Menard, *Sweet Negotiations: Sugar, Slavery, and Plantation Agriculture in Early Barbados* (Charlottesville, Va., 2006), xii; Christopher Tomlins, *Freedom Bound: Law, Labor, and Civic Identity in Colonizing English America, 1580–1865* (New York, 2010), 2–27. For Virginia's early trade with Barbados, see Coombs, "The Phases of Conversion," *WMQ*, 3d Ser., LXVIII (2011), 343; and Hatfield, *Atlantic Virginia*, 141–164. I agree with the critique in Jerome S. Handler and Matthew C. Reilly, "Contesting 'White Slavery' in the Caribbean: Enslaved Africans and European Indentured Servants in Seventeenth-Century Barbados," *New West Indian Guide*, XCI (2017), 30–55. I also agree that the status of slaves was established in custom long before any slave laws were passed; see Handler, "Custom and Law: The Status of Enslaved Africans in Seventeenth-Century Barbados," *Slavery and Abolition*, XXXVII (2016), 233–255.

with the Spanish [an important concession] that they could hardly have failed to acquire the notion that Negroes could be enslaved." This easily made association of blacks and slavery, garnered from the Portuguese and Spanish, is one facet of the "unthinking decision" that Jordan posits.[14]

From the early sixteenth century onward, Spanish settlers and their enslaved laborers grew tobacco, a product on which, of course, Virginia would base its economy. As early as the 1530s, African and Afro-Caribbean slaves on Hispaniola cultivated the plant "behind the fields of their masters... because they say that when they stop working and take the tobacco their fatigue leaves them." By the late sixteenth century, settlers, slaves, and Indians were producing so much tobacco that a thriving contraband trade had developed with northern Europeans. In the early seventeenth century, as a way to prohibit this illicit trade, Spanish authorities banned tobacco growing in certain parts of the Caribbean, forcibly relocated some settlers, and inadvertently diverted a growing commerce eastward—to Trinidad, the Orinoco Basin, and Guiana. In response, the English established settlements in Guiana and grew tobacco there, learning from Spanish settlers and their enslaved workers how to cultivate and cure the mild, high-yielding strains raised in those areas. "Trinidado" became synonymous with tobacco in common English usage, and "Orinoco" would become the name for a strain of profitable tobacco grown in Virginia. Virginians (and Bermudians) owed much of their newfound technical expertise, such as learning to pack tobacco in twisted rolls, to Spanish growers, particularly slaves; and the English colonists' quick learning curve, along with Spanish restrictions on foreign shipping, helped create an opportunity that Virginians and Bermudians seized. By 1617, Robert Rich, Bermuda's largest landholder, reported that tobacco was being cultivated successfully on the island, attributable in part to the "good store of neggars... brought from the West Indies"—almost certainly the Spanish settlements.[15]

---

14. A. C. de C. M. Saunders, *A Social History of Black Slaves and Freedmen in Portugal, 1441–1555* (Cambridge, 1982), 1, 54–57, 59–61; Guasco, *Slaves and Englishmen*, 91–96; Debra Blumenthal, *Enemies and Familiars: Slavery and Mastery in Fifteenth-Century Valencia* (Ithaca, N.Y., 2009), 4, 95–101; Gustav Ungerer, *The Mediterranean Apprenticeship of British Slavery* (Madrid, 2008), 11, 15, 19–27, 31–32, 64–69; Jordan, *White over Black*, 56–63.

15. Gonzalo Fernández de Oviedo y Valdés, *Historia general y natural de las Indias*, ed. Juan Pérez de Tudela Bueso (Madrid, 1992), I, 116, quoted in Marcy Norton and Daviken Studnicki-Gizbert, "The Multinational Commodification of Tobacco, 1492–1650: An Iberian Perspective," in Peter C. Mancall, ed., *The Atlantic World and Virginia, 1550–1624* (Williamsburg, Va., and Chapel Hill, N.C., 2007), 256; Robert Rich to Nathaniel Rich, May 25 [19?], 1617, in Ives, ed., *Rich Papers*, 25; Philip D. Morgan, "Virginia's Other Prototype: The Caribbean," in Mancall, ed., *Atlantic World and Virginia*, 342–380; Joyce Lorimer, "The English Contraband Tobacco Trade from Trinidad and Guiana, 1590–1617," in K. R. Andrews, N. P. Canny, and P. E. H. Hair, eds., *The Westward Enterprise: English*

The English borrowed much more than tobacco from the Spanish and Portuguese. The very terminology for addressing blacks—calling them "Negroes," which in time became synonymous with slaves—was a portentous adoption, one that was incorporated into English from the Hispanic languages in the mid-sixteenth century. Other terms, such as "pickaninny" and "mulatto," entered the language soon thereafter. Of the one hundred or so Africans listed by name in various early Virginia sources, a quarter had Iberian names such as Antonio, Angelo, Manuel, Isabella, Maria, and Magdelina. In the first half of the seventeenth century, an era in which there was little codification of slavery in Virginia, Iberian customs seem to have prompted fairly frequent manumission, toleration of free blacks, tacit acceptance of some racial intermixture (though the acceptance did not last long), the use of Africans for colonial defense, and a willingness to consider incorporating African peoples into the Christian community. Some slaves were allowed to earn money; some even bought, sold, and raised cattle; still others used the proceeds to purchase their freedom. Perhaps some of the earliest black immigrants had absorbed Iberian notions about the relation between slavery and freedom, in particular that freedom was a permissible goal for a slave and self-purchase a legitimate avenue to liberty. Free blacks seem to have formed a larger share of the total black population in the seventeenth century than at any other time during slavery. By the 1660s, in some Eastern Shore counties, perhaps a sixth of the black population was free.[16]

However, the English also learned that sometimes it was best to repudiate the Spanish example. Rather than impose the yoke of bondage on Indians and Africans, the English on occasion made allies of them. English interlopers in the Spanish Caribbean repeatedly sought out free and enslaved blacks as military allies, intermediaries, and guides. The most dramatic alliance took place in Panama in 1572 between Sir Francis Drake and the runaway slaves, or cimarrons, described as "certaine valiant Negroes fled from their cruel masters the Spaniards." By 1577, if the Spanish are to be believed, the maroons were "as Lutheran as the English," crying, "I English; pure Lutheran," as they destroyed Catholic

---

Activities in Ireland, the Atlantic, and America, 1480–1650 (Detroit, 1979), 124–150; Walsh, *Motives of Honor*, 35, 97; David Wheat, *Atlantic Africa and the Spanish Caribbean, 1570–1640* (Williamsburg, Va., and Chapel Hill, N.C., 2016), 110.

16. Jordan, *White over Black*, 61; April Lee Hatfield, "A 'Very Wary People in Their Bargaining' or 'Very Good Marchandise': English Traders' Views of Free and Enslaved Africans, 1550–1650," *Slavery and Abolition*, XXV (2004), 1–17, esp. 2; Heywood and Thornton, *Central Africans*, 276; Guasco, *Slaves and Englishmen*, 210; Goetz, *Baptism of Early Virginia*, 61–111. Another possible borrowing concerns a subset of slaves—those owned by religious, educational, and business organizations. See Jennifer Oast, *Institutional Slavery: Slaveholding Churches, Schools, Colleges, and Businesses in Virginia, 1680–1860* (New York, 2016), esp. 14.

insignia. In that year, the Spaniards came across a camp of thirty Englishmen and more than eighty maroons "cooking a quantity of pork in kettles and amusing themselves together." An easygoing camaraderie had seemingly developed between the two groups. Thereafter, however, a powerful Spanish counteroffensive soured the maroons on the English to the point that they were said to "despise" them and viewed them as their mortal enemies. This volte-face strongly suggests the pragmatic quality of the earlier bonds. When Drake returned in 1596, the maroons and others actively opposed him. Indeed, when some of Drake's party tried to draw water in the river outside Nombre de Dios, Pedro Yalonga, describing himself as a "black slave," stepped forward and killed "the sergeant major of the English armada." Former allies had become staunch opponents. Africans and people of African descent, as historian of the early Spanish Caribbean David Wheat points out, now "defended towns that were, in many ways, their own." The English self-presentation as liberators, and their alliance with blacks against whites, was short-lived, a marriage of convenience rather than, in distinguished historian Edmund Morgan's words, an "alliance [that] seems to have been untroubled by racial prejudice."[17]

Throughout the early colonial period in the circum-Caribbean, most Englishmen apparently accepted both the legality and propriety of slavery. Occasionally they might express sympathy for Africans or Indians, but their hatred of the Spanish, rather than a lack of racial prejudice, was its primary inspiration. Englishmen understood that Africans were valuable resources and accepted unhesitatingly their status as slaves in Spanish and Portuguese America. They saw Africans in various roles: serving as cooks, domestics, and laundresses; working as ranch hands and raising food crops; laboring at sea as canoemen, sailors, caulkers, pearl divers, and dockhands; and occupying skilled positions as carpenters, seamstresses, blacksmiths, masons, and musicians. They likely heard sentiments similar to those of city council members in San Juan, Puerto Rico, who in 1534 described their reliance on enslaved Africans as a necessary evil, "Like one who has the wolf by its ears," but then declared emphatically, "In the end we cannot live without black people." In the early seventeenth century, nearly forty thousand workers of African descent inhabited Spanish Caribbean seaports and rural areas. In 1622, the province of Cartagena alone held more than twenty thousand blacks. English interlopers could hardly miss their

---

17. Edmund S. Morgan, *American Slavery, American Freedom: The Ordeal of Colonial Virginia* (New York, 1975), 10–18 (quotations on 10, 13); Guasco, *Slaves and Englishmen*, 12–13, 80–91, 97–98, 112–113, 119–120; Morgan, "Virginia's Other Prototype," in Mancall, ed., *Atlantic World and Virginia*, 375–377; "Pedro Yalonga," May 24–June 12, 1596, AGI-Panama 44, n. 56 (2), fols. 1r–12r, as quoted in Wheat, *Atlantic Africa*, 2; see also Wheat, *Atlantic Africa*, 4.

Table 1. Destinations of Disembarked Africans, 1551–1650

Years	Mainland North America	British Caribbean	French Caribbean	Spanish America	Brazil	Total
1551–1575	—	—	—	35,000	3,000	38,000
1576–1600	—	—	—	143,000	27,000	170,000
1601–1625	—	600	—	169,000	156,000	326,000
1626–1650	100	27,000	500	86,000	164,000	278,000
TOTALS	100	28,000	500	433,000	350,000	812,000

SOURCES: *Voyages: The Trans-Atlantic Slave Trade Database,* http://www.slavevoyages.org. For Spanish American data, see http://slavevoyages.org/voyages/nJsv3kiC. All other information is from http://slavevoyages.org/estimates/g4thyuEg. Rounding produces small discrepancies.

presence. Slaves were therefore ubiquitous in the Iberian world. And wherever slavery existed, a slave trade was necessary to sustain the viability of the institution.[18]

IBERIANS DOMINATED THE EARLY TRANSATLANTIC SLAVE TRADE, which had been in existence since at least 1505, when two shipments of captive Africans arrived at Hispaniola. At first the numbers were small, and nearly all were destined for Spanish America. In the third quarter of the sixteenth century, on average about two thousand Africans were forcibly shipped across the Atlantic each year, with more than nine of ten destined for the Spanish Americas (see Table 1). The last quarter of the sixteenth century saw a quadrupling of the overall trade—or an annual average of eight thousand Africans—conveyed across the Atlantic, with Brazil receiving its first significant set of shipments. Even then, four of every five Africans went to Spanish rather than Portuguese America. Furthermore, the first quarter of the seventeenth century witnessed a near doubling of the trade—an average of thirteen thousand Africans were shipped across the Atlantic annually. But by then Brazil received almost as many Africans as Spanish America. The union of the Spanish and Portuguese crowns (1580–1640) facilitated a surge in the transatlantic slave trade. When Virginia received its first Africans, the Spanish slave trade was at its peak (not to be replicated or exceeded until Cuba's sugar economy took off in the nineteenth century) and the trade to Brazil was flourishing. Overall, from 1505 to 1650, more

---

18. Vicente Murga, comp., *Historia documental de Puerto Rico,* I, *El concejo o cabildo de la ciudad de San Juan de Puerto Rico (1527–1550)* (Río Pierdras, Puerto Rico, 1956), as quoted in Wheat, *Atlantic Africa,* 5. See also Wheat, *Atlantic Africa,* 7, 12, 15; Guasco, *Slaves and Englishmen,* 119.

than one million Africans were forcibly transported across the Atlantic, with 56 percent going to Spanish America and 41 percent to Brazil.[19]

The period 1626–1650 is the only quarter century in the entire history of the slave trade (1505–1867) that saw a decline in slave shipments. In those twenty-five years, the slave trade to Spanish America halved in size. The collapse of the Iberian Union was part of the explanation, disrupting supplies to Spanish America, but more important was the decline in Spanish gold and silver output that happened to coincide with the separation of the Spanish and Portuguese crowns. In addition, the Native American population began to increase after gaining some immunities to the diseases Europeans and Africans brought with them. As a result, the demand for imported labor weakened rather than strengthened. At the same time, Brazil's slave shipments rose slightly, as Portuguese ships now targeted just the one colony; furthermore, Pernambuco was then the premier sugar-producing region of the world, and so demand for Africans remained high in that area. But, in 1630, the Dutch invaded Pernambuco (as well as occupied Luanda in the 1640s and attacked Portuguese shipping more generally), which disrupted trade during their roughly two-decade occupation. These counterforces help to explain why Brazil's slave shipments remained steady from the first to the second quarter of the seventeenth century. The decline in African imports into Spanish America meant that during the period 1626–1650 Portuguese Brazil's slave trade was twice the size of its Spanish American counterpart. Virginian hopes after 1619 that more Africans would become available were severely dampened by this shakeout in the Iberian slave markets. Furthermore, the second quarter of the seventeenth century saw the first serious British intervention in the slave trade, aimed almost entirely at supplying its burgeoning West Indian colonies. Increased competition and decreased supplies—a 15 percent decline in the number of exported Africans from the first to second quarters of the seventeenth century—resulted in Virginia's difficulty in adding many Africans to those it received in 1619.[20]

Another feature of the early transatlantic slave trade was the dominance of a single African provenance zone. In the early sixteenth century, Upper Guinea was the most important source of slaves for the transatlantic market. In the second quarter of the sixteenth century, nine of every ten Africans destined for

19. Borucki, Eltis, and Wheat, "Atlantic History and the Slave Trade," *AHR*, CXX (2015), 433–461.
20. John J. TePaske, *A New World of Gold and Silver*, ed. Kendall W. Brown (Leiden, 2010), 112–113; David Eltis and David Richardson, eds., *Extending the Frontiers: Essays on the New Transatlantic Slave Trade Database* (New Haven, Conn., 2008); Davis, *Inhuman Bondage*, 77–111; Eltis and David Richardson, *Atlas of the Transatlantic Slave Trade* (New Haven, Conn., 2010), esp. maps 23, 92–96, 131, 138, 141. For additional limits circa 1660 on the number of slaves reaching the colony, see Coombs, "The Phases of Conversion," *WMQ*, 3d Ser., LXVIII (2011), 348–349.

the New World came from this one region. It was the area of Africa closest to the Caribbean and South America, so voyages were shorter to and from this part of the coast. The founding generation of Africans in the Caribbean and Mexico left overwhelmingly from northern Upper Guinea, the region known as the "Rivers of Guinea," a large territory stretching southward from the Senegal River and encompassing Senegambia and Sierra Leone. Many ethnic groups—Jolofs, Mandings, Biafras, and Brans—inhabited the region, and collectively they spoke numerous languages. By the last quarter of the sixteenth century, Senegambia shipped almost three times as many Africans as in the previous quarter century. Although still the dominant exporting zone, Senegambia began losing its near monopoly of the trade in the late sixteenth century, and by the end of the century it supplied only 55 percent of Africans shipped across the Atlantic. If Jamestown had been founded a generation earlier, it would have drawn the majority of its Africans from Upper Guinea.[21]

Toward the end of the sixteenth century and the beginning decades of the seventeenth century, West Central Africa—a vast slaving region extending from Cap Lopez southward and including the present-day countries of Gabon, the Republic of Congo, the Democratic Republic of Congo, and Angola—rose to prominence as the main supplier of Africans to the New World. This dramatic shift, sometimes described as the "Angolan wave" by scholars, was particularly evident in the first quarter of the seventeenth century, when almost nine of ten Africans destined for the New World came from West Central Africa. Virginia was hardly alone in obtaining its first Africans from that region, which remained the dominant exporting zone in the second quarter of the seventeenth century, by then accounting for three-quarters of the Africans shipped across the Atlantic. Insofar as Virginia obtained additional captives, they tended to come from "Angola," the term often used to describe the whole region.[22]

West Central Africa came to dominate the supply of transatlantic slaves for many reasons. One drawback to Upper Guinea was the risk traders ran of slave revolt, which happened far more often among captives from Senegambia than among those from Angola. Upper Guinea shipments were typically two-thirds male and two-thirds to three-fourths adults, ratios that were popular with American planters but that increased the odds of revolt along the African coast. The relative youthfulness of West Central Africans helps to explain why so few

---

21. Wheat, *Atlantic Africa*, 20–67.
22. Ibid., 68–103; Heywood and Thornton, *Central Africans*, ix–x, 39–41, 49–108; Arlindo Manuel Caldeira, "Angola and the Seventeenth-Century South Atlantic Slave Trade," in David Richardson and Filipa Ribeiro da Silva, eds., *Networks and Trans-Cultural Exchange: Slave Trading in the South Atlantic, 1590–1867* (Leiden, 2015), 101–142.

ethnonyms existed among them and why revolts were infrequent. Moreover, wars in West Central Africa greatly increased the number of captives exported from the region. Accordingly, turnaround times for slaving vessels to this region tended to be shorter than to others. A series of Portuguese military campaigns and wars of conquest led to large surges in the flow of captives. The rise of the Imbangala—fierce mercenary bands who fought with the Portuguese—augmented this trend. In addition, Brazil's sugar sector expanded significantly in the first quarter of the seventeenth century, and the export of West Central Africans to Brazil rose sixfold to meet the demand. The Portuguese now focused on Brazil and the South Atlantic routes to West Central Africa. Finally, the Spanish crown systematized the delivery of slaves to its American colonies by giving an asiento, or contract, to a single holder. The number of Africans sent to Spanish America rose from 120,000 in the last quarter of the sixteenth century to 168,000 in the first quarter of the seventeenth century—not as dramatic as the Brazilian surge, but evidence that Spanish America still absorbed many Africans. During the early seventeenth century, as Wheat observes, "Portugal's colonization of Angola and Spanish colonization of the Caribbean mutually reinforced one another."[23]

Competition along the African coast also increased in the second quarter of the seventeenth century. By the 1640s, Dutch and English slave traders, in particular, began supplying the Spanish colonies. Both of these slaving powers had a strong presence on the Gold Coast and Bight of Benin, and they drew on those two parts of the African coast to supply the Spanish. Also in the second quarter of the seventeenth century, the Bight of Biafra exported more Africans than did Senegambia. The decline of Senegambia as the once all-powerful exporting region was rapid and conclusive, although it remained an important supply zone for the English until 1660. West Central Africa's dominance was also on the wane by the middle of the seventeenth century, with the Bight of Biafra coming to the fore. A mix of Africans became typical as the seventeenth century progressed, especially with coastwise shipments from the Caribbean (where transatlantic shipments had a different composition that drew primarily from the Gold Coast, Bight of Benin, and West Central Africa) (see Table 2).

One last feature of the early slave trade was its haphazard, irregular, and predatory character. In the 1560s, John Hawkins and his associates mounted four slave-trading expeditions directly to Africa in which they brought about thirteen hundred Africans into the Spanish Caribbean. Seeing these Africans

---

23. David Richardson, "Shipboard Revolts, African Authority, and the Atlantic Slave Trade," *WMQ*, 3d Ser., LVIII (2001), 69–92; Eltis, *Rise of African Slavery*, 180–181, 285–292; Wheat, *Atlantic Africa*, 17 (quotation), 79, 93.

Table 2. Embarkation Regions of Africans, 1551–1650

Years	Senegambia	Sierra Leone	Windward Coast	Gold Coast	Bight of Benin	Bight of Biafra	West Central	Total
1551–1575	40,000	2,000	—	—	—	3,000	3,000	48,000
1576–1600	125,000	—	—	—	—	8,000	77,000	210,000
1601–1625	41,000	—	—	—	4,000	10,000	335,000	390,000
1626–1650	30,000	1,000	—	3,000	5,000	33,000	263,000	335,000
TOTAL	236,000	3,000	—	3,000	9,000	54,000	678,000	983,000

SOURCES: *Voyages: The Trans-Atlantic Slave Trade Database,* http://slavevoyages.org/estimates/ z4s72voG, with data on the origins of arrivals in Spanish America added from http://slavevoyages.org/ voyages/GrI2NTP7. I thank David Eltis for providing me with this table. Rounding produces small discrepancies.

as legitimate prey, to be acquired by force (if necessary) and often sold under threat of force, the English viewed their human cargo as nothing other than "very good marchandise," as Richard Hakluyt put it. Hawkins's voyages were not especially successful—his last was a disaster—so thereafter English ship captains increasingly preyed on the slave ships of others and sold their captives to Spanish planters or raided plantations and then ransomed back the slaves to their owners. Pillaging a well-established Spanish American empire became the primary goal; a parasitical quality characterized the early English slave trade. The dispersal of Africans often took place on pirate or privateering vessels, not on merchant ships. As historian Greg O'Malley puts it, "In the resulting illicit commerce, the captives were twice stolen—enslaved in Africa for sale to Atlantic traders and then seized in American waters by pirates who viewed African people as loot." Many captives suffered more than one journey: a long transatlantic voyage followed by an inter-American sequel that could last as long—or even longer. In 1619, the corsairs on the *White Lion* and *Treasurer* took at least six or seven weeks to reach Virginia from the Bay of Campeche. Sales of Africans in early Virginia, as O'Malley emphasizes, probably "had less to do with planters' demand for enslaved laborers than with the privateers' desire for a market in which to vend stolen Africans." Furthermore, accepting a proffer rather than actively seeking a supply "may go some way toward explaining the slow development of codified slave law and strict enforcement of a color line in seventeenth-century Virginia." Other privateers brought "twice stolen" captives into Virginia. In 1628, English privateer Arthur Guy, aboard the Massachusetts-based ship the *Fortune,* captured a Portuguese slaver, "an Angola man with many negroes, which the captain bartered in Virginia for tobacco." In the 1630s, at least sixteen instances of English privateers' capturing slavers bound for Spanish America can be traced.[24]

Two seemingly opposing interpretations emerge from these patterns. The first emphasizes homogeneity and uniformity, owing to the prominence of West Central Africans in early Virginia. Leaving mostly from the same port, Luanda, and becoming "Angolas" in the New World, these newcomers have been described by historians Linda Heywood and John Thornton as "the most homogeneous group of Africans to enter the Americas in the whole history of the slave trade." A common background, it is argued, magnified their cultural impact. They spoke closely related languages; they shared much, whether dress, cuisine, or political forms. Furthermore, from at least 1575, when the Portuguese conquest of Angola began, West Central Africans experienced "an intense engagement with European culture." This early contact in Africa—reflected in everything from languages, to naming practices, to religions—facilitated their integration into a New World colonial setting. The distinguished Africanist Jan Vansina has suggested that West Central Africans "provided the common glue" binding together African American communities. Seen as "bearers of an Atlantic Creole culture," perhaps best exemplified in the blending of Catholic and African beliefs and practices, they were prime candidates for cultural incorporation.[25]

An alternative view emphasizes heterogeneity and diversity, owing in part to the dynamic nature of life in seventeenth-century Angola and in part to the prominence of privateering as the chief method of acquiring slaves in a place such as Virginia. Early modern Angola was a region of dislocation and disjuncture; rather than transferring a homogeneous set of cultural practices to the New World, the forced migrants at best developed, in African historian Joseph Miller's words, "ad hoc strategies of assembling new communities out of refugees of the most disparate backgrounds." In addition, most Africans who came to Virginia in the first half of the seventeenth century—like those on the *White Lion*—did so in a two-step process: a transatlantic passage followed by an intercolonial voyage. This pattern prolonged the agony of journeying from Africa to America, added to the mortality rate, increased isolation, and subjected captives

24. Harry Kelsey, *Sir John Hawkins: Queen Elizabeth's Slave Trader* (New Haven, Conn., 2003), 13–115; I. A. Wright, ed., *Spanish Documents concerning English Voyages to the Caribbean, 1527–1568* (London, 1929), 95–112; Kenneth R. Andrews, *Trade, Plunder, and Settlement: Maritime Enterprise and the Genesis of the British Empire, 1480–1630* (Cambridge, 1984), 116–124; Heywood and Thornton, *Central Africans*, 5–48; Guasco, *Slaves and Englishmen*, 68–71, 87, 93, 102–103; Gregory E. O'Malley, *Final Passages: The Intercolonial Slave Trade of British America, 1619–1807* (Williamsburg, Va., and Chapel Hill, N.C., 2014), 86, 88, 90; Walsh, *Motives of Honor*, 119.

25. Heywood and Thornton, *Central Africans*, esp. 2, 49, 238; Jan Vansina, "Foreword," in Linda M. Heywood, ed., *Central Africans and Cultural Transformations in the American Diaspora* (New York, 2002), xi.

to additional sorting and mixing. Taking into account a convoluted, two-stage arrival provides a much bleaker assessment of potential cultural continuities from Africa than does the emphasis on a common West Central African heritage. It suggests that many African newcomers only slowly became accustomed to their new environments. For most migrants in the early years, adjustments were especially slow and painful. Deracination and alienation seem likely; or, as O'Malley puts it, "transshipment via pirate or privateer added to culture shock."[26]

Both perspectives see Africans in early Virginia as particularly eligible candidates for incorporation, which was further encouraged by the special circumstances of plantation life in the fledgling colony. Black slaves lived scattered on small units where they were often outnumbered by white servants. The two groups soon came to speak the same language, and the level of exploitation each group suffered inclined them to see the other as sharing the same predicament. Racial prejudice was not yet strong enough to stop cooperation between the two. Not only did many black slaves and white servants work alongside one another, but they also ate, caroused, smoked, ran away, stole, and made love together. They fraternized with one another. On some plantations, particularly in the Southwest, Native Americans were among the enslaved. The archaeological record, particularly the prevalence of colonoware tobacco pipes, suggests a mixing of Native materials, European imports, and African aesthetics. Made of local terra-cotta clay and often incised with a five-pointed star motif, these tobacco pipes were ubiquitous in early Chesapeake settlements. All the major social groups—Indians, Europeans, and Africans—made and decorated them, a testament to a vibrant cultural syncretism.[27]

HISTORIANS HAVE BEEN ESPECIALLY INTERESTED IN THE RISE OF slavery in the Chesapeake, Winthrop Jordan observed, because it emerged slowly. His contention still holds true, despite historian John Coombs's impressive demonstration that some planters invested in slavery much earlier than once thought. Coombs describes "a complex process, with multiple overlapping

---

26. Joseph C. Miller, "Retention, Reinvention, and Remembering: Restoring Identities through Enslavement in Africa and under Slavery in Brazil," in José C. Curto and Paul E. Lovejoy, eds., *Enslaving Connections: Changing Cultures of Africa and Brazil during the Era of Slavery* (Amherst, N.Y., 2004), 92; James H. Sweet, "African Identity and Slave Resistance in the Portuguese Atlantic," in Mancall, ed., *Atlantic World and Virginia*, 225–247; O'Malley, *Final Passages*, 85–113 (quotation on 108).

27. Philip D. Morgan, *Slave Counterpoint: Black Culture in the Eighteenth-Century Chesapeake and Lowcountry* (Williamsburg, Va., and Chapel Hill, N.C., 1998), 21–22; Audrey Horning, *Ireland in the Virginian Sea: Colonialism in the British Atlantic* (Williamsburg, Va., and Chapel Hill, N.C., 2013), 345–346; Kathryn Sikes, "Stars as Social Space? Contextualizing 17th-Century Chesapeake Star-Motif Pipes," *Post-Medieval Archaeology*, XLII (2008), 75–103.

phases and significant subregional diversity." Overall, the transition to slavery was still a steady, incremental growth, a long, drawn-out process. Thus, Jordan is correct to say that, in the case of Virginia and Maryland, it is possible "to watch Negro slavery *develop*, not pop up full-grown overnight." Indeed, he continued, "The concept of Negro slavery there was neither borrowed from foreigners, nor extracted from books, nor invented out of whole cloth, nor extrapolated from servitude, nor generated by English reaction to Negroes as such, nor necessitated by the exigencies of the New World. Not any one of these made the Negro a slave, but all." This is a fairly comprehensive list, and it can be largely endorsed. An intense demand for labor was the prime sine qua non, the indispensable precondition for the plantation slavery that arose in the Chesapeake. Joined to it were Iberian precedents, a rich English heritage of dependency, intercolonial borrowings, Africans' vulnerable status, and racial prejudice. But, unquestionably, the most important factor was the Iberian example, because it explains much about the growth of not just slavery but also the slave trade.[28]

If viewed from the perspective of the entire Western Hemisphere and of the long history of the transatlantic slave trade, the year 1619 hardly seems pivotal. Firsts should be acknowledged, but so should processes. In any case, Hispaniola in 1505 received the first Africans in the hemisphere (from Seville in Spain); the first transatlantic slave voyage from Africa to the Americas probably took place in 1520; the first Africans to set foot on North American soil arrived in 1526; and Bermuda in 1616 was the first English colony to import Africans. Taking a long perspective, the decision to embrace slavery seems a foregone conclusion. As economic historian Barbara Solow notes, "What moved in the Atlantic [between the sixteenth and nineteenth centuries] was predominantly slaves, the output of slaves, the inputs to slave societies, and the goods and services purchased with the earnings on slave products." If not 1619, another year, probably in the 1620s, would have seen the introduction of slavery into Virginia. On the other hand, as Davis notes, "The Africanization of large parts of the New World was not the result of concerted planning, racial destiny, or immanent historical design, but of innumerable local and pragmatic choices made in four continents." Market constraints and workforce options made it likely that the Chesapeake would develop slavery, but contingency and accident, such as the chance arrival of a privateer, played a role. Planters chose to invest in slavery—

---

28. Coombs, "Phases of Conversion," *WMQ*, 3d Ser., LXVIII (2011), 332–360 (quotation on 360); Jordan, *White over Black*, 72. For more on Spain's role in early Virginia's development, see J. H. Elliott, "The Iberian Atlantic and Virginia," 541–557, and Stuart B. Schwartz, "Virginia and the Atlantic World," 558–570, both in Mancall, ed., *Atlantic World and Virginia;* and William S. Goldman, "Spain and the Founding of Jamestown," *WMQ*, 3d Ser, LXVIII (2011), 427–450.

and, to that degree, engaged in "thinking decisions"—although surely many simply followed the example of their neighbors or emulated their rivals, or succumbed, in Jordan's words, to "certain social pressures generated by the American environment." Such possibilities led him to label the enslavement process an "unthinking decision." Wesley Frank Craven, the distinguished historian of early Virginia, thought it "an especially apt caption."[29]

29. António de Almeida Mendes, "The Foundations of the System: A Reassessment of the Slave Trade to the Spanish Americas in the Sixteenth and Seventeenth Centuries," in Eltis and Richardson, eds., *Extending the Frontiers*, 63–94; Peter H. Wood, *Black Majority: Negroes in Colonial South Carolina from 1670 through the Stono Rebellion* (New York, 1975), 3; Davis, *Slavery and Human Progress*, 52; Barbara L. Solow, ed., *Slavery and the Rise of the Atlantic System* (New York, 1991), 1; Jordan, *White over Black*, 44–45; Wesley Frank Craven, *White, Red, and Black: The Seventeenth-Century Virginian* (New York, 1977), 76; Anthony S. Parent, Jr., *Foul Means: The Formation of a Slave Society in Virginia, 1660–1740* (Williamsburg, Va., and Chapel Hill, N.C., 2003), 2.

Bermuda and the Beginnings of Black Anglo-America

MICHAEL J. JARVIS

The year 1619 is an important date within a national historical conversation about race, but it does not mark the beginning of Black Anglo-America. The Atlantic island of Bermuda, rather than Virginia, holds the dubious distinction of being the first English colony to import an African, in July 1616—deliberately so, in a ship that an English company sent specifically to acquire him. His arrival was soon followed by others: four additional English vessels called at Bermuda over the next three years and landed at a minimum another seventy Africans and Hispanic Africans looted from Iberian ships and Spanish colonies in the Caribbean. By the time Virginia's "20. and odd Negroes" arrived, Bermuda had integrated a sizable black population within its economic, social, labor, and religious landscape. This essay argues that what happened on a small, oft-overlooked mid-Atlantic island during those three years matters greatly to the history of Virginia, and, by extension, that of the United States.[1]

Bermuda lies some six hundred miles east of North Carolina, a tiny outpost at a natural intersection of major North Atlantic wind and current patterns. The uninhabited twenty-square-mile island cluster was first discovered around 1503 by Spanish mariner Juan Bermudez, for whom it was named, during a homeward-bound voyage from the Caribbean. Dangerous variable currents, locally tempestuous weather, and extensive reefs led to dozens of Iberian shipwrecks and to Bermuda acquiring another name: The Isle of Devils. Although several plans were proposed, Spain never colonized this important island lying athwart the main shipping route from the Caribbean to Europe. Other than the brief stays of curious visitors and shipwrecked castaways, Bermuda remained uninhabited throughout the sixteenth century.

---

1. Susan Myra Kingsbury, ed., *The Records of the Virginia Company of London*, 4 vols. (Washington, D.C., 1906–1935) (hereafter cited as *RVC*), III, 243.

It is fitting, then, that Bermuda's permanent settlement started with a shipwreck. In July 1609, the Jamestown-bound *Sea Venture*, flagship of the Virginia Company's Third Fleet, encountered a hurricane a week from its destination and survived a hellish three-day ordeal to limp onto Bermuda's eastern reef and thus avoid sinking with all hands. Religiously inclined Englishmen readily saw God's hand favorably disposed to English colonization through this miraculous deliverance of the *Sea Venture* castaways from certain death to Bermuda's welcoming shores. Over the next ten months, Virginia's newly appointed governor, Sir Thomas Gates, explored the island, catalogued its many natural resources, and coordinated the labors of 150 sailors and settlers to build replacement vessels and complete their journey to Jamestown. When he arrived in Virginia in May 1610, however, he found the colony on the verge of collapse. The vast majority of settlers had died during the winter "Starving Time," and those who survived were besieged by Powhatan Indians. Gates's infusion of food from Bermuda and the arrival of the Fourth Fleet days later saved Jamestown from becoming another Roanoke, but the troubled colony's future remained uncertain.

The Virginia Company immediately circulated news of the *Sea Venture* castaways' preservation and the revelation that Bermuda was a promising paradise rather than a home to devils. It used this favorable narrative to distract investors and the London public from the horrors that had befallen Virginia that same year. And it worked. Sir Thomas Gates himself returned to England to recount his extraordinary odyssey, and Puritan ministers pointedly called upon Englishmen to settle an island that God had particularly revealed to their nation. The Virginia Company secured a new charter that included Bermuda in its domain and in 1612 launched an expedition to permanently settle the island. For the next three years, Bermuda and Virginia were tightly integrated colonial initiatives of the same parent company. Arguably, the immediate profits and positive impressions that Bermuda generated kept the languishing Virginia side of the company's enterprise alive. And, although the company struggled to recruit Englishmen to venture into Virginia (a war zone through 1614), it found no shortage of volunteers willing to go to healthy, uninhabited Bermuda.

Bermuda under the Virginia Company, 1612–1615

Unlike Virginia, Bermuda's early settlement was fast, relatively easy, and quite successful. Although this owed much to the island's abundant natural resources, manageable size, and lack of a hostile Native population, it also reflected valuable lessons that English colonizers had learned from Virginia's mistakes. Bermuda's first fifty settlers included men, women, and families; a minister to address their spiritual needs; and a governor armed with strong authority over his wards. (Virginia's all-male 1607 founders had an ill-conceived administration with elected presidents and jockeying councillors based in an unhealthy location.) Governor Richard Moore, the Virginia Company's chosen commander, rarely made use of his potential powers, however, and led mainly by example and by building consensus. Upon arrival in July 1612, Moore made a solemn compact with his fellow settlers to bind them all to God, England, the Virginia Company, and one another, pledging to worship God, keep holy the Sabbath, "live together in doing that which is just, both towards God and Man," and maintain "the good estate of a Christian Church and well governed Commonwealth." Eight years before Plymouth-bound saints and strangers created the Mayflower Compact, Bermuda's first colonists formed a Christian commonwealth in Bermuda and drafted arguably the first written constitution in English America.[2]

The new settlement benefited greatly from the experiences of three castaway sailors who had opted to remain in Bermuda after the *Sea Venture*'s wreck and who had extensively explored the islands and reefs, created a farm, amassed a large food supply, and pioneered the cultivation of corn, pumpkins, and "a great deale of" high-quality Spanish tobacco, which they had found growing wild elsewhere in Bermuda. The sailors had also found an enormous lump of ambergris (a highly valued sperm whale secretion used in making perfume and medicines) worth between eight thousand and ten thousand pounds sterling, which Moore seized for the Virginia Company. Sent back to England in installments, the ambergris provided the Virginia Company with much-needed infusions of cash, reconfirmed their providential views of Bermuda's settlement, and more than covered the cost of outfitting Moore's expedition.[3]

During his three-year tenure, Moore quickly put the colony on a sound, se-

---

2. [Silvester Jourdain], *A Plaine Description of the Barmudas, Now Called Sommer Ilands, with the Manner of Their Discoverie* . . . (London, 1613), G1v. Moore's compact was available to Plymouth-bound settlers in 1620 who faced a far more ambiguous civil arrangement settling outside the Virginia Company's chartered borders.

3. [Jourdain], *Plaine Description*, F1v; Peter Force, comp., *Tracts and Other Papers, Relating Principally to the Origin, Settlement, and Progress of the Colonies in North America: From the Discovery of the Country to the Year 1776* . . . , 4 vols. (Washington, D.C., 1836–1846), III, 17–20; [Nathaniel Butler], *The Historye of the Bermudaes or Summer Islands*, ed. J. Henry Lefroy (London, 1882), 20–23, 26, 28; John Smith, *The Generall Historie of Virginia, New-England, and the Summer Iles* (1624), in Philip L. Barbour, ed., *The Complete Works of Captain John Smith (1580–1631)*, 3 vols. (Williamsburg, Va., and Chapel Hill, N.C., 1986), II, 351–352; John Chamberlain to Sir Dudley Carleton, Oct. 27, 1613, in Norman Egbert McClure, ed., *The Letters of John Chamberlain*, 2 vols. (Philadelphia, 1939), I, 482–483; Don Diego Sarmiento De Acuna to Philip III, Oct. 5, 1613, and Council of War to Philip III, Oct. 10, 1613, in Henry C. Wilkinson, "Spanish Intentions for Bermuda, 1603–1615: As Revealed by Records in the Archives of the Indies, Seville, Spain," *Bermuda Historical Quarterly*, VII (1950), 75, 79; Kingsbury, ed., *RVC*, II, 46–49.

cure, and profitable footing. A London guild member and master carpenter by trade, he organized his settlers into teams focused on farming, fishing, and fort building. England's occupation of Bermuda had drawn angry threats from Spain, which protested encroachment on an island it claimed and promised to extirpate Moore's colony. In response, the governor quickly erected forts at the entrances to Bermuda's few accessible harbors. Although settlers complained about working on public projects rather than their own fields, Moore was vindicated in late 1613, when he scared off two approaching Spanish scouting vessels by personally firing cannon shots at them from a just-finished fort on Castle Island.

The Virginia Company provided—sometimes overwhelmed—Moore with new settlers, including numerous middling craftsmen and even a few gentlemen and their families. All told, more than 620 colonists arrived in the first two years; unlike in Virginia, almost all lived on to clear fields, build houses and forts, and otherwise contribute to the settlement's success. Indeed, Bermuda's capital, the Town of Saint George, was larger in size and had a greater population than Jamestown in 1615. And whereas Jamestown's residents hunkered down behind walls in what was essentially still a military outpost, Saint George's (as it is colloquially known) resembled a medieval English village, sprawling along meandering roads and centered around a church and common square. Unlike Virginians quartering in large barracks, early Saint Georgians lived as families in many small households, working quarter-acre lots granted by the Virginia Company.

When Moore left in June 1615 after his governorship expired, he could take great pride in his accomplishments. In less than three years, he had established a sizable town boasting a church, storehouse, watchtower, and public dock and built nine forts to guard it. He had rebuffed Spanish scout ships and forestalled further invasion attempts. He left the colony with everything it needed for its continued survival and success: strong defenses, an urban administrative center, an orderly, law-abiding society, and a promising staple crop, tobacco.

The Bermuda Company

While Moore labored, insiders within the Virginia Company formed other plans for the new colony. Between 1612 and 1615, the small group of a dozen or so merchant and noble investors that directed Bermuda's colonization grew increasingly confident of the island's future and less sure about the company's expensive, unprofitable mainland Virginia venture. In early 1615, Bermuda's backers formally severed their ties with the Virginia Company and created a new joint-stock corporation, the Bermuda Company (also known as the Somers Islands Company, named for the *Sea Venture*'s late admiral, Sir George Somers), with

117 investors. On June 29, 1615, James I issued a royal charter that gave them near-complete control of the island colony. Sir Thomas Smith, the new company's governor, presided over a shareholder group overwhelmingly composed of Virginia Company veterans who brought new ideas and approaches to colonization. Over time, three distinct factions emerged with conflicting visions of Bermuda's development. Robert Rich, second earl of Warwick, was drawn to Bermuda's maritime location and sought to use it as an Iberian commerce-raiding base in the mold of Sir Francis Drake. Parliamentary leader Sir Edwin Sandys hoped to take advantage of Bermuda's temperate climate to develop a diversified range of profitable agricultural products. A leading London merchant involved in numerous other global ventures, Sir Thomas Smith most closely followed Virginia Company business strategies, emphasizing earnings from intercolonial shipping and specialized high-profit staple exports. A significant portion of the new company investors—Puritan-leaning religious men mindful of the many instances of divine favor manifested in Bermuda's recent history—also had non-material motives in mind. For them, colonization amounted to a mandate to continue developing Governor Moore's Christian commonwealth.[4]

Granted near-absolute authority over the colony, the Bermuda Company sought a strong and decisive new governor. Sir Thomas Smith chose Daniel Tucker, an experienced Virginia survivor who had earlier served as Jamestown's cape merchant, provost marshal, "Truck M[aste]r]" (Indian trader), councillor, and vice admiral. A soldier, planter, and entrepreneur who could make the colony prosper, Tucker received a commission that restructured civil government within Bermuda and gave him sweeping authority and a directive to diversify the island's economy beyond tobacco cultivation. He was to implement universal mandatory church attendance, complete a land survey to convert most of Bermuda into private property allotted to each company shareholder, and "punishe and correct" any who opposed his efforts. He sailed for the islands in February 1616 with perhaps a hundred planters and indentured servants in two vessels.[5]

4. [Butler], *Historye of the Bermudaes,* 44–46; Smith, *Generall Historie,* in Barbour, ed., *Complete Works,* II, 358; Richard Norwood, "Insularum de la Bermuda Detectio," in Champlin Burrage, ed., *John Pory's Lost Description of Plymouth Colony in the Earliest Days of the Pilgrim Fathers* (Boston, 1918), 6; Bermuda Company (BC) charter, June 29, 1615, in J. H. Lefroy, ed., *Memorials of the Discovery and Early Settlement of the Bermudas or Somers Islands, 1515–1685,* 2 vols. (1877–1879; rpt. Toronto, 1981), I, 83–100.

5. [Butler], *Historye of the Bermudaes,* 69–70; Smith, *Generall Historie,* in Barbour, ed., *Complete Works,* II, 190, 282; Kingsbury, ed., *RVC,* I, 214; Constitutions and Instructions to Daniel Tucker, Feb. 15, 1615/16, in Lefroy, ed., *Memorials,* I, 105–119. As treasurer of the Virginia Company (1607–1616), Smith was very familiar with Tucker's past service and experience.

Governor Daniel Tucker's Bermuda

When Tucker arrived in May 1616, he found that the six acting governors whom Moore had left in charge had done little other than feast on the company's stores and neglect forts and fields; two of the six had even abandoned their post "to fiddle upon [piratically raid] the West Indies" in a stolen pinnace. Tucker made a bold landing, and within days he began imposing the strict disciplinary regime he had known in Virginia. Finding the settlers "abhorring all exacted labour," Tucker enacted the martial law code that Sir Thomas Dale had instituted in Virginia. By midsummer, he had turned the settlers living in Saint George's (transformed by fiat into servants indentured to the Bermuda Company for five years) into a disciplined workforce that assembled daily to the beat of a drum. From dawn until nine o'clock in the morning and from three o'clock until sunset, they cleared fields, felled trees, planted crops, squared timbers, sawed boards, and built boats under Tucker's personal supervision. For this work Tucker paid them wages in "base-mony [copper coins]" (colloquially called "hogge mony" for the boar stamped on one side) that they could spend in the company's store. Tucker was highly motivated to make them work: instead of a fixed salary, the company gave him one-twentieth of all crops and goods that company servants produced. Tucker alienated most of Moore's original settlers by confiscating their private gardens in order to force dependency on company supplies and imprisoning those who protested.[6]

Tucker further flexed his power when he convened Bermuda's first assize in June 1616, a few weeks after his arrival. John Wood, a French joiner, had "saucely and arrogantly" complained of overwork to Tucker while drunk and allegedly threatened his life. The governor charged Wood with "mutiny and rebellion" and hanged him "to lett the rest knowe that . . . his authoritie extended to life." It was the first execution in the colony's history. At other assizes, Tucker sentenced the convicted to become "perpetuall slaves unto the cullony" in accordance with Dale's martial code and hanged a settler who stole a piece of cheese. Tucker's swift, harsh justice and absolute authority made settlers "take heed how they provoked" their hot-tempered governor. Morale plummeted. With no relief from

---

6. [Butler], *Historye of the Bermudaes*, 47 ("fiddle"), 70–75, 76 ("hogge mony"); Smith, *Generall Historie*, in Barbour, ed., *Complete Works*, II, 362–363; Richard Norwood, *The Journal of Richard Norwood, Surveyor of Bermuda*, ed. Wesley Frank Craven (New York, 1945), 58; Lewis Hughes, *To the Right Honourable, the Lords and Others of His Majesties Most Honourable Privie Councell* (London, 1625), A4v, [A5v]. For the Virginia code that Tucker enacted, see William Strachey, *For the Colony in Virginea Britannia: Lawes Divine, Morall, and Martiall, etc.* (1612), ed. David H. Flaherty (Charlottesville, Va., 1969).

hard labor, five wily craftsmen tricked Tucker into letting them build a small boat and then ran away with it, escaping their "slavery" via a desperate seven-week Atlantic crossing to Ireland. Most public servants, however, remained trapped under Tucker's harsh rule.[7]

Having restored order through fear and harsh discipline, Daniel Tucker turned his attention to diversifying Bermuda's economy and developing new commodities. The Bermuda Company had outfitted him with gardening equipment; grapevine cuttings; seeds for growing herbs, onions, orange trees, mulberry trees, and lemon trees; treatises on silkworms and making silk; and live cattle. Tucker had a vested interest in agricultural experimentation since he personally profited from his share of "all the Tobacco and other fruits of the ground" produced on company lands. The company also sent experts—a chirurgeon (doctor), several veteran whale harpooners, and a "skilful planter and curer of tobacco"—and provided Tucker with the pinnace *Edwin*, with orders to dispatch it to the Caribbean to trade for cattle, tropical plants, and "negroes to dive for pearles."[8]

The First Black Bermudians

The *Edwin*'s voyage brought the worlds of African slavery and English American settlement together, with important consequences for interracial relations, cultural interaction, and the legal, social, and working conditions of black Bermudians. Daniel Tucker sent the pinnace to the Caribbean in July 1616, and it returned a month later with plantains, sugarcane, figs, pineapples, and other tropical plants, "all of which wer presently replanted" in Saint George's, as well as "one Indian and a Negroe (the first thes Ilands ever had[ ])." It was a momentous moment in Anglo-American history: while diversifying Bermuda's economy, Tucker's human imports also racially and culturally diversified Bermudian society. In a mere decade, uninhabited Bermuda had become home to all three races bordering the Atlantic rim.[9]

---

7. [Butler], *Historye of the Bermudaes*, 69, 75–84, 89–90; Smith, *Generall Historie*, in Barbour, ed., *Complete Works*, II, 362; Hughes, *To the Right Honourable . . . Privie Councell*, [A5v] ("perpetuall slaves"); Daniel Tucker (DT) to Nathaniel Rich (NR), July 14, 1616, in Vernon A. Ives, ed., *The Rich Papers: Letters from Bermuda, 1616–1646* (Toronto, 1984), 8; Instructions to Tucker, Feb. 15, 1615/16, in Lefroy, ed., *Memorials*, I, 112–116; Bermuda Assize Proceedings, June 1616 and October 1617, Bermuda Colonial Records (BCR), 9 vols. and 6 fragments (A–F), I, fols. 1–2, 6–7, Bermuda Archives, Hamilton, Bermuda (BA).

8. Instructions to Tucker, Feb. 15, 1615/16, in Lefroy, ed., *Memorials*, I, 115–117 (quotations on 112, 115–116).

9. [Butler], *Historye of the Bermudaes*, 78, 84–85, 87; Smith, *Generall Historie*, in Barbour, ed., *The Complete Works*, II, 369; Lewis Hughes (LH) to John Delbridge, Dec. 23, 1618, Papers of Robert

The decision to find and bring a Native American and people of African descent into Bermuda was deliberate, made in England by worldly company investors already familiar with the enslavement of workers throughout Spanish America and the technical skills these laborers possessed. Several of the investors had heavily backed Elizabethan privateering in the 1590s, when English captains had taken hundreds of black slaves as booty during raids. Given the new company's focus on agricultural and economic diversification, it made perfect sense to acquire men experienced in cultivating staples that England was then importing from Spain. Investors further believed that Bermuda had extensive pearl oyster beds on its reefs and hoped to emulate Spain's enormously profitable pearl fisheries at Margarita Island and along Venezuela's Pearl Coast. Thus, Anglo-America's earliest slave system was planned in advance, motivated by a logical business strategy aimed at augmenting profits in an already thriving colony.[10]

And then there was tobacco. Bermuda was the first English colony to cultivate high-grade Spanish tobacco, which *Sea Venture* castaways found growing wild on the north shore of Saint George's. The three sailors who occupied Bermuda between 1610 and 1612 raised "a great deale of Tobacco" for their own consumption and potential export. Governor Moore expanded experimentation with tobacco during his tenure and shipped several hundred pounds of "pudding tobacco" (finished in large, fat rolls resembling English dessert puddings) in 1613, several years before John Rolfe (himself a *Sea Venture* castaway who likely grew tobacco in Bermuda) conducted his tobacco experiments in Virginia. Although one wing of Bermuda Company investors strove to diversify Bermuda's economy, Sir Thomas Smith and other practical merchants saw tobacco as the most reliable commodity for investors and Bermudian settlers alike, since it could be grown immediately on minimally cleared land and produce quick returns for shareholder-landlords anxious to recoup the costs of dispatching and supplying settlers. Rats that had plagued Bermuda in 1615 and 1616 had left tobacco fields alone, making it the default crop for new planters. But Bermudians still struggled

---

Rich, Earl of Warwick, Mss. 9202, Small Special Collections, University of Virginia, Charlottesville. The *Edwin* probably also carried cassava, which appeared on the island soon after its return. It is unclear with whom the *Edwin* traded, since most Caribbean islands had been depopulated of Native Americans. A cimarron (runaway slave) community or Spanish settlers in Hispaniola seems most likely, since the rest of its cargo was cut lignum vitae wood, but the ship might also have trafficked with Leeward Island Carib Indians.

10. Molly A. Warsh, "Enslaved Pearl Divers in the Sixteenth Century Caribbean," *Slavery and Abolition*, XXXI (2010), 345–362.

to produce marketable tobacco: although settlers had been growing it for seven years by 1617, they still couldn't reliably cure the leaf.[11]

Settlers and investors both realized that Bermuda would become an immensely profitable colony if they could overcome this technical hurdle. Demand for tobacco was high in England, and at two to five or more shillings a pound (equivalent to a skilled workman's daily wage) it was a lucrative commodity indeed. Englishmen spent more than two hundred thousand pounds on tobacco in 1615, and "upwards of 7000" taverns, inns, alehouses, and "tobacco houses" sold the leaf in greater London alone. Bermuda was poised to supply this booming market. The Bermuda Company dispatched botanical treatises and Samuel Tickner, a tobacco expert, "to teach his skill unto all," but neither worked. Abstract European knowledge was no substitute for practical experience.[12]

The arrival of Africans able to cure tobacco marked a decisive turning point in the colony's history. The Indian and African men who arrived in the *Edwin* in August 1616 were probably specialist divers taken from Margarita Island or Venezuela's Pearl Coast, but they were also familiar with tobacco smoking and cultivation. They were but the first of many to arrive over the next three years.[13]

English ships landed dozens of skilled black cultivators in Bermuda between 1617 and 1619 as the island became a base for pirates. As early as 1614, Daniel Elfrith, an English captain serving the earl of Warwick, was warmly welcomed in Bermuda with a Spanish prize frigate in tow, and this news spread quickly among English mariners. Although England and Spain were at peace, European seafarers knew that attacks on Iberian ships and settlements beyond the mid-Atlantic Line of Amity would not trigger a formal war. When the Bermuda Company gave John Powell command of the *Hopewell*—"a smale bark (but an excellent

---

11. [Jourdain], *Plaine Description*, in Force, *Tracts*, 20.

12. Kenneth R. Andrews, ed., *English Privateering Voyages to the West Indies, 1588–1595*..., Works Issued by the Hakluyt Society, 2d Ser., no. 111 (Cambridge, 1959), 194; Marcy Norton, *Sacred Gifts, Profane Pleasures: A History of Tobacco and Chocolate in the Atlantic World* (Ithaca, N.Y., 2008), 155–156; Instructions to Tucker, Feb. 15, 1615/16, and Bermuda Company to Tucker, 1616, in Lefroy, ed., *Memorials*, I, 116, 120; John Ferrar, Account of Tobacco Imported into London, 1614–1621, Ferrar Papers (FP) 320, Magdalene College, Cambridge, microfilm (Wakefield, U.K., 1992); C. T., *An Advice How to Plant Tobacco in England*... (London, 1615), A3r; Edward Bennett, *A Treatise Devided into Three Parts, Touching the Inconveniences, That the Importation of Tobacco out of Spaine, Hath Brought into This Land*... (London, 1620), A2. Bermudians successfully cured and exported several hundred pounds of blackened, twisted, and braided rolls of "pudding" tobacco resembling Spanish exports in 1613, but this was just a small fraction of a larger tobacco crop, much of which was not worth exporting. A 1615 treatise promoting a domestic English tobacco industry bemoaned Bermudian attempts to "imitate the Spaniards in juicing" their otherwise "excellent" tobacco; Virginia, notably, had produced no tobacco to critique; see C. T., *Advice*, B4r.

13. Instructions to Tucker, Feb. 15, 1615/16, in Lefroy, ed., *Memorials*, I, 115–116; [Butler], *Historye of the Bermudaes*, 84–85; Linda M. Heywood and John K. Thornton, *Central Africans, Atlantic Creoles, and the Foundation of the Americas, 1585–1660* (New York, 2007), 299–312.

sayler)"—in August 1616 and sent him to the Caribbean to "trade with the native Indians there for cattel," it tacitly expected him to use his craft for raiding purposes as well. During his voyage, Powell captured Portuguese and Spanish ships as well as a "good store of neggars."[14]

The black men and women in Powell's prizes arrived in May 1617, just as planters were harvesting their tobacco crops. Likely from Venezuela or Hispaniola, the captives were well versed in tobacco cultivation and dramatically improved the quality and quantity of that year's crop. Warwick's cousin and resident agent in Bermuda, Robert Rich, learned that one of Powell's captives, Francisco, had shown exceptional skill while working for Tucker on company land. Rich begged his investor brother in London to buy him: "His judgment in the cureing of tobackoe is such that I had rather have him than all the other negers that bee here." Rich set Francisco's value at £100—the price of two hundred acres of land or eight company shares—and promised that, with Francisco's help, "our tobackoe this yeare will farr surpasse in quantyty and goodness" all previous shipments. He apparently secured the tobacco expert on his own the following summer, along with Black James, a man skilled in cultivating many "west endy [West Indian] plants." The two farmed Rich family shares (land tracts) in Southampton Tribe thereafter and lived on farms of their own with their wives. Together they "made" 1,350 pounds of tobacco in 1620—an impressive yield compared to the 100- to 200-pound crops of their white neighbors. A subsequent Rich family agent even placed newly arrived Englishmen under Francisco and James's tutelage. Powell's other black "prizes" lived with Daniel Tucker in Saint George's and taught their techniques to planters and company servants in late 1617, after which Tucker sent the best to privatized land on the main island to further disseminate curing knowledge. Robert Rich's acquisition of Francisco and James paralleled a more general diffusion of vital Hispanic African skills throughout the island. The 1618 crop reflected their contribution. Bermudian tobacco exports topped 30,000 pounds that year.[15]

---

14. [Butler], *Historye of the Bermudaes*, 85–88, 93–95, 98; Robert Rich (RR) to NR, May 25 [19?], 1617, in Ives, ed., *Rich Papers*, 25. Upon Powell's return to England, the Bermuda Company "disowned . . . and held irregular and beyond his commission" his captures and stripped him of his pay and "all such goods . . . as were left behind" in Bermuda for violating his charter-party agreement. Powell's Hispanic African captives thus conveniently became company property. Powell later scouted Barbados and helped Anglo-Dutch merchant William Courteen colonize that island. The "Line of Amity" emerged from 1559 Franco-Iberian treaty negotiations (Jorge Cañizares-Esguerra and Erik R Seeman, eds., *The Atlantic in Global History, 1500–2000* [New York, 2006], 5).

15. RR to NR, May 25 [19?], 1617, and Feb. 22, 1617/18, Thomas Durham to NR, circa Jan. 1619/20, John Dutton to NR, Dec. 4, 1621, in Ives, ed., *Rich Papers*, 17, 58–59, 172–173, 176, 234; [Butler], *Historye of the Bermudaes*, 110. Although Butler put Bermuda's 1617 crop at 30,000 pounds, it was closer to 40,000: Lord Sackville noted a combined Virginia and Bermuda crop of 49,528, including 1,000

In disseminating Spanish curing techniques, Bermuda's first black residents set the island's tobacco apart from that of the Chesapeake, where planters independently developed a different cure. Francisco and his peers coated their tobacco with a brine solution (perhaps seawater) and hung it up to "ferment" (dry), then twisted it into tightly braided rolls. (Settlers had been twisting tobacco since 1613, but apparently without success.) The finished product closely resembled the Spanish leaf it copied. In February 1619, the East India Company sold a thousand pounds of improved tobacco "transported from the Bermudas in the form of rolls" for six shillings a pound. Rolling made the colony's tobacco more appealing to London vendors, since it required no further processing and could be sold immediately. The former Spanish slaves also probably taught English craftsmen to make mechanical "tobacco wheels" to braid cured leaves together into rolls (see Figure 1). By midcentury, most Bermudian households had a wheel. Chesapeake tobacco, by contrast, was shipped loose in hogsheads and required further processing and blending in England. As late as 1618, Virginian growers were still struggling to find a successful curing process. Although raised from the same plant species, Virginia and Bermuda tobacco had become distinctly different brands by the early 1620s: dull-brown Chesapeake leaf arrived compressed in barrels, while Bermuda's shiny black ropes of strong-flavored tobacco came coiled in chests or boxes. The divergence stemmed from the timing of the arrival of the two colonies' first black residents. Whereas Bermuda's first Africans arrived early enough to impart their curing techniques, by the time Virginia's first Africans landed in August 1619, white Chesapeake planters had already devised a different tobacco cure.[16]

With tobacco as a successful staple, Bermuda rapidly achieved full colonization. Planters' success in 1618 motivated most company members to recruit English settlers to develop their land. They sent another nine hundred colonists between 1619 and 1621, doubling the population. Tobacco quickly became the local

---

pounds of expensive six-shilling-per-pound roll tobacco that was certainly Bermudian and 9,419 pounds that came from Virginia ("Lord Sackville's Papers respecting Virginia, 1613–1631," *American Historical Review*, XXVII [1922], 498).

16. Court Minutes of the East India Company, Feb. 26, 1619, and Mar. 12, 1619, in Great Britain, Public Record Office, *Calendar of State Papers*, Colonial Series, *East Indies, China, and Japan, 1617–1621*, ed. W. Noel Sainsbury (1870; rpt. Vaduz, 1964), III, nos. 608 and 622, 251–252, 257; J[ohn] H[ardy], *A Description of the Last Voyage to Bermudas in the Ship Marygold*, S. P. Commander (London, 1671), 18; Kingsbury, ed., *RVC*, III, 93. On Spanish curing methods, see Joyce Lorimer, "English Trade and Exploration in Trinidad and Guiana, 1569–1648" (Ph.D. diss., University of Liverpool, 1973), 265–266. For Bermudian tobacco, see Michael J. Jarvis, "'In the Eye of All Trade': Maritime Revolution and the Transformation of Bermudian Society, 1612–1800" (Ph.D. diss., College of William and Mary, 1998), 94–103; John Bartram, *A Short History of Tobacco, with Some Hints for Its Cultivation and Curing in Bermuda* (Hamilton, Bermuda, 1882).

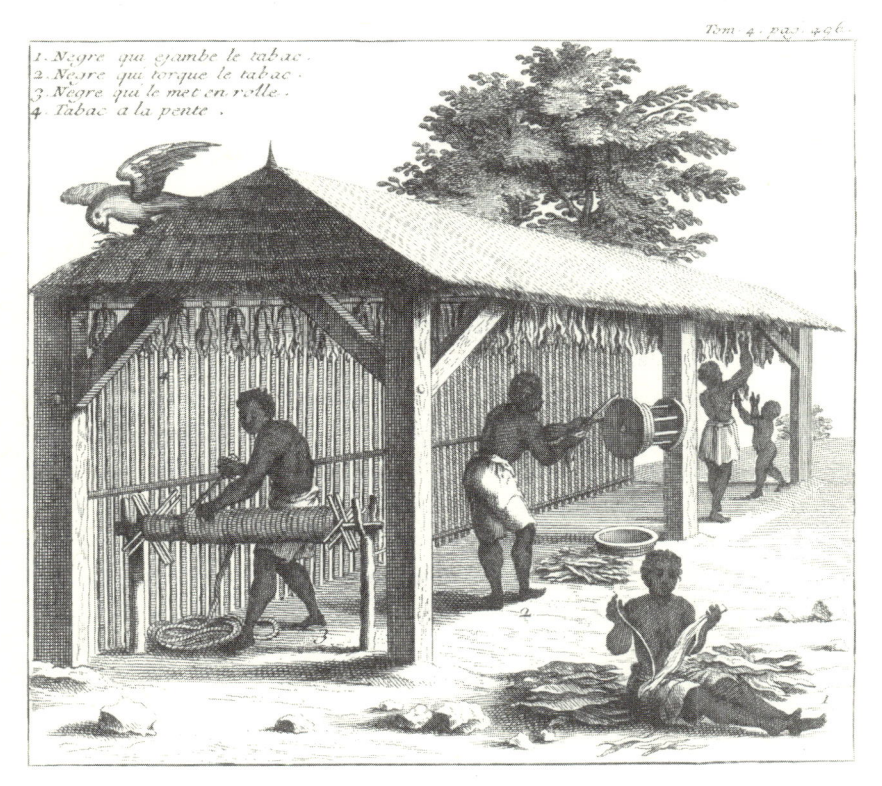

Figure 1. "Preparation of Tobacco." From Jean Baptise Labat, *Nouveau voyage aux isles de l'Amerique,* 4 vols. (Paris, 1722), IV, 496. Enslaved men, women, and children deveining, drying, braiding, and rolling tobacco in the Spanish manner. Courtesy, John Carter Brown Library at Brown University

currency, enabling settlers to conduct business and settle debts locally. By 1620, Bermudians had abandoned the company's "hogge mony" and used pounds of tobacco to value everything from daily wages and tax levies to criminal fines. Tobacco enhanced the company's magazine shipping system (through which it regularly supplied its colony) by giving settlers the means to purchase retail goods they needed. Although islanders complained about the company's high prices, they had regular opportunities to buy necessities, bring in additional servants and family members, and send their crops to London at set rates. Tobacco, in short, became the foundation of Bermuda's early economy and a magnet to attract additional English investment. Black knowledge fundamentally shaped the island's early economic success.[17]

17. Kingsbury, ed., *RVC,* III, 145, 181–186, 639.

"Too Wrathful and Furious in His Passions"

Although Daniel Tucker oversaw the shift to private land and helped to perfect Bermudian tobacco by circulating skilled black cultivators, he made many enemies in Bermuda and London alike because of his authoritarian tactics and explosive temper. Trouble started as London investors shifted hundreds of servants in Saint George's onto their private land shares on the main island, removing them from Tucker's direct command. Company servants who remained in Saint George's resented working on company land and public projects when they would rather lease, clear, and farm unoccupied private shares a few miles west. Tucker continued to claim labor from now-private servants for various public works projects, however, and frequently pressed "a levye of men out of the tribes [private land]" to repair forts and build roads. When local company agents complained about the disruption this caused, Tucker lashed out. When he heard in 1617 that bailiffs Lewis Pollard and Robert Rich were planning to refuse to send men when next Tucker demanded them, he arrested the two and convicted them of sedition in a sham trial. Fearful of angering the powerful earls of Pembroke and Warwick, whom the two served, Tucker pardoned them on the gallows but forced both to publicly recant their words and beg forgiveness.[18]

Daniel Tucker's ultimate downfall stemmed from putting personal enrichment over company interests. As Richard Norwood, the Bermuda Company's surveyor, laid out four hundred private shares of twenty-five acres each for the company's investors on the main island, Tucker ensured that a small "Overplus" would fall in the especially fertile land between Sandys and Southampton Tribes (see Figure 2). When the company hired him, Tucker negotiated to be paid three shares (seventy-five acres) at the end of his three-year term. By manipulating Norwood's survey, Tucker ensured that his tracts would be among the best in Bermuda. As soon as the survey was completed, Tucker began building a massive mansion on the site, using company servants to cut a "great store of timber" from company land and drafting "the choysest worckmen" from private shares to build him "a very substantiall and brave caeder house." Tucker forced scores of private tenants and servants to dig a cellar and well, cut shingles, and clear land around it and then transferred his agricultural experimentation from Saint George's to his own property. No longer working for the company's benefit,

---

18. LH to John Delbridge, Dec. 23, 1618, Papers of Robert Rich; RR to NR, May 25 [19?], 1617, RR to NR, Feb. 22, 1617/18, LH to NR, March 1617/18, and DT to NR, Mar. 10, 1617/18, in Ives, ed., *Rich Papers*, 25, 49, 99, 106–107; [Butler], *Historye of the Bermudaes*, 89–90, 96, 98–103, 114–115, 294; Bermuda Assize Proceedings, May 15, 1617, October 1617, March 1, 1617/18, and July 1618, in Lefroy, ed., *Memorials*, I, 126–130; Smith, *Generall Historie*, in Barbour, ed., *Complete Works*, II, 369; Grievances of Pembroke Tribe circa 1621, FP 1475e.

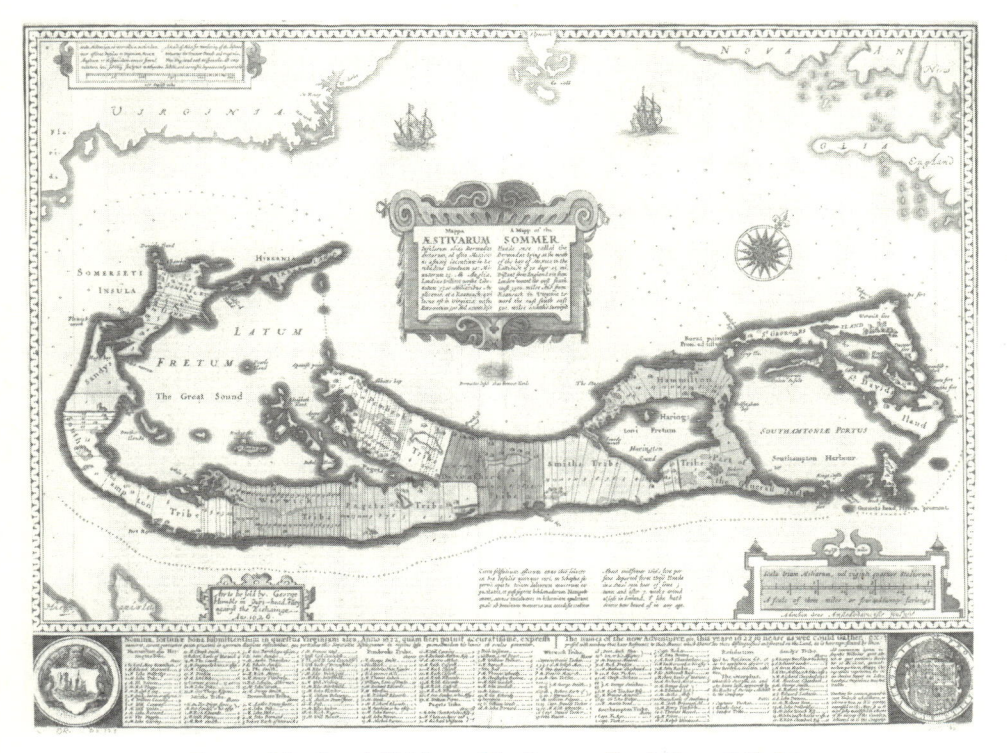

Figure 2. John Speed, "A Mapp of the Sommer Ilands Once Called the Bermudas . . ." (London, 1626). Richard Norwood's 1616/17 survey of Bermuda divided the island into four hundred "shares" (private property land tracts) of twenty-five acres each and paved the way for the colony's rapid, full occupation. Courtesy, John Carter Brown Library at Brown University

Tucker kept four company servants and possibly some of Powell's black captives at work planting sugarcane fields and tending a vineyard. For nearly a year, building Tucker's Overplus Mansion caused a "great slackinge and disturbance of the general bussinesse of the country, and extreame suffrance of the poore labouring people."[19]

While Tucker set himself up as lord of Bermuda, the colony's sole church, located in Saint George's, remained "but a thache hovell" that leaked when it

19. [Butler], *Historye of the Bermudaes*, 88, 90, 109–111; DT to NR, May 22, 1617, Mar. 10, 1617/18, RR to NR, Feb. 22, 1617/18, Mar. 10, 1617/18, in Ives, ed., *Rich Papers*, 39, 52, 85, 98–99. Rich family tenant Edward Dun lost nineteen weeks "workinge at the forts and makinge of highwayes," which is why he remitted "little Tobaco" as rent (Edward Dun to NR, Mar. 10, 1617/18, ibid., 94). John Smith gives only a brief neutral report on Tucker's Overplus house in his *Generall Historie*, perhaps because he and Tucker had been friends in Virginia in 1608 (Smith, *Generall Historie*, in Barbour, ed., *Complete Works*, II, 372).

rained. Bermuda's few ministers did what they could to maintain their Christian commonwealth and defend suffering workers, but they found Tucker "too wrathful and furious in his passions towards every bodie, and wedded to much to his owne will." One clergyman lamented: "I have heard men of good understanding and sober cariage say, that they had rather beg theire bread in England, than live here, where theire lives, goods, and libertie doth depend on the will of one man that hath noe government of his passions." As complaints against Tucker multiplied, the company began to look for a new governor.[20]

Mindful of his many critics, Daniel Tucker became increasingly worried over the fate of his mansion when the Bermuda Company did not confirm his legal ownership. In December 1618, an anxious Tucker departed Bermuda for London to personally secure it. He arrived in the midst of a heated battle within the Bermuda Company over the colony's future and his own administration. Although he ultimately obtained title to his mansion, he lost his governorship to the earl of Warwick's candidate, Nathaniel Butler.[21]

The Summer of 1619

By the time Nathaniel Butler reached Bermuda, his patron had made the island an active anti-Spanish privateering base. Warwick dispatched Captain Daniel Elfrith to Virginia in the heavily armed ship *Treasurer* in the fall of 1618, and from there he went to Bermuda. When he arrived, Tucker's acting governor, Miles Kendall, gave Elfrith provisions from the public store to support a privateering cruise to the West Indies, in consort with another English warship, John Jope's *White Lion*. In July, the two vessels captured the Portuguese slaver *San Juan Bautista* en route from Luanda to Veracruz with Angolan slaves and afterward headed for Virginia. While Jope landed Virginia's infamous "20. and odd Negroes" at Jamestown in August 1619, Elfrith, after a brief stop at Point Comfort, returned to Bermuda, where he added twenty-nine Africans to Bermuda's already substantial black population.[22]

The *Treasurer*'s August arrival closely followed that of yet another English vessel bearing a human cargo. The previous month, an English pirate named

20. [Butler], *Historye of the Bermudaes*, 111–115; Hughes, *To the Right Honourable . . . Privie Councell*, A5v; Smith, *Generall Historie*, in Barbour, ed., *Complete Works*, II, 372; LH to NR, circa March 1617/18, in Ives, ed., *Rich Papers*, 105–108.

21. [Butler], *Historye of the Bermudaes*, 116–132; Wesley Frank Craven, *An Introduction to the History of Bermuda* (1938; rpt. Bermuda, 1990), 118–120.

22. Kingsbury, ed., *RVC*, III, 243. See Emily Rose, "The Conflicted Politics of Slavery: The First Africans in British North America," paper presented at the conference, "Virginia in 1619: Legacies for Race, Commonwealth, and Empire," Dartmouth College, Hanover, N.H., Apr. 28, 2017; and introduction to this volume.

Kirby entered Bermuda and made "a gift" of fourteen black men and women (no doubt taken at sea or seized from Spain's Caribbean colonies) to Kendall in return for cannons and provisions from the colony's public store. In the nine months between Tucker's departure and Butler's arrival, English mariners operating under foreign letters of marque or as outright pirates had swelled the ranks of black Bermudians with nearly fifty new arrivals, bringing the total number to a hundred or more—about 10 percent of Bermuda's population.[23]

Nathaniel Butler's appointment seemed destined to convert Bermuda fully into an anti-Spanish raiding base. Warwick's handpicked choice had both land and naval military training and arrived in the *Warwick*, a newly built, state-of-the-art warship. As he took stock of the colony and began rebuilding the island's forts (anticipating Spanish reprisals likely to follow that summer's raiding), he readied his patron's namesake frigate for a winter cruise. Spanish America was spared, however, after an unseasonably late hurricane struck the island in November, sinking the *Warwick* and damaging the *Treasurer* beyond repair. Although Butler continued to improve Bermuda's defenses, the colony ceased being a haven for pirates and privateers owing to strict Bermuda Company orders to refuse them entry. Accordingly, the flow of captured Africans into the island abruptly stopped for nearly a decade. Bermuda's sizable black 1616–1619 charter generation thus constituted a tightly focused cohort, bound together through their closely spaced arrivals, common living and working conditions, timing of integration near the dawn of settlement, and subsequent isolation as both white and black migration into Bermuda effectively ceased in the 1620s.[24]

Slaves? The Ambiguous Status of Early Black Bermudians

Bermuda's first black residents arrived in 1616, but their social and legal status remained ambiguous for at least a decade. Although colonial authorities familiar with Roman and Iberian American slavery deemed black Bermudians bound and subordinate, the term "slave" appears rarely in documents from the first decades of settlement. It was first used in a penal context in October 1617, when Daniel Tucker made Nicholas Gabriel, a white man, a slave to the colony after his capital conviction for sedition. "Symon the Negro"—either the original 1616 diver or one of Powell's 1617 arrivals—was sentenced to become "a slave to the colony during the governor's pleasure" at the same assize for a sexual offense

---

23. [Butler], *Historye of the Bermudaes*, 147–148; Kingsbury, ed., *RVC*, II, 407.
24. Piotr Bojakowski and Katie Custer Bojakowski, "The *Warwick*: Results of the Survey of an Early 17th-Century Virginia Company Ship," *Post-Medieval Archaeology*, XLV (2011), 51; "Warwick, 1619: Shipwreck Excavation," National Museum of Bermuda, https://warwick1619.wordpress.com.

having "to do with a child in carnal copular." Later complaints indicate that Tucker enslaved other white lawbreakers. The absence of the word "slave" in records means little, however, since Bermudians commonly used the Spanish term *negro* (rather than Moor, "blackamoor," or African) to identify black islanders, a label encompassing racial, ethnic, and bound status within the Iberian Atlantic world. Nathaniel Butler, for instance, conflated race and slavery in a January 1621 letter: "If it were not for the accidentall Negroes [left by the pirate Kirby] (a fortune cast upon my selfe by all due), I wer not able to rayse one pound of Tobacco this yeare for the defrayeing of any publicke worck.... These Slaves are the most proper and cheape instruments for this plantation that can be, and not safe to be any wher but under the Governours eye." Elsewhere calling "negroes ... a most necessary commoditie for thes Ilands," Butler objectified Africans, but it is unclear whether he valued them more for their specialist knowledge or their open-ended servitude.[25]

Emerging English and established Spanish conceptions of slavery further crystallized in 1621 when the Spanish ship *San Antonio* was wrecked on Bermuda's western reefs. Black slaves were among the seventy Spanish castaways who sojourned in Bermuda while awaiting passage to Europe. Dispersed among white planter households, Spanish lodgers daily modeled slave-master interactions to their Bermudian hosts. And at least one early Bermudian resident had personally experienced slavery in North Africa: Walter Deane had been a galley slave aboard a Turkish warship in 1622, when the Virginia-bound *Tiger* rescued him. Deane was just one of thousands of English sailors and American-bound passengers who were captured and enslaved during the decades that Virginia and Bermuda were settled. Daniel Tucker's enslavement of white and black offenders alike reflected the ubiquity of bondage in the early-seventeenth-century Atlantic world.[26]

---

25. Bermuda Assize Proceedings, October 1617, I, fol. 6, BA; NB to NR, Jan. 12, 1620/21, in Ives, ed., *Rich Papers*, 229; [Butler], *Historye of the Bermudaes*, 144. Miles Kendall used the term "Moores" in petitioning for Kirby's black captives, but his word choice is unusual ([Butler], *Historye of the Bermudaes*, 243). For scholarly debate on the legal status of early black Bermudians, see Cyril Outerbridge Packwood, *Chained on the Rock* (New York, 1975), 1–9; James E. Smith, *Slavery in Bermuda* (New York, 1976), 12–19; Virginia Bernhard, *Slaves and Slaveholders in Bermuda, 1616–1782* (Columbia, Mo., 1999), 1–2, 18–33; and Clarence V. H. Maxwell, "Race and Servitude: The Birth of a Social and Political Order in Bermuda, 1619–1669," *Bermuda Journal of Archaeology and Maritime History*, XI (1999), 39–55.

26. [Butler], *Historye of the Bermudaes*, 265–266, 274, 278; "Interrogatories to Be Ministered to the Masters of Ships ...," and "A Certificate from Capt Elfrey on Behalfe of Walter Deane," in Lefroy, ed., *Memorials*, I, 246, 256–257; Deposition of Walter Deane, BCR, fragment A, fol. 27, BA. On Spanish conflations of "slave," "Negro," and "slavery" within the Iberian world, see Michael Guasco, *Slaves and Englishmen: Human Bondage in the Early Modern Atlantic World* (Philadelphia, 2014), 91–109; and Heywood and Thornton, *Central Africans*, 255–258, 287–288, 312–327.

White Bermudians did not enslave the black men and women who arrived between 1616 and 1619; rather, they accepted and maintained their already-enslaved status. Black Bermudians had been enslaved through prior capture in Africa or by English pirates and privateers, or they had inherited that status at birth within Spanish America. The core traits of later English racial chattel slavery—perpetual bondage and the denial of English civil rights—had not yet coalesced in the 1620s. Bermudian lawmakers only formally articulated them by statute in 1764, a century and a half later. But white officials and planter-agents clearly viewed the island's Negroes as subordinates whose labor was subject to white appropriation and their persons movable between shares. Effectively, they were much like white indentured servants but with unfixed terms of servitude, and legally their servile status was assumed from the outset.[27]

It was unclear, however, who "owned" black Bermudians' time and claimed the authority to direct and profit from their specialized work. This ambiguity helped some of them gain considerable autonomy. The *Edwin's* "Indian" and "Negro" and Powell's "good store" of black men and women were explicitly obtained for or claimed by the Bermuda Company. Accordingly, Governors Tucker and Butler directed their work on the company's behalf. Most "company negroes" (as they came to be called) lived in Saint George's in a "longhouse" built next to the governor's mansion and cultivated tobacco, sugarcane, and experimental tropical crops on nearby company land. Men also probably tended company-owned livestock, and women performed domestic duties in the governor's house. Although Miles Kendall claimed Kirby's fourteen Negroes were a personal gift, Nathaniel Butler seized them as company property, since the "gift" was actually payment for corn that Kendall had taken from Bermuda's public grain reserve. Sir Edwin Sandys ultimately obtained six of the fourteen for Kendall, making him Bermuda's first resident slaveowner. They moved with him to Sandys Tribe and worked land that Kendall leased from Sandys.[28]

27. William M. Wiecek, "The Statutory Law of Slavery and Race in the Thirteen Mainland Colonies of British American," *William and Mary Quarterly*, 3d Ser., XXXIV (1977), 258–260; Jonathan A. Bush, "Free to Enslave: The Foundations of Colonial American Slave Law," *Yale Journal of Law and the Humanities*, V (1993), 417–470; Bush, "The First Slave (and Why He Matters)," *Cardozo Law Review*, XVIII (1996), 598–629; Bermuda Assembly, "An Act for the Better Government of Negroes, Mulattoes, and Indians, Bond or Free, and for the More Effectual Punishing Conspiracies and Insurrections of Them," February 1764, in Manuscript Acts of Bermuda, 352–359, W. M. Bell Collection, box 4, Library of Congress, Washington, D.C.

28. RR to NR, May 25 [19?], 1617, in Ives, ed., *Rich Papers*, 25; BC Court Meetings, Jan. 11, 22, 1620/21, July 5, 17, 1622, FP 350; Edwin Sandys to Henry Wriothesley, earl of Southampton, Aug. 10, 1622, FP 402; John Welch, deposition, Sept. 18, 1700, C.O. 37/5, fol. 118, The National Archives, Kew, U.K. ("company negroes," "longhouse"). Kendall also sought Nathaniel Rich's help in obtaining the fourteen men, improbably asserting that Kirby had not stolen them but rather found them "flotinge on the sease" (Miles Kendall to RR, Jan. 17, 1619/20, in Ives, ed., *Rich Papers*, 123). Even before the

In 1622, the Bermuda Company restructured colonial officers' salaries by allotting them the use of company land and laborers in lieu of pay; most company slaves thereafter worked alongside white company servants on land granted to the governor, secretary, marshal, ministers, and fort commanders for their use while in office. Owned by a distant, abstract corporation an ocean away, Bermuda's first black residents performed a variety of tasks under temporary overseers—and as experienced specialist cultivators might have even directed the labors of white servants. The frequent turnover in colonial offices because of factional company politics resulted in company slaves working with or for many different local masters, but their daily work and residence in Saint George's changed little.

The twenty-nine Angolans that Elfrith took from the *San Juan Bautista*, by contrast, belonged to the earl of Warwick and were supervised by his Bermudian agents. The *Treasurer* was Warwick's privateer, and the slaves were his "prize goods," but a third of them (nine slaves) fell to Elfrith and his men as their share of plunder. Warwick gave the sailors cash payments (essentially buying the slaves from them), but Elfrith and Nathaniel Butler chose to keep two Negroes each. (It is unclear whether Elfrith and Butler obtained absolute ownership of these men or merely the use of their labor while they were in Bermuda.) Rich family agents treated the Angolan men and women the same as white tenants and servants, setting them up on independent farms, placing them to serve in other tenants' households, or hiring them out.[29]

Except for Kendall's six and Elfrith's two, Bermuda's earliest black residents were all bound to absentee owners living two thousand miles away. The relationships that developed between black bondspeople and their immediate supervisors—company officers or Rich family agents—resembled those of later eighteenth-century plantation slaves and overseers in that local white authority was limited to the direction of black labor, rather than ownership and absolute

---

1622 company restructure, individual officers had claimed black labor as their prerogative; in 1620, Provost Marshal Thomas Atwell was "allowed one man and a Negro woman" besides fees of office (List of Diverse Martial Officers, n.d. [circa 1620], BCR, fragment C, fol. 49, BA). On the emergence of chattel slavery in Bermuda, see Bernhard, *Slaves and Slaveholders in Bermuda*, 38–52; Maxwell, "Race and Servitude," *Bermuda Journal of Archaeology and Maritime History*, XI (1999), 51–65.

29. NB to the earl of Warwick, Oct. 9, 1620, in Ives, ed., *Rich Papers*, 188. To discredit Warwick, Sir Edwin championed several *Treasurer* sailors who demanded a third of Warwick's negroes (BC Court Meetings, Jan. 11, 22, 1620/21, July 5, 17, 1622, FP 350; Sandys to Southampton, Aug. 10, 1622, FP 402). The *Treasurer*'s men stated that twenty-seven blacks were landed—two fewer than Warwick's agent reported. The Bermuda Company eventually recognized Warwick's claim to "all the negroes left ther [in Bermuda]" and ordered Butler to deliver them "to the right honorable the Erle of Warwick, his officers, or servants, as his lordship himself shall direct" ([Butler], *Historye of the Bermudaes*, 211).

control over their persons. Lifelong servitude, inheritable slave status, and other features of chattel slavery crystallized in the 1630s when another wave of slave-bearing privateers sold captives outright to individual Bermudian planters. Yet the notion that black Bermudians could be bought and sold was already in place: Robert Rich had, after all, set the value of expert tobacco curer Francisco at one hundred pounds in 1618.[30]

The working and living arrangements of black individuals and families mirrored those of white tenants and servants also (albeit temporarily) bound to the company, English landlords, and local agents. Company Negroes cohabited with white servants in a large building adjoining the governor's house in Saint George's. When they were hired out, slaves lived in white households elsewhere on the island. A decade later, in 1632, the governor's company-provided slaves included eight black couples and their thirteen young children, underscoring how early family formation and natural increase were creating an indigenous black community. Black bondspersons owned by the Rich family could not choose where and for whom they worked, but at least some received wages. In May 1617, Robert Rich hired Jack "to worke abought my howse for one whole yere . . . 6 howers in the day for mee, and the other [hours] to employ himself to his best advantage." Rich paid Jack four hundredweight of corn and 20 pounds of tobacco a year for his half-day's labor, wages equal to those of two white men he also hired. In 1622, two company-bound black divers salvaging items from the *San Antonio* wreck received daily wages. Paget landlord Owen Arthur paid two black men 260 pounds of tobacco for curing his tenants' tobacco in 1625, revealing that skilled black curers were still circulating among the tribes and taking fees for transforming planters' dried bundles into Spanish-style rolls.[31]

Although most of Warwick's Angolan bondsmen lived in white tenants' homes, agents set up at least three black families in independent households. When tenant Thomas Durham sought to hire three black men and a woman from among Sir Nathaniel Rich's enslaved workforce in 1620, he noted that "ould Fransisco and James, the Negros, with theire wifes" were farming two of Rich's

---

30. RR to NR, Feb. 22, 1617/18, in Ives, ed., *Rich Papers*, 59.
31. Roger Wood Letterbook, [1632], BCR, fragment F, fol. 88, BA; "Correspondence of Governor Nathaniel Butler concerning the Spanish wrack in Virginia" (1622), "A True Note of the Severall Voyages Made by Me William Seymor . . . " (1622), and "A Copie of the Overseers Note of Pagets Tribe Sent unto the Governor" (1626), in Lefroy, ed., *Memorials*, I, 252, 254, 386; RR to NR, May 25 [19?], 1617, and Thomas Durham to NR, October or November 1620, in Ives, ed., *Rich Papers*, 23, 214–215. Warwick agent Thomas Dutton hired out Negroes on the same terms as indentured servants. Rich's Jack built a tobacco barn and sawed timber for his house; his private earnings went to "clereing up the store"—paying for goods advanced to him on credit (RR to NR, May 25 [19?], 1617, in Ives, ed., *Rich Papers*, 23).

Southampton shares. Negro Antony farmed another share until Daniel Elfrith obtained its lease and displaced him. Rich family agent John Dutton even sent English newcomers to "co-act" with these black farmers and learn their cultivation techniques. Working their own fields and heading their own households, Francisco, James, and their families lived more like tenants than servants and enjoyed considerable autonomy thanks to the large tobacco crops they produced.[32]

Growing local black autonomy troubled Bermudian assemblymen, however, and they responded in 1623 by drafting An Act to Restrayne the Insolencies of the Negroes—the first racially discriminatory law passed in English America. The law addressed allegations that black bondspersons were circulating unsupervised at night, stealing pigs, potatoes, and other provisions, and carrying weapons and tools "not meete to be suffered to be carried by such vassalls." It established that black Bermudians were subject to English common law, ordering tribe magistrates to punish them "as the lawe in such case requireth." Assemblymen also revealed the convergence of race and slavery in their language, stating that a black offender's "m[aste]r or owner" was legally responsible for theft or damage he or she committed. They further banned black bondsmen from buying, selling, bartering, or exchanging goods and tobacco without their masters' consent, ostensibly to stop them from fencing stolen goods.[33]

Although explicitly mentioning race, much of the act reflected wider public concerns about indentured servants and landless free men possessing arms, stealing provisions, tobacco, livestock, alcohol, tools, and expensive imported goods, and living as masterless men now that all of Bermuda's private land was occupied. The act did not ban black Bermudians from owning property, trading, or living on their own; rather, it only required white oversight—regulation consistent with the status of indentured servants. Other laws that the 1623 assembly passed forced landless men to become tenants on unoccupied shares, made stealing tobacco a felony, banned trade between planters and the crews of visiting ships, outlawed gambling and killing wild hogs, and restrained the movements of all Bermudians. White "boyes" (servants) and Negroes were both required to have written passes to use the ferry connecting Saint George's with

---

32. RR to NR, March 1617/18, Thomas Durham to NR, October or November 1620, John Dutton to NR, Dec. 4, 1621, in Ives, ed., *Rich Papers*, 81–82, 215, 217–218, 233–234. Elfrith tried to take over Francisco's and James's cleared shares, but Dutton successfully advocated on the black men's behalf. When Hugh Wentworth moved from Southampton to Warwick in 1623, he surrendered Mingo and his wife to Rich agent Thomas Downham, suggesting the black couple was tied to the Southampton share (Agreement between Hugh Wentworth and Thomas Downham, Feb. 3, 1623/24, BCR, fragment B, fol. 37, BA).

33. "An Act to Restrayne the Insolencies of the Negroes," May 1623, in Lefroy, ed., *Memorials*, I, 308–309.

the main island. Magistrates were ordered to whip white "hired servants, apprentices, and boyes" who broke the law. As colonial leaders strove to establish a legal and social order, they extended the traditional patriarchal authority that agents and household heads exercised over white servants to black bondspersons as well. To redress problems springing from the absentee ownership of black Bermudians, assemblymen made local agents and tenants legally responsible for black slaves living in their households. The 1623 act established a racial hierarchy wherein all black Bermudians were placed under specific white masters' authority but were not subject to white authority in general. Indeed, many white settlers held a similar social status, and some had even less autonomy. And all Bermudians were subject to a uniform, color-blind English common law code.[34]

Dependence

Despite growing local social stratification, all Bermudians were dependent in significant ways. They collectively relied on tobacco and an overseas market for their livelihood and on outside shipping for many basic necessities. And, despite assurance of their rights as English subjects under the colony's 1615 charter, all Bermudians were subject to the near-absolute authority of the Bermuda Company and its deeply divided leaders. External political and economic pressures in the 1620s transformed Bermuda's diverse early settler population into a common people with shared problems, interests, and lives. Although local issues and allegiances to warring Bermuda Company factions sometimes divided them, Bermudians increasingly shared a distinctive colonial creole identity rooted in their common dependencies.

An analysis of early Bermudian society underscores how exceptional freedom was at the dawn of English colonization. Given the ubiquity of different types of bondage and contractual obligations within England and the large sums spent colonizing the island, it is not surprising that most Bermudians were bound. Apprenticeships, service indentures, tenants' lease obligations, military conscription, and the state's forcible binding of vagrants were common in England and particularly targeted the young and the poor. Bermuda Company members who spent considerable funds sending personnel and supplies to their shares legally bound even their principal agents with indentures defining duties and terms of service. John Ferrar's 1616 contract with his agent, George Bostock, bound the latter for eight years and required him to furnish Ferrar with accounts of goods

---

34. Acts of the 1623 Assembly, in Lefroy, ed., *Memorials*, I, 299–313; [Butler], *Historye of the Bermudaes*, 228.

sold and tobacco rents upon two months' notice. Sir Nathaniel Rich bound his own brother with a commission defining his powers and responsibilities in managing the family's lands. From governor and ministers down to lowly storekeepers and ferrymen, all colonial officials were company employees who could be summarily dismissed at will. Most settlers emigrated as servants bound to the company or to individual landlords for set terms. In 1616, company leaders bound all company servants placed on private shares to new five-year indentures, demonstrating their unilateral power to dictate service terms. Islanders were further constrained by company bans on travel and relocation: no agent, tenant, or servant could return to England without advanced written permission from the company or their landlord, nor could they move between shares without approval. Leases gave tenants incentives to work hard and make long-term improvements, but they also tied them to particular tracts for years or decades. Indentures, leases, and company control of oceanic travel fixed every settler to specific people and places within a rather small colony, and their common pursuit of tobacco tied them all to English ships and markets.[35]

Why Bermuda Matters

Bermuda was the first English colony where Englishmen and people of African descent lived and worked together. Africans were well integrated into Bermuda's thriving settlement by the time Virginia became the second. The first black Bermudians were valued and respected for their specialized skills and were conspicuous in the streets and fields of Saint George's, Bermuda's capital and only port. At least some had embraced Christianity. Several attended congregational church services in Southampton Parish in 1620 and were likely present in Saint George's church as well. Bermuda's economic prosperity and rapid rate of settlement in the late 1610s owed much to black Bermudians. Their ability to cure Spanish tobacco was paramount, but numerous other innovations—ranging from detoxifying cassava and keeping caught fish alive in "crawls" (artificial fishponds) to weaving palmetto hats and baskets and sleeping in hammocks—improved the daily lives of English newcomers unfamiliar with the subtropical environment on the island they now called home.

35. George Bostock, Indenture, 1616, FP 69; Daniel Tucker to NR, July 14, 1616, RR to NR, May 25 [19?], 1617, in Ives, ed., *Rich Papers*, 8, 27, 30. On different types of English servitude, see William Blackstone, *Commentaries on the Laws of England* (Oxford, 1765), I, 410–416. In the 1610s and 1620s, indentures bound persons from a wide social spectrum and outlined training and professional obligations rather than merely a period of years of service. After the Bermuda Company ordered that criminals charged with capital offenses be sent to England for trial, Butler joked that "the only way [for many settlers] to get home gratis is to steal a hen here" (Ives, ed., *Rich Papers*, 158).

Bermuda's emergent biracial society matters to Virginia and early English colonial history because this was likely the first place where many English emigrants encountered people of African descent. Until the Virginia Company's demise in 1624, the Virginia and Bermuda Companies worked closely together and routed many Virginia-bound ships via Bermuda to take on water and refresh passengers mid-voyage. England-Bermuda-Virginia-England shipping circuits persisted throughout the seventeenth century. Accordingly, many future Chesapeake colonists' first impressions of Africans were formed in Bermuda, where they saw "Company Negroes" working fields surrounding Saint George's, instructing white settlers to grow tobacco, cassava, and other exotic plants, forming families, attending churches, and interacting on roughly equal terms with white islanders. They likely saw black fishermen or divers from their ships at work sailing boats between Town Harbour and the surrounding reefs. Black Bermudians, in short, were highly visible within Bermuda's thriving colony and society, providing a model for English colonists bound to Virginia and elsewhere to consider, emulate, adapt, or ignore.

The documentary record for Bermuda and Virginia in the 1620s is frustratingly incomplete, and the relationship between the two colonies and their emergent multiracial societies and slave systems must therefore be speculative. It is clear, however, that ships, passengers, and merchants regularly moved between the two colonies and no doubt shared ideas about early black laborers, their agricultural techniques, cultural backgrounds, and their standings within their respective colonial communities. Although the timing and means are unclear, Warwick apparently shifted several Africans from Bermuda to cultivate land in Virginia and perhaps work their magic on tobacco there. And, when the fertility of Bermuda's fields faltered in the mid-1620s, dozens of island planters relocated to the Chesapeake, transplanting living and farming techniques and racial attitudes regarding black fellow islanders to Virginia soil. We cannot quantify exactly how these many Bermuda-Virginia connections shaped how Virginians defined and interacted with Africans there, but Bermuda's precedents and practices were clearly the most prominent and observable to many if not most early Chesapeake settlers before 1630.

Although separated by eight hundred watery Atlantic miles and considered separately by most historians today, the white and black worlds of Bermuda and Virginia were intimately linked in 1619 and in ensuing decades—and both developed in the shadow of Iberian America, where African slavery had been ubiquitous for more than a century. Slavery, racial understandings, bondage, and, ultimately, the emergence of distinct new creole identities and divergences from English values and interests began with these sister colonies exchanging tobacco, personnel, ideas, and practices from 1612 onward. Virginians, in short, were no strangers to Africans when they first arrived in August 1619 because their Atlantic island peers had already come to possess, cohabit, and learn from them—much to their colony's benefit. English colonizers deliberately imported Africans as bondsmen to help Bermuda succeed, but it was their specialized knowledge, rather than mere labor, that they sought and respected.

"Poore Soules"
Migration, Labor, and Visions for Commonwealth in Virginia

MISHA EWEN

On Fleet Street, in the City of London on August 24, 1618, a small child named William Larratt was arrested for the crime of vagrancy. On this summer evening, William was in the city apparently unaccompanied, although he later said that his mother was alive and "dwelleth in the country at Westminster," perhaps some two or three miles from where he was found. It was a watchman, whose job was to walk the streets of London at night scouring the city for vagrants and nightwalkers, who stumbled upon the boy. The lord mayor of London had recently issued a precept to all aldermen in the City of London, ordering them to instruct constables to "forthwith walk the streets within their several precincts, and . . . apprehend all such vagrant children both girls and boys as they shall find in their streets and in the markets or wondering in the night to be apprehended by the watch, and them to commit to Bridewell." After William was arrested, Constable Cleyton took him to the Bridewell house of correction, which was no more than a few minutes' walk from where he was found. There, William told the Bridewell governors that he was born in Houndsditch, underneath the old Roman walls of the city, which was some distance away from both his mother and where he was now sleeping. That night, William was admitted to Bridewell and no doubt whipped and punished for his vagrancy, but not before the governors ordered him, "a little boy," to be transported to the Virginia colony and bound there as a servant. Vagrants who were admitted to Bridewell were usually punished and put to work, perhaps thrashing hemp or cleaning the streets, before they

---

I would like to thank the editors of this volume for organizing the conference at Dartmouth College that led to the publication of this volume and for their continued support. I would also like to thank the other contributors to this volume and the anonymous reviewers for their helpful comments. Funding from the Arts and Humanities Research Council, which I received while at University College London, and from the Leverhulme Trust, during my time as a research assistant at the Centre for Political Economies of International Commerce, University of Kent, supported this research.

were—often quickly—released. This time, William's fate was to be bound for the colony, like thousands of poor children in England over the course of the seventeenth century.[1]

Policymakers in England saw the forced migration to Virginia of the poorest members of society, like William, in terms of redemption. Pauper apprenticeship was a supposedly charitable practice that occurred against a backdrop of new paternalistic measures to help the poor in early modern England. The free and forced migration of subjects from the domestic to the colonial realm was viewed as a means to palliate social and economic ills at home while ensuring that the newly founded commonwealth in Virginia could flourish. Individuals would be saved and the health of the domestic body politic simultaneously restored through a raft of measures that fell under the rubric of social reform and improvement, of which transportation "beyond the Seaes" was just one. It was not only England's poor that the state and Virginia Company conspired to have transported to the colony, of course, but criminals, too. Yet, as vagrancy was considered to be a crime, the line between pauper and rogue was often blurred. This practice of transporting prisoners and the poor overseas also received wider support in sermons and in print. In promotional literature, writers substantiated the view that colonization would prove to be transformative for the lives of the poor in England: in the New World, a wealth of opportunity for work and Christian redemption awaited them.[2]

In the City of London, the Bridewell house of correction emerged as a focus for the supply of bound laborers, including servants as well as pauper apprentices. From 1617 to 1626 alone, the Bridewell governors ordered 381 prisoners, who we know very little about, to be sent to the Virginia colony. After prisoners, especially children, received orders for transportation, their historical record usually falls silent. None of the servant indentures drafted between the Common Council of London and the Virginia Company concerning children imprisoned at Bridewell and transported to Virginia have survived. Moreover, when they

1. "Minutes of the Court of Governors," Aug. 24, 1618, CLC/275/MS33011/006, fol. 65, "Corporation of London, Court of Common Council: Journals," July 1618, COL/CC/01/01/031, fol. 382, and September 1618, COL/CC/01/01/031, fol. 396, all in London Metropolitan Archives (hereafter cited as LMA). See also Robert C. Johnson, "The Transportation of Vagrant Children from London to Virginia, 1618–1622," in Howard S. Reinmuth, Jr., ed., *Early Stuart Studies: Essays in Honor of David Harris Willson* (Minneapolis, Minn., 1970), 137–151; Steve Hindle, *The State and Social Change in Early Modern England, c. 1550–1640* (Basingstoke, U.K., 2000), 164; A. L. Beier, *Masterless Men: The Vagrancy Problem in England, 1560–1640* (London, 1985), 167; and John Wareing, *Indentured Migration and the Servant Trade from London to America, 1618–1718: "There Is a Great Want of Servants"* (Oxford, 2017).

2. W. L. Grant and James Munro, eds., *Acts of the Privy Council of England, Colonial Series*, I, *1613–1680* (Hereford, U.K., 1908), 11 (quotation); Thomas Festa, "The Metaphysics of Labor in John Donne's Sermon to the Virginia Company," *Studies in Philology*, CVI (2009), 76–99.

arrived in the colony, children were often simply recorded as either "boy" or "girl." Many were partially or wholly illiterate, meaning that they did not leave documentary evidence of their time in the colony, thus compounding their anonymity. Only sometimes is it possible to recover material fragments of their time as servants in Virginia, with receipts of items purchased by the Virginia Company and excavations at Jamestown shedding light on their lived experiences. Several children were apprenticed at the glasshouse, where they received six pairs of children's hose; four boys who were bound by the Virginia Company and sent to Bermuda similarly received clothing, shoes, and bedding. The voices of children carried little weight when they were ordered for transportation and are easily lost in the history of Jamestown, too.[3]

It was under the leadership of Sir Edwin Sandys, who replaced Sir Thomas Smith as treasurer of the Virginia Company in 1619, that transporting bound servants to the colony was pursued with greater urgency. With the abolition of martial law and the advent of the General Assembly in 1619, free English colonists had greater social and political freedoms than ever before in Virginia. Many more planters were now persuaded to emigrate to the colony, and the promise of an increasing supply of bound labor was a key reason that they were persuaded to do so. New policies were put in place by the General Assembly, including the headright system, which rewarded planters with fifty acres for each individual they transported, as well as servant indentures. These contracts were negotiated between servants and their masters and usually stipulated a period of four years of service, during which servants were to receive adequate food, clothing, and lodging. At the end of the term of service, servants would customarily receive payment, also known as their "freedom dues." These indentures were, at any time, assignable to another master, prompting some servants to complain that they were treated no better than "slave[s]." Nevertheless, the introduction of new measures concerning migration and the successful campaign that the Virginia Company executed in print, in Parliament, and in local parishes ensured that more migrants, those who would be bound as well as those that were free, were persuaded to "adventure" their persons.[4]

---

3. "Corporation of London, Court of Common Council: Journals," July–September 1618, fol. 396, LMA; John Ferrar, Virginia Population, Livestock, [circa 1619], Ferrar Papers (FP) 138, William Webb, Account and Warrant, July 1621, FP 292, Webb, Account and Warrant and Receipt, July 1621 and Oct. 16, 1621, FP 294, Virginia Company Archives, http://www.virginiacompanyarchives.amdigital.co.uk. Certainly not all of these orders resulted in passage to Virginia. See Paul Griffiths, *Lost Londons: Change, Crime, and Control in the Capital City, 1550–1660* (Cambridge, 2008), 473.

4. David R. Ransome, "'Shipt for Virginia': The Beginnings in 1619–1622 of the Great Migration to the Chesapeake," *Virginia Magazine of History and Biography*, CIII (1995), 443–458; Christopher Tomlins, *Freedom Bound: Law, Labor, and Civic Identity in Colonizing English America, 1580–1865*

Children like William were just one part, then, of an expansive and varied group of individuals who migrated to Virginia in the seventeenth century. The historian John Wareing has estimated that between 1,400 and 1,500 children traveled to the colony by 1627, but over the course of the seventeenth century around 350,000 English and Welsh migrants made the voyage of four thousand miles from English ports to the Chesapeake, accompanied by 7,000 Scots and 20,000 to 40,000 Irish. The migration of all free and unfree settlers was essential for population growth and to plant and cure tobacco, Virginia's staple commodity. From 1619 to 1622, the stage was set with the voyage of 3,570 settlers to Virginia. The year 1619 marked the arrival of the first indentured servants and enslaved Africans in English North America, and, for the first time, greater numbers of women. With the arrival of servants and women, the "Infant-Commonwealth" that the Virginia Company envisioned gained flesh and took shape.[5]

The colony's first decade was a desperate struggle for survival. Hunger, disease, and war with Native Americans depleted the settler population and destroyed morale. The lack of women also meant that Jamestown continued to resemble a military outpost more than a civil society. Women's absence hindered natural population growth as well as the formation of families and stable communities. Yet, despite such demographic and environmental challenges, the colony quickly transformed beyond recognition between 1619 and 1622, owing to the arrival of thousands of new colonists. In 1619, colonists who had departed England aboard the *Bona Nova* came ashore. The individuals on this ship represented a broad range of social, economic, and geographic backgrounds from across England and Wales, including Ambrose Griffith, a thirty-year-old sawyer from Gloucestershire, who traveled alongside John Vaughn, a cutler, aged eighteen, from Devonshire. Trained as smiths, cooks, tanners, silk weavers, drapers, and shoemakers, the men aboard the *Bona Nova* were bound to work on Virginia Company land and had talents that would help the colonial economy to flourish. Women, who were transported at the company's cost to marry planters, followed soon after. However, not everyone who sailed into the Chesapeake Bay in this period did so willingly. Among the new arrivals in August 1619 were the first Africans in English North America, men and women

---

(Cambridge, 2010), 262; Sandra L. Dahlberg, "'Doe Not Forget Me': Richard Frethorne, Indentured Servitude, and the English Poor Law of 1601," *Early American Literature*, XLVII (2012), 1–30 ("slave," 18).

5. Wareing, *Indentured Migration*, 21, 31; James Horn, "British Diaspora: Emigration from Britain, 1680–1815," in *The Oxford History of the British Empire*, II, *The Eighteenth Century*, ed. P. J. Marshall (Oxford, 1998), 28–52, esp. 30–31; Susan Myra Kingsbury, ed., *The Records of the Virginia Company of London*, 4 vols. (Washington, D.C., 1906–1935) (hereafter cited as *RVC*), III, 219 (quotation).

who were captured and enslaved in Angola. Then in 1620, vagrant children who had been imprisoned at Bridewell, the so-called Duty Boys (that included girls), sailed aboard the ship of the same name.[6]

As the occupations of the *Bona Nova*'s passengers suggest, the colony needed skilled workers to develop industry. The Virginia Company hired men from Staffordshire to establish an ironworks, while German carpenters, Italian glassmakers, French vignerons, and Polish pitch and tar makers were sought to set up lucrative trades. Migrants with knowledge of agriculture and industry settled in Virginia as "tenants-at-half" from 1619 onward, including the Italian glassmakers. They served the colony for seven years, returning half of all their profits to the Virginia Company. There was also a small class of workers, with much-needed skills, who secured their passage to the colony and also commanded wages. Humphry Plant, a carpenter and sawyer from Gloucestershire, for example, received payment of forty shillings from the Berkeley Hundred planters before his voyage to Virginia in order to pay his debts in England. Employers also provided for the wives and children of their skilled servants, including the carpenter Thomas Dancy, who traveled from London to Portsmouth with his wife and child at the cost of the Virginia Company. The shipwrights William Gainsbie and Thomas Nun were similarly fitted out with supplies, as were their wives, Mary Gainsbie and Margery Nun, who received clothing, a hat, and some money for further supplies. In the seventeenth century, commentators often lamented the character of Virginia's early migrants, yet their scrutiny was not entirely fair, as many early settlers, men and women alike, carried with them valuable expertise.[7]

The Virginia Company was not only concerned with whether settlers had acumen in agriculture, industry, or household production to grow the colonial economy; it wanted to establish a civil society in Virginia that mirrored England, and the settlement of women and bound laborers was an essential component in this plan for a commonwealth. The colony remained a strikingly male-dominated society throughout the seventeenth century, but in the

6. Karen Ordahl Kupperman, *The Jamestown Project* (Cambridge, Mass., 2007), 225, 277; Kupperman, "Apathy and Death in Early Jamestown," *Journal of American History*, LXVI (1979), 24–40; Ransome, "'Shipt for Virginia,'" *VMHB*, CIII (1995), 446–449; David R. Ransome, "Wives for Virginia, 1621," *William and Mary Quarterly*, 3d Ser., XLVIII (1991), 3–18; Johnson, "Transportation of Vagrant Children," in Reinmuth, ed., *Early Stuart Studies*, 140–144.

7. Keith Pluymers, "Atlantic Iron: Wood Scarcity and the Political Ecology of Early English Expansion," *WMQ*, 3d Ser., LXXIII (2016), 389–426, esp. 413; "The Treasuror, Councell, and Company for Virginia, to the Governour of Virginia," May 17, 1620, FP 173, Virginia Company Arvhives; Kingsbury, ed., *RVC*, I, 493, 499, II, 115, III, 187; James Curtis Ballagh, *White Servitude in the Colony of Virginia: A Study of the System of Indentured Labor in the American Colonies* (1895; rpt. New York, 1969), 20–21, 28, 35; Robert Palmer, Account and Receipt, Aug. 1, 1621, FP 297, and John Cuff, Bill of Lading (copy), [circa June 1622], FP 272, Virginia Company Archives; Alison Games, *Migration and the Origins of the English Atlantic World* (London, 1999), 82.

first two decades of colonization this imbalance was particularly stark. Writing to the Virginia Company investor Sir William Herrick in 1614, Thomas Harrison suggested that women held the key to the success of establishing a settled colony; he envisioned that "if they do transport as many women; as men; nay rather more . . . when they shalbe over settled theare; our country-men, will of thear owne motion delyver passage continuously." Finally, in November 1619, the Virginia Company declared its intention to transport one hundred women to the colony, and, with the financial assistance of company investors, ninety women set sail for the colony in the spring of 1620, followed in the summer of 1621 by fifty-seven more. The Virginia Company believed it could effectively *"tye* and *roote* the Planters myndes to Virginia by the bonds of wives and Children." It was a common metaphor to imagine the commonwealth as a tree, made up of several important roots; thus, in language inflected by Renaissance humanism, the company suggested that the commonwealth needed tending if it was to flourish. As the wording of both documents suggests, then, women were understood to bring about the "settled status" of colonies not only by guaranteeing that men would invest long-term in the colonization project but also by ensuring that the next generation of settlers would inherit the language and customs of England.[8]

Yet the women who arrived in this period had personal motivations for voyaging to Virginia. They relied on their own faculties to seek out opportunities in Virginia, including Abigail Downing, a widow who voyaged to the colony in 1623. She paid the cost of her passage so that she would be "free to dispose of her self when she commeth to Virginia," with the intention of marrying an "honest man." Neither was she misled about conditions in Jamestown, promising to "take pains and . . . do all service that is fit" in order to "earn her diet." In England, opportunities to marry and start families in independent households were hindered by the economic and social climate. Population growth accelerated in the late sixteenth and early seventeenth century at the same time that real wages fell, leaving many underemployed and impoverished. Without decent earnings, couples could not afford to settle down. The thirteen women, aged between sixteen and twenty-eight, who departed for Virginia aboard the *Marmaduke* in 1621 would have been acutely aware of this reality. Whereas 17.4 percent of women born in 1586 would never marry, of those born in 1606 the proportion had increased to 23.6 percent. So, although the Virginia colony might have been

8. Thomas Harrison to William Herrick, Mar. 5, 1614, MS.Eng.hist./744, fols. 263–264, Bodleian Library, Oxford; Ransome, "Wives for Virginia," *WMQ*, 3d Ser., XLVII (1991), 3, 5; "A Coppie of the Subscription for Maydes," July 16, 1621, FP 280, Virginia Company Archives; Janice Liedl, ed., *The Tree of Commonwealth by Edmund Dudley* (Ontario, 2012), http://www.academia.edu/8158734; Sarah M. S. Pearsall, "Gender," in David Armitage and Michael J. Braddick, eds., *The British Atlantic World, 1500–1800* (Basingstoke, U.K., 2002), 113–132, esp. 114–115.

desperately short of women, women in England were increasingly desperate for opportunities themselves. In the colony, however, women were guaranteed marriage and the status that it afforded. For example, each woman aboard the *Marmaduke* was provided with two "coyfe" caps, a form of headdress that only a married woman was permitted to wear.[9]

If the migration of women was meant to encourage the creation of households, then the migration of bound white laborers was essential in order for male householders to fully serve their commonwealth. Transporting indentured servants and pauper children to Virginia would increase the supply of labor to produce vital commodities for trade, thus freeing up planters for other responsibilities, not least, as the investor and company administrator Sir John Danvers suggested, in "places of government." Indeed, the establishment of the General Assembly in 1619 gave free planters "a hand in the governing of themselves." The innovations in migration policy in 1619 concerning women and bound laborers were thus very much connected, both practically and ideologically. Women and servants were both essential to the establishment of households, which were, as the historian Phil Withington has explained, the "base from which men served their commonwealth." Yet contemporary ideas about the commonwealth are also key to understanding the domestic context surrounding forced migration to Virginia. In Parliament and printed literature, the Virginia Company and its supporters presented the company's policies as socially responsible, as serving the common weal. The company challenged the notion that colonial servitude was for profit or private interest alone. Rather, migration to Virginia, whether forced or free, was a matter of public good.[10]

Exploring pauper apprenticeship in greater depth illuminates how arguments concerning servitude and the commonwealth in England and Virginia intersected and also how "push" factors in England shaped early migration to Virginia. Binding poor children as pauper apprentices and transporting them to Virginia was related to efforts to solve problems concerning poverty, under-

9. Nicholas Ferrar to Lieutenant Parkinson, n.d. [circa 1623], FP 520, Virginia Company Archives; Keith Wrightson, *Earthly Necessities: Economic Lives in Early Modern Britain* (New Haven, Conn., 2000), 197, 223–224; Maids in Marmaduke, August 1621, FP 306, Virginia Company Archives. On married women's coif caps, see Laura Gowing, *Common Bodies: Women, Touch, and Power in Seventeenth-Century England* (London, 2003), 58.

10. "A Briefe Declation [sic] of the Plantation of Virginia duringe the First Twelve Years . . .," [February 1623/24], FP 532, and Sir John Danvers, Proposal for Virginia, April 1620, FP 166, Virginia Company Archives; Warren M. Billings, *A Little Parliament: The Virginia General Assembly in the Seventeenth Century* (Richmond, Va., 2004), 6–7; Kingsbury, ed., *RVC*, III, 107–108; Phil Withington, *The Politics of Commonwealth: Citizens and Freemen in Early Modern England* (Cambridge, 2005), 214–215; Edmond J. Smith, "Socially Responsible and Responsive Business in Seventeenth-Century England," in William A. Pettigrew and David Chan Smith, eds., *A History of Socially Responsible Business, c. 1600–1950* (London, 2017), 65–93, esp. 67.

employment, and vagrancy in early modern England. When the governors of Bridewell ordered children to be sent to the colony, they believed that they were cleansing the City of London of unwanted and unoccupied waifs and strays. During sermons in parish churches across the country, in printed literature sold at St Paul's Cathedral churchyard, and in the House of Commons, supporters of colonization argued that "by trans-planting the rancknesse and multitude of increase in our people" to Virginia, both England and the poor could be relieved. In this respect, the Virginia Company and English state were not acting in entirely innovative ways. In 1609, the Virginia Company had discussed sending vagrant children to the colony, influenced by the recruitment of fifteen hundred poor children in Lisbon to serve as indentured servants in the Portuguese East Indies. Recruiting servants from among England's poor would continue to be practiced across English North America, too. The Council for New England, a joint-stock company that was chartered in 1620 and granted authority to colonize the region, pressed the crown for permission to do the same in 1623.[11]

The Virginia Company and the English state introduced measures to transport the poor to North America that coincided with a marked increase in structural poverty and vagrancy across England in the late sixteenth and early seventeenth century. Incidences of vagrancy rose by as much as 65 percent between the 1570s and 1630s, and the problem was also strikingly related to age, with 67 percent of vagrants apprehended between 1570 and 1622 under the age of twenty-one and 43 percent under sixteen. In 1619, James VI/I had an encounter of his own with vagrant children in Newmarket, Suffolk, and afterward advised the Virginia Company to transport them to the colony. The problem was especially visible in London. In *The Poore Orphans Court,* published in 1636, the Puritan printer Michael Sparke lamented the condition of "these poore Orphans, whose Court is kept in a Cage, or under a Stall, or in S[aint] Paul's amongst the formes." Writing to John Ferrar, George Thorpe also vividly described the bad physical state of poor children who were transported to the colony in 1621—"diseased with olde solcers," "broken-belied" and "maymed"—which served to reflect the very real ills that gripped the country they had just left.[12]

With greater numbers of young migrants arriving in London and becoming trapped in cycles of poverty and deprivation, servitude and a new start in Virginia seemed a viable cure. Measures to relieve the poor in England were

---

11. Council of Virginia, *A True and Sincere Declaration* ... (London, 1610), A4r; Abbot Emerson Smith, *Colonists in Bondage: White Servitude and Convict Labor in America, 1607–1776* (Chapel Hill, N.C., 1947), 147; Dahlberg, "'Doe Not Forget Me,'" *EAL,* XLVII (2012), 10.

12. Hindle, *State and Social Change,* 51; Beier, *Masterless Men,* 76; M[ichael] S[parke], *The Poore Orphans Court* ... (London, 1636), A3v; George Thorpe to John Ferrar, [April? 1621], FP 239, Virginia Company Archives.

implemented a long time before the English arrived at Jamestown in 1607. In the sixteenth century, there were new ordinances for the relief and regulation of the poor, including the statutory basis for houses of correction in 1576. It was the introduction of the English Poor Laws in 1598 and 1601 that marked a watershed, as they provided the framework for provision in local parishes. The able-bodied were put to work, those that could not work received poor-relief payments, and pauper children and orphans were fostered out or apprenticed in menial trades. The Poor Laws also facilitated a change in attitudes toward the English poor, whose condition was no longer seen as a threat to the social fabric but as an opportunity. Thousands of poor children in London were put to work making pins, while Bridewell inmates were tasked with thrashing hemp, spinning cloth, and cleaning the streets. In local parishes, too, the poor were provisioned with supplies for work schemes. These reforms were not always successful, but apprenticing pauper children proved to be an exception. It was this particular aspect of the Poor Laws that set the precedent for the forced migration of poor children to Virginia. The English were not only familiar with the concept of forcibly binding poor children into service, but the Virginia Company drew on the precedence of the Poor Laws as well as the authority of houses of correction, local constables, and churchwardens to smooth the way.[13]

Pauper apprenticeship had a long history in early modern England. It was first introduced under the 1547 Vagrancy Act, which stipulated that girls up to the age of twenty and boys up to the age of twenty-four should be forced into apprenticeship. Under the 1563 Statute of Artificers, the practice of forcing youths into work was once again revitalized. This time, children aged ten to eighteen without occupation were entered into the service of a master until they were at least twenty-one. Pauper apprenticeship was legislated again under the 1601 Poor Laws, and toward the end of the 1610s there was a concerted effort to enforce the practice, with instructions in articles to justices of the peace in Norfolk and Suffolk in 1617 and West Riding and Lancashire in 1618 showing that there was increased pressure. Simultaneously, the City of London turned toward the colony for relief by agreeing to indenture children as young as eight to the Virginia Company, a practice that was propelled by, and integrated with, poor-relief policies in England. Indeed, the Common Council of London discussed raising a levy from each taxpayer, an eighth of their annual poor-rate assessment, to pay

---

13. Hindle, *State and Social Change*, 58, 163; Paul Slack, *Poverty and Policy in Tudor and Stuart England* (London, 1988), 8–9, 30, 127; Wrightson, *Earthly Necessities*, 167, 216; Griffiths, *Lost Londons*, 7; Steve Hindle, *On the Parish? The Micro-Politics of Poor Relief in Rural England, c. 1550–1750* (Oxford, 2004), 173, 177–179; Pamela Sharpe, "Poor Children as Apprentices in Colyton, 1598–1830," *Continuity and Change*, VI (1991), 253–270, esp. 253–254.

for poor children's transportation. Churchwardens, overseers of the poor, and constables in "every several parish of this city" would collect this money, which would then be "paid over to the alderman of that ward."[14]

The Virginia Company appealed to the relevant authorities to implement its practice of pauper apprenticeship. It first petitioned the Common Council in July 1618 "for taking up of vagrant boys and girls that lie and beg in the streets of this city having no place of abode nor friends to relieve them and for the transporting of them to Virginia to be employed." The petition prompted a flurry of activity across the City of London. In September, City of London aldermen instructed the constables in their wards to arrest any vagrant children they found and commit them to Bridewell. Soon after, the Common Council agreed that one hundred children "such as have no means of living or maintenance shall be taken up and transported to Virginia there to be educated and brought up at the charge of the said company." In the first instance, the governors of Bridewell ordered seventy-five boys and twenty-four girls for transportation to Virginia, and the children sailed to the colony in the winter of 1618 and early spring of 1619. Another group of more than sixty children, including two girls, were imprisoned in Bridewell between December 18, 1619, and January 15, 1620. Reports soon reached the company that these children had attempted to revolt, however, possibly with the assistance of their agitated friends and family. Sir Edwin Sandys, the company treasurer, wrote to the secretary of the king's Privy Council, Sir Robert Naunton, on January 28, 1620, entreating that those who were unwilling to go to Virginia could be forced. Sandys complained that, although one hundred children, "out of their superfluous multitude," were ready to be "transported" to Virginia, "now it falleth out that among those children, sundry being ill disposed, and fitter for any remote place than for this citie," were unwilling to go. He pleaded that they were individuals "of whom this citie is especially desirous to be dysburdened; and in Virginia under severe masters they may be brought to goodnes." His plea did not fall on deaf ears, and the Privy Council granted the City of London and the company authority to transport the youths against their will, ordering on January 31, 1620, that if any continued to be "obstinat" they could be punished and shipped to Virginia "with as much expedition as may stand with conveniencie."[15]

14. C. S. L. Davies, "Slavery and Protector Somerset; the Vagrancy Act of 1547," *Economic History Review*, XIX (1966), 533–549; Simon P. Newman, *A New World of Labor: The Development of Plantation Slavery in the British Atlantic* (Philadelphia, 2013), 31–32; Tomlins, *Freedom Bound*, 79; Hindle, *On the Parish?* 205, 253; "Corporation of London, Court of Common Council: Journals," September 1618, COL/CC/01/01/031, fol. 396, LMA.

15. "Corporation of London, Court of Common Council: Journals," July 1618, COL/CC/01/01/031, fol. 374v, Sept. 15, 1618, COL/CC/01/01/031, fol. 382, and September 1618, COL/CC/01/01/031, fol.

Although binding poor children as indentured servants was discussed in redemptive, even paternalistic, terms, such language did little to belie their cruel treatment, as many were forced to go to Virginia against their will. Yet, despite the apparent disregard for either the children's or their parents' consent, the decision to transport vagrant children from London did entail some consideration for their welfare. Discussion between the Virginia Company and Common Council of London over the terms of their indenture demonstrates there was scrutiny of the conditions that the children would live under in Virginia. The Virginia Company had to assure the council that the children would fare better in the colony than in the City of London, promising that they would be "educated and brought upp in some good trade and profession . . . to gett their livinge and mayntaine themselves when they shall attayne theire severall ages or be out of theire apprenticeshippe." Indeed, in England pauper apprentices typically received no education or training, nor were they entitled to freedom dues at the end of service. The company, on the other hand, agreed that, at the end of their indenture in Virginia, the children would be granted tenancy on fifty acres of land and provided with a house, a year's worth of corn to eat and more to plant, a cow, clothing, household items and tools, as well as weapons to defend themselves. After a further seven years, the company would provide them with their own "bounde apprentices . . . to helpe and asist them in their labour." Following this agreement between the Virginia Company and Common Council, the Privy Council proclaimed on January 31, 1620, that "the Citty deserveth thankes . . . for redeemeing so many poore Soules from mysery, and ruyne." Although conditions in the colony would be trying, servitude in Virginia was thus presented as an opportunity for both moral and material betterment.[16]

Pauper apprenticeship received support in the early seventeenth century at the local level from law enforcers and overseers of the poor. To begin with, the individuals who usually carried out arrests were local unpaid householders, including constables, beadles, and the night watch, and they were personally invested in the transportation of vagrants. The officers were elected by their community and policed their own neighborhoods, so they had communal interests

---

396, all in LMA; Johnson, "Transportation of Vagrant Children," in Reinmuth, ed., *Early Stuart Studies*, 138, 140–144; Sir Edwin Sandys to Sir Robert Naunton, Jan. 28, 1620, SP 14/112, fol. 86, The National Archives, Kew, U.K.; Grant and Munro eds., *Acts of the Privy Council*, I, 29.

16. Draft of Decree, Quarter Court, Feb. 2, 1619/20, FP 153, Virginia Company Archives; Grant and Munro, eds., *Acts of the Privy Council*, I, 28. See also "Corporation of London, Court of Common Council: Journals," September 1618, COL/CC/01/01/031, fol. 396, Dec. 18, 1619, COL/CC/01/01/032, fols. 125–126, LMA. In English law, seven years was the minimum age for pauper apprenticeship, although children were usually aged eight and older. See Steve Hindle and Herndon, "Recreating Proper Families in England and North America: Pauper Apprenticeship in Transatlantic

in mind when they arrested vagrant children on what were effectively their own doorsteps. In practical terms, they had been given authority to physically remove a social problem. Across parishes, binding pauper children to the Virginia Company would relieve taxpayers and overseers of their responsibilities toward the local poor. Although the city was faced with an initial cost of £3 4s. to outfit each poor child on their voyages, taxpayers avoided what was potentially a lifetime of financial support. The mayor ordered aldermen to instruct churchwardens to find out which families in their parishes were "overcharged and burdened with poor children" and whether they would consent to their transportation to Virginia, "thereby to ease them of that charge where they shall be well used and provision made for their good education and future maintenance." Parents were threatened that, if they did not consent to the transportation of their children, their parish poor-relief payments, which they relied on for sustenance and survival, would be suspended: "Take such order that they receive no further relief from the parish wherein they inhabit." The coercion of poor parents and their children was masked as paternalism, or what Patricia Crawford describes as "civic fatherhood." Yet the number of children apprenticed in the seventeenth century suggests that this practice received sufficient support from administrators at the local level, who understood it in terms of providing local as well as national social and economic benefits.[17]

At times, though, orders for transportation prompted a reconfiguration of who bore responsibility for vagrant children, thus testing the limits of the state's and the Virginia Company's authority. There were different social mechanisms at play, often undetected by historians, that caused orders for transportation to be bypassed. In some instances, the parish's responsibility toward its poor was reasserted. William Larratt, for example, who was first arrested in August 1618 and ordered for transportation, subsequently reappeared before the Bridewell governors on February 26 and July 3, 1619, suggesting that he had been released after punishment, despite the order for his transportation to Virginia. The entry in February recorded that he had been brought in from Fleet Street (again), but this time the governors ordered him to be sent to the "churchwardens and

---

Context," in Ruth Wilson Herndon and James E. Murray, eds., *Children Bound to Labor: The Pauper Apprenticeship System in Early America* (Ithaca, N.Y., 2009), 19–36, esp. 21.

17. Keith Wrightson, "Two Concepts of Order: Justices, Constables, and Jurymen in Seventeenth-Century England," in John Brewer and John Styles, eds., *An Ungovernable People: The English and Their Law in the Seventeenth and Eighteenth Centuries* (New Brunswick, N.J., 1980), 21–46; "Corporation of London, Court of Common Council: Journals," Dec. 18, 1619, COL/CC/01/01/032, fol. 125, and Jan. 10, 1619/20, COL/CC/01/01/032, fol. 128, LMA; Patricia Crawford, *Parents of Poor Children in England, 1580–1800* (Oxford, 2010), 235. See also Dahlberg, "'Doe Not Forget Me,'" *EAL*, XLVII (2012), 10; and Griffiths, *Lost Londons*, 284–286.

overseers for the poore, where he was borne." On William's third arrest, the governors repeated the order. It seems that they wanted his parish to provide for him rather than transport him to Virginia. If William was returned to his parish, under the Poor Laws he could have been fostered or bound out as a pauper apprentice much closer to home. In 1619 and 1620, other children, including Gryffin Beale and Arthur Chaundlor, after receiving similar orders for transportation to Virginia, also reappeared before the governors, suggesting they had been sent away after punishment. Thus, despite the apparent willingness of local constables to arrest vagrants and carry them to Bridewell and of parish overseers to bind children to the Virginia Company, orders were not strictly followed. In the climate of the 1620s, when the Poor Laws were enforced more regularly, it seems that the Bridewell governors were unwilling to let authorities closer to home shirk responsibility toward vagrant children. No doubt the English state and promoters of colonization really did believe that they were saving poor children from poverty and "ruyne" in England, but, nonetheless, the policy proved to be controversial, despite its apparent advantages.[18]

Certainly, the Virginia Company felt the need to publicly promote its practices. During the 1621 Parliament, the company adopted an appropriately paternalistic stance to persuade the House of Commons that transporting poor people to Virginia was a real solution to England's vagrancy problem. Following a bill presented on April 30 concerning how best to relieve the poor in England's towns and countryside, Sir Edwin Sandys suggested that venting the poor from towns to the countryside would be "like the turninge of a sicke man from one side of the bedd to the other, the maladie still remaynes." Building upon the claim made by the Virginia Company a decade earlier in *A True and Sincere Declaration* that for the poor in England "there is left no vent, but age," Sandys pressed his colleagues in the House of Commons to accept that "the poore that can not be sett on work maye be sent to Virginia": "Never was ther a fairer gate opened to a nation," he argued, "to disburden it selfe nor better meanes by reason of the abundance of people to advance such a plantation."[19]

18. For William Larrat, see "Minutes of the Court of Governors," Aug. 24, 1618, CLC/275/MS33011/006, fol. 63, Feb. 26, 1618/19, CLC/275/MS33011/006, fol. 101, July 3, 1619, CLC/275/MS33011/006, fol. 130v, LMA; for Gryffin Beale or Beadle, see "Minutes of the Court of Governors," Aug. 24, 1618, CLC/275/MS33011/006, fol. 63, Jan. 29, 1619/20, CLC/275/MS33011/006, fol. 168v, LMA; for Arthur Chaundlor, see "Minutes of the Court of Governors," Oct. 10, 1618, CLC/275/MS33011/006, fol. 75, Feb. 12, 1620, CLC/275/MS33011/006, fol. 170v, LMA; Claire S. Schen, *Charity and Lay Piety in Reformation London, 1500–1620* (New York, 2002), 191; Michael J. Braddick, *State Formation in Early Modern England, c. 1550–1700* (Cambridge, 2004), 113; Kingsbury, ed., *RVC*, I, 479.

19. Wallace Notestein, Frances Helen Relf, and Hartley Simpson, eds., *Commons Debates 1621*, 7 vols. (New Haven, Conn., 1935), IV, 274–275, V, 113–114 (quotation on 113); Council of Virginia, *True and Sincere Declaration*, A4r.

In promotional literature, too, writers exploited domestic concerns for the health of the body politic to make the case for binding the poor overseas. Robert Gray, in his sermon *A Good Speed to Virginia* (1609), suggested that England was in danger, as "our multitudes like too much bloud in the body, do infect our countrey with plague and povertie." Gray's allusion to Galenic theory, and his claim that the "humors" of the body politic were dangerously imbalanced, would not have gone unnoticed. John Donne employed almost identical imagery when he argued that forcing the idle poor to labor in Virginia would drain "the ill humors of the body," resulting in "good bloud" afterward. Writers were also attuned to the economic hardship that the poor faced and argued that transportation was a means to alleviate their desperation, which so often pushed them to commit crimes. Robert Johnson, in *Nova Britannia* (1609), suggested that, "having no meanes of labour to releeve their misery," the idle poor were compelled to "swarme in lewd and naughtie practises." He concluded, "If we seeke not some waies for their forreine employment, wee must provide shortly more prisons and corrections for their bad conditions." Writers stressed that labor itself could redeem the English poor: like Native American children, who would receive a Christian education at Henrico College, the poor would also be converted.[20]

While stock images of the body politic were employed, those who debated such issues in petitions and promotional literature were also influenced by real-world examples of poverty and hardship. Michael Sparke wrote about what he had witnessed, in his case in the City of London, and argued for a remedy so that the poor would not be forced to beg or steal to survive. Sparke dedicated his *Greevous Grones for the Poore* (1621) to the Virginia and Somers Island Companies, who through Christian charity, he said, had transported "mean and decayed persons." Sparke praised the work that the Virginia Company had already done to employ the poor, describing them as a "rotting sore [which] hath runne farre of late" in that "famous Plantation." Similarly to Gray and Johnson, Sparke framed his arguments in relation to the body politic, but perhaps more so than his contemporaries he argued for sympathy toward the poor, writing, "The Impotent with the lame foote, is to bee defended and sustained by every member of the body of this Commonwealth."[21]

Despite the emphasis on vagrancy in London, such issues were not confined

20. R[obert] G[ray], *A Good Speed to Virginia* (London, 1609), B4r; John Donne, *A Sermon upon the Eighth Verse of the First Chapter of the Acts of the Apostles Preached to the Honourable Company of the Virginian Plantation, 13 Novemb. 1622* (London, 1624), 21; Festa, "The Metaphysics of Labor," *Studies in Philology*, CVI (2009), 97; Robert Johnson, *Nova Britannia* . . . (London, 1609), D1r–v; Peter Walne, "The Collections for Henrico College 1616–1618," *VMHB*, LXXX (1972), 259–266, esp. 261.

21. M[ichael] S[parke], *Greevous Grones for the Poore* . . . (London, 1621), A3v, C1v.

to the capital. Richard Eburne, the author of *A Plaine Path-way to Plantations* (1624), who lived in the parish of Henstridge, Somerset, drew on local examples. Eburne was a vicar in Somerset, and between 1624 and 1625 he petitioned both Parliament and a local gentleman, Sir Robert Phelips, the member of Parliament for Somerset, concerning colonies. In his petition to Parliament he wrote of the possibilities they provided to strengthen England against other nations, including Spain, and also dispose of "the excessive and intolerable number of the poor people that burden our land." In his letter to Phelips he stressed the latter point, enclosing with his letter "an instance or example of it, and for it in the parish where I dwell." He clearly anticipated that this local example would stir the interest of Somerset's MP, who could petition the House of Commons for reform. In this note, Eburne argued that, although fifty or sixty years before the majority of the parishioners in Henstridge had lived comfortably on farms and in cottages, now many were dwelling in cramped, put-together coachhouses built on waste ground. For the first time, too, there were "inmates," presumably in either a hospital or house of correction, as well as a charge of forty pounds per year on the parish for poor relief. No doubt, in the course of serving his parishioners—delivering sermons at church as well as overseeing poor relief—Eburne had become intimate with the realities of life-cycle poverty. There was no denying that the material lives of the laboring poor in England had greatly worsened. As Eburne saw it, plantations were the cure and so needed to be carefully sustained.[22]

Visions for the "common weal" repeatedly crept into and imbued debates on colonization and migration. On the one hand, contemporaries considered what was the best way to advance the common good or "weal" in England, including how to relieve the poor, but they also considered how they would go about establishing a commonwealth in Virginia itself. Contemporaries did not treat these issues distinctly, and neither should historians. According to Sir John Danvers, a close ally of Sir Edwin Sandys, both land and servant labor were key to building the "foundations of places of entertainment of Judicious and worthy men," who would take up "those places of government in that Common Wealth." This outcome would, no doubt, be "the more strength to the government and to the confirming of mens mindes that what is maturely advised or promised heere shall be performed there w[i]th justice." Yet Danvers envisioned expanding on

22. Richard Eburne, *A Plaine Path-way to Plantations* . . . (London, 1624); "Petition of Richard Eburne, a Poor Minister in County of Somerset, to Parliament," n.d., 1624, DD\PH/212/45, fol. 50, Richard Eburne to Sir Robert Phelips, Apr. 21, 1625, DD\PH/219/63, fol. 121, "Note by Richard Eburne, Vicar of Henstridge," n.d., 1625, DD/PH/225/15, fol. 30, all in Somerset Record Office, Taunton, U.K.

practices already in place to forcibly apprentice poor children and bind prisoners as indentured servants in Virginia. He proposed that the company should cooperate with the knight marshal, an officer in the royal household, to forcibly apprentice idle people, who "lived loosely," in order to undertake "the hardest labor" for planters in Virginia. It is clear that bound service, by force or coercion if necessary, was viewed by the Virginia Company as a fundamental component in the foundation of a commonwealth in Virginia. Contemporaries within and outside the company did not view bound labor through an entirely economic lens, then; rather, they understood that it had repercussions for society and governance in Virginia, not least by enabling men to serve their commonwealth through the newly established General Assembly.[23]

In England, too, the forced migration of the poor was considered in much broader terms. Although it was viewed as a paternalistic, even charitable, measure, it was also necessary for the maintenance of the health of the domestic body politic. According to promoters, without the opportunity that plantations provided, social and political breakdown in the commonwealth was inevitable. Thus, in the years immediately following the creation of the General Assembly in 1619, the condition of the poor in England, domestic social reform, migration, and colonial governance were intimately connected issues that also significantly shaped the outlook of colonial legislators. Through exploring the English social history archive, including the minutes taken by the Bridewell governors and Common Council of London, parliamentary debates, promotional literature, petitions, and colonial projects, we can see just how connected policy debates on both sides of the Atlantic were.

Virginia's earliest legislators did, by their own admission, achieve their vision for commonwealth with some success. On September 30, 1619, John Pory, the colony's secretary, in a letter to his patron Sir Dudley Carleton, boasted of "the very principle and rudiments of our Infant-Commonwealth." The supply of a white labor force was a key part of this accomplishment and played an indispensable role in bringing about the permanence of the Virginia colony. Despite the Virginia Company's apparent failures—it was dissolved in 1624, and the colony came under direct crown control in 1625—it succeeded in establishing an English foothold in North America. Between the 1630s and 1660s, unprecedented numbers of emigrants voyaged to the Chesapeake colonies as the demand for labor to produce tobacco continued to grow. Throughout the seventeenth century, however, colonists continued to be mostly single, male, and bound in service. Society in the "commonwealth" of Virginia did not develop, in this respect,

---

23. Danvers, Proposal for Virginia, April 1620, FP 166, Virginia Company Archives.

beyond its "Infant" condition, to quote Pory, for some time. Although women arrived in greater numbers from the 1650s onward, the Chesapeake colonies did not become self-sustaining until the final years of the seventeenth century.[24]

In the absence of a company to direct migration to the Virginia colony, supplying a labor force fell almost entirely into private hands. In the middle decades of the seventeenth century, swelling demand for servants engendered illicit practices, including "spiriting," or forcing individuals aboard ships. In this lucrative and notorious trade in servants, canny "spirits" in Bristol, London, and elsewhere found a means to profit. At the same time, the state's role in supplying indentured servants to its colonies ceased, with the last sent at public cost in 1642. It would be wrong to assume, though, that government involvement in coercing and forcing people to migrate ceased altogether. The English state could not ignore that, as its empire grew, so did its demand for bound labor. The government-chartered Royal African Company's trade in chattel slavery as well as the continued forced transportation of prisoners and, after 1718, penal servitude met the demand.[25]

There is no doubt that increased free migration to the colony, including that of women, and the articulation of visions for the commonwealth in Virginia, which rested on understandings of colonial governance as reliant on bound labor, are some of the significant legacies of Virginia in 1619. Pauper apprenticeship also had an enduring legacy, however, in the early English and later British Empire and right through to the twentieth century. This early experiment in supplying bound labor to Virginia had a lasting impact on welfare policies and responses to poor families in Britain. Yet it also determined that colonization was clearly understood, from 1619 onward, more than it had been before, as bringing about wider social, as well as economic, benefits to the commonwealth—whether at home or overseas.[26]

24. Kingsbury, ed., *RVC*, III, 219; Wesley Frank Craven, *Dissolution of the Virginia Company: The Failure of a Colonial Experiment* (New York, 1932); James Horn, "Tobacco Colonies: The Shaping of English Society in the Seventeenth-Century Chesapeake," in *The Oxford History of the British Empire*, I, *The Origins of Empire: British Overseas Empire to the Close of the Seventeenth Century*, ed. Nicholas Canny (Oxford, 1998), 170–192, esp. 180, 183–184.

25. John Wareing, "'Violently Taken Away or Cheatingly Duckoyed': The Illicit Recruitment in London of Indentured Servants for the American Colonies, 1645–1718," *London Journal*, XXVI, no. 2 (2001), 1–22; Wareing, *Indentured Migration and the Servant Trade*, 178; William A. Pettigrew, *Freedom's Debt: The Royal African Company and the Politics of the Atlantic Slave Trade, 1672–1752* (Williamsburg, Va., and Chapel Hill, N.C., 2013); Griffiths, *Lost Londons*, 473; Hamish Maxwell-Stewart, "Convict Transportation from Britain and Ireland, 1615–1870," *History Compass*, VIII, no. 11 (2010), 1221–1242.

26. John E. Murray and Ruth Wallis Herndon, "Market for Children in Early America: A Political Economy of Pauper Apprenticeship," *Journal of Economic History*, LXII (2002), 356–382; Kristen Grace Lashua, "Children at the Birth of Empire, c. 1600–1760" (Ph.D. diss., University of Virginia, 2015), 311–313.

Private Plantation
The Political Economy of Land in Early Virginia

PAUL MUSSELWHITE

The Virginia Company's decision to begin the widespread distribution of private land to colonists is one of the most consequential—yet overlooked—aspects of the story of 1619. The decision has been taken for granted. We have long known that English colonial promoters coveted land to settle the kingdom's burgeoning population and that a rhetoric describing the Americas as empty land was used to justify English invasion. The granting of private land has therefore seemed inevitable and the logic—that private landownership spurred people to labor and innovation—apparent. Depending on one's perspective, it might appear to be a first American victory for the efficiency of free enterprise or a tragically unavoidable step in the development of capitalism that would dispossess millions of Native people and enslave millions of Africans. The common thread, though, is that the events of 1618–1619 represented a straightforward step on the road to individual landownership, the embrace of private interests, and the development of large commercial agricultural estates. In reality, the Virginia Company was wracked with uncertainty about the appropriate way to distribute land and control private enterprise. Since the Elizabethan era, "plantation" had been seen as a civic project for the good of the realm and the glory of God, and it was not at all clear how private landownership should fit within that project. Questions about land distribution emerged from contemporary debates about whether commercial interests were compatible with the pursuit of the common good. Exploring rival visions of landownership in 1619 reveals a critical debate within the company over political economy that would begin to redefine "plantation" as a private space and, in the process, shape the English Atlantic economy.[1]

1. For previous scholarship on the allocation of private land, see Philip Alexander Bruce, *Economic History of Virginia in the Seventeenth Century* . . . , 2 vols. (New York, 1895); Wesley Frank Craven, *A History of the South*, I, *The Southern Colonies in the Seventeenth Century, 1607–1689* (Baton Rouge, La., 1949); Susie M. Ames, *Studies of the Virginia Eastern Shore in the Seventeenth Century* (Richmond, Va., 1940), chap. 2; W. Stitt Robinson, Jr., *Mother Earth: Land Grants in Virginia, 1607–1699* (Williamsburg, Va., 1957); Irene W. D. Hecht, "The Virginia Company, 1607–1640: A Study in Fron-

There was no such thing as purely private land in England. The realm was an immensely complex patchwork of land tenures held with different conditions and divergent rights to use common resources such as pastures and mills. The century that bracketed the settlement of Virginia was also marked by radical shifts in these patterns: the dissolution of church property led to the reallocation of land to the gentry and to newly empowered corporate boroughs, and these changes spurred efforts to rationalize landholdings and enclose common fields. The way people thought about landownership and agricultural enterprise was changing. Many were moving away from an ideal of stasis and balance in rural communities and toward the virtue of maximizing labor and pursuing improvement. But, at the same time, these innovations met with stiff resistance and stoked fears about their implications for the realm's stability. Even English colonization efforts in Ireland did not provide a straightforward guide; approaches there were complicated by existing Irish and Old English land titles. The many different patterns of commerce and landownership across England and Ireland were therefore, not local traditions existing in static isolation, but rather the result of a long-running national debate about commerce and civic order that was brought to bear on the project of American plantation.[2]

Unsurprisingly, given the volatile English context, it is extraordinarily difficult to pin down the precise moment when "private" land was granted to Virginia's colonists and investors. In the second half of the 1610s, as colonists and inves-

---

tier Growth" (Ph.D. diss., University of Washington, 1969); and Lorena S. Walsh, *Motives of Honor, Pleasure, and Profit: Plantation Management in the Colonial Chesapeake, 1607–1763* (Williamsburg, Va., and Chapel Hill, N.C., 2010), chap. 1. For the positive pro-enterprise spin, see Murray N. Rothbard, with the assistance of Leonard P. Liggio, *Conceived in Liberty*, I, *A New Land, a New People: The American Colonies in the Seventeenth Century* (New Rochelle, N.Y., 1975), chap. 3. For the classic negative depiction of private interests as part of Virginia's founding pathology, see Edmund S. Morgan, *American Slavery, American Freedom: The Ordeal of Colonial Virginia* (New York, 1975); and T. H. Breen, "Looking Out for Number One: The Cultural Limits on Public Policy in Early Virginia," in Breen, *Puritans and Adventurers: Change and Persistence in Early America* (Oxford, 1980), 106–126.

2. J. A. Yelling, *Common Field and Enclosure in England, 1450–1850* (Hamden, Conn., 1977); Joan Thirsk, *Economic Policy and Projects: The Development of a Consumer Society in Early Modern England* (Oxford, 1978); Andrew McRae, *God Speed the Plough: The Representation of Agrarian England, 1500–1660* (Cambridge, 1996); Keith Wrightson, *Earthly Necessities: Economic Lives in Early Modern Britain* (New Haven, Conn., 2002); Paul Slack, *The Invention of Improvement: Information and Material Progress in Seventeenth-Century England* (Oxford, 2015). For Ireland, see Philip S. Robinson, *The Plantation of Ulster: British Settlement in an Irish Landscape, 1600–1670* (New York, 1984); and Nicholas Canny, *Making Ireland British, 1580–1650* (Oxford, 2001). Some historians have portrayed the Chesapeake's pattern of landholding and economic culture as emerging from a particular regional subculture in the predominant arable areas of early modern England; see, for example, David Hackett Fischer, *Albion's Seed: Four British Folkways in America* (Oxford, 1989), 207–418; and Christopher Tomlins, *Freedom Bound: Law, Labor, and Civic Identity in Colonizing English America, 1580–1865* (Cambridge, 2010). For the critical importance of varying land tenure regimes in European colonization of the Americas more generally, see Allan Greer, *Property and Dispossession: Natives, Empires, and Land in Early Modern North America* (Cambridge, 2018).

tors recognized the profitability of tobacco agriculture, everyone involved in the Virginia Company understood that the organization of landownership would define the colony's development. Beginning in 1617, a small number of men led by acting governor Samuel Argall sought to organize Virginia into private manorial estates. Their actions triggered a wave of opposition that coalesced around investor and newly elected company treasurer Sir Edwin Sandys, who laid out an ambitious plan for reorganizing Virginia's relationship between landownership and political power through local corporate institutions. Sandys's reforms are most famous for establishing the Virginia General Assembly, which first met in 1619, but in fact they had little to say about representation and individual rights. They primarily sought to restructure the relationship between landownership, commercial agriculture, and political order. For the next five years, claims to land rights, control over the tobacco trade, and the management of labor were all shaped by Argall's and Sandys's competing visions of landownership. Neither of these models ultimately prevailed in its entirety, but the adaptation of particular details from both manorial and civic corporate traditions helped to give definition to the new phenomenon of private plantations that were established along the James River in the 1620s.[3]

IN ORDER TO UNDERSTAND WHY PRIVATE LANDOWNERSHIP WAS SUCH a complex and fraught issue for the Virginia Company, we must appreciate the extent of the company's ambitions. Despite its establishment as a joint-stock corporation, the company aspired to much more than short-term profit. As the essays in this volume by Andrew Fitzmaurice and Alexander Haskell attest, contemporaries understood the venture as an effort to build a new English commonwealth in America—an endeavor that had critical geopolitical and spiritual significance. Company leaders were not unconcerned with the practical problems of economics and profit, but they were more focused on balancing the pursuit of profit with the broader public good. In this respect, they were hardly unique. As a society grappling with its ties to long-distance trade, early modern England was awash with bodies regulating the increasingly complex world of commerce, from traditional manor courts and trade guilds to newer urban corporations. But which institutions and ideas were essential to maintaining the balance of profit and public virtue in Virginia depended on how profit was conceptualized: whether it lay purely in exchange or whether it emerged from production. Thus, the transition to a planting economy in Virginia and

---

3. Susan Myra Kingsbury, ed., *The Records of the Virginia Company of London*, 4 vols. (Washington, D.C., 1906–1935) (hereafter cited as *RVC*), III, 158.

the rapid profitability of tobacco raised regulatory challenges as it reorganized expectations about what profit was, where it would accumulate, and how it would be distributed.[4]

The Virginia Company initially envisioned profit in narrow terms. When the company was formed in 1606, its prospects for income were based on importing valuable luxury commodities. Although permanent settlement was always an objective, promoters' initial hopes for riches lay in the discovery of gold, trade with Native people, and the identification of a northwest passage to Asia. When these failed to materialize, leaders recognized that they would need to invest in longer-term efforts to produce agricultural commodities with English labor. After 1609, the company's rhetoric and planning shifted toward building a new commonwealth in Virginia, supported by a broader base of investors and waves of new migrants. Because population growth had made labor abundant and cheap in England, however, company leaders did not perceive a need to change their economic calculus: Virginia was still a source for cheap commodities that the company could vend in England to replenish its coffers and reward its collective shareholders. England's indigent poor need only be clothed and fed and they would cultivate exotic crops. Colonists who adventured their persons would technically become shareholders coequal with those who invested money, but there was no mechanism for returning profit to the colony, and presumably the assumption was that all individuals would eventually return to England or designate partners who could claim their shares. As one promotional pamphlet noted, there was to be "no adventure, or goods returned in private." The instructions issued to Sir Thomas Gates in 1609 were unequivocal that he should ensure "returne of commodyty" to the company in London—no consideration was given to profit margins in Virginia.[5]

As long as the company was limited to this static extractive vision, a joint-stock structure seemed appropriate to regulate its commerce. Joint-stock companies were an established way for merchants to raise capital for new ventures

---

4. Wrightson, *Earthly Necessities*, 153–158. See also Andrew Fitzmaurice, *Humanism and America: An Intellectual History of English Colonisation, 1500–1625* (Cambridge, 2003); and Alexander B. Haskell, *For God, King, and People: Forging Commonwealth Bonds in Renaissance Virginia* (Williamsburg, Va., and Chapel Hill, N.C., 2017).

5. R[obert] J[ohnson], *Nova Britannia: Offring Most Excellent Fruites by Planting in Virginia, Exciting All Such as Be Well Affected to Further the Same* (London, 1609), D4r; Kingsbury, ed., *RVC*, III, 22; Virginia Company, "Instructions Given by Way of Advice," 1606, in Philip L. Barbour, ed., *The Jamestown Voyages under the First Charter, 1606–1609*, 2 vols. (Cambridge, 1969), I, 49–54; Theodore K. Rabb, *Enterprise and Empire: Merchant and Gentry Investment in the Expansion of England, 1575–1630* (Cambridge, Mass., 1967), chap. 1; Karen Ordahl Kupperman, *The Jamestown Project* (Cambridge, Mass., 2007), 217–228; Alison Games, *The Web of Empire: English Cosmopolitans in an Age of Expansion* (Oxford, 2008), chap. 4.

by selling shares to non-merchant investors. But, as Andrew Fitzmaurice's essay in this volume notes, formal incorporation also served a crucial civic purpose. Corporations pursued goals that were larger than individual private profit, and, by voluntarily entering into such projects, investors bound themselves into consciously constructed and participatory institutions, effectively creating new forms of sovereignty that could police the trade of both members and non-members within the company's sphere. While the Virginia enterprise was merely focused on generating profit in London through trade, a joint-stock company seemed like the best vehicle for organizing Atlantic merchants and interested investors and directing their energies toward the colonial endeavor.[6]

As the Virginia project evolved after 1609, however, it became clear that the colony's structure did not neatly fit within the existing joint-stock model. Virginia's early struggles are infamous: war with the Powhatans, the Starving Time, the difficulties in motivating workers to labor. From a political-economic perspective, the key question was whether a joint-stock structure could facilitate economic regulation when the commodities that might be produced would require English labor. The Virginia Company aspired to build a commonwealth in America and was the first joint-stock endeavor in which a significant portion of the shareholders—who had adventured their persons (as planters) rather than their fortunes to join the company—were located an ocean away. In theory, these individuals shared a common corporate bond with the shareholders back in England that should have encouraged them to labor for the colony. But, in practice, those adventuring their persons had little interest in profits accruing in London, and the supplies sent back to the colony included only the bare necessities, even after tobacco began to be cultivated in the mid-1610s. Understood in this way, Virginia's famous problems with truculent workers were really a result of applying a joint-stock corporate model to what quickly became an agricultural endeavor.

The company's leaders recognized that they would need to adapt the corporate model to incentivize colonists to labor. They were deeply vexed by the early Jamestown colonists' seeming indigence, framing it as a moral failing and a result of deficient leadership, and famously turned to strict martial law as a means to instill discipline. However, they also held out the prospect of land grants as a tangible reward for colonists who invested their labor. They initially did so within the framework of the joint-stock corporation. In the promotional

---

6. See Henry S. Turner, *The Corporate Commonwealth: Pluralism and Political Fictions in England, 1516–1651* (Chicago, 2016), chap. 4; Phil Withington, *Society in Early Modern England: The Vernacular Origins of Some Powerful Ideas* (Cambridge, 2010), chap. 7; and Philip J. Stern, *The Company-State: Corporate Sovereignty and the Early Modern Foundations of the British Empire in India* (Oxford, 2011).

pamphlet *Nova Britannia* (1609), company official Robert Johnson sought to attract new investors and colonists to Virginia by promising that at "the ende of seven yeeres ... wee purpose (God willing) to make a division by Commissioners appointed, of al the lands graunted unto us by his Majestie, to every of the Colonie according to each mans severall Adventure." Johnson explained, though, that the promise of private land was intended to strengthen the colonists' work ethic and commitment to the common cause of the company during the intervening years, because "there growes a greater benefit to the planters (by bestowing their labours cheerefully) to make returne of stocke [to the company], for hereby the sooner they freeing us [investors in London] from disbursements [of profits], the more our shares and portions will be lessened in the Divident of stocke and land at seven yeeres end, whereby the lesse comming to us, the more will be to them." By promising to pay down the English investors and increase the distribution of land to colonists, the company was seeking to ensure that both groups received equal and appropriate benefit from any potential profit generated by the joint-stock. For the next few years, profit of any kind remained elusive in Virginia, however, so these promises remained vague, and leaders on both sides of the Atlantic took little action to prepare for the division of land.[7]

When colonists began cultivating tobacco in the mid-1610s, the disjunction of interests between merchants and settlers only worsened. Tobacco planters, regardless of their status within the company, effectively became sellers interested (often by desperate necessity) in maximizing the return of supplies and manufactured goods that they received for their crops. The merchants leading the enterprise in London were buyers, increasingly low on funds and bound to seek the largest margin they could on each tobacco shipment. By 1615, planter Ralph Hamor, in his *True Discourse of the Present Estate of Virginia*, was conceptualizing colonists as independent economic actors, explaining that they needed to be supplied with better English goods to be persuaded to return commodities "to the Merchant." A distinctly unstable market was forming in the colony. As a luxury commodity, tobacco was particularly vulnerable to price fluctuations. Production rose (both in Virginia and Bermuda) and quality varied widely based on the skill and experience of the individual farmer. As a result, prices in London began to drop, creating uncertainty and opportunities for exploitation and self-interest, which were much feared in the early modern marketplace. Over the next few years, colonists complained about the terms of trade offered by company merchants. To contemporaries, the tightening grip of tobacco over

---

7. J[ohnson], *Nova Britannia*, D4v, E[1]r. For the labor problem, see Edmund S. Morgan, "The Labor Problem at Jamestown, 1607–18," *American Historical Review*, LXXVI (1971), 595–611.

the colony's economy, far from being a relief, was a clear sign that something was wrong with Virginia's civic and economic structure.[8]

The London merchants who led the company sought to address the problem by hiving off the corporation's commercial functions into a subsidiary joint-stock. Known as the Magazine, this company was to be constituted from a smaller number of merchant stockholders who would exercise a monopoly over Virginia's trade. The Magazine could concentrate on regulating the colony's tobacco trade like any other trading company, seeking to stabilize prices and generate profit in England and merely contributing a portion of its profits to the Virginia Company's broader civic mission. In practice, however, the Magazine did little to regulate trade within the colony, and it explicitly excluded planters from the negotiations over setting a "fair" price for their tobacco. One of the private traders excluded from the Virginia trade by the establishment of the Magazine, Captain John Bargrave, noted that it was intended to "set prizes" and that colonists had their goods "sould and bought before their faces." Most leaders in the colony shared his concerns about the Magazine.[9]

The most direct way to acknowledge the distinct interests of colonists and offer them a concrete stake in the enterprise was through granting private estates. Landownership, though, called for its own system of civic regulation. The commercialization of English agriculture in the second half of the sixteenth century had created an insatiable demand for land and generated a new focus on the "improvement" of estates through more efficient cultivation methods and new industries. A key step in improving an estate was to enclose common fields, restricting communal usages and offering private landowners more control over the way they managed their lands, which encouraged them to invest in improvements. However, enclosure, like mercantile commerce, was predicated upon the pursuit of private profit, which existed in tension with civic ideals. Commonwealth thinkers of the mid-sixteenth century, most famously Sir Thomas More, had universally condemned enclosure as a threat to the common good of English society. But, by the end of the century, political philosophers and policymakers around the Elizabethan court were taking a more nuanced view; just like the merchant community, they sought to frame the innovation in ways that would benefit both private interests and the broader public.[10]

This framing took a number of different forms in contemporary England and

---

8. Raphe Hamor, *A True Discourse of the Present Estate of Virginia* . . . (London, 1615), 17–18.

9. Kingsbury, ed., *RVC*, III, 519. Even the Magazine's agent, Abraham Piercy, complained about its organization; see ibid., I, 240–241.

10. Wrightson, *Earthly Necessities*, 182–186, 233–234 (quotation); McRae, *God Speed the Plough*, chaps. 1, 5, 6.

Ireland. Many improving landlords argued that their investment was self-evidently in the public interest because it employed the poor and increased the output of the realm. They acknowledged that enclosing lands broke down some traditional communal bonds but claimed to be serving their communities' interests by eschewing the "plodding and common course" of agriculture. This was not entirely a self-serving façade. For some upwardly mobile tenant farmers, the opportunities afforded by enclosure did help them flourish by allowing them to rent clearly defined properties where they could invest in improvements. Thus, by one measure, the attentive and knowledgeable rentier landlord acted as a safeguard of the public good in an updated, market-oriented version of traditional patriarchal hierarchy. This model was readily adapted to the sixteenth-century colonization of Ireland, where English nobles received large estates in exchange for hands-on management and infrastructure development designed to improve productivity.[11]

Other contemporaries, however, placed less faith in the gentry and nobles alone to maintain the public good in a commercializing society. Enclosure was therefore accompanied by the strengthening of bodies such as parishes and corporate boroughs. These local institutions amassed considerable resources and took seriously the role of translating civic principles into local regulation, governing domestic markets in goods and labor. England's large number of new incorporated boroughs were at the forefront of this process. The emerging gentry and merchant classes who dominated them embraced civic humanist ideals and saw themselves as leaders of discrete commonwealths, balancing private and public interests, particularly through the management of marketplaces. Corporate towns also amassed their own estates (becoming improving landlords themselves) and used the profits generated to pursue public infrastructure. The local corporate community thus represented an alternative framework for structuring landownership and regulating the private interests that it would unleash in Virginia's emergent agricultural economy.[12]

It was not at all clear which model of "private" landownership the colony should embrace. John Rolfe's experiments in tobacco agriculture in Virginia are often portrayed as a godsend, allowing the colony to realize its original purpose of profits. But shifting to an agricultural economy raised fundamental questions

11. John Norden, *The Surveyors Dialogue Divided into Five Bookes*... (London, 1607), 226; Wrightson, *Earthly Necessities*, 182–190. For the tension between the undertaker and servitor models in Ireland, see Canny, *Making Ireland British*, chaps. 3–4.

12. Patrick Collinson, "The Monarchical Republic of Queen Elizabeth I," *Bulletin of the John Rylands University Library*, LXIX (1987), 394–424; Mark Goldie, "The Unacknowledged Republic: Officeholding in Early Modern England," in Tim Harris, ed., *The Politics of the Excluded, c. 1500–1850* (New York, 2001), 153–194; Steve Hindle, *The State and Social Change in Early Modern England* (New York, 2002). For urban corporations, see Phil Withington, *The Politics of Commonwealth: Citizens and Freemen in Early Modern England* (Cambridge, 2005).

about the company's civic structure. The transition to private landownership was part of a recognition of that reality, but the form that private estates would take and their relationship with the state, the company, and the empire were very much up for negotiation. There was no straightforward vision of the independent small freeholder ready to be embraced.

IN THE YEARS BETWEEN 1614 AND 1619, AS COLONISTS EVENTUALLY found a profitable agricultural commodity, they did not simply inaugurate a bonanza in land patents. Company leaders focused intensely on the organization of landownership as foundational to Virginia's civic order. Two divergent visions of private land in Virginia emerged, one built around manors and the other around incorporated towns. Private motives and the promise of riches drove some of the individuals who advocated these rival plans, but both were explicitly framed by civic concerns for establishing the appropriate balance between profit and the public good in the allocation of land.

The first distribution of private land in the colony was the result of on-the-ground innovation. In 1613, Deputy Governor Thomas Dale, commanding the colony's new town of Henrico at the falls of the James River, wrote to company leaders explaining his continued difficulties in getting the colonists to work. Despite Virginia's infamous martial law, Dale had found it impossible to motivate his men to plant corn; in response, he designated a number of them as "farmers" and allocated responsibility for individual gardens in exchange for a portion of their harvest. The plan was controversial because Dale noted that he would have instituted it the previous year "if I had, had my only wyll." By 1614, though, Dale expanded the system of private plots across the colony. Ralph Hamor explained that "every man in the Colony" received "three English Acres of cleere Corne ground" and remarked that when colonists had been "fedde out of the common store and laboured jointly" they had lacked the motivation to work, but after the allocation of private estates their productivity had increased tenfold. Crucially, colonial leaders saw this new private enterprise, not as an end in itself, but as a means to encourage the pursuit of the public good of the company as a whole; Hamor noted that allowing farmers to sell their surplus kept them in "strength and heart, able to performe such businesses, as shall be imposed upon them" for the colony.[13]

Dale, however, was not prepared to wait for these longer-term effects. In 1614, he embarked on a more ambitious plan. He established a new settlement just

---

13. Thomas Dale, "Letter from Henrico, 10 June 1613," in Edward Wright Haile, ed., *Jamestown Narratives: Eyewitness Accounts of the Virginia Colony, the First Decade, 1607–1617* (Champlain, Va., 1998), 758–782; Hamor, *True Discourse*, 16–18.

downriver from Henrico, but, instead of granting the colonists there individual plots, he bound them together as the corporation of Bermuda City. This new corporate city received a communal title to "many miles of Champion [unenclosed land], and woodland." In exchange, members of the corporation were required to perform "duties and services" for the colony. The exact terms of the charter have not survived, but Bermuda City did have a mayor, aldermen, and a recorder (senior legal representative) and was clearly expected to be a self-governing community. When John Rolfe described Virginia's various settlements in 1617, he noted who "hath the commaund" in each place, reflecting continued martial governance in much of Virginia, but he pointedly wrote that Deputy Governor George Yeardley "for the most part liveth" in Bermuda City and did not mention anyone in "commaund" at the corporation. It is unclear where exactly Dale got the idea for the local corporation, but he was drawing on the growing importance of corporate towns in England. The same model had already been highly influential in the settlement of Ireland. Bermuda City thus united on a local level, through landownership, the private interests of individual planters and the public good of the colony. It represented a dramatic departure for Virginia's civic structure. Hamor described it as "a businesse of greatest hope, ever begunne in our Territories there."[14]

Not everyone shared Hamor's optimistic outlook on the corporate system of landholding. Two men in particular, Samuel Argall and John Martin, both of whom had extensive experience in the colony, were opposed to Dale's reforms and saw them as an encroachment upon their rights and responsibilities as veteran leaders in Virginia. Argall and Martin returned to London in 1616, where they pressed their case for individual grants. They asserted their claims on the basis of the company's 1609 promise to distribute private land to stockholders after seven years. Rather than receiving this land as part of a corporate communal grant, they lobbied the company to transform Dale's system by allowing them to patent for themselves large landed estates with authority equal to "any lord of any manours in England."[15]

14. Hamor, *True Discourse*, 18, 31–32; John Rolfe, *A True Relation of the State of Virginia Lefte by Sir Thomas Dale Knight in May Last 1616* (New Haven, Conn., 1951), 38–39; "A Briefe Declaration of the Plantation of Virginia . . . ," in *Colonial Records of Virginia* (Richmond, Va., 1874), 76. For corporate towns in Ulster, see Thomas Blenerhasset, *A Direction for the Plantation in Ulster* (London, 1610); Withington, *Society in Early Modern England*, 214–215; R. J. Hunter, "Towns in the Ulster Plantation," *Studia Hibernica*, no. 11 (1971), 40–79; Robinson, *Plantation of Ulster*, 157–158; Audrey Horning, *Ireland in the Virginian Sea: Colonialism in the British Atlantic* (Williamsburg, Va., and Chapel Hill, N.C., 2013), 289–313.

15. Kingsbury, ed., *RVC*, III, 163. Although the terms agreed to by Argall and Martin have not survived, an agreement made by Lord Zouche in 1617 lays out a large manorial land grant that was likely based on the Argall / Martin model; see Kingsbury, ed., *RVC*, III, 77. For the Warwick faction,

Argall and Martin were firmly allied with the pro-expansion group of aristocrat investors in the Virginia Company, which was led by the earl of Warwick, and it was likely with their support and encouragement that the two men envisioned a more hierarchical manorial structure of landownership. Warwick and his allies had recently been at the forefront of imposing a similar structure on Virginia's sister colony, Bermuda (the Somers Islands). Land in Bermuda had been divided into grants allocated to the small pool of wealthy English shareholders in the Somers Islands Company, but almost none of these prominent individuals intended to settle in the islands, and so a system of manorial tenantry was guaranteed. In early 1616, the Somers Islands Company had refined plans for this manorial system, resulting in a systematic survey of the islands, with each shareholder receiving a twenty-five-acre sliver of land. In contrast to the corporate communities of freemen that Dale had begun to develop in Virginia, Bermuda landlords were to send tenants to the colony who, despite being mostly young men, were organized into groups termed "families" under the oversight of older colonists in order to reinforce patriarchal hierarchy. Argall and Martin's manorial plan for Virginia was a natural extension of this system and a rejection of the local corporate structure Dale had erected.[16]

Early in 1617, Argall returned to Virginia with a clear agenda to reorganize the structure of landownership. The company's leaders had sent him as deputy governor, alongside returning governor Lord De La Warr, but, when De La Warr died on the Atlantic crossing, Argall had a free hand to institute radical reforms. Argall immediately targeted Bermuda City. He wrote that Virginia was in a "ruinous condicon" and singled out the city, claiming that the corporation's autonomy hindered his pursuit of public projects. Within three weeks of his arrival, Argall had relocated most of the Bermuda City residents to Jamestown. In response, the citizens (members of the corporate borough) formally complained that he was expropriating land and resources "belonging to them" as a corporate community. The deputy governor dismissed the complaints and effectively undermined the authority of the corporate structure by commissioning a military provost marshal to govern the settlement. Over the next year, Argall replaced the corporate model with a vision of manorial estates governed by personal patronage. He used the land grant he had received from the company to establish a community that he named Argall Town, near Jamestown, and relocated

---

see Wesley Frank Craven, *Dissolution of the Virginia Company: The Failure of a Colonial Experiment* (New York, 1932), 121–140.

16. J. H. Lefroy, ed., *Memorials of the Discovery and Early Settlement of the Bermudas or Somers Islands, 1515–1685*, 2 vols. (London, 1877–1879), I, 83–98, 109; Wesley Frank Craven, "An Introduction to the History of Bermuda," *William and Mary Quarterly*, 2d Ser., XVII (1937), 338–362.

company assets and tenants to his new community. He also resettled free planters who had become bound to him through debts they accrued for the English goods he imported (in defiance of the Magazine's monopoly). No records of individual land grants survive from Argall's tenure, but he did convey private property (cattle and houses) to those working on his land. This suggests that Argall was not denying individual colonists all claims to private property and returning them to the status of company servants; rather, he was acknowledging their ownership of resources and improvements while denying their ownership of land, thus laying the foundations of a permanent tenantry.[17]

Argall's actions should not be seen merely as naked self-interest. Although his plans were clearly designed to enrich his own fortune, Argall consistently asserted that his approach was the only effective way to balance private interests with the company's broader objectives. As a responsible manorial landlord, he erected high-quality housing for his tenants in a compact, defensible community. He also encouraged economic innovation, introducing experimental crops and seeking to limit tobacco production. The efficiency of Argall's scheme was impressive, befitting an English improving landlord. He embraced that status explicitly when he reported to the company in London that he had "improved almost everything." Argall's ally John Martin also reflected this mindset when he christened his estate Martin's Brandon; a brandon was a torch or lantern, and so the name conveyed Martin's sense of his own trailblazing leadership. Both men viewed their careful management of the tenants on their private estates as a crucial public service.[18]

Nonetheless, when news of Argall's actions began to filter back to London in the winter of 1617–1618, company officials responded with fierce opposition. Some leaders, particularly Treasurer Sir Thomas Smith and Alderman Robert Johnson (who ran the Magazine), were still wedded to the extractive model of colonial economics, and for them Argall's crime lay in directing colonists' trade away from the Magazine and toward his own network of merchant allies. Argall's reforms also attracted the ire of Sir Edwin Sandys, another prominent politician who had long been an investor in the Virginia and Bermuda projects.

---

17. Kingsbury, ed., *RVC*, II, 44–45, 50–55, 284–285, III, 71, 73, 76, 91–92, 119–120, 175–176, 247, 255–256. Argall redirected new arrivals to his private estate; see Ivor Noël Hume and Audrey Noël Hume, *The Archaeology of Martin's Hundred*, 2 vols. (Philadelphia, 2001), I, 18–21. Argall briefly sought to reform the Magazine, but soon bypassed it; see Kingsbury, ed., *RVC*, II, 52–53, III, 78.

18. Kingsbury, ed., *RVC*, III, 73–74, 92 (quotation). For the quality of the structures Argall built, see Henry Chandlee Forman, "The Bygone 'Subberbs of James Cittie,'" *WMQ*, 2d Ser., XX (1940), 475–486; Alain Charles Outlaw, *Governor's Land: Archaeology of Early Seventeenth-Century Virginia Settlements* (Charlottesville, Va., 1990), 3–9; and Charles E. Hatch, *The First Seventeen Years: Virginia, 1607–1624* (Williamsburg, Va., 1957), 36–37.

Sandys was stirred, not by Argall's imposition upon the company's profits, but by his incursion upon what Sandys broadly defined as the "publique." His complaints centered on Argall's decision to relocate tenants onto his private estate and undermine the corporate structure that bound planters to public lands. Without the rents tenants paid for public lands, the colony lacked the resources to support local civic institutions that could regulate commerce and support public projects. For Sandys, "the maintayning of the publiq in all estates" was "of noe lesse importance, even for the benefitt of the Private, then the roote and body of a Tree are to the perticuler branches." Argall's actions had reinforced his conviction that the balance of public and private interests "in all estates"—not merely on a broad theoretical level, nor simply within the company's corporate leadership back in London—was fundamental to the success of Virginia.[19]

It was in this context that the famous reforms of 1619 were conceived. Sandys and his allies took control of the company during the latter half of 1618 and acted quickly to resurrect Dale's vision of the municipal corporation. Sandys advocated for the selection of George Yeardley, who had previously resided in Bermuda City, as the new governor for the colony. He also crafted Yeardley's instructions, which required the new governor to expand the Bermuda City model to the company's three other main settlements in Virginia—Jamestown, Henrico, and Elizabeth City. Although these instructions, which Virginia's planters christened the "Great Charter," are most famous for instituting the first General Assembly in 1619, their primary goal was to strengthen corporate communities, which would anchor private landholding and trade within local public communal institutions. The plan for a General Assembly was merely an outgrowth of the new corporate foundations, and the body was intended as a forum for debate between the new vibrant corporate commonwealths, rather than between the planters as discreet private individuals.[20]

The main role of the incorporated boroughs was to carefully control the shift toward privatized landholding. According to Yeardley's instructions, all planters who had traveled to Virginia at their own expense, or who had completed their service to the company, were to receive at least fifty acres of land, but all of these small private land grants were to be located within one of the company's

---

19. Kingsbury, ed., *RVC*, I, 267–268. For Smith and Johnson's critique, see Kingsbury, ed., *RVC*, II, 51–53; for Sandys's critique, see Instructions to Governor Sir George Yeardley, Nov. 18, 1618, Ferrar Papers (FP) 91, Virginia Company Archives, http://www.virginiacompanyarchives.amdigital.co.uk; and Kingsbury, ed., *RVC*, II, 400–405.

20. Kingsbury, ed., *RVC*, III, 98–109 (esp. 99–102). For evidence that Sandys masterminded the reforms, see "A Report of S[i]r George Yeardlyes[,] Going Governor to Virginia," Dec. 5, 1618, FP 93, Virginia Company Archives. Sandys had previously commissioned Rolfe's account of the workings of the Bermuda corporation that was completed in 1617; see Rolfe, *True Relation*, dedication.

incorporated boroughs, and grantees were required to reside in the town itself as active citizens of the corporate community. To help guard against the conflicts that might arise with private landownership, the company granted each corporation forty-five hundred acres of public land. This public land would be rented to new colonists who would be transported to Virginia to serve as tenants for seven years. New arrivals would thereby benefit from access to land, accommodation in public guesthouses (which each corporation was ordered to erect), and a place within an existing civic community. This tenancy was envisioned, not as a permanent status, but as a transitional step toward freeholding. Furthermore, in a crucial departure from earlier common property in Virginia, and from the model then operating on the island of Bermuda, public land was not primarily intended to generate profit for the company in London. Instead, it was to be a shared profitable enterprise under the management of the new corporate bodies, which would accumulate public capital. Managing the public enterprise would give ambitious colonists the resources to test new crops and industries that they could not afford to sponsor alone, and it would complicate the market in the colony's one booming staple—tobacco—by giving every corporate member a stake in the price of both their own crops and the common community stock. Accumulation of rental property of this kind had underpinned the flourishing of English borough corporations, driving the improvement of rented land while also allowing corporate leaders to erect new civic infrastructure. This, then, was the manifestation of Sandys's conviction about the importance of the public not simply to social cohesion and order but also to economic improvement and the profitability of private enterprise.[21]

Sandys's new vision was not limited to the company's four boroughs. Another key part of the reform plan was to invite private groups of Virginia investors to pool resources to settle large new land grants called "particular plantations." Unlike Argall's manorial estates or the land shares granted by the Somers Islands Company, particular plantations were intended to also be structured according to a corporate model. Each plantation was required to send colonists to settle as a compact community that would receive its own corporate charter to establish a system of civic self-governance. To support this structure, each new particular plantation was also promised an additional free endowment of "fifteen hundred Acres of Burough Land for the public use," which would pay local officials and support infrastructure development. No new landowners in Sandys's redesigned Virginia venture, then, were to be free from concern with the "public use" of

---

21. Kingsbury, ed., *RVC*, I, 268, III, 92, 99–102. For expansion of English borough estates, see Robert Tittler, *The Reformation and the Towns in England: Politics and Political Culture, c. 1540–1640* (Oxford, 1998); and Withington, *Politics of Commonwealth*, chap. 2.

the land. New promotional material, intended to attract planters and investors, also emphasized this point. One pamphlet explained that the company had "infranchise[d] the fower townes allready in being, and all other plantations begun, or heereafter to bee erected, into corporations, under the name of burroughs or citties" and allocated them "publique landes" and that only after this process had been completed would officers in Virginia "lastly... sett downe what landes or im[m]unities every p[er]son is presently to enioye... and what duties they are tyed to." Provision of private land and private rights was an outgrowth of the corporate system. The company's new pitch was not about attracting investors in search of cheap land and liberal individualism; it appealed to those familiar with the associational structures of early modern England.[22]

The company leadership also envisioned this network of corporate plantations, supported by public land, as the foundation for a structure of economic regulation. Yeardley's 1618 instructions were thin on details about the corporations' jurisdictional authority, but in a private letter to Yeardley Sandys admonished him to use the new structure to encourage planters "to applie themselfs to an industrious coorse of life, in foloing their busines each in his severall place" and to "draw the people from ... the excessive planting of Tobacco." In early 1620, the company agreed to allow all of Virginia's new corporations to draft ordinances for "the better orderinge and dyrectinge of their Servants and buisines." This new system of local corporate regulation was critical because Sandys and his allies aimed to abolish the commercial monopoly exercised by the Magazine. They were generally suspicious of monopolies and believed that the Magazine served the interests of a narrow merchant clique within the company, rather than the good of the whole colony. However, by removing the monopoly they did not intend to place their trust in free trade. Instead, they were relying on the regulatory capacity of the corporate system in Virginia. As local civic societies with common economic interests, corporations were empowered to monitor and administer their marketplaces, just as English corporate boroughs did through courts of piepowder. Each step the company took to undermine and abolish the Magazine during these years was closely tied to parallel efforts to strengthen the colony's corporate communities. John Smith, in his account of the Virginia reforms, emphasized that the corporate plan coincided with an ef-

22. Kingsbury, ed., *RVC*, I, 268, III, 104–106; "A Report of S[i]r George Yeardlyes[,] Going Governor to Virginia," Dec. 5, 1618, FP 93, Virginia Company Archives. See also "A Declaration of the State of the Colonie and Affaires in Virginia..." (1620), in Peter Force, comp., *Tracts and Other Papers, Relating Principally to the Origin, Settlement, and Progress of the Colonies in North America* (New York, 1947), III, no. 5. Particular plantations were also referred to as "Societies" (Kingsbury, ed., *RVC*, III, 310, 463), a term which was increasingly popular with commonwealth thinkers to describe consciously constructed communities; see Withington, *Society in Early Modern England*, chap. 4.

fort to prevent the abuse of laborers and the forestalling and engrossing of the market in the colony.[23]

Many investors embraced the company's new corporate plan, and between 1619 and 1621 a slew of new particular plantations were established. A group of Gloucestershire investors, whose plans for a particular plantation are especially well documented, explicitly took up the corporate model. The Gloucestershire consortium agreed with the company "to transport at their owne costs and charges divers psons into Virginia, And there to erect and build a Towne" and within seven years to give it "[le]tres and grants of incorporacion." The investors instructed their first contingent of planters to establish Berkeley Town by inaugurating rituals, building a common hall for meals and religious devotions, and creating a hierarchy of offices to strengthen the community's corporate bonds. The plantation, therefore, was to be an agricultural enterprise, but one rooted in a civic vision underpinned by a combination of private and public landownership. Far from being cumbersome Old World pretensions that were bound to wither away, as historians have often viewed them, these provisions were at the heart of a very particular effort to wrestle with the challenges of commerce and order in the new colony.[24]

The transformation of Virginia's pattern of landownership and political organization in 1619 was a product of profound debate within the company about the relationship between commerce and political order. Early Virginia was riven with divisions about the best way to stimulate private enterprise and improvement while safeguarding the common good. Argall had focused on the oversight of improving landlords who could restrict planters' pursuit of their short-term private goals, whereas Sandys and his allies placed their faith in corporate institutions to regulate commercial exchange and support economic development. Both of these approaches recognized and sought to mold the distinct economic interests of planters by controlling the way they exercised rights over land. However, both strategies integrated planters into the larger English commercial world in radically different ways.

---

23. Copy of Instructions to Sir George Yeardley, Dec. 2, 1618, FP 92, Virginia Company Archives; Kingsbury, ed., *RVC*, I, 303, 394–396; John Smith, *The Generall Historie of Virginia, New-England, and the Summer Isles* . . . (1624), in Philip L. Barbour, ed., *The Complete Works of Captain John Smith (1580–1631)*, 3 vols. (Williamsburg, Va., and Chapel Hill, N.C., 1986), II, 268–269, 283. Sandys had long been an opponent of monopolies; see Theodore K. Rabb, *Jacobean Gentleman: Sir Edwin Sandys, 1561–1629* (Princeton, N.J., 1998), 86–97. For attitudes toward monopoly, see David Harris Sacks, "The Greed of Judas: Avarice, Monopoly, and the Moral Economy in England, ca. 1350–ca. 1600," *Journal of Medieval and Early Modern Studies*, XXVIII (1998), 263–307.

24. Kingsbury, ed., *RVC*, III, 130, 131, 133, 197–198, 200, 207–210. For the Berkeley project, see James Horn, *Adapting to a New World: English Society in the Seventeenth-Century Chesapeake* (Williamsburg, Va., and Chapel Hill, N.C., 1994), 78–80; and Walsh, *Motives of Honor*, 49–51.

IN THE AFTERMATH OF THE 1619 REFORMS, THE STRUGGLES BETWEEN these rival sets of ideas and institutions only intensified. Beginning in 1619, Sandys and his allies sent waves of new colonists to serve as tenants and populate the corporate structure they had erected, but these women and men met with disease and catastrophic mortality rates, reaching a crescendo with the March 1622 Powhatan assault on the colony. In the face of these setbacks, it is easy to attribute the colony's survival and growth to planters' pragmatic adjustment to the harsh realities and profitable opportunities that arose amid the destruction. Virginia after 1619 has been portrayed as a lawless booming frontier where the norms of English life were set aside. In fact, though, officials were not so quick to abandon their deep-seated convictions about how land and commerce should be organized, and factions on both sides of the Atlantic interpreted the setbacks in the colony in light of these conflicting visions. This ongoing struggle was crucial in laying the foundations for the concept of the private, commercially oriented plantation estate in English America.

Opposition to Sandys's corporate plan developed quickly. It came from the leading London merchants who operated the Magazine and from the Warwick faction, who had supported Argall's plans. Both groups pointed to the colony's struggle to diversify the economy and the continuing high mortality figures as evidence of the failure of the corporate system. One of Warwick's allies in the colony, John Pory, reported that planters refused to labor for corporate communal projects. Robert Johnson, treasurer of the Magazine, concluded that Sandys's plan was cultivating "divers ffactions, and disordered people" who sought "onely to reape a benefitt to themselves." In the aftermath of the 1622 Powhatan attack, critics found more evidence to support this contention. The inability of most boroughs to defend themselves clearly demonstrated the weakness of the corporate structure. Another of Warwick's allies, Nathaniel Butler, made this point in "The Unmasked Face of our Colony in Virginia," which described the aftermath of the attack and pointed to the corporations' failure to maintain infrastructure such as streets, wharves, and houses. Sandys's opponents built upon these vivid images and argued that his faith in incorporated boroughs had led him to completely surrender control of the colony.[25]

These arguments were well placed to gain traction in the early 1620s because they meshed with conclusions the king himself was reaching about his own realm. Facing increasing opposition in Parliament, James I and his courtiers were becoming skeptical of corporate independence. Lord Chancellor Francis Bacon argued that corporate citizens were merely private subjects who might be

25. Kingsbury, ed., *RVC*, II, 374–376 ("Unmasked Face"), III, 301–303 (Pory), 581–588, IV, 85 ("divers ffactions"), 93, 135–136, 174–182.

beneficial to the state's commerce but who should have no role in governance and public affairs, which were the natural province of "gentry and noblemen." Royal skepticism about English corporate authority heightened in the early 1620s, when members of Parliament representing corporate boroughs, including Sandys himself, led opposition to crown policies in Parliament. When James dissolved Parliament in January 1622, reports began to circulate at court blaming the kingdom's "pettie corporancons" and describing them as lawless "Receptacles for Theeves."[26]

Sandys's opponents also fleshed out the alternative vision for the colony that had been developed by Argall and Martin. In a 1620 petition to the company, a group of experienced colonial leaders, including Argall, Sir Thomas Gates, and Captain Daniel Tucker (a former governor of Bermuda), claimed that they were "willing and ready" to return to Virginia, but only if there was a radical change in the colony's organization. They demanded that the colony be placed under the government of men recognized for their "Eminence, or Nobillitye," who could temper the colonists' "vulgar and servile Spiritts." More fully fleshed-out plans for restructuring the colony around a gentry class were developed in the aftermath of the 1622 attack. In late 1622, John Martin, who had received the manorial grant for Martin's Brandon back in 1616, proposed a plan to subjugate the Powhatans and bring order to the planter community using England's county gentry. He proposed that each English county "send over 100 men a peece to posesse" one of the thirty-two towns within the Powhatan empire, converting them to parallel Virginia shires "undr the Comaund of some Noble Generall." The English counties would nominate "Justices of peace ... and other Officers under them as here in England" so that Virginia's order would be rooted in an established gentry hierarchy. Martin's plan was not simply a reimposition of military rule. It was filled with new ventures for economic diversification and development. However, it completely rejected the local municipal corporate form. Another longtime investor in the Virginia project, Captain John Bargrave, constructed an even more elaborate scheme. Bargrave's plan focused upon establishing an orderly hierarchy dominated by a transatlantic gentry class who would be compelled to own land on both sides of the Atlantic. A new Magazine collectively owned by the gentry planters, with the ability to accrue capital in London and establish a commercial bank, would also bolster the control of the resident planter elite. These schemes had evolved from Argall's and Martin's

26. Francis Bacon, "Of Empire," quoted in Withington, *Politics of Commonwealth*, 63; "A Rememberance for my Hoble Good Lord Chancellor of England," Ellesmere MSS7922, Huntington Library, San Marino, Calif.; Rabb, *Jacobean Gentleman*, chaps. 8–9; Robert Ashton, *The City and the Court, 1603–1643* (Cambridge, 1979), chaps. 3, 5.

initial claims to manorial estates, but they remained rooted in the idea that entrusting authority to improving landlords was the best way to balance public and private interests in pursuit of economic development.[27]

Resistance was not just coming from armchair critics in England; leaders in Virginia were also quick to raise concerns with Sandys's corporate plan. Early signs suggested some progress toward Sandys's vision. John Rolfe reported in early 1620 that "the Governor hath bounded the lymyttes of the 4. Cerporacions." However, the General Assembly did not take any further action to draw up corporate constitutions. The Burgesses instead urged the company to "sende men hither to occupie their landes belonging to the fower Incorporations, as well for their owne behoofe [benefit] and proffitt as for the maintenance of the Counsel of Estate." The General Assembly had identified a crucial problem: the extensive acreage that the English felt entitled to appropriate in early Virginia and the high levels of mortality meant that access to labor rather than land was the true measure of wealth. Company leaders had failed to account for the ready availability of ostensibly "empty" land that made tenancy an unattractive option for planters after they completed their service to the company. As a result, the vision of common land as an endowment for corporations could not succeed without a persistent supply of new tenants. Sandys eagerly complied with entreaties to send more laborers, but the result was a glut of ill-prepared immigrants who made unproductive tenants. Yeardley soon complained that managing these men and women took up too much of his time. Many other planters agreed; they shunned Sandys's plan for accommodating new tenants in public guesthouses and favored settling them on their private estates instead.[28]

Practical issues with the tenancy arrangements were only part of the story; other planters in Virginia refused from the outset to fall in with Sandys's conception of their enterprise. The most overt resistance came, unsurprisingly, from John Martin, who had no intention of adapting his manorial estate to fit within the new corporate structure that Yeardley was instructed to impose. When

---

27. Kingsbury, ed., *RVC*, III, 231 (quotation), 707–710 (quotation on 708), IV, 223–224, 408–435; John Bargrave, "A Treatise Shewing Howe to Erect a Publique and Increasing Treasurie," MSSHM962, Huntington Library. Two other proposals from the same period also suggested establishing a noble landowning class; see "A Project from Mr Caswell for Creating Noblemen in Virginia," July 1619, FP 121, and John Danvers, Proposal for Virginia, April 1620, FP 166, Virginia Company Archives. For Bargrave, see also Peter Thompson, "Aristotle and King Alfred in America," in Peter S. Onuf and Nicholas P. Cole, eds., *Thomas Jefferson, the Classical World, and Early America* (Charlottesville, Va., 2011), 193–218; and Haskell, *For God, King, and People*, 224–234. For Martin, see Aaron K. Slater, "The Ideological Origins of the Imperial State: Republicanism, Rights, and the Colonization of Virginia, 1607–1660" (Ph.D. diss., New York University, 2011), 181–185.

28. Kingsbury, ed., *RVC*, I, 394–396, III, 122–129 (esp. 124), 158–161, 245. For discussion of these problems, see Walsh, *Motives of Honor*, 106–110.

Martin attempted to send delegates from Martin's Brandon to the 1619 General Assembly, he was given an ultimatum: he could either accept and adopt the corporate structure, with the limits that this placed upon his personal authority, or he could withdraw his delegates. He chose the latter. Martin was an extreme example, but other new particular plantations also framed their projects in manorial rather than corporate terms. Even though they had initially committed to Sandys's corporate plan, when the leaders behind the Berkeley (Barkly) Town project eventually drafted a plan for their plantation, it called for the appointment of officers such as "steward of the household" and "clarke of the kitchin," which were more in keeping with a manorial structure.[29]

Despite this opposition in both London and Virginia, Sandys and his allies did not relent in their pursuit of the local corporate vision. The events of March 1622 only strengthened company leaders' convictions; upon receiving word of the attack, they insisted that the best method of defense was to have planters quickly repopulate the corporate boroughs. This was, company leaders argued, the method "most effectuall for the engageing of this State, and securing of Virginia," and they repeated their demand that corporations build guesthouses to help support new arrivals who might strengthen the communities. Ultimately, though, Sandys and his allies in the company leadership were losing the power to enforce their will: they lacked funds to send new colonists and they were facing scandals and investigations at home.[30]

Caught between Sandys's ambitions and those of his opponents, colonists in Virginia framed a hybrid vision of plantation enterprise. Some parts of Sandys's plan endured—in particular, the freedom of trade in the colony, which colonists would fight to maintain over the next twenty years. Moreover, despite their ambitious schemes, Sandys's opponents found it impossible to establish a full-fledged manorial system of tenantry. Private freehold estates would become the norm. Crucially, though, the route to a grant of fifty or one hundred acres—and the status of small planter—was not what Sandys had envisioned. Rather than serving as tenants on public land and transitioning to freeholders within a corporate structure, immigrants became subject to the new system of indentured servitude that bound them to labor for a term of years. By 1625, more than 40 percent of the colony's population were bound laborers. The fifty-acre land grants promised to new immigrants under the 1618 reforms (which came to be termed headrights) went to the established planters who paid for their Atlantic passage. Once they reached the end of their service (if they survived), most were cut loose to search for opportunities anywhere in the colony. For the first

29. Kingsbury, ed., *RVC*, III, 162–164, 207–210.
30. Ibid., III, 666–673 (quotation on 669).

Africans who arrived in Virginia in the summer of 1619, the system of servitude and slavery was even more restrictive.[31]

The shift to headrights and indentured servitude was partly driven by the problems with tenancy and colonial leaders' improvisation, but it was framed by conscious engagement with the debates over landownership and civic order that had gripped the colony for the past decade. Virginia leaders insisted that indentured servitude would address the shortcomings of the corporate model and thus shore up its foundations rather than undermine it. Late in 1621, Captain Christopher Newce of Elizabeth City proposed replacing the company's tenantry system with a two-stage process of labor management. Newly arrived laborers would be rented to established planters as servants who would serve four to seven years to cover their transportation costs, during which term they would be "Cherished, menteyned, and Instructed in the waies and Courses of this Country," supposedly improving their survival rates. After their terms expired, these individuals would be transferred back to the company's lands as tenants who would generate public revenue for the corporations. Newce's plan sought to combine the growing demand for servant labor with the civic concerns of Sandys' corporate plan, and he claimed that it would thereby "restore the fier in the hartes of the Adventurers." Sandys and his allies resisted the proposal, but planters on the ground continued to strengthen the system of servitude, framing it as the most appropriate method for regulating labor and maintaining civic order in the tobacco market.[32]

---

31. The success of the free trade element of Sandys's agenda owed to Warwick's continued support for that particular policy; see Kingsbury, ed., *RVC*, IV, 53–57. For the struggle against new monopolies, see Robert Brenner, *Merchants and Revolution: Commercial Change, Political Conflict, and London's Overseas Traders, 1550–1653* (Princeton, N.J., 1993), chaps. 3, 4. Scholarship on the development of indentured servitude and the headright system has tended to portray it as a pragmatic adaptation to circumstances. The classic account is Edmund Morgan, "The First American Boom: Virginia, 1618 to 1630," *WMQ*, 3d Ser., XXVIII (1971), 169–198. David W. Galenson has traced the roots of indentured servitude to both English precedent and local adaptation, but he also considers the initial establishment of the system as unselfconscious, predicated on the assumption that the Virginia Company's "purpose was the simple one of maximizing its profits"; see Galenson, *White Servitude in Colonial America: An Economic Analysis* (Cambridge, 1981), 5–15 (quotation on 11). For the percentage of servants and slaves in 1625, see Irene W. D. Hecht, "The Virginia Muster of 1624/5 as a Source for Demographic History," *WMQ*, 3d Ser., XXX (1973), 65–92. Some planters did grant their servants land at the expiration of their terms of service, as a "custom of the country," but this was not guaranteed by statute and relied upon individual negotiation; see Warren M. Billings, "The Law of Servants and Slaves in Seventeenth-Century Virginia," *Virginia Magazine of History and Biography*, XCIX (1991), 45–62 (esp. 51–52). For the status of early Africans in Virginia, see Philip D. Morgan's essay, "Virginia Slavery in Atlantic Context, 1550 to 1650," in this volume; and Michael Guasco, *Slaves and Englishmen: Human Bondage in the Early Modern Atlantic World* (Philadelphia, 2014), chap. 6.

32. [Capt. Nuce?], "Propos[it]ions to Be Tendred to the Company of Virginia for Alteringe Ther Present Condic[i]ons w[i]th Ther Tenants in Virginia," [Nov.? 1621], FP 336, Virginia Company Archives. For the Company's response, see Kingsbury, ed., *RVC*, III, 479, 489, 647.

In the aftermath of the 1622 Powhatan attack, colonists' preference for private estates was reinforced. Surviving planters gravitated to the estates of the colony's proven military leaders who provided defense and provisions in the midst of war and the subsequent famine. One such figure was William Harwood, who during the post-1622 period became known as the "Governor" at Martin's Hundred, one of the corporate settlements devastated by the 1622 Powhatan attack. After the attack, Harwood converted the nascent corporation into a palisaded estate. Plantations such as Harwood's displaced the corporate structure that Sandys had envisioned, but they were not the large manorial seats that Argall and some of his allies had favored. They were independent estates pursuing private commercial interests in the tobacco trade. It was no coincidence that it was in this moment, after the debate over the nature and purpose of private land, that the term "plantation," so long used to connote a public colonial project with civic ends, began to be applied to a commercial agricultural enterprise. Whereas "plantation" had previously been used synonymously with "city," "town," or "hundred," land patents in the 1620s began referring to plantations tied to individuals. The estate of George Sandys (treasurer of the colony and brother of Sir Edwin Sandys) was referred to as "his plantacon," and even humbler planters such as Richard and Isabell Pace, who patented only two hundred acres, described their land as "the plantation called Paces Paine." The decision to term individual estates as "plantations" was a conscious effort to legitimate private enterprise within a rich civic framework. The extent and nature of the civic authority private planters claimed and the degree to which private plantations should be regulated at a local and an imperial level would be topics of intense debate in the Chesapeake for the remainder of the century.[33]

THE TRANSITION TO PRIVATE LANDOWNERSHIP IN VIRGINIA DURING the 1610s was a drawn-out process in which early modern English debates about commerce and enclosure confronted the economic realities of the Chesapeake. It was not a single defining moment when a pent-up liberal capitalist demand for land and riches inevitably flooded the low-lying coastal plain of the Powhatan empire. Once it became clear that English colonists in Virginia would be

33. Charles T. Hodges, "Private Fortifications in 17th-Century Virginia: A Study of Six Representative Works," in Theodore R. Reinhart and Dennis J. Pogue, *The Archaeology of 17th-Century Virginia* (1993; rpt. Richmond, Va., 2007), 183–221; Hume and Hume, *Archaeology of Martin's Hundred*, I, chap. 3 (esp. 135–138); J. Frederick Fausz, "The Powhatan Uprising of 1622: A Historical Study of Ethnocentrism and Cultural Conflict" (Ph.D. diss., College of William and Mary, 1977), chap. 5 (esp. Table V.1); *Oxford English Dictionary Online*, s.v. "Plantation," www.oed.com (the first use of the term for private land relates to John Martin's estate); Nell Marion Nugent, *Cavaliers and Pioneers: Abstracts of Virginia Land Patents and Grants, 1623–1666* (Baltimore, 1963), 3, 10.

cultivating staple crops, the terms on which they would control their land and labor and the manner in which the market for their goods would be regulated became crucial civic questions. This essay has sketched out two broadly distinct positions that emerged in this debate: one vision of corporate, self-governing communities of freeholders with diverse and complementary economic interests supported by hefty endowments of public land, and another of improving landlords and stable hierarchies of tenants. The origins of English America's private staple-producing plantations lay in the middle ground between these two visions. Both approaches built upon the experience of developing commercial agriculture in England, and thus we cannot describe one as more "modern," or "progressive," or "capitalist" than the other; instead, they capture the complex intersection of civic commonwealth thought and the emerging science of political economy at this crucial moment. The leaders of the Virginia Company, both in England and Virginia, were deeply engaged with these debates. Furthermore, although the system of freehold land tenure and bound labor took hold in the Chesapeake from the early 1620s, the viability of tenancy and local corporate organization would continue to be tested in other parts of the English Atlantic over the next few decades.[34]

By emphasizing pragmatism, economic determinism, and inevitability in the development of the plantation system, even if we do so with an air of disapproval, we minimize the culpability of those who manipulated and adjusted the company's plans to build a world of private plantations under a veneer of civic rhetoric. Any true reckoning with the bonds between slavery and capitalism must acknowledge the evolution of the concept of "plantation." The physical and conceptual spaces that enslaved Africans would occupy in America for the next two and a half centuries were created through a conscious process of reframing ideas about the public good and private interest in English society. Newly established private plantations helped redefine and justify commercial practices and labor regimes that were essential to making the staple production of luxury goods in the Americas a viable proposition. Their creation, though, stretched the limits of contemporary ideas about economic regulation and civic order in England.

34. For continuing experiments with tenancy, see Karen Ordahl Kupperman, *Providence Island, 1630–1641: The Other Puritan Colony* (Cambridge, 1993), chap. 5. For the application of corporate structures to labor management and land allocation in New England, see Barry Levy, *Town Born: The Political Economy of New England from Its Founding to the Revolution* (Philadelphia, 2009), esp. chap. 1.

"A Part of That Commonwealth Hetherto Too Much Neglected"

Virginia's Contested "Publick" and the Origins of the General Assembly

ALEXANDER B. HASKELL

On April 21, 1624, a group of Virginia planters stood before a crowded court of Virginia Company members in London and made a forceful appeal for the integrity of Virginia's General Assembly in any matters that related to the "publique." Resentment against this small group of colonists happened to run high at this moment, for the planters had just submitted a "Mallitious Scandalous false and leaude [lewd]" petition to James I that the members were certain would contribute to the company's downfall, given that its future already rested precariously on a quo warranto suit then making its way through the king's courts. Yet the planters' remarks about their assembly not only aroused little opposition among the company's gathered lords, knights, gentlemen, merchants, and London citizens but, on the contrary, elicited their strong affirmation. Led by John Boyse, a gentleman colonist who had served as the burgess for Martin's Hundred in the Virginia Assembly's first meeting in July and August 1619, the planters argued before the company that recent impositions placed on their tobacco violated their firm understanding that "all taxation" in the colony "ought to have binne by a Generall Assembly." Along the same lines, any resources reserved for "puplique Uses should be Seine [sanely, or gravely] dispended by Some of them Selfes appoynted by the Generall assembly to the right use." Rather than reject these sentiments, company members fully agreed with them. To the planters' allegations that building the colony's forts had required excessive levying of their labor and that their "goods" had sometimes been "taken away by the Governors Command," the company's leaders responded that they "liked not that Course if it was Soe: for it was fitt that all leavies and Taxactins [taxations] should be

I am grateful to the organizers and participants of the conference "Virginia in 1619: Legacies for Race, Commonwealth, and Empire" and thankful as well to my colleagues in the Early Modern World Seminar at the University of California, Riverside, for helpful comments on an earlier draft.

given and dunne by the Generall assembly . . . and men appoynted to See it expended to the use [for which] it was gathered." To company members and planters alike, the General Assembly's role as a steward of the colony's public assets was beyond dispute.[1]

This illuminating exchange of beliefs about the Virginia General Assembly's purpose offers a useful starting point for reexamining that body's origins. The fragmentary nature of the evidence surrounding the company's authorization of the assembly in 1618 has left this chapter in the colony's political history stubbornly ambiguous. Few extant records speak directly to why company members chose to establish the assembly at this time or what ends they envisioned it performing. As a result, historians have understandably concluded that the assembly was initially an ill-defined institution that amounted to little more than an adjunct of the company's own decision-making apparatus. On the logic that whatever motives accounted for the creation of such a mundane body must have been correspondingly prosaic in nature, scholars have generally accepted Wesley Frank Craven's 1932 argument that little more was involved in the founding of the assembly or in the other reforms introduced in 1618 than the company's concern for its own solvency and future profit-making pursuits. Yet the planters and company members who waxed exuberantly about the assembly's responsibilities on that spring day in 1624 left little doubt that they perceived the institution in vigorously political terms. Unequivocal about the role the assembly should perform, they agreed that its function lay fundamentally in overseeing the raising and apportioning of the goods and services needed for local governance. Those shared resources—referred to collectively as the public—were central to how contemporaries conceived of the assembly as well as key to the circumstances behind its founding. Propelled by a particular Renaissance understanding of the public as a necessary concomitant of a divinely favored state, the assembly's founders took action when the colony's public itself seemed fatally compro-

---

1. John Ferrar to [Sir Francis Wyatt], [early May 1624] (draft), Ferrar Papers (FP) 539, Virginia Company Archives, http://www.virginiacompanyarchives.amdigital.co.uk; Susan Myra Kingsbury, ed., *The Records of the Virginia Company of London*, 4 vols. (Washington, D.C., 1906–1935) (hereafter cited as *RVC*), II, 519; H. R. McIlwaine, ed., *Journals of the House of Burgesses of Virginia, 1619–1658/59* (Richmond, Va., 1915), [vii]. The petition by John Boyse's group posed a threat during the quo warranto proceedings because the planters directed their blame for the colony's difficulties at the company's current leadership, thus implicitly taking sides in what had become an intensely partisan conflict among the company's officers. Sir Edwin Sandys's circle faced especially strong opposition from Robert Rich, earl of Warwick's party after Rich's 1618 raid on Virginia's public stock, an event that this essay posits as a major factor in the creation of Virginia's General Assembly. Such opposition contributed to the verdict by the King's Bench on May 24, 1624, that Sandys's faction was guilty of mishandling—usurping, in the language of the quo warranto writ—the privileges that James I had originally granted them through royal charter.

mised. At bottom, the story of the assembly's beginnings is an account of an effort to ensure that the colony had a meaningful public at all.[2]

In 1618, a convergence of factors led a group of Virginia Company members to lash out at what they regarded as the company's worrying drift away from the state-building goals that had animated it from the outset. Sir Edwin Sandys, the veteran parliamentarian, was the central figure behind this campaign, along with his allies, including Henry Wriothesley, third earl of Southampton, and John Ferrar. These men took the lead in authorizing the assembly as a way of reviving a vision of colonization that they associated closely with the earliest years of the Jacobean Virginia venture. The original prime mover behind the colonizing endeavor at the beginning of James's reign, Secretary of State Robert Cecil, earl of Salisbury, had given the enterprise an outsized aura of political and religious importance that continued to hold massive appeal for the Sandys circle. At the heart of this idealized outlook was the lofty expectation that Virginia would one day take its place among the king's great states, thereby providing a robust counterpart to the Spanish monarchy's American dominions.[3]

Yet developments in 1616–1618 had convinced Sandys that the colonizers' earlier commonwealth-forming goal was newly endangered and that the only tenable step was to "sett up the publiq againe." The "Publick," Sandys argued, was "a part of that Commonwealth hetherto too much neglected, and I would that neglect had been all the falt." Encompassing everything from common lands, forts, and a proposed college to government-sponsored servants, cattle, and corn, Virginia's public suddenly faced three new threats. First, the company's longtime merchant leadership had begun by 1616 to prioritize quick profits over the longer-term work of securing Virginia's political foundations. Second, while King James's commitment to the colony had never been dependable, his treasurers by 1617 were starting to eye corporate bodies like the Virginia Company

---

2. Wesley Frank Craven, *Dissolution of the Virginia Company: The Failure of a Colonial Experiment* (New York, 1932). For more recent studies that place less emphasis than Craven did on economic motives and give greater credit to Sandys's public-mindedness while still adhering to Craven's broad analysis, see Warren M. Billings, *A Little Parliament: The Virginia General Assembly in the Seventeenth Century* (Richmond, Va., 2004); Theodore K. Rabb, *Jacobean Gentleman: Sir Edwin Sandys, 1561–1629* (Princeton, N.J., 1998), 319–352.

3. Craven acknowledged the pervasiveness of the discourse on state formation, only to dismiss it as irrelevant to the colonizers' true intents: "To attribute to them any idea of creating a body politic either politically or economically independent of the company and of England is to credit them with an idea that is compatible neither with contemporary theories of colonization nor with reason" (Craven, *Dissolution of the Virginia Company*, 49). For alternative interpretations of contemporary theories of colonization that try to understand such commonwealth rhetoric rather than disregard it, see Alexander B. Haskell, *For God, King, and People: Forging Commonwealth Bonds in Renaissance Virginia* (Williamsburg, Va., and Chapel Hill, N.C., 2017); and Andrew Fitzmaurice, *Humanism and America: An Intellectual History of English Colonisation, 1500–1625* (Cambridge, 2003).

with fresh appreciation for how their profits might be diverted into royal coffers. Third and most dramatic of all, the Puritan aristocrat Sir Robert Rich and his client, Virginia governor Samuel Argall, staged a remarkable raid in early 1618 on the colony's common stores. Driven by an apocalyptic determination to weaken the Spaniards and thereby ready the world for the prophesied defeat of the Antichrist in the form of the Roman Catholic pope, Rich had given scant regard to Virginia's state-building efforts when he sent his warship to the colony for provisions en route to the West Indies and left the colony's public resources more or less depleted. It was against this backdrop of multiple encroachments on Virginia's common goods that Sandys introduced the colony's General Assembly. A means of jealously safeguarding the planters' shared stock, the assembly was at the same time an assertion that the colony possessed the political substance that warranted such a public sentinel in the first place.[4]

SANDYS'S COMMITMENT TO VIRGINIA'S PUBLIC HARKED BACK TO HIS earliest days of involvement in the colonizing endeavor, when the earl of Salisbury first set about refashioning American colonization at the outset of James I's reign. Salisbury had taken the lead in launching the Jacobean Virginia colonizing project, propelled in that endeavor by his frustration at the failures of the Elizabethan colonizers for leaving the queen's sovereign claims in the New World shamefully unsecured. As Salisbury put it, Sir Humphrey Gilbert's and Sir Walter Ralegh's "weake" attempts at establishing English dominion on the other side of the Atlantic had left Spanish pretensions in the region unanswered, as though this "glorious state of ours" was "rather broched by the vertue of our Ancestors, then of our owne worthiness." Especially worrisome was the damage done to England's imperial kingship, that special power, increasingly referred to in this period as sovereignty, that Salisbury considered an integral part of what made England a state in the first place. Royal imperium was meant to be an extraordinary puissance granted by God, but that sin-purging strength was hardly on display in conquests that came up as lamentably short as Gilbert's and Ralegh's ineffectual colonizing ventures. The lesson that Salisbury had learned from such disappointments in planting English imperium abroad was that Elizabeth's colonizers' pusillanimity arose from their status as "private men," that is, persons who took on sovereign responsibilities without sufficient public standing. Captains who wielded the queen's sovereign sword in far-off parts of the world with only the barest semblance of her support and little backing from

---

4. Kingsbury, ed., *RVC*, I, 267; Sir Edwin Sandys to Sir Lionel Cranfield, Sept. 9, 1619, in "Lord Sackville's Papers Respecting Virginia, 1613–1631, I," *American Historical Review*, XXVII (1922), 498.

the broader commonwealth invited defeat and disgrace. Hence, Salisbury's turn to that other key component of the state: the public. His intent was to clothe Jacobean Virginia in the mantle of a solidly public and state-backed enterprise, while treating the colony itself as a commonwealth in the making.[5]

Salisbury's turn to the public to save the colonizing venture was consistent with his broader political and ecclesiastical commitments. On the one hand, he was part of a new generation of late Renaissance politicians who lavished attention on the state as a divinely sanctioned means of holding people to their civil and religious duties. Praised by one of his admirers as a "well governed Statist," he drew many of his political insights from a late-sixteenth-century literature on statecraft by authors like Louis LeRoy, Jean Bodin, Giovanni Botero, and Justus Lipsius. These authors had scoured history for examples of human polities that did or did not satisfy God, weighing in particular which civil inventions seemed to align with Providence and which ones evidently defied God's will. One of their fundamental conclusions was that sovereignty was not the only element of the state that was divinely appointed. Other aspects of the ways humans had organized their polities over time also enjoyed God's approval and thus were similarly deserving of reverence. Bodin identified families as one such sacred part of the polity and held, as a corollary, that the private property of households should be deemed sacrosanct. But he also devoted considerable attention to what those families shared in common, such as "their markets, their churches, their walks, wayes, lawes, decrees, judgements, voyces, customs, theaters, wals, publick buildings, common pastures, lands, and treasure." This was the public, the wide assortment of resources, institutions, and norms that belonged to all the polity's members and in relation to which everyone, including even the king himself, was private. On the basis of such reasoning, Salisbury was prepared to see the public as possessing a legitimating weight all of its own, and thus much of his politics was focused on trying to uphold England's imperial crown while simultaneously safeguarding the commonwealth.[6]

---

5. "Reasons to Move the High Court of Parlament to Raise a Stocke for the Maintaining of a Collonie in Virgenia," 1606, in David B. Quinn, ed., with the assistance of Alison M. Quinn and Susan Hillier, *New American World: A Documentary History of North America to 1612*, 5 vols. (New York, 1979), V, 168–169. For a fuller discussion of Robert Cecil, earl of Salisbury's efforts to move beyond the disappointments of Elizabethan colonization through an extensively reimagined Jacobean colonizing project, see Haskell, *For God, King, and People*, 137–198. The likelihood that Salisbury was the author of "Reasons to Move the High Court of Parlament" is suggested ibid., 159.

6. Richard J[oh]nson, *A Remembrance of the Honors Due to the Life and Death of Robert Earle of Salisbury, Lord Treasurer of England, etc.* (London, 1612), [A3v]; J[ean] Bodin, *The Six Bookes of a Commonweale*, trans. Richard Knolles (London, 1606), 11. Salisbury's admiration for sixteenth-century statecraft writers like Jean Bodin and Giovanni Botero is developed further in Haskell, *For God, King, and People*, 141–155, 160, 167.

On the other hand, the same providential reasoning that made the public so important to Salisbury's politics also made it inescapably central to his religiosity. Drawn to post-Reformation establishmentarianism, he viewed settled institutions that enjoyed public approbation and state authorization as the nearest thing in this still-corrupt world to true faith. His connection to Sandys probably owed as much to their shared establishmentarian Protestantism as to their mutual interest in a public-centered politics. Sandys was closely connected to the theologian Richard Hooker, and in 1593 he personally took in hand the task of publishing the four books of Hooker's great apologia for establishmentarian faith, *Lawes of Ecclesiasticall Politie*. That same year, Sandys joined Cecil in supporting a bill in Parliament directed against Separatists, radical Protestants who rejected the settled church for their own interpretation of God's will. Such a rigid spurning of worldly institutions was a route to endless confusion, in the view of Hooker and his disciples. Later, Salisbury would attract to Virginia's cause a number of church figures who shared his establishmentarian beliefs and were similarly invested in staking out a firm position between Catholic error and Protestant extremism. Clergymen like Richard Hakluyt and William Crashawe and major church leaders such as George Abbot, archbishop of Canterbury, were among these like-minded supporters of the Virginia endeavor. The minister William Symonds would sum up their establishmentarian ecclesiology succinctly in a 1609 sermon before the Virginia Company in which he railed against the papal "Antichrist," while also ruing those Separatists who were in such a hurry to usher in the millennium that they wanted to "place earth in heaven," "abolish kings," and "bring all to a Popularity." For Salisbury and his admirers, the godliness of the civil order sometimes needed to be saved even from the godly.[7]

Salisbury's determination to challenge Spanish Catholic power without succumbing to Protestant anti-worldliness influenced his decision to approach Virginian colonization as an exercise in state formation. He knew from books like Botero's *Delle relationi universali* (1591), which he had his client Robert Johnson translate in 1601, that the Spaniards' own influence in America rested upon such a state-building program. In that work, America appeared as the one part of the world where the Spanish king "hath no corrivall able to make head against him" and where he had proven himself an undisputed "absolute lord," especially in his

---

7. William Symonds, *Virginia: A Sermon Preached at White-Chappel, in the Presence of Many, Honourable and Worshipfull, the Adventurers and Planters for Virginia, 25. April. 1609* . . . (London, 1609), 14, 50. On Sir Edwin Sandys's relationship with Richard Hooker and early participation with Cecil in opposing Separatists, see Rabb, *Jacobean Gentleman*, 10–11, 13–18, 31. For the centrality of establishmentarian philosophy to early Virginia, see Haskell, *For God, King, and People*, 2–3, 15, 18, 40, 46, 108, 142, 225–227, 234–235, 239–240, 276, 278, 280–283.

willingness to plant one "great and stately kingdome" after another. To confront Iberian pride by forging a comparably impressive polity on the banks of the Chesapeake Bay was a far more effective and honorable strategy, in Salisbury's view, than the private exploits of great men.⁸

Salisbury forged his embrace of state-led endeavors partially in response to one of Elizabeth's own brash adventurers, Robert Devereux, second earl of Essex. Facing criticism for his failed attack on the Spanish in the Azores in 1597, Essex made little apology for his largely singlehanded crusade, which had received only tepid support from the queen. Instead, he asserted that he and his fellow aristocratic captains (including Ralegh, who had accompanied him on the voyage) possessed "greatnesse of minde," a peculiarly stout Christian resolution that God gave to "men of action" to uphold them in their constancy and allow them to transcend those worldly interests that most men's "little mindes" hungered after, like "love[,] ease[,] pleasure[,] and profit." Salisbury and his circle responded that greatness of mind had been their era's singular failing, for such an exalted understanding of the individual adventurer's calling differed from pride only by degree. Johnson put the argument in print in 1601, asserting that "this greatnesse of mind, if it be not accompanied with vertue, maketh men daungerouslie bad and terrible." When he later served as one of the Virginia Company's most active members and apologists, Johnson slyly repeated that argument by associating such self-aggrandizing behavior with the Spaniards: "Their greatnes of minde arising together with their money and meanes, hath turmoiled all Christendome these fourtie yeares and more." In place of the Elizabethans' greatness of mind, Salisbury stressed the value of public associations that brought especially upright and honorable minds into concert. To fashion Virginia into a solid and rising kingdom rather than a mere solitary crusader's turbulent conquest would require weighing in forcefully in favor of a sober, state-centered politics.⁹

Salisbury first introduced his public-oriented approach to colonization in a proposal that he circulated, apparently in early 1606, suggesting that Parliament

---

8. *The Worlde; or, An Historicall Description of the Most Famous Kingdomes and Common-Weales Therein* . . . (London, 1601), 36–37; Giovanni Botero, *Delle relationi universali di Giovanni Botero Benese prima parte* . . . (Rome, 1591). On Robert Johnson's role in translating Botero's book, see Andrew Fitzmaurice, "The Commercial Ideology of Colonization in Jacobean England: Robert Johnson, Giovanni Botero, and the Pursuit of Greatness," *William and Mary Quarterly*, 3d Ser., LXIV (2007), 791–820.

9. [Robert Devereux, second earl of Essex], *An Apologie of the Earle of Essex, against Those Which Fasly and Maliciously Taxe Him to Be the Onely Hinderer of the Peace, and Quiet of His Countrey* ([London], [1600]), B3r; Rob[ert] Johnson, *Essaies; or, Rather Imperfect Offers* (London, 1601), B4r–B4v; J[ohnson], *Nova Britannia: Offring Most Excellent Fruites by Planting in Virginia, Exciting All Such as Be Well Affected to Further the Same* (London, 1609), B3r–B3v.

raise and maintain a "publique stocke" for the Virginia endeavor. If Parliament had accepted his proposal, it would have effectively made that body the colony's treasurer, responsible for managing the costs associated with planting a new dominion overseas. Salisbury made clear that he regarded the plan as an alternative to the individualistic exploits of the Elizabethan colonizers. "Collonies ... fownded for a publique-well" were preferable to a venture "where private men are absolute signors of a voiage," because public backing permitted overseas settlements to "continewe in better obedience, and become more industrious." He hinted too in his repeated insistence of the honorableness of money gathered by "publique consent" that he was distancing colonization from its earlier associations with dreaded monarchical impositions. Elizabeth had given Ralegh just such royal license in 1585 to gather and impress whatever supplies and personnel he desired for his Virginia voyage in the counties of Devon and Cornwall and in Bristol. A regular stock maintained by Parliament would allow the colonizers to avoid such unwelcome provisioning raids on families and communities, thereby abiding by Bodin's axiom that the private property of households and the public treasuries of commonwealths are sacred.[10]

Salisbury was familiar with Bodin's analysis and clearly relied directly on his prescriptions for a rightly ordered public. On the basis of his research into human political arrangements that enjoyed divine sanction, Bodin had ordered different methods for raising public moneys along a moral spectrum. The first and most "honest and sure" basis for the polity's wealth were rents from common and royal lands. Salisbury acknowledged this emphasis on the favorability of rents in the very opening of his 1606 proposal, conceding their desirability but also explaining that island countries like England where land was limited had little choice but to rely on trade to augment the public treasury. On Bodin's moral hierarchy, traffic and merchandizing were also acceptable bases for state revenues, the first involving extracting riches to feed into royal or public coffers and the latter centering on the customs duties levied on the imports and exports of private traders. However, he conspicuously gave these sources of income a low ranking, probably because of lingering suspicions of merchants as unduly self-interested actors. Bodin especially loathed impositions because they "oppress[ed]" subjects. Unlike taxes levied by assemblies, which were accept-

---

10. "Reasons to Move the High Court of Parlament," in Quinn, ed., *New American World*, V, 168; for the publication's likely date of 1606, see Quinn's introductory remarks, ibid. For the queen's requisition order, see "Signet Letter for Sir Walter Raleigh," June 10, 1585, in David Beers Quinn, ed., *The Roanoke Voyages, 1584–1590: Documents to Illustrate the English Voyages to North America under the Patent Granted to Walter Raleigh in 1584*, Works Issued by the Hakluyt Society, 2d Ser., no. 104 (London, 1955), I, 156–157.

able as long as they really were "gifts" or voluntary offerings rather than forced subscriptions, impositions struck at the livelihood of subjects without any promise of benefiting them in turn. Only in cases of great necessity, like war, were impositions "religious and godly," because only then did the commonwealth's preservation outweigh all other considerations. In general, although Bodin was no constitutionalist and took for granted that God gave sovereignty to rulers absolutely and inviolably, he preferred consensual over forceful methods of raising public resources. Given that commonwealths were, in his word, "holy," such a volitional approach to maintaining the polity's welfare was effectively a divine imperative.[11]

Salisbury took such Bodinian reasoning seriously enough to endow his plan for a Virginian stock with a distinctive moral logic. On the one hand, he treated the public as granting colonization a very particular sort of legitimacy, especially by freeing it from associations of greed that circled relentlessly around mere private undertakings. The latter were "ignominious" because they were "presumed to ayme at a lucre," whereas an overseas voyage intended for "publique service ... carrieth more reputacon with it." Accordingly, Salisbury wanted merchant adventurers to make up only one small part of the investors loaning money for Virginia's public treasury, for Parliament's management of that stock on behalf of the colony was meant to indicate that the "whole state," not one particular group of lenders, was "interested in the benefit of it." On the other hand, for such moneys to be truly public they needed to comport with the commonwealth's own much-touted reciprocal bonds. Thus, the taxes that Parliament would need to levy for the colony were not to "be raised upon the sweat of the poore, or industrie of the husbandman[,] Artificer, or tradisman" or directed at commonwealth necessities like food or apparel. Likewise, all persons who contributed to the fund should expect some future dividend for their generosity toward the public. The king, for instance, would receive a share of the proceeds in exchange for his willingness to commission the officers needed to collect the revenues. Even persons who abused the poor for "emoderate gaines," whose fines would help pay the colony's expenses, would be included in this eventual payout, as though their original vice had been rendered virtuous and worthy of recompense once it was made useful to the commonwealth. Salisbury hoped that commerce between the king's two states would eventually give this feedback loop of mutual benefits a permanent footing, with the English wool and cloth that traveled to Virginia and the American commodities making their way back

---

11. Bodin, *Six Bookes of a Commonweale*, 1, 650, [657], 663; "Reasons to Move the High Court of Parlament," in Quinn, ed., *New American World*, V, 168.

to England each pouring a steady stream of assets into public coffers in the form of customs duties. However, Salisbury had no illusions about the massive costs that his scheme would incur up front, and he justified those expenses in relation to what always mattered most to his plan: the political challenge that Virginia was meant to pose to Spanish power. As he acknowledged, only a "publique purse, and a Comon consent to prosecute an accion" could raise the "compotent some of monie" that Virginia would need to stand firm against such "forraigne states." However, the Parliament that met in early 1606 was evidently deaf to such reasoning, for the absence of any record of discussion of the matter suggests that the members declined even to give Salisbury's proposal serious consideration.[12]

Unable to rely on Parliament's assistance, Salisbury turned to the institutions and arrangements for which the Jacobean Virginia venture would ultimately become known. By no means giving up his determination to lend the colonizing effort the public stature it had formerly lacked, he now turned for that commonwealth backing to other bodies like the Virginia royal council and the Virginia Company. Salisbury was undoubtedly responsible for the inclusion of these two colonizing entities in James's letters patent of April 10, 1606, a document that was itself probably Salisbury's or his clients' handiwork, given the king's own wariness about participating in an enterprise with such delicate diplomatic implications. Conscious that Spanish ambassadors pressed the king on his commitment to Virginia and uncertain "how far his Majestie wilbe pleasd to avow it, which may intimate disavowing," Salisbury and his circle were all the more purposeful in surrounding the colonizing venture with tangible signs of public support. They were concerned not only with the practical needs of funding and directing the venture but also with the trickier issue of upholding the project's fragile legitimacy. The Council of Virginia was useful in this regard by linking the colony symbolically to the king, despite his disappointing ambivalence. Meanwhile, the Virginia Company functioned as a means of raising and managing the large sums needed for forging a new polity overseas while also presenting itself to the realm as an impressive public organization in its own right. Modeled only loosely on the era's trading companies, the Virginia Company was really a stand-in for the treasurer's position that Salisbury had originally envisioned Parliament as performing. Headed by a treasurer, rather than the governor that

---

12. "Reasons to Move the High Court of Parlament," in Quinn, ed., *New American World*, V, 168–169. It is not clear which English laws Salisbury had in mind in suggesting that fines imposed on exploiters of the poor could serve as one valuable source of funding for Virginian colonization. Possibly he meant statutes like An Act to Redress the Misemployment of Lands, Goods and Stocks of Money Heretofore Given to Charitable Purposes (1601), an Elizabethan law that James I perpetuated in a 1604 proclamation, or perhaps royal proclamations such as a 1604 one directed against bakers, brewers, innkeepers, and butchers who unlawfully increased their prices.

typically led trading companies, and following the joint-stock model of opening membership to anyone willing to pay for a single share of its collective funds, the company portrayed itself as basically the commonwealth in microcosm. As one pamphlet put it, "What voiage ever was there which had so many honourable undertakers, and of so many sorts and callings, both of the *Clergie* and *Laitie, Nobilitie, Gentrie,* and *Commonaltie, Citie* and *Countrie,* Merchants and *Tradesmen, Private persons* and *Corporations*? as though every kinde and calling of men desired to have their hands in so happie a worke." In conspicuously relegating merchants to the bottom rungs of this hierarchy of participants, Salisbury's group made clear that the company was the embodiment of the public as a whole rather than simply those interested in commercial gain.[13]

Yet, if the Virginia Company helped maintain Virginia's status as a public endeavor, it did so only in close connection with the idea that the colonizers really were engaged in the grand project of founding a new state. That aim appeared prominently in the colony's promotional materials, which encouraged English subjects to lay the "foundation of a *Common-wealth*," "builde up fast Virginias state," and recognize that "the same God that hath joyned three Kingdomes under one *Casar,* wil not be wanting to adde a fourth." Sustaining that state-building objective proved difficult, however, especially once Salisbury's leadership no longer provided the endeavor with its original coherence. When he succumbed to illness on May 24, 1612, the Virginia venture lost not only its most influential link to English government but also a figure capable of holding together the wide array of clients and allies in church and state who had given the enterprise its initial momentum. In the unpredictability left by Salisbury's death, a few core supporters like Sandys sought to preserve the secretary of state's vision. Their alertness to circumstances and groups that threatened to steer colonization away from its original public orientation would set the stage for the creation of Virginia's assembly.[14]

---

13. Kingsbury, ed., *RVC*, III, 2; W[illiam] Crashaw[e], *A Sermon Preached in London before the Right Honorable the Lord Lawarre, Lord Governour and Captaine Generall of Virginea, and Others of His Majesties Counsell for That Kingdome, and the Rest of the Adventurers in That Plantation, at the Said Lord Generall His Leave Taking of England His Native Countrey, and Departure for Virginea, Febr. 21, 1609* (London, 1610), I[1]r. On the significance of councils to Renaissance-era colonization, see Alexander Haskell, "Councils, Providence, and Political Legitimacy in Early Virginia," in Jacqueline Rose, ed., *The Politics of Counsel in England and Scotland, 1286–1707*, Proceedings of the British Academy (Oxford, 2017), 211–228.

14. [Counseil for Virginia], *A True and Sincere Declaration of the Purpose and Ends of the Plantation Begun in Virginia . . .* (London, 1610), 25; "Londons Lotterie: With an Incouragement to the Furtherance Thereof, for the Good of Virginia, and the Benefit of This Our Native Countrie, Wishing Good Fortune to All That Venture in the Same, to the Tune of Lusty Gallant" (London, 1612); Councell of Virginia, *A True Declaration of the Estate of the Colonie in Virginia . . .* (London, 1610), 66–67.

ALTHOUGH SANDYS HAD BEEN INVOLVED WITH THE VIRGINIA PROJECT since joining the royal council in 1607, his activities in the Virginia Company intensified around 1616 when he took on the leadership position known as assistant. Participating more in day-to-day operations, including helping to expand the public lottery that for the last four years had provided the colonial venture with one of its major funding sources, he became increasingly concerned about the diminished condition of the company's stock. Later he would write that he and others had come to see the colony as "weake and the Treasury utterly exhaust" and to worry that "this great Action" would "fall to nothinge." By the time he took over the position of treasurer from the London merchant Sir Thomas Smythe on April 28, 1619, Sandys was declaring regularly, as though reciting a mantra, that Virginia's "publique was gone" and "the fruite of full 12 years labour and above one hundred thousand marks expences" wasted. It was against this backdrop of anxieties about the dramatic depletion of the colony's common assets that Sandys had taken the lead in advancing the reforms of 1618 that included establishing the General Assembly. However, what had prompted his hand in this regard was not mere company negligence or mismanagement. Rather, Sandys had perceived growing signs that the very idea of Virginia as a future state was being undermined, a subversion of Salisbury's vision that simultaneously raised the question whether the colony needed a public at all. In establishing an assembly in Virginia to function as a custodian over its own treasury, Sandys was not only safeguarding the colony's public store over the long term but also making a vivid statement about the continuing viability of Salisbury's conception of the colony as a state-in-the-making.[15]

Sandys's suspicions about Virginia's attenuated resources focused initially on the colony's longtime merchant leadership. Smythe and his deputy Robert Johnson, Salisbury's old hired pen, had been involved in the Virginia Company from the beginning. Both men had served Salisbury in various respects, and their experience— especially in the late 1590s in helping to found the East India Company—probably explains why he later entrusted them with chief oversight over the stock managed by the Virginia Company. Yet Smythe's merchant status apparently generated some unease among Salisbury's other clients. For instance, William Strachey, a member of Virginia's Council of State and early secretary in the colony, wrote a dedicatory poem in *For the Colony in Virginea Britannia: Lawes Divine, Morall, and Martiall, etc.* (1612) that went out of its way to convey that Smythe was not approaching Virginia as he would one of his usual com-

---

15. Rabb, *Jacobean Gentleman*, 330; Kingsbury, ed., *RVC*, I, 350.

mercial enterprises. "Vent[u]ring your Purse for profit" was a perfectly honorable behavior in an arena like the East Indies, Strachey wrote, but in the case of Virginia, where establishing the sacred bonds of commonwealth prevailed over moneymaking, "you traffique not with men, but God." This instinctual suspicion of traders as concerned above all for their private good was initially offset by the impressive numbers of noblemen and gentlemen who sat on the royal council and attended the Virginia Company general courts. However, the loss of Salisbury's direction threatened to unravel this relationship between the two groups. Later, after factionalism in the company had grown to even greater heights, John Donne, dean of Saint Paul's, would characterize this infighting as ultimately a contest of mutual slights, the traders exclaiming ruefully to Sandys's circle, "You have playd the *Gentlemen;* and they in equal reproach, You have playd the *Merchant.*" Feelings of dishonor were close to the surface in this environment, where the very capacity of merchants for sustained moral conduct was at question.[16]

Although Sandys appears to have worked generally well with the merchants, not least in advancing the 1618 reforms while Smythe was still treasurer, it was nevertheless the case that his vision for the colony was markedly different from theirs. This contrast became especially clear when in 1616 Smythe introduced a number of organizational changes that tended to shift public burdens to private hands. In confronting the company's mounting debt, he established the Magazine, where provisions entering the colony could be exchanged for local commodities. Rather than a public institution, the Magazine operated as a monopoly under the direction of, and according to prices set by, Smythe, Johnson, and a few other associates. Meanwhile, Smythe encouraged the planters to think of themselves first and foremost as producers. He promoted a primary focus on tobacco cultivation, granted colonists their dividends in land, and fostered a brisk trade through the Magazine rather than nurturing public resources or institutions. On June 8, 1617, John Rolfe wrote to Sandys to describe the predictable results of these changes in the colony. While industriousness had spiked and "men cheerefully labor about their grounds," nevertheless those same inhabitants scarcely had "ragges to cov[e]r their naked bodyes," and their public infrastructure, "in buildings, fortyficac[i]ons, and of boats," was similarly "much ruyned" and in "greate want." In short, Smythe was gradually transforming Vir-

16. William Strachey, *For the Colony in Virginea Britannia: Lawes Divine, Morall, and Martiall, etc.* (London, 1612), unpaginated dedicatory poem; John Donne, "A Sermon upon the Eighth Verse of the First Chapter of the Acts of the Apostles: Preached to the Honourable Company of the Virginian Plantation, 13. Novemb. 1622" (1624), in Donne, *Foure Sermons upon Special Occasions* (London, 1625), 35.

ginia into little more than an outpost for gathering and trading commodities, a far cry from Salisbury's original state-building vision.[17]

Sandys was alarmed by this fundamental change in the Virginia venture. By early 1618 he had called for an intensive investigation into Smythe's accounts and had become one of the most energetic of the auditors. Eyewitnesses marveled that he and some of his fellow inspectors pored over the records "five dayes of the week, from between nine and ten of the clock in the morning, till five or six in the evening, for the space of nine moneths," all in the hope of finding "a very considerable sum, to be charged on Sir Th. Smith." The audit found plenty of evidence of Smythe's sloppy bookkeeping but little proof of wrongdoing. By Smythe's boast, all that could be shown was that Virginia's stock was "indebted to him, and not he to it" and that his "painfull goverment" had always been approved in the company's general courts. But malfeasance had never really been the issue, for the merchants had simply begun approaching the colony as they would any of their commercial enterprises. Rumors that swirled around the audit acknowledged this fact unsympathetically by accusing the Smythe group of revealing themselves to be self-interested merchants after all. These reports "suggested that the Marchants as they termed them who then swayed the Courts affected nothinge but their owne immoderate gaine though w[i]th the poore Planters extreame oppression as appeared by their Magazine." Some of the planters were indeed unhappy. When John Boyse's group later stood before the Virginia Company in 1624, they made clear that they also resented the colony's transformation into a narrowly mercantile project. According to one onlooker, "They Spoake many bitter things that all was turned to private ends in Virginia and littell care for publique." Sandys was thus not the only person to be troubled by the commercialization of the colony, though the planters' complaints indicate how difficult Sandys himself would find restoring the colony's public after he replaced Smythe as treasurer in 1619. Building up Virginia's public would prove to be a challenge that spanned not just years but entire generations, and it was partly for this reason that Sandys sought to take that task out of the hands of profit-seeking merchants and place it in an assembly that promised to last the ages.[18]

The merchants' reworking of the colonial venture, however, was not the only factor that prompted Sandys to defend Virginia's public, for he was also spurred

---

17. Rabb, *Jacobean Gentleman*, 327–328; Kingsbury, ed., *RVC*, III, 71.

18. Rabb, *Jacobean Gentleman*, 331–332; Josias Foster, "An Account and Observation Taken by A. W., a True Friend and Servant to Sir John Danvers, and the Parliament-Interest," in *Copy of a Petition from the Governor and Company of the Sommer Islands*... (London, 1651), 6; Kingsbury, ed., *RVC*, II, 404, III, 523–524; Ferrar to [Wyatt], [early May 1624] (draft), FP 539, Virginia Company Archives.

to action by the king's own changing relationship to the colonial endeavor. Perennially uncertain in Salisbury's day, James's patronage of the Virginia venture grew even more complicated in the late 1610s as his own finances worsened and the Virginia Company's evolving legal status placed new pressures on the colonizers' stock. The king's revenue problems were well known, and company officials like Sandys were undoubtedly aware of the creative tactics that Sir Lionel Cranfield, one of James's most indefatigable treasurers, was employing to locate untapped sources of royal income. One of these strategies involved targeting incorporated communities on the grounds that their royally awarded privileges left them beholden to their king. By late 1617, Cranfield had forced the ancient trading company the Merchant Adventurers of London to pay upward of eighty thousand pounds to win back their recently revoked corporate rights, a strong-arm move that suggested something of his resolve in pursuing corporate wealth, even if the Virginia Company lacked comparably rich reserves. However, Virginia was about to become much more vulnerable to such machinations because of the limited duration of its freedom from taxes.[19]

Like many corporations, the Virginia Company had enjoyed a seven-year tax exemption, a privilege commonly awarded to royally chartered endeavors that promised to benefit the public. Because the company received a letters patent in 1612, that tax-free status would end in 1619. Officials had already taken steps to address this looming deadline, having appealed to the Privy Council in December 1617 for an extension. Although that petition had failed, Sandys seems once again to have started planning for the long term, in particular by putting in place various safeguards intended to discourage the crown from treating the colony as simply a convenient source of royal income. His thinking in this regard basically mirrored Salisbury's original vision of Virginia and England as fellow British states standing tall on opposite sides of the Atlantic, engaging in a mutually beneficial commerce and satisfying their reciprocal public needs through customs duties. Yet, Sandys's awareness that Virginia might imminently fall prey to the king's desire for profits, just as it had almost succumbed to the similar poaching of the merchants, now gave new urgency to the problem of insulating that state-building project against all such short-sighted interventions.[20]

---

19. Robert Brenner, *Merchants and Revolution: Commercial Change, Political Conflict, and London's Overseas Traders, 1550–1653* (Princeton, N.J., 1993), 211; Menna Prestwich, *Cranfield: Politics and Profits under the Early Stuarts* (Oxford, 1966), 176–177.

20. Emily Rose, "The End of the Gamble: The Termination of the Virginia Lotteries in March 1621," *Parliamentary History*, XXVII (2008), 175–197; *Acts of the Privy Council of England*, XXXV, *1616–1617*, ed. J. V. Lyle (London, 1927), 400, *British History Online*, http://www.british-history.ac.uk/acts-privy-council/vol35.

In light of this fear that the king's treasurer privileged immediate economic returns over long-range political goals, Sandys instituted the Virginia General Assembly as one key component of his broader agenda of holding firm to the imperiled idea of Virginia as a future state. It was scarcely an accident that the instructions drafted on November 18, 1618, to Governor Sir George Yeardley that announced the assembly's authorization framed the act as consistent with the company's long-standing efforts "to prepare a way and to lay a foundation whereon A flourishing State might in process of time by the blessing of Almighty God be raised." That message needed to be trumpeted, for only acceptance of Virginia's commonwealth status would allow for the kind of public that the colony required, that is, a public with all the sober stateliness and rich resources necessary to sustain a kingdom able to challenge the Spaniards' own American states. Even after setting the assembly in place, Sandys pursued a number of other ends intended to reinforce that larger state-making plan. Two of these objectives, neither of which ultimately succeeded, included a request for new letters patent from the king and, in a nod to Salisbury's earlier hope of recruiting Parliament to the colonial cause, an appeal for parliamentary confirmation of that charter. Sandys also took every opportunity to call upon the colony's supporters for greater patience as well as the recognition that a Virginia kingdom, if founded correctly, would benefit all of its individual constituents. "The maintayning of the publique in all estates [states]," he asserted in a speech to the company in November 1619, was "of noe lesse importance, even for the benefitt of the Private, then the roote and body of a Tree are to the perticuler branches." That statement was almost certainly directed not only at investors but also at the crown, a reminder that James was ultimately but one of the private parties that Virginia's public was meant to serve.[21]

Yet the greatest assault on the colony's common resources ultimately came, not from the company's merchants nor the king, but from another company member whose aristocratic status and Puritan beliefs would contribute to his disruptiveness. Sir Robert Rich, scion of Robert Rich, third Baron Rich, was also a kinsman of the second earl of Essex, Salisbury's onetime rival and the epitome of the headstrong Protestant militantism that Salisbury's establishmentarianism had so vigorously opposed. The younger Rich, soon to be elevated to second earl of Warwick, likewise embraced a bellicose Puritanism, which lent his energetic involvement in a wide range of English colonizing ventures a distinct millenarian edge. Patron to fiery preachers like the Somers Islands

---

21. Kingsbury, ed., *RVC*, I, 267–268, III, 98; Rose, "End of the Gamble," *Parliamentary History*, XXVII (2008), 188–189.

clergyman Lewes Hughes, who had allegedly declared that "the Government of the Church of England by Bishops was Antichristian and that the Booke of Common prayers was butt an Old wives tale," Rich pursued colonization with an anti-popish fervency that was more reminiscent of the Elizabethans than the new breed of wary statesmen like Salisbury and Sandys. Thus, whereas Salisbury had tiptoed around the diplomatic intricacies of colonization in the wake of the Anglo-Spanish peace of 1604 that he had personally helped to negotiate, Rich in 1616 gleefully led roving expeditions against Spanish ships, regardless of the diplomatic repercussions. Bypassing King James altogether, he embarked on these maverick exploits under a commission from the similarly belligerent Protestant duke of Savoy, Charles Emmanuel I. Such heedlessness of the state in pursuing a godly cause was precisely the kind of zealous independence that establishmentarians like Salisbury and Sandys most distrusted, and thus it is not surprising that Sandys was also quick to pick up on troubling signs that Rich had begun to cast his own eye covetously on Virginia's common stock.[22]

The particular Virginian assets that interested Rich were not the tobacco proceeds that had caught Smythe's attention nor the potential tax revenue that enthralled Cranfield; rather, it was the public resources that had been gradually accumulating in the colony itself. Eager to do battle with the Spanish in the West Indies, Rich sought men and provisions for a voyage, and by early 1618 he evidently had come to discern just such a supply in the numerous servants, cattle, and corn reserves that had been set aside in and around Jamestown for various public needs. One of his loyal clients, Samuel Argall, happened to be the colony's deputy governor, and it was undoubtedly Argall who not only had helped to identify this attractive cache but also was ready to corral it on board Rich's 130-ton vessel the *Treasurer* once it arrived from England en route to the Caribbean. The ship, under the direction of Captain Daniel Elfrith, had left England under a cloud of suspicion when its publicized nature as a fishing expedition was belied by the "notorious and manifest" absence of salt, hooks, or lines and the equally conspicuous presence of shot, powder, ordinance, waistcloth, and "streamers" and "flagges," no doubt emblazoned with Rich's coat of arms. Once the *Treasurer* departed England, orders hastily went out to the recently

22. Douglas Bradburn, "The Eschatological Origins of the British Empire," in Bradburn and John C. Coombs, eds., *Early Modern Virginia: Reconsidering the Old Dominion* (Charlottesville, Va., 2011), 15–56; Barbara Donagan, "The Clerical Patronage of Robert Rich, Second Earl of Warwick, 1619–1642," American Philosophical Society, *Proceedings*, CXX (1976), 388–419; Kingsbury, ed., *RVC*, II, 406. The Somers Islands was the name by which the English at this time commonly referred to Bermuda. The name honored Sir George Somers who, as admiral of Virginia, was among the officers of that colony who were marooned on the islands in 1609 and whose ten-month stay there helped spur English colonizing efforts in the region.

appointed Virginia governor Thomas West, third Baron De La Warr, then sailing to the colony on the *Neptune,* to intervene. He succeeded in intercepting the vessel and arranging for the two ships to sail to Virginia together, but he died unexpectedly on June 7, before reaching the colony. When the *Neptune*'s captain, Edward Brewster, arrived in Virginia, he attempted to carry out De La Warr's commands to protect Virginia's public store, but Argall, recognizing Rich's authority more than the company's, reacted in bold defiance of Brewster's efforts. Court-martialling the captain, Argall went so far as to have Brewster condemned to death. Barely escaping the colony with his life, the captain returned to England in early 1619 after Argall commuted his sentence to banishment. Yet by that time the colony's "publique"—the "ffruite of ffoureskore Thousande pounds charge," as the company later put it—had found its way into Argall's hands, who had "converted ... wholly to his owne pryvate use and possession [that is, to Rich's purposes]; the verie publique Lands Cultivated, the Companies Tenants and Servants, their Corne, Rents and Tributes of Corne[,] their Kine and other Cattle, [and] their Stores and Provisions." Meant to support an emergent state, the colony's public goods had instead become the cargo for a Puritan English pirate expedition that, according to one unnamed Somers Islands minister, aimed at "the robbinge of the Spanyards (as beinge lyms of Antechrist)." In one fell swoop, an apocalyptically motivated voyage had left Virginia with virtually its entire public foundation plundered.[23]

When the Sandys circle instituted the colony's General Assembly, then, it did so under circumstances that were profoundly political and in which the single objective of protecting Virginia's public assets cut across the otherwise wide-ranging types of threats the colony then faced. The overwhelming concern of the moment was to salvage a state-building enterprise that had suddenly become deprived of the very bedrock of common resources upon which such a project needed to rest. Toward the end of 1618, Sandys and his group wrote several slightly varying sets of instructions in preparation for Yeardley's voyage for Virginia to take up his post, and these directions left little doubt that the assembly had become part of a broader campaign to revive the colony's injured

23. Kingsbury, ed., *RVC,* I, 367, II, 402, III, 419–421 (quotation on 419). How exactly Samuel Argall purloined the colony's public stock remains elusive, in large part because of the veil of obscurity that quickly settled over the raid and its relationship to the high-ranking Sir Robert Rich. The Sandys circle had little doubt that Argall was simply a pawn in Rich's militant Puritan machinations, but Rich's aristocratic status and political prominence made it difficult to blame him directly for the near "overthrowe of the wholl Plantation" (Instructions to Governor Sir George Yeardley, Nov. 18, 1618, FP 91, Virginia Company Archives). As Sandys's ally Nicholas Ferrar would state a number of years later, it was Argall's "greatest freinds and abettor," that is, the powerful Riches, "from whom that matter had its originall" (Nicholas Ferrar, Memorandum concerning Disputes in Virginia Company, [May? 1623], FP 481, Virginia Company Archives).

public and thereby restore the state-founding enterprise itself. Numerous initiatives were directed at replenishing the "public Store" of corn and cattle, returning servants to the public lands, and encouraging a more diversified economy that did not center exclusively on tobacco. The Magazine was itself to become a public institution to avoid the "wrongs and sinister practises" of the recent past. The company's ongoing efforts to persuade the king to see the colony as more than a source of tax revenues also received indirect mention, including in several references to James's eagerness for the planters to cultivate silk. Yeardley had enjoyed an encouraging audience with the king before leaving for the colony, in which James had made clear he knew and approved of the 1618 "lawes and orders," including, presumably, the establishment of the assembly. Likewise, he had pointedly commanded Yeardley to take special care "to preserve the store (especially that belonging to the publique)" while at the same time preventing "Novelty or singularity" in religion, an indication that he was well aware of the distinctively paired threats the colony had just confronted. All the king wanted for now, in return for his liberality to the planters, was for them to "raise more ritch and staple commodities" than tobacco, and especially to "cherish up silkewormes," desires that were fully in keeping with the idea of Virginia as a rising state that would one day enjoy with England a mutually beneficial trade.[24]

On the other hand, the instructions also made clear that the assembly was entering a perilous world in which neither its authority nor the colony's commonwealth status could be taken for granted. Yeardley was to arrive in the colony not only as the herald of good news about the king's patronage and the authorization of the assembly. He was also there as an interrogator and punisher, ordered to question Argall and especially to implicate Rich. The questions he was to ask spoke to the pronounced fragility of the colony's public order: By "what authoritie" did Argall act? On what grounds did he "disgrace the Companie of Virginia and his Majesties Counseil here"? Was it true that he "hath denyed to hold anie authoritie from them or under them"? What had "become of the publique Tenants or Servants" as well as the "Companies Tobacco garden"? Whatever role the assembly might ultimately play in the colony, one hope in the Sandys circle was assuredly that it might at the very least give some greater weight to local rule, eliminating the kind of harrowing uncertainty that Rich's raid had both exploited and exposed.[25]

24. Kingsbury, ed., *RVC*, III, 98; Counseil for Virginia, Copy of Instructions, Dec. 2, 1618, FP 92, Virginia Company Archives; "A Report of S[i]r George Yeardlyes[,] Going Governor to Virginia," Dec. 5, 1618, FP 93, Virginia Company Archives.

25. Counseil for Virginia, Copy of Instructions, Dec. 2, 1618, FP 92, Virginia Company Archives. See also Virginia Company, Instructions to Governor Sir George Yeardley, Nov. 18, 1618, FP 91, Virginia Company Archives.

The assembly would meet for the first time at Jamestown on July 30, 1619, bringing together Governor Yeardley, the Council of State, and twenty-two elected burgesses into a single deliberative body to consult on the colony's laws. It was a political creation of a distinctively Renaissance stamp. An indication of this was one of Sandys's ardent hopes for the colony, that it could become, in effect, a pure instance of Bodin's ideal commonwealth, a state that derives its public funds completely from common lands. According to Sandys, he was drawing on "the laudable Example of the most famous Common Wealthes both past and present," perhaps an acknowledgment that he was relying on Bodin's own rich analysis of those polities. Based on that research, Sandys went on, "our intent is to Ease all the Inhabitants of Virginia forever of all taxes and public burthens as much as may be and take away all occasion of oppression and corruption" by allotting and laying "out A Convenient portion of public lands for the maintenance and support as well of Magistracy and officers as of other public charges both here and there from time to time arising." This was a heady vision, full of Christian humanist idealism. But Sandys must have known even in proposing such a plan that the decision to implement it would not ultimately be his to make. In creating the assembly, the company had passed the responsibility of stewardship over Virginia's public largely to the grave members of that body. It would be up to the first assembly of 1619 and the many assemblies that followed to provide the "seine" judgment that preserves and marshals public resources for the common weal.[26]

26. Kingsbury, ed., *RVC*, III, 99.

The Company-Commonwealth

ANDREW FITZMAURICE

Historians frequently remark that the first representative assembly in North America was established in the same year that the first slaves were brought to Virginia, while, at the same moment, Native American people began to be pushed from their lands. The contrasting stories of freedom, slavery, and dispossession are viewed now as paradoxical—what Edmund Morgan described as "the American paradox"—but to early-seventeenth-century English people they were not. Slavery and dispossession were perceived as undesirable but justified by a greater good. Such logic reflected the emergence of reason of state thinking, which placed interest before virtue in political calculations. Reason of state shared a common basis with discourses of popular government in the political thought of necessity and self-preservation that flourished in the early seventeenth century. Indeed, the nexus between reason of state thinking and discourses of popular government had been established since the early sixteenth century, having been brought together in Niccolò Machiavelli's *Discourses on Livy*. Exploring these entangled discourses in the creation of the colony in Virginia helps explain why they were not mutually exclusive. Although popular government and reason of state had a common source in the politics of necessity, both were regarded as potentially dangerous ways of discussing politics, particularly on the national level. Much adventurous thinking about both discourses accordingly occurred away from the national stage, and especially in the semi-sovereign bodies politic that were created by corporations: notably, in chartered companies. Of these, the Virginia Company afforded a space in which early-seventeenth-century English people could put such dangerous ideas into practice.[1]

Early modern European sovereigns were engaged in two struggles over their authority. The first was the effort to impose their dominance over internal rivals

---

For their extensive feedback on this paper, the author would like to thank Quentin Skinner, Noel Malcolm, and Saliha Belmessous as well as the organizers and participants in the conference "Virginia in 1619: Legacies for Race, Commonwealth, and Empire."

1. Edmund S. Morgan, *American Slavery, American Freedom: The Ordeal of Colonial Virginia* (New York, 1975), 6. For reason of state, see Noel Malcolm, *Reason of State, Propaganda, and the Thirty Years' War: An Unknown Translation by Thomas Hobbes* (Oxford, 2007).

for power, both feudal and religious, as well as over contiguous territories. This was the fight for the very foundation of their states. The second was the battle with one another for survival, or self-preservation. Particularly after the Reformation, the society of European nations was a dangerous world characterized by constant conflict in which, as Thomas Hobbes would observe, sovereigns faced off against one another like gladiators. Early modern sovereigns and their apologists defined both of these struggles—for the creation of states and for survival—in terms of the pursuit of glory and greatness. And greatness, they concluded, would be achieved by expansion. It was in these terms that the English understood the creation of a colony in Virginia in 1607. The first decade of the seventeenth century was relatively peaceful in Europe compared to the violence of the preceding decades during the Wars of Religion in France, as well as the wars between Spain and the Low Countries and conflict between Spain and England. It was, however, merely a moment in which tensions simmered before the outbreak of the Thirty Years' War in 1618—a war in which the leaders of the Virginia Company became deeply interested.[2]

The logic of greatness, survival, and reason of state, as well as the language of the commonwealth, were adopted by the seventeenth-century agents of expansion: the Dutch East India Company (Vereenigde Oost-Indische Compagnie, or VOC), the English East India Company, and the Virginia Company, to name three of the most important. These chartered companies saw themselves as semi-autonomous sovereigns and as civil societies in themselves. To incorporate was to create a single legal person from a body politic and thereby create a person who could represent that plurality of people. States were themselves corporations. When early modern authors explained the body politic of the state, they turned to the medieval and Roman law discourse of a fictive body that speaks and acts for the people it represents. All corporations, not only states, were understood to be bodies politic: that is, to be political communities whose members had a duty to act for the common, or public, good. The Church was one of the first medieval communities to be understood as a corporation with a discrete membership that acted for its common good. Over the following centuries, this understanding of corporations as bodies politic was extended to other communities, including cities such as London as well as trading corporations, particularly public joint-stock companies.[3]

---

2. Thomas Hobbes, *Leviathan*, ed. Richard Tuck (Cambridge, 1991), 90.

3. F. W. Maitland, *State, Trust, and Corporation*, ed. David Runciman and Magnus Ryan (Cambridge, 2003). On the state as a corporation, see Runciman, *Pluralism and the Personality of the State* (Cambridge, 1997); and Quentin Skinner, "A Genealogy of the Modern State," *Proceedings of the British Academy*, CLXII (2009), 325–370.

Early English joint-stock companies were charged with overseas trade and exploration. The first of these was the Muscovy Company, chartered in 1555, followed by the Levant Company (1581) and the East India Company (1600). In early modern England, these corporations, like the state, were understood to be "common wealths," from the Roman *res publica:* namely, societies that pursued the shared, or common, values (or the good) of their members. An extensive discourse flourished on the qualities necessary for commonwealths to be maintained and extended. This discourse was articulated equally for the corporate commonwealths of church, city, and joint-stock trading company as it was for the state. In fact, it was articulated more freely in these nonstate bodies politic because they were less constrained by the presumptions of deliberative political discourse in the presence of ambitious claims for monarchical power. Through the language of the commonwealth, these corporations were presented as bodies politic whose citizens (a term used in cities but also at times in chartered companies), or members, were responsible for the conduct of political life, largely through the performance of public office.[4]

By the late sixteenth century, well before plans had been drafted to establish a colony in Virginia through the instrument of a joint-stock company, the language of the commonwealth was no longer dominated simply by the idea of virtue and the performance of public duties. The calculation of interest had an increasingly important role in political debate, particularly at a time when previous generations' optimism about the potential for virtuous action had been eroded by religious war. Governing by interest as well as by virtue was understood to be the means by which commonwealths could not only preserve themselves but also make themselves great. Again, these ideas were employed as much in the context of the numerous nonstate corporate commonwealths as they were for the state itself. Indeed, these were precisely the terms in which the Virginia Company was first imagined and then established.

"Reasons to Move the High Court of Parliament" was one of the earliest works outlining the way in which the Virginia colony was conceived. This docu-

---

4. For the formation of the English corporate system, see Phil Withington, *The Politics of Commonwealth: Citizens and Freemen in Early Modern England* (Cambridge, 2005). For the application of this insight to chartered companies, see Andrew Fitzmaurice, *Humanism and America: An Intellectual History of English Colonisation, 1500–1625* (Cambridge, 2003); and Philip J. Stern, *The Company-State: Corporate Sovereignty and the Early Modern Foundations of the British Empire in India* (Oxford, 2011). Stern's *Company-State* has made the boldest exploration of chartered companies as bodies politic and has been followed by a series of subsequent studies, such as Henry S. Turner, *The Corporate Commonwealth: Pluralism and Political Fictions in England, 1516–1651* (Chicago, 2016); and Steven Press, *Rogue Empires: Contracts and Conmen in Europe's Scramble for Africa* (Cambridge, Mass., 2017). On the centrality of office in early modern political thought, see Conal Condren, *Argument and Authority in Early Modern England: The Presupposition of Oaths and Offices* (Cambridge, 2006).

ment, thought to have been written in 1605 or 1606, endorsed publicly backed colonization and rejected the private ventures that were still pursued despite frequent failures. David Quinn argues convincingly that Edward and Thomas Hayes were the authors of the tract based on content, style, and a letter they had written in early April 1606 to Robert Cecil, the earl of Salisbury. The letter informed Salisbury that they had authored a tract arguing for a new colonizing venture that was neither "private" nor financed by the state and that sought the endorsement of Parliament. Edward Hayes had been engaging in English colonizing enterprises for more than twenty years. He participated in Sir Humphrey Gilbert's 1578 venture to Newfoundland by financing his own vessel in Gilbert's fleet, upon which he lost most of his father's fortune—one motivation for now looking to other means of financing colonizing ventures, as he stated in the letter to Cecil. Before that, he had been a tutor to the son of Sir Thomas Hoby, the translator of Baldassare Castiglione's *Courtier*. To secure such a job, Hayes must have been learned in the *studia humanitatis*—history, moral philosophy, poetry, rhetoric, and grammar—the disciplines that furnished the moral philosophy of the commonwealth, both in terms of the Renaissance ideals of virtue and the new currency of interest.[5]

The title "Reasons to Move the High Court of Parliament" is deceptive and has prompted historians to argue that the tract was written to raise funds for the Virginia colony from members of Parliament. As the original manuscript shows, however, this title was added in 1607 by "T. Gerolyn," who presented the work as his own when he sent it to the parliamentarian Sir Julius Caesar. Thomas and Edward Hayes had said only that their proposal for public funding of a venture "requyreth the Consent of Parliament," and the title they gave the tract was more

5. For consistency with the scholarship, I use the title "Reasons to Move the High Court of Parliament." The manuscript of the tract is in the British Library: "Reasons or Motives for the Raising of a Publique Stocke to Be Imploied for the Peopling and Discovering of Such Countries as Maye Be Fownde Most Convenient for the Supplie of Those Defects Wch This Realme of Englande Most Requireth," [circa 1605–1606], Landsdown MS, fols. 356–357, British Library, London. In a different hand, the back of the manuscript was signed in 1607 by T. Gerolyn, who also, in that place, gave it the title that has subsequently been used, namely: "Reasons to Move the High Court of Parlam[en]t to Raise a Stocke." For a published version, see "Reasons to Move the High Court of Parlament to Raise a Stocke for the Maintaining of a Collonie in Virgenia," 1606, in David B. Quinn, ed., with the assistance of Alison M. Quinn and Susan Hillier, *New American World: A Documentary History of North America to 1612*, 5 vols. (New York, 1979), V, 168–170. See also Edward and Thomas Hayes to the earl of Salisbury, [circa Mar. 25–Apr. 9, 1606], ibid., 167. Alexander B. Haskell argues for Edward Hayes's patron, Robert Cecil, as the author of this tract, or at least for his ventriloquism through the Hayeses; see Haskell, *For God, King, and People: Forging Commonwealth Bonds in Renaissance Virginia* (Williamsburg, Va., and Chapel Hill, N.C., 2017), 159. For Edward Hayes's background and education, see Fitzmaurice, *Humanism and America*, 45–46. On private ventures, see, for example, George Weymouth's proposed 1605 "marchante voyage to Virginia," in Alexander Brown, ed., *The Genesis of the United States*, 2 vols. (Boston, 1890), I, 33.

representative of the breadth of its argument: namely, "Reasons or Motives for the Raising of a Publique Stocke to Be Imploied for the Peopling and Discovering of Such Countries as Maye Be Fownde Most Convenient for the Supplie of Those Defects Wch This Realme of Englande Most Requireth." In the essay, Thomas and Edward Hayes stated that "private purses are cowld Compfortes to adventurers and have ever ben fownde fatall to all interprices hetherto undertaken by the English by reason of delaies, Jeloces and unwillingness to backe that project which succeeded not at the first attempt." Condemning private ventures, the Hayeses declared: "It is honorable for a state rather to backe an exploite by a publique consent, then by a private monopoly." Clearly, one of their objectives was to argue for crown support for the enterprise, and that is the context for the work, and for the idea of a commonwealth, that Alexander B. Haskell explores in this volume. When members of the Virginia Company spoke of commonwealths, however, they could have three different commonwealths in mind—the state, the company itself, and the colony they were establishing—and it is always necessary to parse their use of the term. When this tract spoke of a public enterprise and "public consent," it was not referring to the state. The public envisioned here was the public of a joint-stock company, the body politic of the corporation. The purpose of the piece was to argue that, because corporations were bodies politic, all their members had a stake in their successes. And such bodies politic were best suited to both the foundation and preservation of new colonies: they were "most apt to make a conquest, so are publique weales fitter to howld what is gotten and skilfuller by industrie to inrich it."[6]

The Hayeses then pointed out that the Dutch had very recently achieved great success with joint-stock corporations in the pursuit of overseas expansion: "The Example of the Hollinders is verie pregnant by a maine backe or stocke have effected marvellous matters in traficque and navigacion in fewe years." Indeed, for Hugo Grotius, who was employed by the Dutch East India Company to justify their ventures, the notion that wealth was to be gained through expansion was key to self-preservation, to achieving greatness, and thereby to rivaling Spanish power and saving reformed religion. The preservation and greatness of the body politic that Grotius sought, however, was not only that of the Dutch republic but also that of the body politic of the VOC as an instrument of Dutch power. It must be remembered that a central purpose of Grotius's *Mare Liberum* and his *De Jure Praedae* (which are foundational texts in the law of nations) was to justify the intervention of the Dutch in Asia but specifically to justify the

---

6. Edward and Thomas Hayes to the earl of Salisbury, [circa Mar. 25–Apr. 9, 1606], and "Reasons to Move the High Court of Parlament," both in Quinn, ed., *New American World*, V, 167, 169–169. On different commonwealths, see Fitzmaurice, *Humanism and America*, 71–92.

capture of the Portuguese ship, the *Santa Caterina,* by VOC admiral Jacob van Heemskerk in what are now known as the Straits of Singapore. Accordingly, Grotius made the case that Heemskerk and the Dutch East India Company had a right to pursue their own self-preservation in a state of nature. The preservation of the Dutch state followed from that first right.[7]

The languages of self-preservation and reason of state were similarly powerful in "Reasons to Move the High Court of Parliament." The first reason the Hayeses gave for colonizing was: "All Kingdomes are maintained by Rents or traficque, but especially by the latter." This statement that wealth was the means by which kingdoms were maintained was not conventional in the early seventeenth century. Political discourse from the sixteenth century through to the eighteenth was characterized by a debate about whether the consideration of virtue or expedience (which included wealth) was the best means through which to govern. The classical response to this question, established by the Romans and adopted by Renaissance humanists, was that both qualities were necessary but that in any conflict between them virtue should prevail. Over the course of the sixteenth century, however, pessimism about the possibilities of virtuous government and rivalries between states drove a growing concern with expedience and wealth. Virtue was not dismissed, but it was moderated by questions of interest and reinterpreted, in rather Machiavellian terms, as *prudence,* a key term in reason of state thinking.[8]

Giovanni Botero, the man who introduced the term prudence to political thought, was one of the key figures in recalibrating political argument in this manner. When the Hayeses stated that kingdoms are maintained by "traficque," or trade, they echoed one of the central claims of Botero's political economy at the same time that the debate about the relative merits of virtue and wealth as sources of greatness was still very much alive. This tone and its associations with reason of state thinking was further underlined when the Hayeses expanded on their main themes:

> Where Collonies are fownded for a publique-well maye continewe in better obedience, and become more industrious, then where private men are absolute signors of a vioage, for as much as better men of haviour and qualitie will ingage themselves in a publique service, which carrieth more

---

7. "Reasons to Move the High Court of Parlament," in Quinn, ed., *New American World,* V, 168. For *Mare liberum,* see Hugo Grotius, *The Free Sea,* trans. Richard Hakluyt, with William Welwod's critique and Grotius's reply, ed. David Armitage (Indianapolis, Ind., 2004). For *De jure praedae,* see Grotius, *Commentary on the Law of Prize and Booty,* ed. Martine Julia van Ittersum (Indianapolis, Ind., 2006), 21.

8. Ibid.

reputacion with it, then a private, which is for the most parte ignominious in the end, as being presumed to ayme at a lucre and is subject to emulacon, fraude and invie, and when it is at the greatest hight of fortune, can hardly be tolerated, by reason of the Jelosie of state.

Here again, the public and the "publique-well" (or common good, or common wealth) that are envisaged are not those of the state. The Hayeses were referring to the commonwealth of the company itself. The public service performed by the adventurers is similarly service to the commonwealth of the joint-stock corporation. The essay contrasts the public service performed by adventurers in establishing colonies for the commonwealth of their joint-stock companies with efforts made by adventurers who are not acting for a corporation, and are therefore said to be acting privately, even if they might be said to be acting for the state.[9]

What is remarkable about this passage from "Reasons to Move the High Court of Parliament" is that the comparison was framed in terms of "Jelosie of state." The Hayeses argued that private adventurers, far from performing public acts for the good of the state, excited the "Jelosie of state" when their ventures were successful, or at the "hight of fortune." At the same time, the Hayeses suggested that corporations did not excite the jealousy of the state, presumably because they were themselves bodies politic created by the crown to pursue the common good of their members rather than any person's individual ends (which conformed with the classical notion of corruption). When the Hayeses cast the absence of a rivalry between trading corporation and state as an absence of the jealousy of the state, they were introducing one of the key terms in reason of state thinking to the understanding of the joint-stock company. This body politic, they argued, made colonization a public affair (meaning an affair of the corporation) and thereby evaded the problem of the subjects of the state becoming victims of reason of state thinking. They made no distinction between the political thought of the state as a commonwealth and the corporate company as a commonwealth.[10]

The analysis of interest and expedience in this tract extended into a discussion of the justice of the colony in relation to both the claims of other European states, notably Spain, and the claims of Native Americans. The Hayeses observed

---

9. Giovanni Botero, *Della ragion di stato* (Venice, 1589); Giovanni Botero, *A Treatise, concerning the Causes of the Magnificencie and Greatnes of Cities*, trans. Robert Peterson (London, 1606); "Reasons to Move the High Court of Parlament," in Quinn, ed., *New American World*, V, 168.

10. "Reasons to Move the High Court of Parlament," in Quinn, ed., *New American World*, V, 168. On reason of state and commerce, see Istvan Hont, *Jealousy of Trade: International Competition and the Nation-State in Historical Perspective* (Cambridge, Mass., 2005).

that England's claim to Virginia had been weakened by its failure to follow up discovery with occupation: "The want of our fresh and presente supplie of our discoveries hath in manner taken awaye the title which the Lawe of nacions giveth us unto the Coast first fownde out by our industrie, forasmuch as whatsoever a man relinquiseth mayebe claimed by the next finder as his just property, neither is it sufficient to set foot in a Countrie but to possesse and howld it." The concern here is with the Roman law of prescription. By the sixteenth century, Roman law was recognized as the basis for the emerging law of nations, the conventions that states employed to arbitrate their relations. In Roman law, and in the law of nations, prescription was a category within the broader law of occupation stipulating that anything that belonged to nobody could be possessed by the first person to seize it. Seizure was taken to mean use, so, in cases where a thing was seized and then abandoned, the law of prescription applied, and it became once more subject to possible occupation by the next taker.[11]

This language of occupation was crucial in justifying the new European empires of the sixteenth and seventeenth centuries. For Grotius, the argument of occupation assumed a pivotal place in the law of nations as part of a broader reconciliation between the understanding of justice and the idea of self-preservation, which together drove reason of state thinking. The occupation of territory, and the exploitation of nature that it demanded, was essential to survival, as Grotius and many contemporaries through to John Locke would observe. Occupation, therefore, was a fundamental part of a shift toward an interest-driven discourse of political thought. The centrality of the idea of occupation to the justifications for the Virginia Company's appropriations of territory in America is an important indicator of the prevalence of reason of state thinking in the visions of the company and colony. By 1619, the Virginian colony had appropriated large areas of Powhatan territory, all justified in the name of self-preservation—the self-preservation of the colony itself and that of England. Those justifications were mobilized not simply for English and rival European audiences but also against the Powhatans themselves. The latter claimed their territories with arguments based upon inheritance, occupation, and conquest— terms that were recognizable to the European law of nations and that partly provoked the English arguments for the justice of the enterprise.[12]

---

11. "Reasons to Move the High Court of Parlament," in Quinn, ed., *New American World*, V, 169. On prescription, see Andrew Fitzmaurice, *Sovereignty, Property, and Empire, 1500–2000* (Cambridge, 2014), 43–44, 226–227; and Edward Cavanagh, "Prescription and Empire from Justinian to Grotius," *Historical Journal*, LX, (2017), 273–299.

12. On occupation, see Fitzmaurice, *Sovereignty*. For occupation in Virginia: Andrew Fitzmaurice, "Moral Uncertainty in the Dispossession of Native Americans," in Peter C. Mancall, ed., *The Atlantic World and Virginia, 1550–1624* (Williamsburg, Va., and Chapel Hill, N.C., 2007), 383–409. On Pow-

The concluding remarks in "Reasons to Move the High Court of Parliament" focused on how some of the financial benefits of a successful company and colony could return to the crown. With the prospect of revenue, the Hayeses argued, the king would be more inclined to offer this new body politic his protection "to assist and protect the project." Moreover, they observed, the king's prerogative, which was necessary to create the company, should not be "valued at no thinge." The observations cast the relation between the body politic of the projected company and the crown in terms of the relation between an empire and a dependent sovereign or city. This was a mentality closer to the Holy Roman Empire's multiple jurisdictions than to the modern state. It belonged to a world in which sovereignty was cascading. Early modern colonies, such as Virginia, were established by such fragmented sovereign systems and by their satellites, such as the Virginia Company, rather than by monolithic states. Sovereignty was not only plural and contested on the borders of empire; it was also plural and contested in the metropolitan center. The Hayeses therefore had to remind their audience that the king should also have some stake in the benefits of a newly created commonwealth, or two newly created commonwealths—the company and the colony. They warned that not providing the king with some "convenient porcion" of the profits "would savior to much of affectacion of a populor State." Rather than warning that England might be misconstrued as a republic, the Hayeses were arguing that the new commonwealth could be misconstrued as a "populor State," or republic. This observation, as we shall see, was one of the first of several times over the following years that the members of the Virginia Company were associated with ideas of popular government. Collectively, those associations form part of the context in which the creation of the General Assembly in 1619 must be understood.[13]

When James I granted a charter creating the Virginia Council in 1606 and licensed it to establish two colonies in Virginia, the reality of the arrangements fell well short of the autonomy that had been envisioned in "Reasons to Move the High Court of Parliament." Philip Barbour observed that the king did not find attractive the Hayeses' proposal for "Parliamentary hands poking about in the Virginia project." He certainly had good cause to be concerned that parliamentary leaders might find space in the colony to pursue their own political projects. It is true that the council created by James in 1606 was able to appoint councillors

---

hatan claims to territory, see Fitzmaurice, "Powhatan Legal Claims," in Saliha Belmessous, ed., *Native Claims: Indigenous Law against Empire, 1500–1920* (Oxford, 2012), 85–106.

13. "Reasons to Move the High Court of Parlament," in Quinn, ed., *New American World*, V, 170. On fragmented sovereignty, see Lauren Benton, *A Search for Sovereignty: Law and Geography in European Empires, 1400–1900* (Cambridge, 2010).

and choose its own president as well as remove that president as it judged fit. The council was also given authority over the administration of law in the colonies and in the creation of "such constitutions, ordinances, and officers, for the better order, government and peace of the people of their several collonies." The control over law and the creation of offices were certainly important elements in the government of a body politic. Nevertheless, the Virginia Council was to answer directly to the crown, and the language of the first charter said little about creating a new body politic, either as a corporation or in the colonies.[14]

It has been suggested that, in the two or three years after James I granted the first Virginia charter in 1606, he began to have doubts about how far he was prepared to go to defend the enterprise against the fury of the Spanish. During this period, when the Virginia Council sat down to debate whether it should respond to the uncertain status of the colony in the law of nations (and therefore produce some form of justification of the plantation), it accordingly noted that, if the Spanish ambassador protested against the colony, "it is not conceav'd how far his Ma[jes]tie wilbe pleasd to avow it." Consistent with these fears, from 1607 James began to distance himself from the enterprise. In order to do so, and also to address the problems of government encountered by the first colony, he agreed to the drafting of the second charter of 1609. This document incorporated the Virginia Company as a separate body politic, creating a political society charged with establishing the new colony, and thereby removing direct responsibility for expansionist actions from the sovereign. The title of the new charter made clear what was at stake: "The Second Charter to the Treasurer and Company, for Virginia, erecting them into a Corporation and Body Politic." From the king's nervousness about the "Jelosie" of the Spanish state, a separate political society was thus created that would also evade jealousy between the adventurers and the English state. The Virginia Council was now obliged to report directly to the government of this new commonwealth, this corporation and body politic, and not to the king.[15]

The new leadership of the corporation, or body politic, of the Virginia Company was refined by the third charter (1612), under which the council was superseded by committees and more frequent company meetings. Courts of the

---

14. Philip L. Barbour, ed., *The Jamestown Voyages under the First Charter, 1606–1609*, 2 vols. (Cambridge, 1969), I, 14; "Articles, Instructions, and Orders Made . . . for the Good Order and Government of the Two Several Colonies and Plantations . . .," Nov. 20, 1606, in Brown, ed., *Genesis of the United States*, I, 67, 73.

15. Susan Myra Kingsbury, ed., *The Records of the Virginia Company of London*, 4 vols. (Washington, D.C., 1906–1935) (hereafter cited as *RVC*), III, 2; "The Second Charter to the Treasurer and Company, for Virginia, Erecting Them into a Corporation and Body Politic . . .," May 23, 1609, in Brown, ed., *Genesis of the United States*, I, 208. On James's doubts, see Kingsbury, ed., *RVC*, I, 22.

treasurer and company were to meet on a weekly basis and, for matters of the "weal publick," "four great and general courts" were to be held yearly with the "power to regulate the government (appoint or remove officers, make laws etc)." The 1612 charter admitted a large number of "additional adventurers," including numerous "Cittizens of London." The company was also granted the power to "correct and chastise" "abuses, not to be tolerated in any civil government." Through these two charters of 1609 and 1612, the company, and its colony, was remade as a self-governing body politic with its own legal system and citizens, governed by its own political assembly and officers, whom it had the power to appoint and dismiss. It also gained authority over territory, trade, law, and government in Virginia itself. It shared a monarch with England, as did Scotland, Wales, and Ireland. The negative side of such independence was reflected, notoriously, in the tariffs that were to be imposed on any goods imported by the company into England following an initial waiver period of seven years—a policy placing it "outside the English fiscal system" and on a similar footing to foreign sovereign nations.[16]

In 1618 and 1619, the governments of Virginia and the Virginia Company were reformed further, which included the creation of what would come to be known as the House of Burgesses. These reforms should be seen, not as a rupture from the previous regime, but as the culmination of the establishment in 1609 of the Virginia Company as a new body politic, no less than a new political society, charged with founding another political society in America. The company, accordingly, continued to embrace the language of the commonwealth to explain the nature of the body politic both as a company and as a new plantation. That language was echoed in the daily actions of the enterprise. In 1618, in its "Instructions to George Yeardley," the company stated the overtly political ambition that a "flourishing State might . . . be raised." Yeardley, the new governor of that "state," was charged with creating a "Council of State"—later known as the House of Burgesses—as one of the instruments for governing that state. The "Instructions" made it clear that the model for that new political society was the body politic of the company itself. The aim was to establish "a laudable form of Government by Majestracy [that is, office holding] and just Laws" in the same manner "as we have already done for the well ordering of our Courts here [in the company] and of our Officers and accions." Plantations in the colony were not to be placed "straglingly" but rather should "be united together in one seat and

---

16. "A Third Charter of King James to the Treasurer and Company for Virginia," Mar. 12, 1612, in Brown, ed., *Genesis of the United States*, II, 540–553 (esp. 541 n. 1, 548–550, 551). On tariffs, see Wesley Frank Craven, *Dissolution of the Virginia Company: The Failure of a Colonial Experiment* (New York, 1932), 222–225, esp. 223n.

territory that so also they may be incorporated by us into one body corporate and live under Equal and like Law." The body corporate of the company was the model for the body politic of the colony. Other commonwealths were also held out as models, so that the instruction to establish public lands in order to support "Magistracy and officers," and thereby evade corruption, was to follow the "example of the most famous Common Wealthes both past and present."[17]

In 1619, when Edwin Sandys was elected the new treasurer of the company, he employed again the language of the creation of a new state that had been used in the "Instructions to Yeardley." Sandys's election is generally represented as a response to the misgovernment of the company by the Smythe administration. His election additionally reflected a desire to diversify the economic base of the colony. Sandys's victory should also be viewed in the context of the outbreak in 1618 of the Thirty Years' War—a conflict into which almost all the states of Europe were drawn—which was provoked by the claim of the Elector Palatine, Frederick V, to the throne of Bohemia. The war, which ended only with the Peace of Westphalia in 1648, was initially religious. But, as sovereigns crossed confessional boundaries in order to strengthen their positions, it became progressively more strategic and generated deep cynicism about the art of politics, a cynicism that spurred the growth of writing and discourse about reason of state.[18]

Sandys was one of the members of Parliament who vehemently supported the claims of Frederick V, who was married to James I's daughter Elizabeth. He belonged to a group that included William Cavendish, the earl of Southampton, and Dudley Digges, all of whom were deeply frustrated by James I's equivocation in coming to the support of his son-in-law and daughter, particularly after the disastrous Battle of White Mountain in 1620 when Bohemia was lost. What these men—Sandys, Cavendish, Southampton, and Digges—had in common, apart from their agitation in Parliament for a stronger commitment to the Protestant cause in the war, was that they were all leading members of the Virginia Company. This was not a coincidence. The men met to discuss their plans in Southampton's house in Holborn. They viewed the company and the colony as means to project English power and to take the fight to the Habsburgs; as such, they used the company to pursue their own autonomous foreign policy objectives when confronted by what they saw as the apathy of the state.[19]

---

17. Kingsbury, ed., *RVC*, III, 98–99, 104. On the language of the commonwealth in Virginia, see Fitzmaurice, *Humanism and America*.

18. Malcolm, *Reason of State, Propaganda, and the Thirty Years' War*, 93.

19. Ibid., 77–78; Theodore K. Rabb, *Jacobean Gentleman: Sir Edwin Sandys, 1561–1629* (Princeton, N.J., 1998), 215, 261.

In his speech to the Quarter Court on November 17, 1619, Sandys stated his desire to restore "the Publique now lately decayed." His reference was to the attempt by his administration to expand the public lands of the company and diversify the crops away from the focus on tobacco. But he also used "public" throughout this speech to refer to the public good of the company and the colony and saw the maintenance of public land as fundamental to the pursuit of the public, or common, good. His speech took the form of a historical panegyric of the colony, praising and blaming the virtues and defects of various colonial leaders since Virginia's founding for their contributions to the colony's maintenance and flourishing. Regarding matters "Touching the Publique," Sandys, for example, reminded the Court of Sir Thomas Gates's service, whereby through "his wisedome, valor and industry, . . . in the middst of so many difficulties laid a foundacion of that prosperous estate of the Collonie, which afterward in the vertue of those beginings did proceed." Sir Thomas Dale had built "upon those foundacions" and "reclaymed . . . those idle and disordered people and reduced them to labour and an honest fashion of life," setting up a "Common Garden" for "the good of this Company" and "other Publique workes" for "the goode of the Companie [and] for the service of the Publique." The provision of such public goods had enabled "many perticuler Plantacions to seate in Virginia" with the "hope and promise" of being able to borrow "from the Publique" until such time as they were established. Sandys again identified the provision of public goods with the pursuit of the common good or the common wealth of both the company and the colony. The language of the commonwealth accordingly implied the provision of specific economic and political goods that were to be above the reach of private interests, even as they served those interests. He similarly blamed the manner in which "all these publique provisions" had "beene utterly Laid wast" by the previous administration of the company. The reintroduction of the system of public goods would, he argued, lay the foundation for a "great state" in America: that is, for the greatness that, according to reason of state thinkers and echoed in Sandys's own *A Relation of the State of Religion,* was essential to survival in a dangerous world. Sandys concluded that he "hoped the Publique would agayne be well restored, A foundacion Laid for a future great state." The striking aspect of this ambition to establish a new and great state—a central goal of early modern political thought—was that it was to evolve from the body politic of a company.[20]

---

20. Kingsbury, ed., *RVC,* I, 266–267, 269; Edwin Sandys, *A Relation of the State of Religion* (London, 1605).

The dissolution of the Virginia Company reveals much about the perception of it as a body politic. The company, notoriously, was riven and ultimately destroyed by factions that, it was alleged, acted for their own private interests rather than for the common good. This was the charge brought against Sir Thomas Smythe's administration of the company. Smythe and his allies, according to the Sandys faction, had used the company magazines for their own profit while neglecting the welfare of the colony. Smythe and his son-in-law Robert Johnson responded with charges of corruption against Sandys, including overpayment of the offices of the treasurer and the director of the tobacco monopoly that the company had secured. From 1620, the king began to take interest in the affairs of the company and recommended his own nominees for their offices, but during company elections those recommendations were ignored.[21]

In early April 1623, Johnson, backed by the Thomas Smythe faction in the company (including the earl of Warwick and Nathaniel Rich) and driven by their common hatred and resentment toward Sandys and his associates, petitioned the king to establish a royal commission investigating the affairs of the Virginia Company. The king agreed, and the dissolution of the company began. Sir Edward Sackville, a partisan of the Sandys and Southampton faction, described the backers of Johnson's petition as "traitors" to the company, bringing the language of treason, a language of the state, to the understanding of the corporation as commonwealth. For their part, the Smythe group accused Sandys of attempting to establish a Brownist republic in America, referring to his support for the Puritans waiting in Leiden (these were the English dissenters who had taken refuge in the Dutch Republic and would in 1620 cross the channel to sail on the *Mayflower* and establish the Plymouth colony in New England). The question of popular government, or a republic, was at issue in the accusation against Sandys, as much as that of religious dissent; the two issues were linked. Sir Nathanial Rich recorded a now-notorious conversation with Captain John Bargrave at the earl of Warwick's house in which Bargrave declared that, after long acquaintance with Sandys, he had concluded, "There was not any man in the world that carried a more *malitious* hart to the Govermt of a Monarchie then Sr Ed. Sandys did." According to Bargrave's account, Sandys had claimed that if God "did constitute and direct a forme of Governmt it was that of Geneva"—that is, a Calvinist republic—and had criticized Bargrave for having frowned upon the "frame of the pre[se]nt Govermt of Virginia to as that wch inclines unto if not directly beeing a popular Govermt." Bargrave's meaning was that the Virginia

---

21. Nicholas Ferrar, *Sir Thomas Smith's Misgovernment of the Virginia Company*, ed. D. R. Ransome (Cambridge, 1990); Craven, *Dissolution of the Virginia Company*, 262.

Company and the colony were governed as republics, in practice if not in name. In response to Bargrave's disapproval, Sandys said it was his intention to "erect a free state in Virginia." This was the reason, Bargrave argued, that Sandys had asked the archbishop of Canterbury for permission to send "Brownistes and Separatists" to Virginia: their doctrines claimed "a libertie to disagreeing to the Govermt of Monarches." Sandys aimed to establish a plantation that would "have no Govermt putt upon them but by their owne consents," and he accordingly "aymed at nothing more then to make a free popular state there."[22]

The Sandys faction responded to these charges by attempting to establish that there was nothing inconsistent between popular government and monarchy. They thereby aligned themselves with a well-established Tudor tradition of monarchical republicanism, although in this instance they were arguing for another kind of mixed government: namely, monarchical democracy. On April 12, 1623, before the conversation between Rich and Bargrave, William Cavendish, the son of the earl of Devonshire and a partisan of the Sandys and Southampton faction in the company, had addressed an "extraordinary" court of the company in order to "acquaint them" with the news of Johnson's petition to the king. The officials were informed of the substance of the petition, which they agreed "was against the Company it selfe" (rather than against particular individuals, as Johnson claimed). They accordingly determined that they "ought to justify themselves, and to defend their proceedings" with their own petition to the king. To this end, Cavendish presented two tracts to the court that were the basis of their petition. One was "A Declaration of the Present State of Virginia," which had been written "by some of the Counsell" the previous Christmas. The other was entitled "A Relation of the Late Proceedinges of the Virginia and Summer Ilandes Companies, in Answere to Some Imputacions Laid upon Them." It had been produced by Cavendish himself, with the minutes reporting: "Wch discourse his Lo[rdship] said himselfe had drawne up."[23]

Cavendish's "Relation of the Late Proceedinges of the Virginia and Summer Ilandes Companies" contains an extended and remarkable defense of democracy. He conducts that defense in a way that reminds us that it was possible for

---

22. Craven, *Dissolution of the Virginia Company*, 258, 277, 305; Kingsbury, ed., *RVC*, IV, 194–195.

23. "An Extraordinary Court Held for Virginia and the Summer Ilandes on Satturday in the fforenoone the 12th of Aprill 1623," in Kingsbury, ed., *RVC*, II, 346–348, 351; [William Cavendish], "A Relation of the Late Proceedinges of the Virginia and Summer Ilandes Companies . . . ," ibid., 353. It is very likely that Thomas Hobbes had some part in drafting "Relation." He was Cavendish's secretary at the time, having formerly been his tutor, and he was present at the meeting of the "Extraordinary Court" of the company. On Hobbes and Cavendish, see Malcolm, *Reason of State, Propaganda, and the Thirty Years' War*, 5–9; Quentin Skinner, "Hobbes and the *Studia Humanitatis*," in Skinner, *Visions of Politics*, III, *Hobbes and Civil Science* (Cambridge, 2002), 45–46.

an early modern English person to support one kind of constitution for the kingdom and another for any one of the various other kinds of body politic to which he or she might have belonged, whether church, city, or company. At the same time, those multiple constitutions created the potential for these "many lesser Common-wealths in the bowels of a greater, like wormes in the entrayles of a natural man" (as Thomas Hobbes would later describe such corporations) to introduce radical notions of politics into public debate or, at least, to introduce new ways of understanding how best to maintain a commonwealth and help it to flourish.[24]

Cavendish's treatise opened by recalling the charges brought by the Smythe faction against Sandys and his associates in their management of the monopoly they had secured from the king in 1622 for the importation of tobacco. The Virginia and Somers Islands Companies had sought this monopoly to redress the unfavorable terms that the government had imposed since 1619 on the importation and sale of tobacco in England—terms that were bankrupting the company and threatening its continued survival. In purchasing the monopoly on the distribution of tobacco, however, they had awarded inflated salaries to the managers of the contract: namely, five hundred pounds to Sandys as the director and four hundred pounds to the treasurer, Sandys's ally John Ferrar. Cavendish noted that Smythe, Johnson, and other members of their faction were irate at what they regarded as extortionate salaries but claimed that Sandys and Ferrar had performed public office for many years with "great paines charge and trouble without hope" . . . of "proffitt," for "the good and benifitt of both Plantacions." For the "generall good" they had neglected "so many opportunities for their owne private." The tobacco contract, he argued, was a different matter because it was "a buisines of meer merchandize and of distinct nature from a Plantation and the Goverment therof." Sandys and Ferrar had not sought responsibility for this business but had been chosen by the two companies, Virginia and Somers Islands, who valued their experience and knowledge in such an important matter to their survival. The first step in Cavendish's defense, therefore, was to distinguish between the performance of public and private actions and to portray the Sandys faction as acting for the common good.[25]

The second objection to which Cavendish responded was that the company court had been "overswayed" in the question of the unfavorable tobacco contract by Sandys' claiming that "itt was prest uppon them by the Kinge." Cavendish argued such claims of pressure and forceful persuasion in the assemblies were

24. Hobbes, Leviathan, ed. Tuck, 230.
25. [Cavendish], "Relation," in Kingsbury, ed., RVC, II, 353. On the monopoly, see Craven, Dissolution of the Virginia Company, chap. 8.

"manyfestly false" because "sundry Cittizens"—by which he meant the citizens of the company body politic—had declared that "never in any Society wheresoever they had been, [had they] found that liberty of Speech and vote or the Courte carryed wth that moderacion and Temper as these of Virginia and the Summer Ilands." All decisions by the court on the tobacco contract had been determined by a "generall ereccion of hands." This defense of citizens' acting with freedom of speech in a political assembly (one of several "societies" to which they belonged) was now moving toward the full-throated defense of democracy that was to follow.[26]

Cavendish next turned to the claim that "no buisines can be done in the Courte by reason of faction and wranglinge." In an understanding of government in which virtuous citizens acted in pursuit of the common good, factions were believed to be among the great corrupting forces of good government. Cavendish dismissed the charge, arguing that the company had almost a thousand members and only twenty-six adherents to the Smythe "faction." Moreover, he argued, "what soever they have alleadged as ffaction in the Companies must needs reflect on them selvs because in all Societies well governed the Major p[ar]t doth invovle the consent of the lesser." His meaning here is not entirely clear. On the one hand, he opposes the notion of a tyranny of the majority; on the other, he seems to imply that the Smythe faction had consented, at least tacitly, to the views of the majority through their participation in the assemblies. He articulates a contract theory of government: that is, that all societies "invovle" the consent of the people they govern. The foundation of the contract theory of government was that subjects consent to being governed in order to advance their preservation—making such a contract is an act of self-preservation for the subject. The basis of the contract, one of the pillars of the idea of representative government, lay in the ideas of self-preservation and survival that were central to the reason of state tradition. Cavendish was steeped in the reason of state literature.[27]

Cavendish began his defense against the charge of democratic tendencies in the government of the Virginia Company, and the colony, by reciting the allegation itself: "They alleadge that the Goverment as it now stands is Democraticall and tumultuous and thersfore fitt to be altered and reduced to the hands of some few personns." He then pointed out that the government was none other than that which had been created by James in his letters patent for the corporation,

---

26. [Cavendish], "Relation," in Kingsbury, ed., *RVC*, II, 354–355, 358.

27. Ibid., 355, 357–358. On contract, compare Hobbes, *Leviathan*, ed. Tuck, 94 ("Signes of Contract, are either Expresse, or by Inference"). On Cavendish and reason of state, see Malcolm, *Reason of State, Propaganda, and the Thirty Years' War*.

and it was therefore a "bold censure" to attack "a Goverment ordayned and constituted by such an authority." Before turning to a defense of democratic government, Cavendish accused the accusers of slander because "the Goverment is not Democraticall." The charter was granted by the king and therefore "supreme authority over the people of the Plantations" was held by the king. "The Goverment," he reasoned, "cannot be tearmed Democraticall wher the Kinge onely hath absolute power." Such a government, on the contrary, is "truly Monarchycall." Moreover, the company did not have "absolute power" over its citizens because when they "scape" its laws and punishments they could appeal to "higher Justice," although he did not specify whether that higher justice was the king or English law.[28]

Having thus attempted to blunt the accusations of democracy, Cavendish set about proving the advantages of democratic government. "Itt is true," he continued, "that according to yor Ma[jesty's] Institucion in their Letters Patente the Goverment hath some shew of a Democraticall forme wch is in this case the most just and most p[ro]fitable and the moste apt means to worke the ends and effect desyred by yor Ma[jesty]: for the benifitt encrease and wealth of these Plantacions." Democracy, therefore, would be the best, most just, and most profitable means by which to ensure the foundation and flourishing of these new bodies politic in Virginia and Bermuda. It was "Most just," he argued, because, although the plantations had benefited from the king's "grace," they had not been "made att yor Ma[jesty's] charge or expence but chiefly by the pryvate purses of the Adventurers." The adventurers would never have participated in "such an Accion wherein they interress their owne fortunes" if in the "governinge of their owne buisines their owne votes had been excluded." Democracy was a system of government most appropriate to a body politic in which each citizen had a stake, or interest, in the interest of the whole. He was not claiming that democratic government would produce a republic of virtue, although virtue was not excluded from the system; he was making an interest-based argument for democracy. Again, what we see here is an argument for popular government that is dependent upon the reason of state tradition and its emphasis on interest above virtue.[29]

Turning to the "profit," or expedience, of a system of democratic governance for the plantations, Cavendish continued, "Because of the great supplies wch the necessities of the people there often require and cannott be sent but by the purses of many, who if a few had the managinge of the buisines would and that not wthout reason leave them unsupplyed." In other words, the necessities of the

28. [Cavendish], "Relation," in Kingsbury, ed., RVC, II, 358–359.
29. Ibid., 359.

new body politic were most likely to be met by a large number of people acting in concert who would collectively have deep pockets. Democracy as the best means to satisfy the needs of the people drew on the contemporary emphasis on the self-preservation of the body politic and was consistent with Hobbes's later concern with that idea. What was novel was the notion that democracy was the best means for self-preservation.[30]

Cavendish concluded his thoughts on the expedience of democracy by declaring: "And wheras they [the Smythe faction] cry out against Democraci and call for Oligarchie they make not the Govermt therby either of better forme or more Monarchicall." This statement contains a number of significant points. It recalls the common claim of Elizabethan political thinkers that their government was a monarchical republic, a system of mixed government. Monarchy need not be opposed to popular government, republicanism, or, in this instance, democracy. Cavendish had already made it plain that the bodies politic of the Virginia and Somers Islands Companies, as well as the bodies politic of their plantations, had the king at their head, just as he was at the head of a number of other commonwealths.[31]

Finally, Cavendish proclaimed that, for trading corporations, the advantage of democratic government lay in the ability "to discerne what is the judgement of a Company if ther be not unanimity ther is no way but by pluralitie of voyces and if plurallytie of voyces were not ther would scarse att any time in poynte be unanimitie in any Assembly." His meaning here was that it was impossible to know the will of the people who make up the body politic ("the judgement of a Company") in cases where they do not agree without determining the majority view (a "pluralitie of voyces") through an assembly. He argued, moreover, that, while there may not be unanimity in the opinions of the company's members, there could be no unanimity in the company, or coherence in its purpose, without such a majority rule. He added, however, that the unanimity of the company was nevertheless now undermined by the despair of one faction who had failed to prevail with their "pryvate opinions" and who were ashamed of their "opposicion to publique good." These men, he complained, attempted "to drawe all things into their owne power" through plotting "conspirac[ies]."

30. Ibid.
31. Ibid., 359. The understanding of democracy in early modern England is a little-explored subject, although there is a substantial literature on early modern English "monarchical republicanism," beginning with Patrick Collinson's landmark essay, "The Monarchical Republic of Queen Elizabeth I," *Bulletin of the John Rylands Library*, LXIX (1987), 394–424. See also Markku Peltonen, *Classical Humanism and Republicanism in English Political Thought, 1570–1640* (Cambridge, 1995); Fitzmaurice, *Humanism and America*; Withington, *Politics of Commonwealth*; Mark Goldie, "The Unacknowledged Republic: Officeholding in Early Modern England," in Tim Harris, ed., *The Politics of the Excluded, c. 1500–1850* (New York, 2001), 153–194.

Here, once again, we find the language of betrayal of the state. These men were driven by "envy" aroused by the "change of the Officers and the great change in the State of the Plantacions" and were guilty of having provided "proteccion of personns declared enimies to the Companies."[32]

As a remedy to these ills, Cavendish requested that the "enimies" of the plantations be sent back to the colonies to face trial, suggesting that they were fugitives from justice. His broader point was that English jurisdiction was separate from that of Virginia, underlining once again that the colony was a body politic apart with a common sovereign. In these claims, which he delivered personally to the king, Cavendish also requested that James I otherwise allow the company to be "lefte freely to governe themselves according to their Lawes and letter Patente." Much of his defense confirmed the charges of popular government raised by Bargrave and Rich, albeit attempting to place them in a different light.[33]

Far from agreeing to secure for the company a kind of sovereign semi-autonomy, the crown established a royal commission to investigate the accusations of the Smythe faction. In October 1623, the Privy Council asked the company to voluntarily surrender its letters patent so that the affairs of the colony could be rapidly settled without the delay of legal action. After some attempts at stalling, a meeting of the company's assembly refused to give up the charter of incorporation. A writ of quo warranto, which then brought the matter before the King's Bench, was issued against individuals in the company rather than the company itself—the government's argument was, not that there was a problem with chartered companies, as such, but that authority in this particular company had been usurped by one faction.[34]

On May 24, 1624, the King's Bench issued a decree dissolving the company, and four days later James advised Parliament that its responsibilities had been assumed by the Privy Council. The dissolution of the company caused anxiety in the colony about the autonomy of their own body politic, particularly concerning whether they would be able to maintain the assembly of burgesses. This fear is understandable given the king's dismissal of Cavendish's defense of democratic government, which raised questions about whether the crown saw democracy as the source of the factionalism that had torn apart the company and whether the quasi-republican culture of the company and the colony that had developed since at least the 1609 charter was also responsible for the problems of the 1620s. The anxieties proved to be unfounded; the crown concluded that, insofar as the problems were constitutional, they were caused by the constitu-

32. [Cavendish], "Relation," in Kingsbury, ed., *RVC*, II, 359–360.
33. Ibid., 359–362; "An Extraordinary Court," ibid., 364.
34. Craven, *Dissolution of the Virginia Company*, 311–318.

tion of the company rather than the colony itself. The company's dissolution had little impact on Smythe's and Johnson's corporate autonomy, largely because during Sandys's ascent in the Virginia Company they had focused their investments in the Somers Islands Company and had continued to lead the East India Company.[35]

It is a moot point whether the political thought employed by the Sandys and Smythe factions was substantially different. The Sandys faction was certainly prepared to defend the rule of a popular form of government insofar as that government could be defended as a monarchical democracy. The support for a popular constitution, both within the company itself and in the colony, might be contrasted with the seemingly hard-headed views of the Smythe faction. Those views are best exemplified by Robert Johnson's writings, including his essays and his tracts promoting the Virginia colony. In these pieces, he strongly endorsed contemporary Tacitean political thought, which emphasized the importance of interest in governing politics while diminishing the idea that a commonwealth of virtuous citizens acting for the common good could rise above the corruption of the times. The problem, however, with contrasting the Smythe and Sandys factions in such a manner is that Sandys was also deeply concerned with contemporary ideas promoting the greatness of states, and Cavendish employed the concept of interest in defense of the Sandys faction. Indeed, for Sandys and Cavendish, such ideas were central to their own roles in leading the parliamentary faction that urged James I to provide more aggressive support for the Elector Palatine in his fight against the Habsburgs. Smythe and Johnson, on the other hand, were strongly supportive of the idea of the chartered company (and of the corporation more generally) as an autonomous body politic governed by conventions of political thought that those corporations shared with the state, so long as it served their own ends. When we consider the origins of the first political assembly in Virginia, therefore, it is important to remember that both factions in the Virginia Company had a reason for pursuing their goals through representative forms of government. Both had a stake in an understanding of politics that was based upon interest and virtue. While virtue nourished republican conceptions of government, the concern with interest encouraged political representation as a way of reconciling and harnessing competing interests within the body politic.[36]

35. Ibid., 320–322, 238.
36. On Johnson's Tacitism, see Andrew Fitzmaurice, "The Commercial Ideology of Colonization in Jacobean England: Robert Johnson, Giovanni Botero, and the Pursuit of Greatness," *William and Mary Quarterly*, 3d Ser., LXIV (2007), 791–820. For Sandys and the greatness of states, see Rabb, *Jacobean Gentleman*.

There is a broader question here about how the political thought of the chartered company related to the political thought of the state. The shared corporate ideology of the state and the corporation was the basis upon which the broader ideology of the state, including the emerging discourse of reason of state, could be transferred from state to corporation. More radically, one could argue that the political thought dealing with the state also drew upon the numerous bodies politic within the state, including chartered companies. Understood to be commonwealths in themselves, such companies were fertile grounds for discussions about the best form of commonwealth and the best means to preserve a commonwealth and make it great. When chartered companies were additionally charged with creating new commonwealths overseas, those debates were even more extensive. These lesser bodies politic provided an environment for experimenting with new ideas about politics and the best form of government—including both reason of state and democracy—without directly challenging the jealousies of the state.

"These Doubtfull Times, between Us and the Indians"
Indigenous Politics and the Jamestown Colony in 1619

JAMES D. RICE

On the first morning of the first representative assembly in English America, the speaker of the assembly—John Pory, a much-traveled and well-connected newcomer to the colony who doubled as secretary to Deputy Governor George Yeardley—addressed the twenty-two delegates seated in the choir of Jamestown's church. He explained that their primary task was to "establish one ... uniforme kinde of government over all *Virginia*" by interpreting the newly promulgated Great Charter, by recasting previous instructions from the Virginia Company and its governors as laws applying throughout the colony, and by petitioning the Virginia Company to modify some of the particulars of the Great Charter should they find them "not perfectly squaring wth the state of this Colony."[1]

Pory delivered these introductory remarks somewhat hastily, for, like many colonists that summer, he was "extreame sickly, and therefore not able to passe through long harangues." Perhaps, too, he was already fatigued from a long morning of preliminaries—an opening prayer by the Reverend Richard Bucke and the swearing in and seating of the burgesses—and by the "obstacles" presented by the "antient Planter" Captain John Martin. Martin, a turbulent character who had been in the colony since 1607, held a 1616 patent to a seven-thousand-acre tract on the south shore of the James River called Brandon Plantation, the terms of which made him largely independent of the government at Jamestown. The first obstacle to proceeding with the assembly emerged when two men from Brandon Plantation presented themselves as delegates. Governor Yeardley objected that they should not participate in the making of laws by which the inhabitants of Brandon Plantation were not bound. The assembly dispatched

---

1. "A Reporte of the Manner of Proceeding in the General Assembly Convented at James Citty in Virginia, July 30, 1619 . . .," in H. R. McIlwaine, ed., *Journals of the House of Burgesses of Virginia, 1619–1658/59* (Richmond, Va., 1915) (hereafter cited as *JHB*), 4–6 (quotations on 6). On Pory's career, see William S. Powell, *John Pory, 1572–1636: The Life and Letters of a Man of Many Parts* (Chapel Hill, N.C., 1977).

a message to Martin: unless he agreed to submit to the same "generall forme of governemente" as everyone else, his representatives should be "utterly . . . excluded, as being spies, rather than loyal Burgesses." The second obstacle was an urgent complaint that some of Martin's men had waylaid a canoe of Accomac Indians on the Eastern Shore and robbed them of their corn. "Suche outrages as this," the assembly feared, would "breed danger and losse of life to others of the Colony." The burgesses composed a second message to Martin, this time summoning him to Jamestown to answer for his men's actions.[2]

Having dealt with Martin, Speaker Pory could at last give his opening instructions, and the assembly could finally get down to business. That business, however, was not all that different from the preliminaries. The assembly of July 30–August 4, 1619, gave considerable attention to the personal behavior of colonists, to master-servant relationships, and to the marketing of tobacco. It also devoted much of its time—and nearly 25 percent of the published proceedings of the session—to discussing Native Americans and Indian traders. Far from distracting the assembly from its course, the incident between Martin's men and the Accomacs reflected issues that were central to life in the Chesapeake Bay region. Indian affairs had always been important, especially in the colony's first seven years. The end of the First Anglo-Powhatan War (1609–1614) had marked the beginning of five years of relative peace, during which Indians had appeared relatively infrequently in the colony's records. In 1619, though, something new and troubling was afoot. As Governor Yeardley told Pory, these were "doubtfull times between us and the Indians."[3]

In short, 1619 was a moment of political uncertainty and pressing, unresolved issues throughout the Chesapeake Bay region. The complexity and unpredictability of this state of affairs, and the high stakes involved, were evident in a series of incidents that year involving Indians, English Indian traders, and Jamestown's political leadership. Three of these occasions—Martin's men's theft of corn from the Accomacs, the conviction of a leading Indian interpreter for denigrating Governor Yeardley's authority, and an unexpected overture to the Jamestown colony from the Patawomeck nation on the distant Potomac River—were especially revealing. Each was complicated: there were never "two sides" to the story but rather multiple sides with competing agendas and alternative strategies for navigating such "doubtfull times." For the most part, these episodes played out

---

2. "Reporte of the Manner of Proceeding in the General Assembly," in McIlwaine, ed., *JHB*, 4–6 (quotations on 5, 6); "John Martin I," in Martha W. McCartney, *Virginia Immigrants and Adventurers, 1607–1635: A Biographical Dictionary* (Baltimore, 2007), 479–480.

3. "Reporte of the Manner of Proceeding in the General Assembly," in McIlwaine, ed., *JHB*, 4–17 (quotation on 7). The 25 percent figure excludes the formalities of the opening and closing sessions.

on Native ground and among Native peoples. The key actors included local werowances (hereditary chiefs of the region's Algonquian nations), their paramount chief, Itoyatin (successor to Powhatan, who died in 1618), and Itoyatin's brother and outer chief, Opechancanough (responsible for external affairs). All three events took place in or just beyond Tsenacommacah, the territory encompassed by Itoyatin's paramount chiefdom, rather than at Jamestown.[4]

THE OFFICIAL ACCOUNT OF THE FIRST OF THESE THREE EPISODES, the theft of Indian corn chronicled at the beginning of the assembly's minutes, is—like so much of the documentary record of the Jamestown era—disappointingly terse. By teasing out and contextualizing some of the key details, however, we can appreciate why the assembly considered this such an important affair. It's also possible to get a glimpse of the complex calculations of interest by all of the parties involved in the event, which happened at a key node in the Chesapeake's polycentric Native American diplomatic and exchange system.

Martin's men set out from Brandon Plantation in search of corn in the late spring or early summer, the time of year when food was at its scarcest in the Chesapeake Bay region. Times were even leaner than usual in early 1619, because the previous year's crop had been blasted first by "a great drought," as John Rolfe and then deputy governor Samuel Argall reported, and then by "a cruell storme of haile." It's likely that their need for corn was greater than usual, because Martin's Brandon Plantation was new and not yet fully productive.[5]

Once they were out on the water, Martin's agents had difficulty finding anyone to trade with. Not only was it the wrong time of year, but relations with the Chickahominies—near neighbors of Martin's and previously among the Jamestown colonists' most reliable trading partners—had soured since a 1616 incident in which colonists under the command of Deputy Governor Yeardley killed twelve Chickahominies for refusing to provide them with corn. The English had then threatened to execute another twelve hostages, forcing the Chickahominies to at last produce one hundred bushels of maize. A large group of Chickahominy

---

4. Itoyatin also appears in English documents as "Opitchipam" (or similar spellings). Powhatan was known to his own people during the 1610s as Wahunsonacock, and Pocahontas as Amonute (later Rebecca Rolfe). Since neither is the focus of this essay, however, I've retained the names by which they are most widely known today.

5. John Smith, *The Generall Historie of Virginia, New-England, and the Summer Iles* ... (1624), in Philip L. Barbour, ed., *The Complete Works of Captain John Smith (1580–1631)*, 3 vols. (Williamsburg, Va., and Chapel Hill, N.C., 1986), II, 263 (quotation). On the annual subsistence cycle, see Helen C. Rountree, Wayne E. Clark, and Kent Mountford, *John Smith's Chesapeake Voyages, 1607–1609* (Charlottesville, Va., 2007), 29–32; and James D. Rice, *Nature and History in the Potomac Country: From Hunter-Gatherers to the Age of Jefferson* (Baltimore, 2009), 35–42.

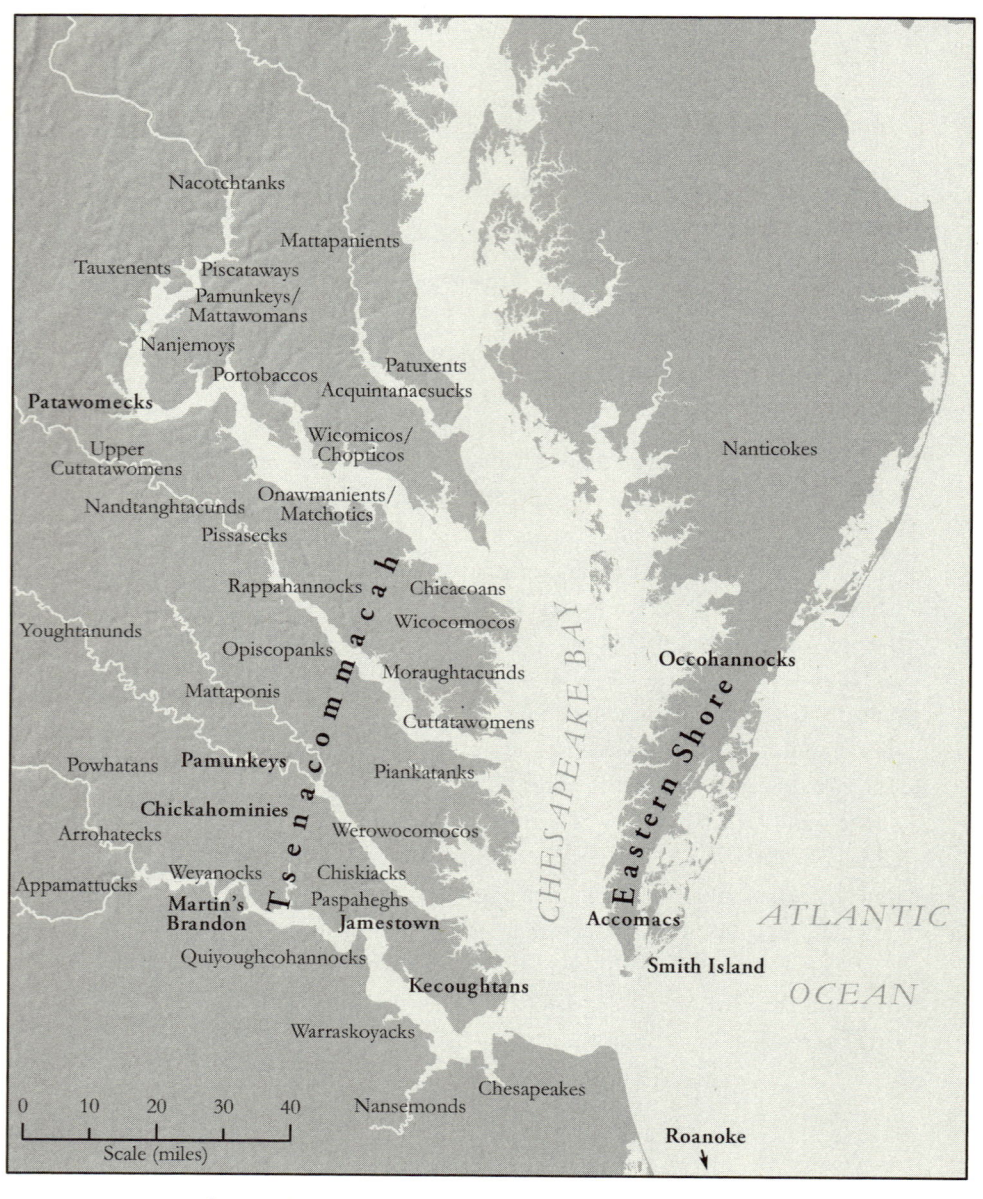

Indigenous Communities in the Chesapeake Tidewater, 1607–1619. Tsenacommacah extended from the fall line of eastern Virginia's major rivers to the Chesapeake Bay and from the Powhatan (James) River to the Potomac River. People and places mentioned in this essay appear in boldface. Drawn by Jonathan W. Chipman

"Runnagados" (renegades) had retaliated by killing nine colonists and making "a massacre of Deere and Hogges" before, according to John Pory, finding refuge under Itoyatin's protection.[6]

Thus Martin's men, led by Ensign James Harrison, sailed out of the James River altogether, bypassing the Chickahominies and other nations on the way to the Eastern Shore. Yet even there they found no corn, frustrated in their search by the lack of willing traders and by shallow creeks that they could not enter with their shallop (a single-masted vessel suited to coastal sailing). Then, just when it seemed that theirs would turn out to be "a harde voiage," Martin's men chanced upon "a Canoa coming out of a creeke," loaded with corn. When the Indians refused to trade, the Englishmen took the food by force, "measuring out the corne wth a baskett they had" and "giving them satisfaction in Copper, Beades, and other trucking Stuffe." The outraged Accomacs complained to Opechancanough "to procure them justice" from the English.[7]

It's not much of a story, as literature. Yet even the bare outline of this episode raises questions about the backstory and immediate context of this brief encounter, explorations of which begin to reveal the diversity and fluidity of indigenous and English approaches to navigating "these doubtfull times." Why, for example, did Martin's agents gravitate to the Eastern Shore? Why did the Accomacs appeal to Opechancanough instead of to the English governor Yeardley? And why did Yeardley panic—what did he fear might happen?

Martin's traders chose the lower Eastern Shore from among numerous potential destinations. Ensign Harrison sailed past a half dozen Indian nations on his way down the James River, and there's no indication that he attempted to contact any of them. (Captain Martin simply "sente his Shallop . . . into the baye," the complaint read.) Once in the bay, they could have entered the densely settled York, Rappahannock, or Potomac Rivers on the Western Shore, but instead they crossed over to the more lightly populated lower Eastern Shore. Martin, a seasoned colonist, knew better than most that the Accomacs and their Occohannock neighbors (who were linked together in an incipient paramount chiefdom or chiefly alliance) had a well-established trading relationship with

---

6. Smith, *Generall Historie*, in Barbour, ed., *Complete Works*, II, 256–257, 264–265, 291 (quotations); Susan Myra Kingsbury, ed., *The Records of the Virginia Company of London*, 4 vols. (Washington, D.C., 1906–1935) (hereafter cited as *RVC*), IV, 117–118; H. R. McIlwaine, ed., *Minutes of the Council and General Court of Colonial Virginia, 1622–1632, 1670–1676* . . . (Richmond, Va., 1924), 480; William Waller Hening, ed., *The Statutes at Large, Being a Collection of All the Laws of Virginia* . . ., 13 vols. (Richmond, Va., 1809), I, 287, 293.

7. "Reporte of the Manner of Proceeding in the General Assembly," in McIlwaine, ed., *JHB*, 5 (quotations); Kingsbury, ed., *RVC*, IV, 515; "James Harrison," in McCartney, *Virginia Immigrants*, 370.

the English that had in the past helped the two Indian nations and Jamestown itself resist incorporation into Tsenacommacah.[8]

Itoyatin's predecessor, his brother Powhatan, had inherited six subordinate chiefdoms along the James and York Rivers at some point between the late 1560s and early 1580s, then expanded his paramount chiefdom over the next several decades until Tsenacommacah encompassed most of today's tidewater Virginia. Powhatan had conquered Kecoughtan (directly west across the fifteen-mile-wide bay from Accomac) in the mid-1590s. If the past was any indication, the Eastern Shore werowances would be the next to fall into a tributary relationship with Powhatan. When the Jamestown colonists arrived in 1607, however, they found that the Accomacs were still an independent nation; they traded regularly with the Powhatans but remained only prospective additions to Tsenacommacah. The bay crossing, navigable but often hazardous for Indian dugout canoes, offered the Accomacs some protection. So, too, did their unusually long and close relationship with the English, which gave them a diplomatic and trading alternative to the Powhatans. By virtue of their location, they were likely among the first people to be visited by European ships in the sixteenth century; the Roanoke colonists, for example, had mapped the lower Eastern Shore in 1585. That the English provided copper and beads—known in Algonquian cultures as instruments for accessing the spiritual sources of all real power—as well as more mundane but useful items such as metal tools, both strengthened the Accomac werowance's hand and created a sense of reciprocity with the English that could be invoked to resist Powhatan and his successors.[9]

The Accomacs returned the favor by helping Jamestown resist incorporation into Tsenacommacah. In December 1607, after several weeks of captivity, council member Captain John Smith had undergone a ceremony in which he

---

8. "Reporte of the Manner of Proceeding in the General Assembly," in McIlwaine, ed., *JHB*, 5 (quotation).

9. David Beers Quinn, ed., *The Roanoke Voyages, 1584–1590: Documents to Illustrate the English Voyages to North America under the Patent Granted to Walter Raleigh in 1584*, Works Issued by the Hakluyt Society, 2d Ser., no. 104 (London, 1955), I, 245–246. For Powhatan's claim to the Eastern Shore, see John Smith, *A True Relation of Such Occurrences and Accidents of Noate as Hath Hapned in Virginia* ... (1608), I, 69, and Smith, *A Map of Virginia: With a Description of the Countrey, the Commodities, People, Government, and Religion* (1612), I, 150, in Barbour, ed., *Complete Works*; William Strachey, *The Historie of Travell into Virginia Britania* (1612), ed. Louis B. Wright and Virginia Freund, Works Issued by the Hakluyt Society, 2d Ser., no. 103 (London, 1953), 57, 68, 104–105; Helen C. Rountree and Thomas E. Davidson, *Eastern Shore Indians of Virginia and Maryland* (Charlottesville, Va., 1997), 30–31, 45, 48–49; and John Banister, "Of the Natives: Their Habit, Customes, and Manner of Living," in Joseph Ewan and Nesta Ewan, eds., *John Banister and His Natural History of Virginia, 1678–1692* (Urbana, Ill., 1970), 373. On the spiritual properties of "prestige goods," see Daniel K. Richter, "Tsenacommacah and the Atlantic World," in Peter C. Mancall, ed., *The Atlantic World and Virginia, 1550–1624* (Williamsburg, Va., and Chapel Hill, N.C., 2007), 29–36.

was proclaimed "a werowanes of Powhatan," who ordered that from this point onward "all his subjects should so esteeme" the Jamestown colonists as "Powhatans." Powhatan expected the English to move to a new town site closer to his capital and to make regular tribute payments. Smith, being a captive, outwardly agreed to the new arrangements but did not follow through beyond an initial payment. Instead, he spent the summer of 1608 exploring the Chesapeake Bay, seeking (among other things) to establish an English foreign policy independent of Powhatan's. One of Smith's first stops was the Eastern Shore, where the Accomacs gave the English a particularly warm welcome. They so "kindly intreated" Smith that he pronounced their werowance "the comliest proper civill Salvage wee incountred." In 1613, Captain (and future deputy governor) Samuel Argall acquired corn ("whereof they had great store") from them in the midst of the Anglo-Powhatan War of 1609–1614. The Accomacs also permitted the English to establish a short-lived saltworks and a fishing camp on an island within their territory in 1616. In 1619, the lower Eastern Shore was still the best possible place for Martin's men to trade for corn in a time of shortages. It was also, for the colony as a whole, one of the worst imaginable places for them to have committed "outrages."[10]

The Accomacs, then, were normally "in league and peace" with the English. But instead of complaining to Yeardley about the theft of corn by Martin's men, the Accomac werowance appealed to Opechancanough "to procure them jus-

---

10. Smith, *The Proceedings of the English Colonie in Virginia, [1606–1612]* . . . (1612), in Barbour, ed., *Complete Works*, I, 220, 224–225 (quotation); "A Letter of Sir Samuell Argoll Touching His Voyage to Virginia, and Actions There: Written to Master Nicholas Hawes, June 1613," in Samuel Purchas, *Hakluytus Posthumus; or, Purchas His Pilgrimes: Contayning a History of the World in Sea Voyages and Lande Travells by Englishmen and Others* (1625; rpt. Glasgow, 1906), XIX, 94 (quotation); Kingsbury, ed., *RVC*, III, 116; Transcription of "John Rolf's Relation of the State of Virginia, 17th Century," reproduced in "Virginia in 1616," *Virginia Historical Register, and Literary Advertiser*, I (1848), 106. See also Rountree, Clark, and Mountford, *John Smith's Chesapeake Voyages*, 80–82; Joe Jones, *Additional Archaeological Survey and Artifact Survey, the Arlington Site (44NH92)* (Williamsburg, Va., 2001), 4, 39; and Anne Floyd Upshur and Ralph T. Whitelaw, "Some New Thoughts concerning the Earliest Settlements on the Eastern Shore of Virginia," *Virginia Magazine of History and Biography*, L (1942), 193–198. The role of Powhatan's daughter Pocahontas in Smith's adoption is much contested, but Powhatan's attempt to incorporate the English as another dependent chiefdom is not in dispute. See Smith, *True Relation*, I, 57, 67 (quotation), Smith, *Proceedings*, I, 248, and Smith, *Generall Historie*, II, 146–152, in Barbour, ed., *Complete Works*; Frederic W. Gleach, *Powhatan's World and Colonial Virginia: A Conflict of Cultures* (Lincoln, Nebr., 1997), 109–122; James Horn, *A Land as God Made It: Jamestown and the Birth of America* (New York, 2005), 61–71; and Karen Ordahl Kupperman, *The Jamestown Project* (Cambridge, Mass., 2007), 228. For opposing takes on the Pocahontas story, see Helen C. Rountree, *Pocahontas's People: The Powhatan Indians of Virginia through Four Centuries* (Norman, Okla., 1990), 38–39; and J. A. Leo Lemay, *Did Pocahontas Save Captain John Smith?* (1992; rpt. Athens, Ga., 2010). The saltworks were at Smith's Island, which lies on the Atlantic side of the lower Eastern Shore (not to be confused with today's Smith Island, which is farther north and is inside the bay).

tice," thus signaling to Yeardley that he should not take their alliance for granted. The governor, who was simultaneously trying to mend fences with the Chickahominies, recognized the high stakes. The Accomacs had fed and otherwise supported the English whenever the colonists' relationship with the paramount chief soured. In return, they expected the English to serve as an effective counterweight against the Powhatans. The Englishmen's "outrages" risked not only strengthening the Powhatans' hand but also alienating an important ally and thus endangering "others of the Colony, w[hi]ch should have leave to trade in the Baye hereafter." It's not so surprising, therefore, that the 1619 assembly's first substantive action was to sanction John Martin.[11]

THE SECOND KEY EPISODE OF 1619 INVOLVING INDIANS AND JAMEStown's political leadership grew out of a conflict between two young English-Algonquian interpreters, Henry Spelman and Robert Poole, and culminated in the conviction of Spelman, by the assembly, for denigrating Governor Yeardley's authority. The official account of this incident is more detailed than that of the springtime theft of Indian corn by Martin's men; thus, the simple question of why a personal feud escalated to the point that the assembly had to adjudicate it yields broader insights into indigenous politics and the Jamestown colony. The Spelman-Poole affair, while deeply personal, also reflected the uncertain state of Powhatan-English relations in 1619—as well as significant divisions within the Virginia Company and at Jamestown over the colony's future direction.

Those whose lives were put in danger by Ensign Harrison's "outrages" against the Accomacs included the colony's three leading Indian interpreters: Thomas Savage, Henry Spelman, and Robert Poole. Savage, who came to Jamestown in 1607, had lived in Powhatan's household for nearly three years and had often served as an interpreter for both Powhatan and the English. After the First Anglo-Powhatan War ended in 1614, he developed close trading connections with the Accomacs and other Eastern Shore nations. Spelman, who arrived in 1609, also lived with Powhatan (briefly sharing a table with Savage) and later with the werowance of one of Powhatan's tributary chiefs. After the war, Spelman specialized in trading along the Potomac River. Last to arrive was Poole, who came to Jamestown in 1611. Although it's not known where he gained his experience, he became the English interpreter for Opechancanough after 1614 ("wholly ymployed by the Governor of messages to the greate King," John Rolfe noted), making him perhaps the most important of the three young men in

---

11. "Reporte of the Manner of Proceeding in the General Assembly," in McIlwaine, ed., *JHB*, 5 (quotation); Kingsbury, ed., *RVC*, III, 157, IV, 514–515.

1619. Between them, Savage, Spelman, and Poole had been present at most of the key events in Anglo-Powhatan relations since 1607. Needless to say, they all knew one another.[12]

Knew, but did not always like. In 1609, Savage and Spelman, increasingly uncomfortable living with Powhatan while war was brewing with the English, fled from his household. They did so with the help of Iopassus, a visitor from the Patawomecks, one of Powhatan's subordinate chiefdoms along the Potomac River. Iopassus was the Patawomeck werowance's brother and served as his outer chief (much as Opechancanough did for his own brothers Powhatan and Itoyatin). He first encountered the English boys while on a diplomatic mission to Powhatan in 1609. When Iopassus returned to Patawomeck, Savage and Spelman slipped away from Powhatan's side and joined Iopassus's retinue on its journey north. Savage, however, had second thoughts and returned to warn Powhatan of Spelman's escape; as a result of this betrayal, Spelman only narrowly avoided recapture. He lived with Iopassus until he was redeemed by Captain Argall during a trading voyage to the Potomac in late 1610. With Spelman acting as interpreter, Argall and Iopassus established an ongoing relationship. Over the next several years, the Patawomecks regularly sold much-needed corn to the English—and even, in 1613, handed Powhatan's visiting daughter Pocahontas over to Argall as a wartime hostage.[13]

The origins of the bad blood between Robert Poole and Henry Spelman are less clear, but by 1619 they were literally mortal enemies. During the 1619 assembly, Poole denounced Spelman for having recently spoken "very unreverently and maliciously" against Yeardley at Opechancanough's "courte." As a result, Poole testified, "the honour and dignity of his [Yeardley's] place and person, and so of the whole Colonie, might be brought into Contempte, by w[hi]ch ... mischiefs might ensue from the Indians." Spelman, called before the assembly to answer these accusations, denied most of Poole's story. He did admit, though,

---

12. J. Frederick Fausz, "Middlemen in Peace and War: Virginia's Earliest Indian Interpreters, 1608–1632," *VMHB*, XCV (1987), 41–64. See also Henry Spelman, "Relation of Virginea," in Edward Arber, ed., *Travels and Works of Captain John Smith, President of Virginia, and Admiral of New England, 1580–1631*, part 1 (Edinburgh, 1910), ci–cxiv; "A Courte Held the First of November 1624," in H. R. McIlwaine, ed., *Minutes of the Council and General Court of Colonial Virginia*, 2d ed. (Richmond, Va., 1979), 28; Kingsbury, ed., *RVC*, III, 244 (quotation); and Karen Ordahl Kupperman, *Indians and English: Facing off in Early America* (Ithaca, N.Y., 2000), 230–237.

13. Spelman, "Relation of Virginea," in Arber, ed., *Travels and Works of Captain John Smith*, part 1, ciii (quotation); Smith, *Generall Historie*, in Barbour, ed., *Complete Works*, II, 25–488; Raphe Hamor, *A True Discourse of the Present Estate of Virginia* . . . (London, 1615), 2–5; Rice, *Nature and History in the Potomac Country*, 81–83. The Patawomeck werowance's name was not recorded. "Iopassus" is sometimes spelled "Japazaws," but the hard *J* ("jay") doesn't exist in Algonquian languages; it's likely meant to be pronounced like the "Jo" in "Johannes."

to telling Opechancanough that the newly arrived Yeardley was a lame-duck governor, merely acting in that capacity until "a Governour greatter than this" arrived.[14]

Even this lesser offense, the burgesses were convinced, put "the whole Colony in danger." Some wished to have Spelman executed, or at least subjected to "sharpe punishments." The majority, however, contented themselves with stripping Spelman of his captain's title and military command and condemning him to seven years of servitude as the governor's interpreter. Spelman "muttered certaine wordes to himselfe" as the sentence was read, showing no remorse for his actions—a response that Pory interpreted as a sign that Spelman had "in him more of the Savage then of the Christian."[15]

Spelman's conviction did not mark the end of his feud with Poole. A few weeks after the 1619 assembly, Poole "perswaded" Governor Yeardley that Opechancanough, if properly approached, would be willing to come to Jamestown on a formal visit. This would have been an extraordinary development, as until then the paramount chiefs (Powhatan and his successor Itoyatin) and their outer chief, Opechancanough, had made a point of meeting English leaders on Indian ground. Yeardley had little choice but to pursue this opportunity. He sent two men to carry a formal invitation to Opechancanough and to serve as "pledges" (hostages) for the chief's safe return from Jamestown. But Opechancanough sent away the two Englishmen "wth frivoulous aunsweres, saying he never hadd any intent to come" to Jamestown.[16]

Opechancanough's curt rejection worried Yeardley, who immediately sent a shallop captained by an experienced Indian trader, William Powell, to Opechancanough's main town of Pamunkey on the eponymous Pamunkey River. John Rolfe joined the delegation—a sign of the importance that Yeardley attached to this meeting—and Spelman went as his interpreter. As the English ship approached Pamunkey, Poole came out to meet it. Once aboard, Poole doubled down on his deception, asking Rolfe and Captain Powell to meet with Opechancanough in person. They begged off, however, and sent Spelman and another Englishman to Pamunkey in their stead.[17]

---

14. "Reporte of the Manner of Proceeding in the General Assembly," in McIlwaine, ed., *JHB*, 15 (quotations). See also Kingsbury, ed., *RVC*, I, 310, III, 251, IV, 514–515.

15. "Reporte of the Manner of Proceeding in the General Assembly," in McIlwaine, ed., *JHB*, 15 (quotations); Kingsbury, ed., *RVC*, III, 242.

16. Kingsbury, ed., *RVC*, III, 244.

17. Ibid., 244–245. Given the wording of the account of Spelman's trial at the assembly, it seems probable that Poole had never left Opechancanough's side—that instead of testifying in person before the assembly he sent a "relation upon oath." See "Reporte of the Manner of Proceeding in the General Assembly," in McIlwaine, ed., *JHB*, 15.

Although his initial reception by Opechancanough and his councillors was "harshe," Spelman somehow managed to turn the situation around. It's not clear whether he met with Opechancanough without Poole present or bested Poole in a direct confrontation. But somehow, in the end (Rolfe reported), Spelman's explanation of the situation "was kindly taken" by Opechancanough. Poole, in contrast, now stood "accused and Condemned" by the Indians "as an instrum[en]t that sought all the meanes he could to breake o[u]r league." They seemed "very weary" of Poole, who (Rolfe was convinced) had "untruly delyvered" all messages "on both sides." Powell and Rolfe had no orders to recall Poole, though, and they feared that he might do even more damage if they confronted him directly—perhaps by persuading the Powhatans to do "some myscheif in o[u]r corne feilds." They would have to "gett him away by fayre means" at some later date. In the meantime, they returned to Jamestown with the good news of Opechancanough's apparent reconciliation with the colonists.[18]

The twists and turns in this series of events reflected the turbulent state of Anglo-Powhatan relations. Although the post-1614 peace had never been trouble free, tensions were on the rise. Opechancanough's role in the aftermath of the 1616 English killings at Chickahominy had provided an early indication of his stance toward the English: he had insisted "with much adoe" (through Spelman as interpreter) that he, and not the English, had "procured their peace." Ever since then, he pointedly emphasized, the previously independent Chickahominies had been paying him tribute and calling him "King." Like Opechancanough's similar assumption of the role of arbitrator after the 1619 robbery of the Accomacs by Martin's men, this version of events was intended to maintain the paramount chief's supremacy by undermining relations between the region's non-Powhatan tribes and the English.[19]

Powhatan's abdication in 1617, coupled with the death of Pocahontas in England that year, had opened the way to a more hard-line stance by his successor Itoyatin and by Opechancanough, who continued as outer chief. Furthermore, an important member of Pocahontas's entourage to England, an influential priest named Uttamatomakkin, had formed a harsh impression of the English during his stay in London and delivered a bitterly unfavorable report to Opechancanough upon his return to Tsenacommacah in 1617. New Virginia Company policies also made compromise less likely. Samuel Argall, who had captained the ship that carried Pocahontas to England, took over as deputy governor after returning from London in 1617 and implemented changes in the distribution

---

18. Kingsbury, ed., *RVC*, III, 245 (quotations), 253, IV, 117–118. The content of Spelman's explanation was not recorded.

19. Smith, *Generall Historie*, in Barbour, ed., *Complete Works*, II, 256–257.

of land (including the introduction of the headright system and the granting of larger parcels of land to government officials and private investors) that enabled English tobacco planters to spread out over a larger area than before. The growing number of colonists living near the larger Powhatan Indian population centers upriver from Jamestown, together with the continuing practice of private trade between Indians and newcomers, led to a "daily familiarity" between the two groups. It did not, however, lead to increased respect.[20]

Itoyatin's and Opechancanough's confidence in Poole, which made him both useful to the English and a suspect in their eyes, likely contributed to the interpreter's oscillating reputation among his fellow colonists. Still another turn in Poole's fortunes, just a few weeks after his apparent disgrace at Pamunkey, suggests as much. In January 1620, Pory relayed to the Virginia Company's treasurer in London, Sir Edwin Sandys, the surprising news that, although Yeardley and the council had fully intended to punish Poole and remove him as interpreter at the first opportunity, when Poole actually visited Jamestown they "were quite of another opinion." For fear of "discontenting Opoechancanough," Pory explained, "we thought it no wayes convenient to call Poole to accounte." Yeardley allowed Poole to return to Pamunkey and to continue as interpreter for Opechancanough. For his part, Opechancanough may have been merely pretending that he was weary of Poole at those moments when the interpreter was out of favor with Jamestown's leaders in order to seem agreeable; as subsequent events would show, Opechancanough had a penchant for lulling English authorities into a false sense of security by feigning consent to their initiatives.[21]

The Poole-Spelman feud also reflected a persistent division within the Virginia Company and at Jamestown over the direction of the colony's diplomacy. As J. Frederick Fausz has noted, Yeardley and Argall embraced different strategies while they were alternating terms as deputy governor during the late 1610s: "Yeardley wanted to secure Opechancanough's firm allegiance and relied on Poole's talents in doing so," whereas Argall "mistrusted the Powhatan-Pamunkeys and preferred to strengthen the Anglo-Patawomeke and Anglo-Accomac alliances through the efforts of Spelman along the Potomac and Savage on the Eastern Shore." Neither Argall nor Yeardley succeeded in permanently resolving the issue, however, for as deputy governors they were but a part of an

---

20. Kingsbury, ed., *RVC*, III, 73–74, 551 (quotation); J. Frederick Fausz, "Samuel Argall," in *The Dictionary of Virginia Biography*, ed. John T. Kneebone et al. (Richmond, Va., 1998), I, 197–199. On changes in the distribution of lands, see Edmund S. Morgan, *American Slavery, American Freedom: The Ordeal of Colonial Virginia* (New York, 1975), 92–97.

21. Kingsbury, ed., *RVC*, III, 253. On Opechancanough's friendliness, see Horn, *Land as God Made It*, 249–255.

ongoing debate in which many, including Virginia Company shareholders in England and colonists on the ground in Virginia, had a voice.[22]

This division over diplomacy was intertwined with a running debate over Jamestown's economic future. The choice, roughly speaking, lay between trying to foster a tobacco-centered economy or a more diverse system. Yeardley's Pamunkey-centered diplomacy fitted best with Jamestown's growing tobacco production. Although the market for Virginia tobacco was not completely established, and there was good reason to fear that Parliament might legislate Virginia's tobacco trade out of existence, tobacco exports nevertheless increased sharply in the late 1610s. Yeardley worried about the proliferation of dispersed tobacco plantations, which intruded ever deeper into Tsenacommacah—"it would behoove us not to make so lardge distances between Plantation and Plantation," he confided to John Pory—but the link between tobacco cultivation and spread-out populations was already well established. The best way to protect people on these scattered plantations was to focus the colony's diplomatic efforts on keeping Opechancanough happy, even if that meant retaining Robert Poole as his interpreter.[23]

Argall's diplomatic orientation toward the northern Chesapeake and the Eastern Shore, in contrast, remained attractive to those who favored an expansion of the Indian trade, fisheries, and other initiatives to diversify Jamestown's economy and broaden its geographic reach beyond the core of Tsenacommacah. The leadership of the Virginia Company in London embraced such plans in the late 1610s. They sent a new burst of directives to set up ironworks, make rope and other naval stores, produce silk and wines, and restore the Eastern Shore saltworks to support an expanded fishery. English ships setting out for Virginia from 1619 onward routinely carried "trucking" goods such as beads, copper, and hatchets. Company officials schemed to bring Italian glassworkers to Virginia to manufacture trade beads, treating "the ffurr and Glasse buissines" as a locally integrated program. An independent group of London investors also financed a substantial fur-trading venture, hiring an agent, interpreters, and a ship to carry on the trade.[24]

22. Fausz, "Middlemen in Peace and War," *VMHB*, XCV (1987), 52 (quotation).
23. "Reporte of the Manner of Proceeding in the General Assembly," in McIlwaine, ed., *JHB*, 7 (quotation). On tobacco production in the 1610s, see Lorena S. Walsh, *Motives of Honor, Pleasure, and Profit: Plantation Management in the Colonial Chesapeake, 1607–1763* (Williamsburg, Va., and Chapel Hill, N.C., 2010), 38.
24. It's easy to underestimate the seriousness of these efforts, partly because the teleological pull of tobacco-and-slaves is so strong and partly because the evidence of economic diversification is inherently more scattered than that regarding tobacco production and marketing. See "A Note of the Shipping, Men, and Provisions Sent to Virginia, by the Treasurer and Company, in the Yeere 1619," XIX, 126–129, "A Note of the Shipping, Men, and Provisions Sent and Provided for Virginia . . . in

The 1619 assembly echoed company officials by paying more attention to the Indian trade and other forms of economic diversification than it did to tobacco. In addition to sorting out the controversies involving Poole, Spelman, and Martin's agents, the burgesses recommended laws prohibiting colonists from pursuing grievances against Indians without the company's permission, regulating the employment and lodging of Indians, encouraging the education of Indian boys in an English "Colledge," policing the Indian trade, and providing for defense against surprise attacks. Additional laws mandated the cultivation of corn, hemp, flax, grapes, and mulberry trees (for silk production), encouraged skilled tradesmen to immigrate, and promoted the breeding of cattle and oxen. That some of these deliberations are difficult to categorize as purely economic or purely diplomatic measures shows just how intertwined the two were. The provision that "No man shall trade into the Baye" without putting up a bond for good behavior, for instance, both gave the governor the power to regulate that trade (an economic measure) and discouraged traders from behavior that might damage the colony's diplomatic relations.[25]

Secretary Pory exemplified the renewed push for diversification. "Three thinges there bee, w[hi]ch in fewe yeares may bring this Colony to perfection," he wrote Sandys: "the English plough, Vineyards, and Cattle." A good start, Pory reported, had already been made in these areas, so much so that Jamestown's cow keeper could afford to wear "freshe flaming silkes" to church on Sundays. Large numbers of cattle were imported, particularly from Ireland, and Virginia ships worked the bay and North Atlantic fisheries (though their work was hindered by a shortage of salt). Pory himself took up lands on the Eastern Shore in 1620, thinking it a fertile place to grow and trade for corn. It was he who reestablished the short-lived 1616 saltworks and fishing settlement on Smith's Island and, along with other investors, sought to open up the fur trade in the northern Chesapeake Bay. Though overshadowed in historical accounts by the rise of tobacco, this turned into a profitable trade. Pory listed current prices for furs and pelts for

---

the Yeere 1621 ...," XIX, 144–149, and "Newes from Virginia in Letters Sent Thence 1621 ...," XIX, 149–157, in Purchas, *Hakluytus Posthumus*; and Kingsbury, ed., *RVC*, II, 15–16 (quotation on 15). See also Kingsbury, ed., *RVC*, I, 423, 484–485, 493–494, 499, 501–502, 504, 507, 566–568, 583, 608, III, 115–117, 178–179, 196, 242–243, 278–279, 299–300, 386, 488, 495, 514–515, 526–527, 530, 581–588, 589–590. See also Smith, *Generall Historie*, in Barbour, ed., *Complete Works*, II, 267, 288–289; Virginia DeJohn Anderson, "Animals into the Wilderness: The Development of Livestock Husbandry in the Seventeenth-Century Chesapeake," *William and Mary Quarterly*, 3d Ser., LIX (2002), 377–381; Martha W. McCartney, "An Early Virginia Census Reprised," *Quarterly Bulletin of the Archaeological Society of Virginia*, LIV (1999), 179, 181; Keith Pluymers, "Atlantic Iron: Wood Scarcity and the Political Ecology of Early English Expansion," *WMQ*, 3d Ser., LXXIII (2016), 389–426.

25. "Reporte of the Manner of Proceeding in the General Assembly," in McIlwaine, ed., *JHB*, 9–14 (quotation on 14).

company officials in London: "bever skins that are full growne, in season" sold for seven shillings apiece, and well-worn pelts that had been broken in cost six shillings per pound. Within a short time, nearly a hundred colonists lived on the Eastern Shore and adjoining islands, "very happily," Pory wrote, "with hope of a good Trade of Furres there to bee had."[26]

There's no denying the deep personal animosity between Poole and Spelman, which is palpable in the documentary record even four centuries later. Yet there was more going on here than a personal grudge; otherwise the 1619 assembly would not have made room in its crowded agenda for Poole's testimony and Spelman's trial. The assembly did so because the conflict between the two young interpreters was thoroughly entangled with the central issues of both Powhatan and English politics—with crucial and difficult decisions to be made about the future of both the paramount chiefdom and the English colony. The chain of connections, then, runs outward from the Poole-Spelman feud to Itoyatin's and Opechancanough's hardening stance toward the English, to debates in London and Jamestown over the colony's diplomatic and economic strategies, and, in a more concrete sense, to John Pory's fur, farming, and fishing ventures on the Eastern Shore.

THE THIRD NOTABLY REVEALING EPISODE OF 1619 BEGAN WITH THE sudden, unannounced arrival of the Patawomecks' outer chief Iopassus at Jamestown in September, several weeks after the assembly had adjourned. The purpose of Iopassus's journey from the distant Potomac River was a mystery to the English, who brushed off most of his "frivoulous messages." They partially acceded, however, to his request that "2. shipps might be speedyly to Patawamack where they should trade for greate stoore of corne": they sent a single ship captained by John Ward, a newcomer to the colony who had been a burgess at the recent assembly, with Spelman as interpreter. Iopassus also insisted that the governor send an Englishman to accompany him back to Patawomeck by an arduous overland route rather than taking passage on an English vessel, to which the English also agreed. When Captain Ward arrived at Patawomeck in October, however, he learned that there was no corn to be had. Angered and perplexed at having been so "deceyved," Ward took corn "by force from Jupasons [Iopas-

26. Kingsbury, ed., *RVC*, III, 220–221 ("three thinges," "fresh flaming silkes"), 238–239 ("bever skins"), 278–279; Smith, *Generall Historie*, in Barbour, ed., *Complete Works*, II, 288–291; "Note of the Shipping . . . in the Yeere 1621," in Purchas, *Hakluytus Posthumus*, XIX, 146 ("very happily"). On the fur trade, see J. Frederick Fausz, "Merging and Emerging Worlds: Anglo-Indian Interest Groups and the Development of the Seventeenth-Century Chesapeake," in Lois Green Carr, Philip D. Morgan, and Jean B. Russo, eds., *Colonial Chesapeake Society* (Williamsburg, Va., and Chapel Hill, N.C., 1988), 47–98; and Rice, *Nature and History in the Potomac Country*, chap. 5.

sus's] Country." Yet, despite the fact that Iopassus had clearly duped the English in some way and the English had stolen his people's corn, the two sides "made a firme peace againe" before the English left the Potomac in late November.[27]

Like the compressed narratives of other key Native-newcomer encounters in 1619, the terse English descriptions of this strange sequence of events raise questions that can only be addressed by looking to the larger context. John Rolfe reported that "a more plentyfull yere then this, it hath not pleased God to send us since the beginning of this Plantacion"—quite a turnaround from the bad harvest of 1618. Why, then, did Yeardley agree to send Ward and Spelman to trade for corn that the English did not much need? Iopassus's behavior is equally baffling: Why did he go to Jamestown himself rather than send an emissary? Why did he insist on returning to Patawomeck by land, and why did he want an Englishman with him? Why, if he hadn't enough corn to trade to the English, did he ask them to come in the first place? And why did Iopassus make "a firme peace againe" with the Englishmen who had just forcibly taken the Patawomecks' corn?

Part of the explanation for these events can be found in a discussion among Yeardley's councillors shortly after Iopassus's visit to Jamestown. Opechancanough, it seemed to them, had "stood aloofe upon termes of dout and Jealousy" of late and "would not be drawne to any treaty at all." This had actually been the case for over a year: as early as July 1618, John Rolfe worried that "Opechankanough will not come at [to] us," which "causes us [to] suspect his former promises." It was a good time, then, for the English to begin cultivating allies—by sending a ship to the Potomac to trade for corn that they didn't need, for example—in case their relations with Itoyatin and Opechancanough went completely bad. But why look to the Patawomecks as trading partners and allies? Were they not part of Itoyatin's paramount chiefdom? Barely. Patawomeck stood near the outer fringe of the paramount chiefdom, some eighty miles from Itoyatin's and Opechancanough's towns. A relatively recent addition to Tsenacommacah and one of the larger and more powerful chiefdoms within Itoyatin's orbit, it was less integrated into the paramount chiefdom than most.[28]

Iopassus's mission to Jamestown had little to do with corn and everything to do with asserting the Patawomecks' independence at this fluid, uncertain moment. By traveling on foot through the heart of Tsenacommacah, conspicuously

---

27. Smith, *Generall Historie*, in Barbour, ed., *Complete Works*, II, 268; Kingsbury, ed., *RVC*, III, 244–247 (quotations on 244, 247); "Reporte of the Manner of Proceeding in the General Assembly," in McIlwaine, ed., *JHB*, 3–4, 6.

28. Kingsbury, ed., *RVC*, III, 228 ("stood aloofe"), 244–245, 247; Smith, *Generall Historie*, in Barbour, ed., *Complete Works*, II, 267 ("will not come").

accompanied by English emissaries, Iopassus advertised that the Patawomecks intended to make their own deals with the English. This was a serious challenge to Itoyatin's authority. The paramount chief did not interfere much in the everyday lives of his subordinate werowances and their people, but he did expect conformity in their relations with outsiders. Iopassus may have been aware that Opechancanough was, at that very moment, considering a massive attack against the English; if so, his overture to the English would have reminded Itoyatin and Opechancanough that, at this juncture, they needed to maintain good relations with the semi-independent Patawomecks. Yet Iopassus's initiative amounted to more than a change of masters. He also made fools of the English by inviting them to trade for corn that didn't exist, thus declaring the Patawomecks' independence from them as well.[29]

The Patawomeck Nation was but one of many recent additions to the paramount chiefdom that had never completely reconciled themselves to their tributary status under Powhatan or Itoyatin. The existence of such partial (and often reluctant) Powhatans and the presence of independent nations such as the Accomacs presented interesting possibilities to the English newcomers. In 1619, Itoyatin, Opechancanough, and the English all recognized that they had to compete for the affections of the Patawomecks and other unreliable Powhatans. Powhatan, for example, had made an "annuall progress through his pettye provinces," including Patawomeck, and Opechancanough continued the practice after Powhatan's death. Meanwhile, the Virginia Company's push to establish a fur trade in the northern Chesapeake was a diplomatic initiative as well as an economic venture, for such exchanges continuously reaffirmed the colony's alliances with the Patawomecks and other potential counterweights to the Powhatans. The grain trade with groups beyond the Powhatan core, which had already done so much to forge connections between the English and the Patawomecks, grew so regular after 1619 that "almost every letter [from Jamestown] tells of that trade."[30]

The independent Accomacs also tended carefully to their relationship with the English amid the uncertainties of 1619. Accomac-Powhatan relations were especially tense in the late 1610s, during which (as John Pory reported) a "few of the Westerly Runnagados [Chickahominies]" who were under Itoyatin's protection "had conspired against the laughing King" (the Accomac werow-

29. Kingsbury, ed., *RVC*, III, 244–245; Rountree, *Pocahontas's People*, 70.
30. On the "annuall progress," see Kingsbury, ed., *RVC*, III, 92, 438 (quotation); Smith, *Generall History*, in Barbour, ed., *Complete Works*, II, 308. On the new fur trade and continuing grain trade in the northern Chesapeake, see Kingsbury, ed., *RVC*, I, 504, 515, 565, 567, 583, 608, III, 157, 238–239, 242, 300, 488, 495–496 ("almost every letter" on 495), 526–527, 530, 535–536, 549, 639–641.

ance). Thus, despite having momentarily turned to Opechancanough to get "justice" for the theft of their corn by Martin's men, the Accomacs consistently reaffirmed and steadily deepened their alliance with the English during these years. Part of Itoyatin's and Opechancanough's animosity toward the Accomacs stemmed from the growing English trade, which was increasingly supplanting the cross-bay trade between the Powhatans and the Eastern Shore nations. The still-youthful interpreter Thomas Savage, who had once lived with Spelman in Powhatan's household, took a leading role in this development—so much so, the Accomac werowance warned Pory, that Opechancanough had "imployed" someone to assassinate Savage for cutting into that trade.[31]

Opechancanough also wanted Savage killed because of a "disgrace hee had done his sonne, and some thirteene of his people." The outer chief's son had gone to the Eastern Shore in pursuit of Thomas Graves, an old planter who had arrived at Jamestown in 1608. Graves had previously served as military commander of the English settlement closest to the Chickahominy towns, where he had somehow earned the enmity of both the Chickahominies and Opechancanough—possibly by playing a role in the killings and kidnappings there in 1616. In 1619 he was on the Eastern Shore, where Opechancanough's son caught up with him. When confronted by four Englishmen led by Savage, however, Opechancanough's son and his twelve companions backed down. To compound Opechancanough's mortification at this apparent cowardice, a hundred "Easterlings" witnessed the Pamunkeys' humiliation. These locals so "derided" them, the Accomac werowance later told Pory, "that they came there [to the Eastern Shore] no more." A few months later, the Accomacs further strengthened their ties with the English by allowing John Pory to seat twenty servants at Accomac as well as a second English settlement of ten men nearby.[32]

Given this cozy relationship, Opechancanough understandably met with a brisk refusal in 1621 when he tried to enlist the Accomacs in a plan to poison English leaders using the extract of a plant found only on the Eastern Shore. Indeed, the Accomac werowance, "no well-willer" of Opechancanough, might have been the person who warned the English that the Powhatans were planning a massive surprise attack against the English settlements and thus forced Ope-

---

31. Smith, *Generall Historie*, in Barbour, ed., *Complete Works*, II, 288–291 ("Westerly Runnagados" on 291). English sources sometimes referred to the Accomac werowance as the "Laughing King"; see Rountree and Davidson, *Eastern Shore Indians*, 44, 51–52.

32. Smith, *Generall Historie*, in Barbour, ed., *Complete Works*, II, 288–290 (quotation on 290); Kingsbury, ed., *RVC*, I, 343–344, 349, III, 585, 641; "Note of the Shipping . . . 1621," in Purchas, *Hakluytus Posthumus*, XIX, 146; Upshur and Whitelaw, "Earliest Settlements on the Eastern Shore," *VMHB*, L (1942), 193–198. On Graves's career, see "Thomas Graves (Granes, Grayes) I," in McCartney, *Virginia Immigrants*, 337.

chancanough to delay his plans until the following year. The rupture between the Accomacs and the Powhatans was now complete: Pory reported that the latter wanted to "invade" the lower Eastern Shore but did not do so because they lacked "Boats to crosse the Bay"—and because the Accomacs' alliance with the English was so strong.[33]

Opechancanough nevertheless persisted in his plans for a general attack against the Virginia colony. Having momentarily lost the opportunity for surprise, he adopted a conspicuously conciliatory demeanor toward the English. He hinted that he might welcome instruction in Christianity, and even appeared to brush off the murder of one of his leading warriors, Nemattanew (also known as Jack of the Feather), by a group of English colonists. Although Opechancanough was, in fact, enraged by the killing, he sent a message that Nemattanew had been too "farr owt of . . . favor" for the Powhatan Indians to make an issue of it. Meanwhile, Itoyatin and Opechancanough planned a great ceremony for "the takinge upp of Powhatan[']s bones" for secondary reburial, in which his remains (which had been left to dry for three years on a scaffold) were cleaned and reinterred in a temple. The event brought together Indians from throughout Tsenacommacah, which presented Opechancanough with the ideal opportunity to plan a coordinated attack "uppon every Plantatione" of the Virginia colony. This time, no one broke ranks in time to thwart the surprise attacks. These fell on March 22, 1622, in a strike that was "so sodaine [sudden]," the Virginia Company's secretary in London wrote, "that few or none discerned the weapon or blow that brought them to destruction." Roughly a quarter of the inhabitants of the English settlements were slain in a single morning.[34]

A fairly straight line can be drawn between, on the one hand, Iopassus's seemingly baffling behavior during and immediately after his sudden appearance at Jamestown in September 1619 and, on the other hand, the Powhatans' March 1622 attack on the English settlements. For, although the Patawomecks and other nations on or just beyond the edges of Tsenacommacah occasionally hedged their bets in the Anglo-Powhatan conflict, they largely followed the course charted by Iopassus and the Accomac werowance in 1619. They tended more closely than usual to their relationships with the English by trading with them even during wartime while at the same time avoiding fighting for either

33. Kingsbury, ed., *RVC*, III, 556 ("no well-willer"), IV, 10; Smith, *Generall Historie*, in Barbour, ed., *Complete Works*, II, 290–291 ("Boats"). For an informed speculation on the identity of this poisonous plant and on the Accomacs' warning of the impending attack, see Rountree and Davidson, *Eastern Shore Indians*, 51.

34. Kingsbury, ed., *RVC*, III, 551–553 ("so sodaine" on 551), IV, 10–11. On secondary reburials, see Helen Rountree, *The Powhatan Indians of Virginia: Their Traditional Culture* (Norman, Okla., 1989), 113.

side, thus exploiting Anglo-Powhatan tensions in the late 1610s and early 1620s in order to become more nearly independent of both.[35]

MANY OF THE PEOPLE WHO HAD BEEN INVOLVED IN THE KEY NATIVE-newcomer events of 1619—the theft of the Accomacs' corn by John Martin's men, the trial of Henry Spelman at Robert Poole's behest, and Iopassus's surprise visit to Jamestown—also played key roles in the aftermath of the Powhatans' March 22, 1622, attacks. John Martin, for example, reacted fiercely to the 1622 massacre. Martin had begun his career as a hard-core Elizabethan privateer and had always been notably hostile toward Indians, even by Jamestown standards. His immediate response to the 1622 attacks was entirely in character: he wrote up a plan for the enslavement and ultimate extermination of the Powhatans while also calling for the revocation of the Virginia Company's charter. In its broad outlines, Martin got what he wanted: Virginia became a crown colony in 1624, in the midst of a ten-year war that went almost entirely the Virginians' way. Martin disappeared from the colony's records in 1629, as the war was winding down.[36]

Robert Poole survived the 1622 attacks and was sent to trade for corn at Patawomeck, where he repaid this important English ally by imprisoning the werowance and attacking the town; under his direction, the English "slew thirty or forty men, women and children." It took considerable effort to undo the damage to English-Patawomeck relations. Poole's violence at Patawomeck led indirectly to the death the following year of Henry Spelman, who was killed and beheaded while trading elsewhere along the Potomac River. Iopassus disappeared from the English records after 1619 and may have already been dead by 1622, but the diplomatic strategy he had developed during his long term as the Patawomecks' external chief disposed the Patawomeck nation to continue its alliance with the English, despite Poole's atrocities and the loss of Spelman. Thomas Savage acquired ever more land and trading connections on the Eastern Shore, where he died in 1633. Itoyatin survived until about 1629. His death at last cleared the way for his younger (though now elderly) brother Opechancanough to become paramount chief. Opechancanough outlived them all (with the possible exception of Poole), surviving to lead a second round of surprise attacks against English plantations in 1644 before he was murdered in an English jail cell in 1646.[37]

35. Rice, *Nature and History in the Potomac Country*, 86–91.
36. Lorri Glover and Daniel Blake Smith, *The Shipwreck That Saved Jamestown: The "Sea Venture" Castaways and the Fate of America* (New York, 2008), 110–111; Kingsbury, ed., *RVC*, III, 253, 705–707; "From Captaine Martyn His Plantation, 27. Decemb. 1619," in Purchas, *Hakluytus Posthumus*, XIX, 134; Rice, *Nature and History in the Potomac Country*, 90–91.
37. Smith, *Generall Historie*, in Barbour, ed., *Complete Works*, II, 313–314 (quotation on 314), 320–321; Kingsbury, ed., *RVC*, IV, 89. On the fates of Savage and Poole, see Fausz, "Middlemen in

Yeardley's warning at the 1619 assembly that these were "doubtfull times" framed the issue in binary terms, as a problematic relationship between only two groups: "us" and "the Indians." Yet most people—Native or non-Native, including Yeardley—knew better. These were doubtful times within "Indian country" as well, for Itoyatin and Opechancanough faced challenges both internally and around the margins of Tsenacommacah. Yeardley's "us" similarly elided differences within the Virginia Company and among the Jamestown colonists over the colony's future. Above all, the theft of the Accomacs' corn by Martin's men, the struggle between the interpreters Spelman and Poole, and Iopassus's unannounced visit to Jamestown all highlighted the importance of reluctant Powhatans and of non-Powhatans who lived near Tsenacommacah.

Recognizing the complexities of the Chesapeake Bay region's multisided and rapidly shifting indigenous politics in 1619 does much to explain the proceedings of the first representative assembly in English America. It is certainly possible to discern the future in those proceedings and in other events of 1619. Tobacco, slaves, land hunger, increasingly powerful independent planters, representative government for the most successful of those planters—it's all there. Yet a closer examination of the records of that crucial year also reveals substantial continuities with the Jamestown colony's first twelve years: the persistent centrality of Native people to life in the Chesapeake Bay region, the keen interest taken by English leaders in the details of indigenous politics, the still-open possibility of an economic future that included Indian producers of maize and furs, a wary respect for Powhatan military might, and a well-founded, lingering suspense about the colony's very survival.

Peace and War," *VMHB*, XCV (1987), 59–62. For Spelman's death, see Rice, *Nature and History in the Potomac Country*, 87–89. On Opechancanough, see Horn, *Land as God Made It*, 286.

Brase's Case
Making Slave Law as Customary Law in Virginia's General Court, 1619–1625

PAUL D. HALLIDAY

He came with them "willingly." At least that was how English sailors described the nameless "negro" who accompanied them from the Caribbean to Virginia in July 1625.[1]

Their woeful voyage had begun the year before, when the *Black Bess* left Flushing with Dutch letters of marque and an English crew eager for shares in Spanish prizes. Once in the West Indies, they took a small frigate. Its hold contained sixty sea turtles, but little else. Fresh meat slaked the crew's hunger, but their "Admirall," Captain John Powell, drove them too hard. In keeping with the semidemocratic ethos of privateering ventures, some decided to head for home.[2]

Captain Nathaniel Jones, second-in-command, agreed to lead them as they departed in a captured Spanish ship. Jones was new to Caribbean waters; his crew was soon trapped in currents and winds he did not understand. As water and food dwindled, they encountered a small Spanish ship with sixteen aboard, among them a Frenchman and a "negro," both of whom "were desirous to goe alonge wth them." It's less clear that the Portuguese pilot they captured was quite so keen, but Jones needed him to get them out of the Caribbean. While stopped along the Florida coast to take in water and more turtles, a storm tore their ship off its anchors and blew them out to sea. Lacking provisions to return to England, they turned to the closest refuge: Virginia. Once there, Jones's crew and their new companions encountered the law of Virginia just as it was being made.

The year 1619 is famous for two developments: the creation of the General Assembly and the arrival of "20. and odd Negroes." But a third, oft-overlooked novelty arose that year: the General Court. Judgments in this court would do

---

1. This story is reconstructed from three sailors' depositions given July 20, 1625. See H. R. McIlwaine, ed., *Minutes of the Council and General Court of Colonial Virginia, 1622–1632, 1670–1676* . . . (Richmond, Va., 1924), 66–68.

2. Ibid. (quotation on 67).

as much to create new law as the assembly. Judge-made, customary law would determine the fate of those first African-Virginians and their descendants.[3]

In their initial hearing on July 21, 1625, the General Court's judges made some quick decisions about Captain Jones's crew. First, they directed that fourteen who sailed with him should "be disposed of" by the governor and his council to such places "as they shall thinke fitt, whereof the *frenchman* to be one." Second, they permitted Captain Francis West—one of the court's judges—to purchase the ship for twelve hundred pounds of tobacco, which Captain Jones and his crew "demanded for her," perhaps in anticipation of an admiralty decision assigning them lawful prize in the vessel. The court directed "the *Spaniard*"—presumably the captured pilot, who as a Portuguese was a subject of Spain's king—to await further orders.[4]

No order concerning "the negro" survives from that July hearing. It appears that the court sent him to work on lands owned by former governor Sir George Yeardley. In a September hearing, the judges commanded that he "remaine wth the La[dy] Yardley till further order" and that he be "allowed" forty pounds of tobacco per month for his work—a handsome sum at current prices. He likely encountered another eight unnamed black servants on the Yeardley property. Two weeks later, "the negro that cam in w[i]th Capt. *Jones*" had a name: Brase. The court now decided his fate. He would "belonge to Sr *ffrancis Wyatt*, Govrnor and, As his servant, Notwthstandinge any sale by Capt *Jonnes* to Capt [Nathaniel] *Bass*, or any other chaleng by the ships company." And at that point, Brase, Captain Jones, and his crew disappear from our view.[5]

Explaining Brase's Case

Brase's case provides the earliest surviving evidence of an English colonial court disposing of an African's labor for nonpunitive reasons. How shall we make sense

---

3. Susan Myra Kingsbury, ed., *The Records of the Virginia Company of London*, 4 vols. (Washington, D.C., 1906–1935) (hereafter cited as *RVC*), III, 243. On the court, see Warren M. Billings, *A Little Parliament: The Virginia General Assembly in the Seventeenth Century* (Richmond, Va., 2004), chap. 9.

4. McIlwaine, ed., *Minutes*, 68–69.

5. Ibid., 71–73. Tobacco ran two to three shillings per pound in 1624–1625; see Edmund S. Morgan, *American Slavery, American Freedom: The Ordeal of Colonial Virginia* (New York, 1975), 108. The census of early 1625 records Africans on the Yeardley property; see Annie Lash Jester and Martha Woodroof Hiden, eds., *Adventurers of Purse and Person: Virginia, 1607–1625* (Princeton, N.J., 1956), 27. Brase might be a corruption of Spanish or Portuguese words; for instance, it might refer to Brazil as a place of origin. *Brazo* or *braço*, Spanish and Portuguese for "arm," perhaps indicated that Brase was a "hand," or laborer, or that he was a *bracero*, someone with a good arm for throwing lances. *Brazalete* might indicate bronze or copper bracelets used in the West African slave trade as currency. Such possibilities suggest he might have been an African creole. My thanks to my colleagues Christina Mobley and Brian Owensby for discussion of the above terms.

of this cryptic record? What happens to our story of the origins of slavery as law across the Anglophone world when we do? To understand what happened to Brase, we must first consider how Virginians conceived judicial authority, then examine how they used judicial authority in these early years. Doing so reveals how the men who served as judges in Virginia held themselves and the law they made in the highest regard. Their idea of their own authority, as much as their ideas of racial difference, encouraged a belief in their virtually unlimited power to dispose of the labor of others. This would have enormous consequences for Brase and for all the Africans who came after him to Virginia; it would establish a pattern that would repeat itself in courts across Britain's burgeoning empire over the next two centuries.[6]

Given the absence of any words describing the judges' reasoning, we can only guess at what legal principles, if any, motivated their work. But we can conclude much from their deeds. Captain Jones—perhaps on behalf of the crew, which would share in the value of any prize—believed that Brase's labor was his to command and to transfer by lawful sale. The court rejected Jones's claim and pursued a different one: that Brase's labor was theirs to command. Behind this claim was an even greater one: that law in Virginia was theirs to make. After all, there was no English law or legal norm permitting a judge to assign an alien—black or white, enemy or friend—to labor.

The judges served their own interests first. In doing so, they violated a bedrock principle of natural and common law: that no one may be a judge in his own cause. They assigned movable property—the ship—to one of their own members; they assigned property in a man's labor to another judge. These conflicts of interest fit a pattern. As we shall see, that's what other Virginians thought as they routinely condemned the court's members for their corrupt ways.[7]

The court's work may have depended on distinguishing among kinds of people. They seem to have separated English subjects from aliens. This probably explains why "fowerteene of those men wch came in w[i]th Capt *Jonnes*"—presumably English sailors—were sent off and not heard from again. The Frenchman, though an alien, joined them. This distinction between subjects and aliens

---

6. In 1617, Bermuda's new assize court sentenced Symon "the negro" to slavery for sex with a minor, "during the Governor's pleasure." This was a criminal matter: here, assignment to slavery was a punishment, not a decision about a law-abiding person's labor status. During the same assize, a white servant had his sentence of hanging commuted to enslavement; see J. H. Lefroy, ed., *Memorials of the Discovery and Early Settlement of the Bermudas or Somers Islands, 1515–1685*, 2 vols. (London, 1877–1879), I, 127; Virginia Bernhard, *Slaves and Slaveholders in Bermuda, 1616–1782* (Columbia, Mo., 1999), 28–29.

7. *Bonham's Case* (1610), 8 Co. Rep. 118a, 77 *The English Reports* . . . (London, 1907) (hereafter cited as *Eng. Rep.*), 652; R. H. Helmholz, "Bonham's Case, Judicial Review, and the Law of Nature," *Journal of Legal Analysis*, I (2009), 325–354.

depended on another distinction: between aliens friendly to England's king and his enemies. Thus, the Frenchman went with the Englishmen, while the Portuguese pilot, as a subject of the king of Spain, who was then at war with England, required further consideration.[8]

The court may have concluded that Brase, having been taken from a Spanish vessel, was an enemy alien. If so, why handle him and the Portuguese pilot so differently? No English legal rule in 1625 distinguished people by race. A judge might separate Christians from "infidels," but this idea—bare dicta asserted in Chief Justice Sir Edward Coke's report of *Calvin's Case* (1608)—was legally dubious. Christian status interested the General Court; their first encounter with an African, ten months earlier, involved John Phillip, "a negro Christened in *England*." Noting Phillip's Christianity probably concerned his ability to swear an oath and thereby give testimony in a case before Virginia's judges. Perhaps infidel status explains the court's decisions about Brase. Probably not. The record is silent, and there is no reason to believe the judges had copies of Coke's *Reports* or would have thought to consult them. We may be safest concluding that, in Brase's case, the General Court was tacitly transforming pervasively negative cultural norms about race into a rule of decision, a rule then unique among English dominions to the nascent customary law of Virginia.[9]

Because the racial principle seemed to be uppermost, we might understand it better by reading Brase's case alongside others concerning Africans, but there were none in Virginia until county courts were established in 1634. This may not matter. After all, what mattered as much as or more than the judges' view of Brase was their view of themselves—their notions about lawmaking and their exalted capacity as judges. Law would be what they declared it to be.

Viewed as a lone episode involving African labor, it's hard to make much of Brase's case. But when viewed in light of the grants of authority by king and company to the people of Virginia and read alongside other cases decided by the General Court, we can watch a profound process unfolding. Unburdened by extensive knowledge of English laws and with no one supervising its work, the court freely mixed ideas from multiple English jurisdictions—common law, equity, the church courts, martial law—with cultural norms, claims of necessity, and naked self-interest to generate an entirely new kind of law, a customary law of Virginia. The most distinctive feature of this customary law involved control

---

8. McIlwaine, ed., *Minutes*, 68.
9. "All infidels are in law *perpetui inimici,* perpetual enemies"; see 7 Co. Rep. 17a (1608), 77 *Eng. Rep.*, 397. See also McIlwaine, ed., *Minutes*, 33; Winthrop D. Jordan, *White over Black: American Attitudes toward the Negro, 1550–1812,* 2d ed. (Williamsburg, Va., and Chapel Hill, N.C., 2012), chap. 1.

of people's labor, and, in particular, innovative controls imposed on the labor of Africans.

Creating Custom

Custom, in the words of the leading law dictionary of the age, was "a lawe or right not written ... established by long use and the consent of our awncesters." Custom occupies the place where extralegal norm shades into law, where rarely articulated social and moral values are asserted as enforceable claims binding on others. In England, custom was "a *discursive field:* a body of ideas that sanctioned claims to rights, office, space, land and resources," as Andy Wood notes. "Most customs were built up, generation after generation, encoding social practices just as they became habitual."[10]

But there was a tension in seventeenth-century ideas about customs, a tension between their presumed ancientness and their susceptibility to creation or change, often by silent means. Customs, in E. P. Thompson's analysis, were intensely local, typically deployed by subalterns against their superiors, with origins lost in the past. In Virginia, custom was certainly local. But in the hands of the General Court, custom was not a weapon of the weak; it was an instrument of rule, wielded to keep certain kinds of people in ever-better-defined places. And there was certainly nothing ancient about Virginia's customs, even if those unwittingly articulated in Brase's case soon became habitual. General Court judges knew they were inventing customs. By the 1620s, they routinely used the language of custom to refer to the ways they handled two aspects of law peculiar to Virginia: terms of service and the valuation of tobacco.[11]

It may seem paradoxical to say we can watch people creating custom, but not according to contemporary ideas. Coke identified "two pillars of custom, one the common usage; the other, that it be time out of mind." Virginians were making a usage common whose time was nonetheless in mind. Claims of prescription, a legal privilege presumed to have been granted in writing lost long ago, required

---

10. John Cowell, comp., *The Interpreter; or, Booke Containing the Signification of Words* (Cambridge, 1607), s.v. "custom"; Andy Wood, *The Memory of the People: Custom and Popular Senses of the Past in Early Modern England* (Cambridge, 2013), 2.

11. J. W. Tubbs, *The Common Law Mind: Medieval and Early Modern Conceptions* (Baltimore, 2000), chaps. 6, 7; E. P. Thompson, *Customs in Common: Studies in Traditional Popular Culture* (New York, 1993), 97–103. One servant's indentures said the terms he agreed to were *"according to the custome of land there holden."* The court referred to the "custome of this Country" for making agreements for the sale of tobacco (1626–1627), and to "the custome usually" used for valuing tobacco in estates of the deceased (1628); see McIlwaine, ed., *Minutes,* 125, 129, 164. By 1635, servants' terms could be referred to in printed indenture forms used in the Chesapeake as "the custom of the country"; see Thomas Cecil, *A Relation of Maryland: Together with a Map of the Countrey* ... (London, 1635), 53–54.

"a lawful beginning." Custom did not: it "ought to be reasonable . . . but need not be intended to have a lawful beginning." Another way to think of custom is to say it was any rule—even one contrary to common law—accepted as law in a particular locale without contravention by a superior judge. Virginians created customs leading to enslavement—laws with no lawful beginning—because no one who might have stopped them did so.[12]

Jurisdiction Unbounded, Discretion Unbridled

A customary law of slavery was born of the reforms of 1619—and of the royal charters, commissions, and instructions given to Virginians during the preceding decade that had failed to impose effective bounds on judicial innovation. Brase learned this before anyone else.

On July 30, 1619, Speaker John Pory opened the first meeting of Virginia's General Assembly by reading two documents. One he called "the greate Charter, or commission of privileges, orders and laws." This was only great in length. But it was undeniably a charter in the unheroic, contemporary sense of the word: "written evidence of things done between man and man." This so-called charter was actually the Virginia Company's November 1618 instructions to their new governor, Sir George Yeardley. It opened by proclaiming their intention, "according to the Authority granted unto us from his Majesty under his great Seal" (the company's 1612 charter), to settle "a laudable form of Government by Majestracy and just Laws." None of the words following defined just laws or outlined a form of magistracy. Far from providing a new constitution, the charter simply detailed who would have land and on what terms.[13]

The other document Pory read, "the commission for establishing the Counsell of Estate and the general Assembly," was more important. This "Ordinance and Constitution" lay the ground for a new General Assembly. It also created the General Court by directing members of the new Council of State to assist the governor "in administracion of Justice." The governor's council would act in two capacities, by two names: making policy as a council and adjudicating disputes as a court. Most analysis of slave law in Virginia starts with the founding of county courts in 1634 or focuses on legislation, though the colony's statutory

---

12. 4 Leon. 242, 74 *Eng. Rep.*, 847; 6 Co. Rep. 60b, 77 *Eng. Rep.*, 345.

13. Magna Carta was called "great," not because of its contents, but because it was longer than the Forest Charter of 1217; see David Carpenter, *Magna Carta* (London, 2015), 5–6; Cowell, *Interpreter*, s.v. "charter"; and Kingsbury, ed., *RVC*, III, 98–99, 158. Wesley Frank Craven deflated the charter's greatness in Craven, *Dissolution of the Virginia Company: The Failure of a Colonial Experiment* (New York, 1932), 52–67.

law of slavery would not begin until 1662. But it was here, before there were county courts or statutes regulating slavery, that Virginians began to craft the customary legal practices that would underpin later county court judgments and legislative codes. They did this innovative work in the General Court.[14]

Several qualities marked the new court's judges. Few had legal experience. Three passed a short spell in one of the Inns of Court in London, where barristers learned their craft. Of these, two never advanced to the bar, thus reflecting a tendency among English gentlemen to spend a year or two in an Inn as part of their education. Of the smaller group of seven court members who presided in Brase's case, only one, Governor Sir Francis Wyatt, had any legal learning, though no sign survives that he had any experience as a lawyer or magistrate. Five of these seven shared a more important characteristic: they employed English indentured servants. One judge, Abraham Piersey, also had seven Africans working on his lands. These judges had an interest in the labor of others; now they would make the law controlling it. Moreover, four of Brase's judges held military rank. The legal text they probably knew best was Sir Thomas Dale's martial law code, derived from the articles of war governing English troops in Ireland and published for use in Virginia in 1612 as *Lawes Divine, Morall, and Martiall*.[15]

---

14. Kingsbury, ed., *RVC*, III, 158, 482–484. This document is dated July 24, 1621. Craven argued that this 1621 text was a copy of the 1618 commission made three years later so that it might be sent with other documents that were prepared when Sir Francis Wyatt became governor. Craven provides no direct evidence for why this text must be the same as that of 1618. But one might surmise that, since the 1621 text explained it was designed to establish these two councils, both of which had been in operation before 1621, this may well be a copy of the 1618 ordinance of creation. See Craven, *Dissolution*, 73–74. For the first statute concerning slave status, see William Waller Hening, ed., *The Statutes at Large; Being a Collection of All the Laws of Virginia...*, 13 vols. (Richmond, Va., 1809), II, 170; Warren M. Billings, "The Law of Servants and Slaves in Seventeenth-Century Virginia," *Virginia Magazine of History and Biography*, XCIX (1991), 54. A 1640 statute denied blacks the possession of weapons, which was a racial rather than slave regulation; see Hening, *Statutes at Large*, I, 226.

15. The number of judges on the court varied. William Ferrers, George Thorpe, and Governor Sir Francis Wyatt spent time in the Inns. Only Ferrers was called to the bar (1618) after entering the Middle Temple (1610); I have found no evidence that he practiced law. Thorpe, a council member until his death in 1622, enrolled in Staple Inn, followed by the Middle Temple. Wyatt, like his father George Wyatt, spent a spell in Gray's Inn. Neither he nor Thorpe was called to the bar. See Joseph Foster, *The Register of Admissions to Gray's Inn, 1521–1889...* (London, 1889), 107; Henry F. MacGeagh and H. A. C. Sturgess, comps., *Register of Admissions to the Honourable Society of the Middle Temple: From the Fifteenth Century to the Year 1944* (London, 1949), I, 73, 95; Reginald J. Fletcher, ed., *The Pension Book of Gray's Inn (Records of the Honourable Society), 1569–1669* (London, 1901); and Charles Henry Hopwood, *Middle Temple Records*, I (London, 1904). For background on the Inns, see Wilfrid R. Prest, *The Inns of Court under Elizabeth I and the Early Stuarts, 1590–1640* (London, 1972), 39–41, 141, 149–153. Seven men were present on one or more of the occasions when Brase's case was discussed: William Claiborne, Raphe Hamor, Samuel Mathews, Abraham Piersey, Capt. Roger Smith, Francis West, and Sir Francis Wyatt. Information about their servants survives in the 1625 census; see Jester and Hiden, eds., *Adventurers*, 28, 29, 38, 62. On Dale's *Lawes*, see John M. Collins, *Martial Law and English Laws, c. 1500–1700* (Cambridge, 2016), esp. 97–105.

We might conclude that the judges who decided Brase's fate knew two aspects of law well: the law concerned with servants and the summary procedures used in martial law. Their experience with the first of these areas of law inspired the judges' presumption that others' labor was theirs to command. Masters and those who would judge disputes between masters and servants were the same people. And the justices' experience of martial law inspired their presumption that they might give orders with little, if any, opposition in Virginia or beyond. In this way, the preemptory nature of justice at the heart of Dale's *Lawes* persisted after 1619.[16]

In their use of summary procedures, the General Court's judges were like justices of the peace (JPs) in England, few of whom had much legal education. But Virginia judges differed from JPs in two crucial ways. First, they were not bound by common law or parliamentary statutes that defined pre-trial criminal process and the procedures JPs followed when regulating everything from alehouses to vagrancy. Second, Virginia's lay magistrates worked without supervision by professional judges, while England's JPs had been subjected to increasing judicial oversight during the three decades or so before 1619. The Court of King's Bench developed a number of tools by which it corrected JPs when they strayed outside their areas of competence. This was *the* major legal development in England of that generation: the imposition on lesser magistrates of an idea and practice of rule-boundedness by professional justices who defined the rules every time they corrected their subordinates. No such practice restrained Brase's judges. The inattention of England's judges allowed Virginia's judges to make distinctive customary laws.[17]

By what authority did the General Court operate? Virginia's first charter, in 1606, conveyed little capacity to make law. The company's council in London would govern itself and its colonies "according to such laws, ordinances, and instructions as shall be ... given" by the king. In the second charter (1609), the king for the first time delegated a capacity to the London council "to make, ordain, and establish all manner of orders, [and] laws." Neither the second nor the third charter (1612) granted Virginians authority to make law. This was given only to the company's leaders in London, who in 1612 were empowered to make

---

16. David Thomas Konig, "'Dale's Laws' and the Non-Common Law Origins of Criminal Justice in Virginia," *American Journal of Legal History*, XXVI (1982), 354–375.

17. On summary process by English JPs, see Robert B. Shoemaker, *Prosecution and Punishment: Petty Crime and the Law in London and Rural Middlesex, c. 1660–1725* (Cambridge, 1991), 35–40. On law reform by judicial supervision of other magistrates, see David Chan Smith, *Sir Edward Coke and the Reformation of the Laws: Religion, Politics, and Jurisprudence, 1578–1616* (Cambridge, 2014), chap. 1. This common law supervision extended to other jurisdictions beyond JPs; see John Baker, *The Reinvention of Magna Carta, 1216–1616* (Cambridge, 2017), chaps. 8, 9.

"laws and ordinances" for Virginia, so long as they "be not contrary to the laws and statutes of this our realm of England."[18]

"Our realm of England" knew a plurality of laws, each complementing the others. There was a law common across England and used in the king's greatest courts in Westminster Hall to resolve debts, broken agreements, and other trespasses. Other courts—Chancery, the Court of Requests—dispensed with common law's rules to decide cases by equity, "a ruled kind of justice, allayed with the sweetnesse of mercy." Church courts, following civil law, oversaw probate, defamation, and marriage; admiralty and martial courts also followed civil law. Towns and manors worked according to local customs often at odds with common law. Thus, in England, different kinds of law ran through different courts. In Virginia, these many kinds of law would be joined together and put into the hands of a single court, the General Court, which thereby enjoyed a sweeping jurisdiction no English court knew.[19]

The chief problem for jurisdictional management in England involved keeping these many tribunals from invading one another's jurisdiction. King's Bench treated nearly all other courts the same way it treated justices of the peace, as subject to its correction. Using prerogative writs, England's leading jurists voided local customs and tightened bounds around courts of equity, church courts, and local courts of all kinds. King's Bench thereby made itself the arbiter of what counted as law in England, declaring its supremacy every time it determined the jurisdiction of other courts.[20]

England's justices would never impose this kind of supervision on colonial magistrates. The Committee for Foreign Plantations managed some aspects of imperial policy after its formation in 1634, though it did not oversee magisterial work. The Privy Council would later provide a venue for colonial appeals in high-value civil cases. But no greater court monitored Virginia's General Court as it adjusted the terms of service of poor English workers or decided the fate of strangers like Brase. England's courts were kept in carefully policed bounds while Virginia's judges, using all the varieties of English law in one court, played

18. Hening, *Statutes at Large*, I, 60–61 (1606), 91 (1609), 103 (1612).
19. Richard J. Ross and Philip J. Stern, "Reconstructing Early Modern Notions of Legal Pluralism," in Lauren Benton and Richard Ross, eds., *Legal Pluralism and Empires, 1500–1850* (New York, 2013), 109–141; Thomas Ash, *Epieikeia* . . . (London, 1609), Aiiij. On equity and civil law, see J. H. Baker, *An Introduction to English Legal History*, 4th ed. (London, 2002), chaps. 6–8.
20. On the prerogative writs, see Paul D. Halliday, *Habeas Corpus: From England to Empire* (Cambridge, Mass., 2010), 74–84. "The common law came to see alternative legal frameworks as possessed of an authority that could be said to be valid just to the extent that the common law itself acknowledged and controlled those alternatives"; see Bradin Cormack, *A Power to Do Justice: Jurisdiction, English Literature, and the Rise of Common Law, 1509–1625* (Chicago, 2007), 27.

freely across a vast jurisdictional terrain. Unbounded jurisdiction swelled their notion of juridical power.[21]

Unbridled discretion inflated their self-worth. The problem began before 1619. The company's 1609 charter ordered Virginians to govern according to their "good discretions ... in cases capital and criminal as [well as] civil, both marine and other; So always, as the said ... proceedings, as near as conveniently may be, be agreeable to the laws, statutes, government, and policy of [this] our realm of ... England." What was good discretion? In 1619, the second edition of what soon became the leading guide for English JPs appeared. In it, Michael Dalton explained that discretion "is a knowledge or understanding to discerne betweene truth and falshood, between right and wrong, between shadowes and substance." He added that magistrates may not use discretion according to their "wills and private affections"; it should "be limited and bounded with the rules of Reason, Law, and Justice."[22]

The company's instructions and the charters on which they were based did little to limit discretion or define the rules of reason to be used by unlearned Virginia judges. Quite the reverse. In 1609, the company instructed Governor Sir Thomas Gates that in judicial matters he should

> P[ro]ceede rather as a Chauncelor then as a Judge rather uppon the naturall right and equity then uppon the niceness and re [letter] of the lawe w[hi]ch perplexeth in this tender body rather then dispatcheth all Causes so that a Summary and arbitrary way of Justice discreetely mingled with those gravities and [fourmes] of magistracy as shall in yor discrecion seem aptest for you and that place, willbe of most use.

In other words, the company told its governor in Virginia not to concern himself with the kinds of rules that so worried the justices of King's Bench when they bound the jurisdiction and bridled the discretion of English magistrates.[23]

We can see how the reforms of 1619 compounded judicial presumption in

---

21. King's Bench made a few fitful attempts at colonial oversight, for instance, by sending habeas corpus in the later seventeenth century on behalf of prisoners in Jamaica and Barbados. The court was unable to compel the writs' return, not because its oversight was unlawful, but because of distance. See Halliday, *Habeas Corpus*, 268–271. On the Committee for Foreign Plantations, see Ken MacMillan, *The Atlantic Imperial Constitution: Center and Periphery in the English Atlantic World* (New York, 2011), 6. On Privy Council appeals, see Mary Sarah Bilder, *The Transatlantic Constitution: Colonial Legal Culture and the Empire* (Cambridge, Mass., 2004).

22. Hening, *Statutes at Large*, I, 96; Michael Dalton, *The Countrey Justice* ... (London, 1619), 20. The first edition of 1618 contained a more limited discussion of discretion.

23. Similar wording was used in Lord De La Warr's instructions; see Kingsbury, ed., *RVC*, III, 15, 27–28.

Virginia by examining the instructions Sir Francis Wyatt received when he became governor in 1621. The company directed Wyatt to "provide that Justice bee equallie administered to all his Ma[jes]ties subjects" and that the General Court give "free accesse ... to all suiters to make knowne ther perticuler grevances, bee itt against what person soevr." Once there, Wyatt was to ensure that "a due course" was taken to do parties "right and Justice." Whether there was truly "free accesse" and equal treatment of suitors would be a contentious issue in the years ahead. After all, Wyatt received "absolute power and authoritie ... to direct determine and punish at his good discretion any emergent bussnes neglect or contempt of authority in any kind." Language of constraint—"equallie administered," "due course," "right and Justice"—was overawed by language of unboundedness—"absolute power," "good discretion," "any..."—that no English justice or magistrate could have imagined using.[24]

Nothing limited Wyatt; nothing limited Gates after 1609, nor the General Court after 1619, except whatever struck them as "aptest." What seemed aptest in 1625 was that Brase should "belonge" to Wyatt. Legally unfounded decisions like the one in Brase's case did not happen in isolation. We may not have other cases concerning Africans in the 1620s, but, when we watch judges with "absolute power," when we see the vast jurisdiction and discretion they used in other areas of law, especially servant cases, we start to see patterns. These patterns reveal how Brase's case came to be resolved as it was and demonstrate its significance in generating a customary law of slavery.[25]

Improvising Customary Law in the General Court

To extract as much meaning as we can from the limited record of Brase's case, we must see it against the backdrop of all the court's other work. Doing so reveals three prominent features of the judges' approach to judging. First, because they occupied such an open jurisdiction, law was theirs to make as they pleased. Second, as in most courts, they responded vigorously to any contempt of their authority; unlike in other courts, they imposed horrifying punishments to demonstrate their dominion over all who came before them. Finally, the judges' partiality and self-dealing was plain for all to see. Their willingness to do as they pleased in defiance of contemporary values about judicial self-restraint helps to

---

24. Ibid., 469, 472–473, 478–480. On the language of law's due course, see Paul D. Halliday, "Birthrights and the Due Course of Law," in Lorna Hutson, ed., *The Oxford Handbook of English Law and Literature, 1500–1700* (Oxford, 2017), 587–603.

25. McIlwaine, ed., *Minutes*, 73.

explain their comfort imposing an order with no precedent in English law on a helpless African. But that order would become a precedent for generations to come. No custom accounts for their treatment of Brase; they had to invent one.

Some of the General Court's jurisdictional improvisation and exercise of discretion arose from the limited capacity of writing to fix the terms of agreements. Oral testimony of a document's existence might have to stand in for the document itself, contrary to common law's discomfort with oral evidence about written agreements. The need to accept oral evidence resulted from the exigencies of colonial life, which produced a fair amount of soiled, sodden, or lost paper and parchment. Peaceable Sherwood put it poetically when he testified about a missing deed whose "toren pages" he saw "swiming do[wne] the river"; he then offered his memory of the words those pages recorded. In 1625, after opening papers from England needed to settle a disputed will, the General Court found them "soe defaced and imprfect that they cannot bee recorded." No matter. They proceeded to resolve the issue, without the writing on which all had depended just moments before. More significant, the judges resolved factual questions, in which the reliability of oral evidence had to be independently assessed, without the help of a jury, thus taking to themselves both the finding of fact and law.[26]

Even oral land deals might be recognized in the General Court. Lacking a written deed, landholders sometimes came to court and, in the manner of a bargain and sale, made a deal. By appearing before the court, such sales would be registered. In one instance, relying on oral testimony in the absence of a deed went deeper: not only to the transaction before the court but to an earlier, unrecorded transaction on which the current seller based his title. The court accepted the testimony of one witness to the seller's ownership, allowed the sale to proceed, and then ordered a patent for the purchaser. A string of oral titles had been made into written title on the strength of one person's testimony. Again, no jury weighed the value of the testimony on which all hinged. Three of the four unusual transactions of this kind that occurred on January 24, 1625, concluded with property in the hands of General Court judge Sir George Yeardley. This

---

26. See testimony of Nicholas Greenhill to the making of an acquittance (that is, the cancellation of a bond for debt upon payment) between Lt. Harrison and Rowland Loftis, in McIlwaine, ed., *Minutes*, 38–40. Common law courts were loath to admit oral testimony in cases of canceled bonds on the principle that performance of a written agreement required evidence of the same kind as the agreement itself: written agreements required written conclusions to those agreements; see Baker, *Introduction*, 324–325. For soaked or defaced papers, see McIlwaine, ed., *Minutes*, 29, 64. The General Court did not use juries in the 1620s in civil matters. Juries saw inconsistent use in other matters; see McIlwaine, ed., *Minutes*, 5 (felony), 34 (to determine Company rents), and 38, 54 (inquisitions post mortem).

suggests how influence might have inspired unusual creativity to ensure durability of title where before there had been none.[27]

Contracts gone bad were sometimes addressed by novel combinations of common law and equity, producing what looks more like compromise results of arbitration than judgments of common law or customary courts. Such results may have made sense in the circumstances Virginians faced. But they also violated a basic idea about common law decision making, that judges should not "arrogate unto themselves authoritie to use their discretion, and to play (as it were) the Chauncelours": a reference by the legal writer William Lambarde to the idea that common law should not be undermined by the use of equitable procedures or principles. Once again, we discover that such novel transactions often involved one of the court's judges or a family member. The more we look, the more we see unusual procedures deployed to serve those who sat in judgment.[28]

Testamentary cases reveal more clearly the unification of jurisdictions that made the General Court so unusual. Probate was a church court matter in England. When settling estates in Virginia, the court routinely straddled the line separating common law from ecclesiastical law. Similarly, a remarkable amount of the court's work involved ill-chosen words. In England, objectionable language was often handled under the church courts' jurisdiction of defamation; Star Chamber examined cases of perjury or sedition. The General Court operated in the area of overlap between these jurisdictions, while throwing in some common law practices as well.[29]

We move from defamation to contempt of court in the 1625 case of Luke Eden, who used "unreverent speche ... to the great abuse of the Governor and the rest of the Counsell beinge then in Courte." While contempt of common law courts typically resulted in fines or imprisonment, the General Court displayed

---

27. McIlwaine, ed., *Minutes*, 44–45; John Baker, *The Oxford History of the Laws of England*, VI, *1483–1558* (Oxford, 2003), 675–676. Though registration in court by bargain and sale was a different form of registration, arguably the most important Great Charter innovation was the order to enroll all grants made under the company's seal "into your records to be kept there in Virginia"; see Kingsbury, ed., *RVC*, III, 106. Deed registration would become routine in the empire long before it would be practiced in England, where it was not established until 1897; see A. W. B. Simpson, *A History of the Land Law*, 2d ed. (Oxford, 1986), 280–283.

28. William Lambard[e], *Eirenarcha; or, Of the Office of the Justices of Peace* ... (London, 1581), 65. One example involved an order to pay part of a debt when cattle died after delivery to the purchaser. One of the parties was the brother of Capt. Raphe Hamor, a court member; see McIlwaine, ed., *Minutes*, 9, 11, 17.

29. McIlwaine, ed., *Minutes*, 30–31. Edward Smith's 1625 accusation against two others for stealing a hog ended in perjury charges against him. One of the accused was committed for the alleged felony, thus putting him in danger of execution. Smith was later found to have spoken in "malice" and was ordered to be whipped, a punishment commonly used in Star Chamber defamation or perjury cases (ibid., 54).

its most zealous jurisdiction-mixing creativity in punishing people like Eden. The court's order against him for contempt displayed just such a combination: martial law's practice of being laid neck and heels and the common law practice of levying fines and requiring bonds for good behavior. Edward Sharpless, the council's own clerk, received rougher treatment. After he gave papers of the Council of State to visiting English commissioners investigating government behavior in Virginia in 1624, the court ordered him pilloried: his ears were nailed to the boards, then cut off. At the same session, Richard Barnes was disarmed and his tongue bored for "base and detracting speeches" against the governor. These were Star Chamber punishments. But there was more: Barnes was also to pass through a gauntlet of forty men, where he would be mauled by each as he went by; he was then to be "footed out of the fort"—all standard martial law fare. The court concluded with a penalty typically imposed under common law: a demand that Barnes sign a bond for good behavior. While such cases combined practices of multiple jurisdictions, the humiliating treatment of the intersex Thomas or Thomasine Hall drew from no English court of any kind. Left to themselves, Virginia's judges improvised.[30]

The judges punished Virginians when they pointed out the court's irregular proceedings. John Lamoyne was ordered to apologize and to pay a fine of twenty pounds after he suggested that a search of someone's private papers was improper. For attacking their proceedings in a shipboard sodomy conviction, the judges ordered Edward Nevell to stand in the pillory, lose his ears, and spend a year in servitude to the colony. Others were punished by assignment to service; those who were servants already might find their terms extended.[31]

"Reproachfull Speeches" against the court involved more than claims of injustice; they involved accusations of oppression and self-interest. William Tyler was condemned for declaring that the court would not do "poore men any right." The judges allowed one of their own—Captain Ralph Hamor—to testify that Tyler had said the court "would shew favor to great men and wronge the poore." Tyler's contempt hit close to home. As we've seen, the General Court generated a new procedure for registering property to suit one of its most prominent members, former governor Yeardley. And it may be important that one of the few felonies prosecuted in the 1620s involved theft of property belonging to Yeard-

30. The treatment of Sharpless remained controversial; see McIlwaine, ed., *Minutes*, 14, 21, 57, 61–63, 194–195. On martial law punishments, see Collins, *Martial Law*, 126. Hall was given a shaming sentence: to go about in public in a combination of men's and women's attire; see Kathleen Brown, "'Changed ... into the Fashion of Man': The Politics of Sexual Difference in a Seventeenth-Century Anglo-American Settlement," *Journal of the History of Sexuality*, VI (1995), 171–193.

31. McIlwaine, ed., *Minutes*, 39, 52, 81, 85, 93. In the last case, Sir George Yeardley benefited when one of his servants, Thomas Hatch, had his service extended for contempt.

ley; perhaps there was something in Tyler's charge of favoring great men. An examination of the court's oversight of labor agreements suggests there was.[32]

White Servants before the General Court

Charters, commissions, and instructions conveyed jurisdiction to the General Court in vague terms. But one area was spelled out with care: purview over terms of service. The 1618 instructions to Governor Yeardley required recipients of company lands to present a "true Certificate" of people they transported to Virginia. Upon arrival, the names of these servants were "to be entered by the Secretary into a Register book for that purpose." Among the Virginia Assembly's first actions in 1619 was to confirm this order and to supplement it by requiring all new immigrants to report the "termes or conditions" of their service to the colony's secretary. These commands were emphasized in Governor Wyatt's 1621 instructions, which expressed only one clear subject-matter jurisdiction in his judicial capacity: that he should ensure "that all apparent or proved Contracts made in England or in Virginia betweene the Owners of land in Virginia and ther tenants or servants be truly pformed and the breach of them reformed by due punishment." Just what constituted an apparent contract, a breach, or due punishment would be up to the General Court.[33]

Virginians placed great faith in the idea that writing, in indentures and an official register, would prevent disputes. But indentures did not always help, filled as they were with words whose meanings people might dispute. Consider the indenture by which Robert Coopy bound himself to the proprietors of Berkeley Plantation. Coopy agreed to serve three years in return for transportation to Virginia and a grant of land at the end of his term. Looking closely at the text suggests how fixing words in ink could not fix their meaning. Who knew what constituted the "lawfull and reasonable workes" Coopy agreed to perform? Might Coopy and his masters have different notions of the "diet" and "apparell" he should be given? What "liberties freedomes and priviledges" was he to enjoy as "a freeman there" when his time was finished? Only a court could answer such questions.[34]

---

32. McIlwaine, ed., *Minutes*, 4–5, 18–20. In England, judges might convict for contempt committed in court. But there was no practice allowing them to convict on their own testimony about words spoken elsewhere; see Baker, *Introduction*, 511; and Morgan, *American Slavery*, 125–126.

33. Kingsbury, ed., *RVC*, III, 108, 171, 475. No registry survives. The court sometimes registered indentures in its record, but it usually did so when a servant died, was transferred, or completed a term, not at the outset; see McIlwaine, ed., *Minutes*, 42, 50–51, 124–125.

34. Kingsbury, ed., *RVC*, III, 210–211.

Words like these opened Virginians to conflict, but one new term in indentures did not. In return for free passage to Virginia in 1622, Nicholas Webling promised to work three years for "Edward Bennett *or his assigns.*" These last three words were the most innovative element in Virginia service indentures. To assign meant "to set over a right unto another." In other words, the term of labor agreed in the indenture was salable. Most bonds also included language of inheritance: that one's heirs would take the remainder of the servant's term upon the master's death. Given this, servant terms could be used as security for payment of debts and were subject to seizure if unpaid. Like a lease, a term of labor had become a transferable species of property. One could not sell a person, but one could sell a property interest in labor limited to a fixed spell. This gave extraordinary power to masters and to the judges who decided disputes about such terms. Indeed, masters and judges were often the same people. It would be an easy thing for them to extend this power over an African refugee who washed up on their shores.[35]

Assignability of service was forbidden in England: neither written indentures of service nor customary unwritten agreements for agricultural servants countenanced transfers. As a result, such "buying and selling [of] men and boies" in Virginia was criticized. That they were "sold heere upp and downe like horses" led some to conclude that it was "not lawfull" to carry servants to Virginia. Nevertheless, the language of transfer became standard in indentures after 1619. Worse, abuse of servants by drawing them into unwitnessed oral agreements persisted. Company leaders in London believed that mandatory uniform contracts, made and registered before servants departed for Virginia, might protect workers. Yet a 1622 proposal to this effect came to nothing. Servant law would be left to the General Court to make and enforce as it willed.[36]

The court enjoyed enormous freedom in adjudicating service disputes in the 1620s. The judges often consulted oral evidence when they lacked written evidence of agreements. This practice might work to a servant's advantage: for instance, when a witness to an oral will testified to a woman's intention that her servant should be freed upon her death. The court might insist on seeing writing if they knew it existed, as when it ordered that an indenture be obtained from

---

35. McIlwaine, ed., *Minutes*, 124–125; Cowell, *Interpreter*, s.v. "assign"; Indenture between Richard Lowther and Edward Hurd, July 31, 1627, MSS 1 D2856a2, Virginia Historical Society, Richmond. For servants in or due to an estate, see McIlwaine, ed., *Minutes*, 94, 98, 99, 110, 113.

36. James Horn, *A Land as God Made It: Jamestown and the Birth of America* (New York, 2005), 247; McIlwaine, ed., *Minutes*, 82; Morgan, *American Slavery*, 126–130; Kingsbury, ed., *RVC*, II, 113, 129–131. Traditional annual oral contracts for agricultural service were nontransferable and could only be changed by consent of both parties; see Ann Kussmaul, *Servants in Husbandry in Early Modern England* (Cambridge, 1981), 31–33, 49–51.

England after a servant's copy had been stolen from his chest. Often, examining an indenture led the court to assign further service, as it did for the servant of one of its own members in 1624. In other instances, reading an indenture revealed that a servant was held by the wrong master and thus required reassignment; or when a master died crossing the Atlantic the court might order his executors to employ a servant who sailed with him.[37]

The court treated property in servant labor as entirely fungible. Servants were routinely reassigned from one master to another. When a promised servant was not provided, another might be offered in his or her place. A strong pair of arms attached to a sturdy body was all that mattered. When a body could not be found, other compensation might be accepted. What the minds attached to those bodies thought was irrelevant. At the same session in which Brase was ordered to remain with Lady Yeardley, the court directed reassignments to make up for five servants who absconded from their Virginia-bound ship while still in England.[38]

Shuffling servants about this way was enabled by their silence before the court. On rare occasions, the record shows servants testifying to their understanding of their contracts. But, in general, they leave little trace on the record. They were mute because their assent to the judges' orders was beside the point. Many had been under the age of legal consent when they were indentured; consent had been given by their parents or, in the case of orphans and waifs, by London magistrates. Young white servants were objects in the hands of the judges who made Virginia's customary law after 1619. The judges' grand notion of their authority over white servants must have grown as they dealt with forcibly transported children and felons who arrived in the 1620s. Poor people accustomed to subjection in England would be governed by judges accustomed to unchecked rule in Virginia.[39]

Virginia's judges believed that the full assignability and heritability written into indentures pertained even when masters made oral agreements with new servants or when there were no agreements at all. They presumed to treat servants as interchangeable parts. This was one of many invented customs in

37. McIlwaine, ed., *Minutes*, 28, 30, 52–53, 56, 80, 96, 124.
38. Ibid., 30, 34, 52, 63, 75. One of the masters receiving new servants on one occasion was court member Abraham Piersey; ibid., 71.
39. Kristen Grace McCabe Lashua, "Children at the Birth of Empire, c. 1600–1760" (Ph.D diss., University of Virginia, 2015), chaps. 2, 4; Cynthia Herrup, "Punishing Pardon: Some Thoughts on the Origins of Penal Transportation," in Simon Devereaux and Paul Griffiths, eds., *Penal Practice and Culture, 1500–1900: Punishing the English* (Basingstoke, Eng., 2004), 122–123. One exception to the usual servant silence in court was the puzzling testimony Richard Grove gave addressing confusion that arose during his voyage to Virginia about who his master was to be; see McIlwaine, ed., *Minutes*, 12.

Virginia, made possible by judges who experienced none of the limits on their discretion that English magistrates knew. It would be nothing to extend such customs to Africans and then to transform those customs into a new body of law binding a new body of people to the unbounded wills of Virginia's judges.

Brase before the General Court

The white sailors from whom we know Brase's story left hundreds of words on the court's otherwise spare record. That same record suggests that Brase never spoke. If he did, neither the court's clerk nor its judges thought his words mattered any more than the words of white servants. Like them, Brase was putty in the justices' hands, his words—his consent—meaningless.

The judges' regard for their own power probably increased when they saw Brase, a person all their cultural norms said was due even less consideration than English servants. We get some idea of those norms by examining the census taken in Virginia earlier that year. Most of the nearly two dozen "Negroes" mentioned there were unnamed; the few who weren't had only a forename. The absence of names involved more than racist erasure; it was legal erasure. Without a name, one could not sue or be sued in an English court. White servants with names could and did petition the court. People without names had no legal personhood. Denied names, Virginia's "20. and odd Negroes" and those who followed them could only be objects of Virginia law—like inanimate things—not subjects under the protection of the English king's laws.[40]

The 1625 census records the dates and ships on which white servants arrived, thereby marking when their terms of service began. But no such entries were made for black servants, who were apparently presumed to serve indefinitely. It was the same in Bermuda, where names were omitted from such lists and where language in letters underscored blacks' subjection to whites. They might be "disposed of" or "reserved"; they were "procure[d]," "placed," "deliver[ed]," or "presented" without consent. Such words implied legal claims, even if such claims had not been tested in any court. What remained was to turn those

---

40. Jester and Hiden, eds., *Adventurers*, 3–69; Alden T. Vaughan, "Blacks in Virginia: A Note on the First Decade," *William and Mary Quarterly*, 3d Ser., XXIX (1972), 471–476. Two contexts in English law involved nonliving legal persons who nonetheless had legal, if fictional, names to give them standing before courts. A proper corporate name was the only way to recognize a nonhuman collective person that might sue or be sued; see *The Case of Sutton's Hospital* (1612), 10 Co. Rep. 28b–30a, 77 *Eng. Rep.*, 967–969. The other involved fictional persons—Roe and Doe—who were imagined to exist in support of process on ejectment to examine title to real property; see Baker, *Introduction*, 302. On white servants' petitioning the court, see McIlwaine, ed., *Minutes*, 98, 117. On the entailments of subjecthood, see Hannah Weiss Muller, *Subjects and Sovereign: Bonds of Belonging in the Eighteenth-Century British Empire* (Oxford, 2017), 16–30.

claims—that Africans were at the disposal of English colonists—into legally enforceable practices. The General Court's judges began this work as they made Virginia's customary law, one decision at a time.[41]

The origins of slavery as a variety of law, like so many kinds of law, are hard to pin down because people did not generally deploy legal language of enslavement in its early stages. By their final order, Virginia's judges decided that Captain Jones could not sell Brase to Captain Bass; they rejected one person's claim to another, a claim that perhaps viewed Brase as a slave under Spanish law and now as lawful prize by English admiralty law. Whatever the precise nature of Jones's claim, the judges thought their own was better: that their untrammeled authority over everyone and everything in Virginia might be extended to this stranger. Acting on that claim, they decided that Brase would now "belonge" to Governor Wyatt "as his servant." No custom, no law, could explain this judgment. They had to make one.[42]

Brase in an Empire of Law

Brase's story concerns Virginia's laws at the moment of their genesis. It also concerns law between and within empires. Brase, taken from a Spanish vessel in the Caribbean, probably passed through oversight by Spain's laws on his way to oversight by Virginia's laws. This may explain his "willingness" to go with Captain Jones: his readiness to leave the legalized slavery of Spain's empire in hopes of a better dispensation in England's empire. Doing so meant leaving fully developed laws regulating slavery for a place where slavery, as a matter of property law, had not yet been made. As he sailed off with Jones's crew, he probably could not have imagined that English imperialists would take their first steps to create that law upon his arrival in Virginia. In Spanish colonies, sovereign power drew on medieval codes intended in part to constrain slaves' masters. In Virginia, masters would make law as judges, and thereby make themselves sovereign over those who labored for them. Brase would be the first.[43]

In 1625, the General Court set an imperial pattern, followed over the next

41. Vernon A. Ives, ed., *The Rich Papers: Letters from Bermuda, 1615–1646: Eyewitness Accounts Sent by the Early Colonists to Sir Nathaniel Rich* (Toronto, 1984), 103, 157, 184, 188, 202; Bernhard, *Slaves and Slaveholders in Bermuda*, 26–27. Language in wills in the 1620s, including Sir George Yeardley's, reveals similar assumptions; see Vaughan, "Blacks in Virginia," *WMQ*, 3d Ser., XXIX (1972), 477.

42. McIlwaine, ed., *Minutes*, 73.

43. On English understandings of Spanish experience with enslaved people, see Michael Guasco, *Slaves and Englishmen: Human Bondage in the Early Modern Atlantic World* (Philadelphia, 2014), chap. 3. In Spanish colonies, the thirteenth-century law code, Las Siete Partidas, set a number of restrictions on the treatment of slaves; see J. H. Elliott, *Empires of the Atlantic World: Britain and Spain in America, 1492–1830* (New Haven, Conn., 2006), 107. Later, the Code Noir would perform a

two centuries, of a court fusing in one place all jurisdictions known to English law: a court presided over by people with little if any legal training; a court unconstrained in its use of discretion. Out of incremental decisions made by lay judges would arise a law of slavery across Britain's empire in the decades following Brase's case. Such lay judges would be heralded by their white colonial neighbors as avatars of a commonsense version of English law stripped of the "*abracadabra* of downright law jargon." In Jamaica, Edward Long would celebrate unlearned judges for their knowledge of "the customs, the policy, and equitable laws of Jamaica," the same kind of customary law Virginians made in their General Court beginning in 1619. By the eighteenth century, white colonial masters had come to like their customs quite well. Little wonder—they first made them in the courts where they sat.[44]

In time, colonial assemblies—where master-judges also sat as legislators—would pass statutes codifying those customs. The customary despotism constructed by lay magistrates thus became the tyranny of full-blown slave law. Two centuries after Brase's case, metropolitan critiques of slavery as law and of the practices of colonial lay magistrates converged in the work performed by the Commissioners of Inquiry who visited courts from the Caribbean to New South Wales to make recommendations for judicial reforms. Over and over, those commissioners remarked on the brutality, ignorance, and venality of lay judges. The problem was not new. It grew from a tradition begun two centuries earlier in Jamestown.[45]

Was Brase servant or slave? He was probably both. We know nothing of his legal condition or personal fate after that last order. Did he continue to receive payment for his work, as he had while on the Yeardleys' lands? Did he ever leave the Wyatts, or Virginia? Did white Virginians believe that he could do so lawfully? Did Brase have children; if so, did they remain with Wyatt's heirs? We don't know. We do know that a court presumed it possessed authority to determine his fate, even if no previously known law gave them such authority. This was how customary law was made, beginning in 1619.

---

similar function constraining masters in French colonies; see Malick W. Ghachem, *The Old Regime and the Haitian Revolution* (Cambridge, 2011), chap. 1.

44. [Edward Long], *The History of Jamaica* . . . (London, 1774), I, 70–72. Anguilla's Court of King's Bench is a good example of an eighteenth- and nineteenth-century court that generated a hodge-podge record quite like that of Virginia's General Court in the 1620s; see "Safeguarding Anguilla's Heritage: A Survey of the Endangered Records of Anguilla (EAP596)," https://eap.bl.uk/project/EAP596.

45. Lauren Benton and Lisa Ford, *Rage for Order: The British Empire and the Origins of International Law, 1800–1850* (Cambridge, Mass., 2016), chaps. 1–3. A vivid example of magisterial countenancing of master brutality occurred in Nevis in 1810 (ibid., 43–47).

Virginia and the Amazonian Alternative

MELISSA N. MORRIS

On the last day of April 1620, a ship set sail from Plymouth, England, headed to the New World. It carried more than 120 people, most of whom were to be left in the Americas to establish "trade and plantation." The trip across the Atlantic took seven weeks and resulted in only one death, a favorable outcome by the standards of the day. When John Smith wrote an account of the settlement a few years later, he declared that, when they arrived, "the sight of the Countrey and people so contented them, that never men thought themselves more happie." They found the place "most healthfull, pleasant and fruitfull." In just a few years, some English living in the area had been entirely won over by both "the goodnes of that Country" and the "gentle disposition of the people" and vowed to stay. This settlement, however, was not in North America; it was thousands of miles to the south, along the Amazon River. The group was sent out as the first settlers of the Amazon Company.[1]

In the first three decades of the seventeenth century, all of the major Atlantic empires established settlements in a region they called Guiana, which stretched along the northern coast of South America, from Venezuela to Brazil. The Spanish and Portuguese had founded settlements at the western and eastern ends, respectively, and the Dutch, French, and English saw the vast region in between as an obvious place to establish their own colonies and trading posts. Scholarship has tended to overlook these settlements because they were short-lived and because the region, composed today of three nations not colonized

---

The writing and research for this essay was funded in part by fellowships at the McNeil Center for Early American Studies, the John Carter Brown Library, and the Omohundro Institute of Early American History and Culture. I wish to thank Zach Carmichael, Peter Walker, Paul Musselwhite, James Horn, Peter C. Mancall, and all of the participants of the conference from which this essay emerged, and the editors of the Omohundro Institute for their comments and careful attention to earlier drafts of this essay. Thanks also to Jonathan Chipman for creating the map that accompanies this essay.

1. John Smith, *The True Travels, Adventures, and Observations of Captaine John Smith, in Europe, Asia, Affrica, and America, from Anno Domini 1593 to 1629* (London, 1630), 49, 51; Robert Harcourt, *A Relation of a Voyage to Guiana...*, ed. C. Alexander Harris, Works Issued by the Hakluyt Society, 2d Ser., no. 60 (London, 1928), 144.

Language groups
single underline: Carib
double underline: Arawakan
dashed underline: Tupi
no underline: Other

1. Riffault (French), 1594; France Équinoxiale (French), 1612; São Luis (Portuguese), 1615
2. San Tomé (Spanish), 1600
3. San Josef (Spanish), 1600
4. Leigh (English), 1604
5. Harcourt (English), 1609
6. Purcell's Creek/Tauregue (Irish), 1612
7. Thomas King (English), 1612
8. Sapanow (English/Irish), 1613
9. Fort (Dutch), circa 1613
10. Settlement mentioned in Spanish complaint (English), circa 1613
11. Materu/Orange/Gomoarou/Nassau (Dutch), 1615
12. Amsterdam Merchants (Dutch), 1615
13. P. Lodewycx and Son (Dutch), 1615
14. P. Adriaenszoon (Dutch/English), 1616
15. Belém (Portuguese), 1616
16. Fort Kijkoveral (Dutch), 1616
17. O'Brien (Irish), 1620
18. R. North (English), 1620

Guiana and the Amazon in the Early Seventeenth Century.
Drawn by Jonathan W. Chipman

by Iberians, fits clumsily into histories of Latin America. In the early seventeenth century, however, the Amazon was as likely a place for English interest as Virginia. Rather than a doomed alternative, South America was an attractive competitor to Virginia. Trade and settlement in the region built upon prior English experience there, and South America even offered some advantages Virginia lacked, including a climate suitable for growing tropical commodities and alliance-seeking Natives.[2]

The year 1619 was critical for English interests in Guiana. Although the region was home to a smattering of settlements, attempts to charter a company to oversee and organize them had thus far failed. In 1619, a group of investors led by Roger North, who had been with Walter Ralegh on his ill-fated 1617–1618 last voyage to the region, sought and received a charter to colonize as the Amazon Company. They intended to bring several existing settlements along the river under their control and then to send out new settlers to shore up their claims. The 1620 migrants described above were part of the latter initiative. The Amazon Company's 1619 charter thus demonstrates the appeal of alternatives to Virginia. From the early seventeenth century, South American colonization schemes competed with those to the north. English colonial enthusiasts argued that they would find surer riches closer to the Iberian colonies. The Amazon Company attracted many influential investors but also sparked protests from Spain. The Spanish ambassador to England, Diego Sarmiento de Acuña, Count Gondomar, argued that the English had no right to colonize Iberian territory, and his campaign against the company contributed to its swift demise. Like other events of 1619 for Virginia, the consequences of the Amazon charter and the subsequent failure of the company were gradual. The English continued to have an interest in Guiana, but subsequent colonization efforts

---

2. The historian Joyce Lorimer is a notable exception to the lack of attention given the Guianas; see her introductory essays in Joyce Lorimer, ed., *English and Irish Settlement on the River Amazon, 1550–1646*, Works Issued by the Hakluyt Society, 2d Ser., no. 171 (London, 1989); and Lorimer, "The English Contraband Tobacco Trade from Trinidad and Guiana, 1590–1617," in K. R. Andrews, N. P. Canny, and P. E. H. Hair, eds., *The Westward Enterprise: English Activities in Ireland, the Atlantic, and America, 1480–1650* (Liverpool, 1978), 124–150. Anthropologist Neil L. Whitehead also wrote extensively on the region, focusing on the Caribs, including their relationships with the English and Dutch; see Whitehead, *Lords of the Tiger Spirit: A History of the Caribs in Colonial Venezuela and Guyana, 1498–1820* (Providence, R.I., 1988); and Walter Ralegh, *The Discoverie of the Large, Rich, and Bewtiful Empyre of Guiana*, ed. Whitehead (Norman, Okla., 1997). Historians of the Dutch Atlantic have more frequently included Guiana in their assessments, though scholarship on the early seventeenth century is still comparatively thin; see Mark Meuwese, *Brothers in Arms, Partners in Trade: Dutch-Indigenous Alliances in the Atlantic World, 1595–1674* (Leiden, Netherlands, 2012); L. A. H. C. Hulsman, "Nederlands Amazonia: Handel met Indianen tussen 1580 en 1680" (Ph.D. diss., University of Amsterdam, 2009); and Cornelis Ch. Goslinga, *The Dutch in the Caribbean and on the Wild Coast, 1580–1680* (Assen, Netherlands, 1971).

did not attract the same enthusiasm. For the next several decades, the Guiana colonies remained underpopulated and inessential, while Virginia eventually flourished.[3]

As the essays in this volume demonstrate, 1619 was also a crucial year in Virginia's history: the first meeting of the General Assembly, the arrival of the first Africans, and the first sustained recruitment of marriageable women. All three directed the future of the colony along a particular course, helping to guarantee its permanence. Only after several decades, however, did the full ramifications of these events become clear. Immediately after 1619, Virginia continued to face challenges, culminating in the revocation of the Virginia Company's charter in 1624. The innovations introduced in 1619 took a while to bear fruit, but in that pivotal year Guiana and Virginia were both still plausible candidates to become a primary focus of English colonization.

BY 1619, THE ENGLISH HAD MAINTAINED AN INTEREST IN BOTH VIRginia and Guiana for several decades. For northern Europeans, Guiana had long held an allure. In his 1584 "Discourse of Western Planting," Richard Hakluyt laid out both its strategic and material appeal: "All that parte of America eastwarde from Cumana unto the River of St. Augustine in Bresill conteyneth in lengthe alongest to the sea side [2100] miles, In whiche compasse and tracte there is neither Spaniarde, Portingale, nor any Christian man but onely the Caribes, Indians, and salvages. In w[hi]ch places is greate plentie of golde, perle, and precious stones." Guiana had wealth, and no one was claiming it.[4]

Hakluyt's assessment of easy riches was exaggerated, but his geography was roughly accurate. By the 1590s, the Spanish had established two settlements in the province they called Trinidad y Guayana: one on the island of Trinidad and another along the Orinoco River in present-day Venezuela. These settlements represented the limit of their presence in the region outlined by Hakluyt. From 1570 to 1600, far to the southeast, the Portuguese waged a war against the Potiguar peoples and came to control the land from Bahia to São Roque, in Rio Grande do Norte, on Brazil's easternmost point. In between these settlements lay about twelve hundred miles of coast.

---

3. By the 1650s, English interest in Guiana was renewed before once again being abandoned in favor of less risky imperial interests; see Justin Roberts, "Surrendering Surinam: The Barbadian Diaspora and the Expansion of the English Sugar Frontier, 1650–75," *William and Mary Quarterly,* 3d Ser., LXXIII (2016), 225–256; and Alison Games, "Cohabitation, Suriname-Style: English Inhabitants in Dutch Suriname after 1667," *WMQ,* 3d Ser., LXXII (2015), 195–242.

4. "Discourse of Western Planting, by Richard Hakluyt, 1584," in E. G. R. Taylor, ed., *The Original Writings and Correspondence of the Two Richard Hakluyts,* Works Issued by the Hakluyt Society, 2d Ser., no. 76 (1935; rpt. Nendeln, Liechtenstein, 1967), 255.

Hakluyt, of course, had also championed Virginia as a promising place to colonize. He thought Virginia would have gold, silver, pearls, dyes, and other lucrative commodities and that it might lead to the discovery of a Northwest Passage. Hakluyt was both directly and indirectly responsible for early publications about the colony and encouraged Theodor de Bry to publish Thomas Harriot's *Briefe and True Report of the New Found Land of Virginia* (1588) about the Roanoke colony. He even seems to have contemplated going to Virginia himself, though he never made the voyage.[5]

Initial interest in the North American coast was taken up by Humphrey Gilbert, who was awarded a patent to colonize in 1578 but died before establishing a colony. Ralegh received his half brother's patent and in 1585 sent Philip Amadas and Arthur Barlowe on a reconnaissance voyage that explored coastal North Carolina. The next year, the English settled 108 men at Roanoke, but the group, disillusioned by the lack of easy riches and the presence of resistant Natives, returned to England the following year. Undeterred, Ralegh sent out a second group to settle in 1587, led by governor John White. White then returned to England in August of the same year to request a relief expedition. War prevented Ralegh and White from sending a ship to resupply the fledgling settlement, and by the time White returned in 1590 the colonists were gone. Thus, the initial attempts to colonize Virginia resulted only in the "Lost Colony."[6]

The attempts to settle in Guiana are less familiar to us today, but both regions were well known to interested contemporaries. As in Virginia, Guiana's most illustrious early booster was Walter Ralegh. John Smith was initially slated to go to Guiana as part of a 1605 colonization effort headed by Charles Leigh, but instead he departed for the Americas in 1607, bound for Virginia. In his *Of Plymouth Plantation*, William Bradford recalled how the more famous group of 1620 migrants weighed their own options: "Some (and none of the meanest) had thoughts and were ernest for Guiana . . . others were for some parts of Virginia." While the chief advantage of Virginia was that the English had already begun to colonize it, Guiana's attraction was "that the cuntrie was rich, fruitfull, and blessed with a perpetuall spring, and a florishing greenes; where vigorous nature brought forth all things in abundance and plentie without any great labour or

---

5. Peter C. Mancall, *Hakluyt's Promise: An Elizabethan's Obsession for an English America* (New Haven, Conn., 2007), 195–196; Anthony Payne, "Richard Hakluyt (1552?–1616)," in Lawrence Goldman, ed., *Oxford Dictionary of National Biography*, online ed. (Oxford, 2004); Thomas Har[r]iot, *A Briefe and True Report of the New Found Land of Virginia* . . . (London, 1588).

6. Karen Ordahl Kupperman, *Roanoke: The Abandoned Colony*, 2d ed. (New York, 2007); James Horn, *A Kingdom Strange: The Brief and Tragic History of the Lost Colony of Roanoke* (New York, 2010).

art of man." In the first decades of the seventeenth century, both locations held promise in the eyes of English colonists.[7]

Guiana's reputation as a place with great riches arose from an intermingling of indigenous and Spanish traditions. Columbus had been the first to note, in 1498, that the people of Trinidad "wore pieces of gold on their breasts, and some had some pearls round their arms." To underscore his point, he added: "I rejoiced greatly when I saw these things." He traveled along the coast of Venezuela, inquiring after gold and pearls all the while: "I made great endeavours to know where they collected that gold and they all indicated to me a land bordering on them to the west, which was very lofty but not at a distance. But all told me that I should not go there, for there they ate men." In 1531, Spaniard Diego de Ordás set out with five ships and six hundred men to explore the region between the Amazon and the Orinoco Rivers. Ordás subscribed to a belief, popular at the time, that gold was typically found close to the equator and was placed by God in less hospitable landscapes to encourage their settlement. He thought such a lode would be found at the headwaters of the Orinoco. Storms quickly scattered Ordás's ships, and the expedition came to nothing, but stories of it made their way back across the Atlantic.[8]

Around the same time, the conquistador Gonzalez Jiménez de Quesada heard tales from the Muisca tribe of eastern Colombia about a gilded prince. Like the tribes of Guiana, the Muisca had elaborate goldwork but no obvious source. Quesada determined that the gold might lie farther east, and, years later, Spain granted him a patent to explore a region of present-day Venezuela. In 1569, he led an expedition of two thousand men to the Orinoco but returned to Bogotá three years later with only thirty survivors. Quesada died in 1579, and his encomienda, the right to the labor of a group of Native peoples, passed to his niece's husband, Antonio de Berrío. A stipulation in Quesada's will required Berrío to continue the search. Although he enthusiastically took up the task, his forays into the interior ended in disaster. Still, Berrío established the two settlements mentioned above—San Joséf de Oruña, on Trinidad, and San Tomé, along the Orinoco River—and he governed the province of Trinidad y Guayana from 1592 until his death in 1597.[9]

---

7. Smith, *True Travels*; William Bradford, *Of Plymouth Plantation: The Pilgrims in America*, ed. Harvey Wish (New York, 1962), 43.

8. Cecil Jane, ed., *Select Documents Illustrating the Four Voyages of Christopher Columbus*, 2 vols. (New York, 1988), II, 20, 24; John Hemming, *The Search for El Dorado* (New York, 1978), 10–11; Pablo Ojer, *La Formacion del Oriente Venezolano*, I, *Creación de las Gobernaciones* (Caracas, 1966). The priest Pedro Simón, a longtime resident of Colombia and an important early chronicler of its indigenous peoples (especially the Muisca), wrote an account of Ordás's expedition in 1626; see Simón, *Noticias historiales de las conquistas de Tierra Firme en las Indias occidentales* (Bogotá, 1882), I.

9. Ricardo Piqueras Céspedes, "Antonio de Berrío y las ordenanzas de 1573," *Boletín Americanista*, XLIX (1999), 234; "Antonio de Berrío to the King of Spain," Dec. 2, 1594, no. 3, and "Letter from

Concurrently, English, French, and Dutch explorers began to frequent places along the South American coast east of Colombia. Their initial visits were part of the raiding and illicit trading that became increasingly common elsewhere in the Caribbean during the sixteenth century. The area, however, presented them with unique opportunities. Some ships came to take advantage of the region's natural resources; Dutch vessels, for instance, mined the saltpans near Punta de Araya, on the mainland between Cumaná and Margarita Island.[10]

Other expeditions were intended to attack Spanish settlements. This was especially the case on Margarita Island, whose pearl fisheries attracted raiders like the English pirate John Hawkins. As early as 1586, Spanish settlers appealed to the crown for assistance in building a fort. In April 1587, the cabildo (government council) of Margarita Island wrote to alert Philip II that increased predations had led to death and destruction. They reported that, in October 1591 alone, thirty enemy ships had come near the island. The governor, Juan Sarmiento de Villandandro, wrote that, although his people constantly defended the coast with "weapons in hand," they had not received any new munitions from Spain during his tenure in office. An English account of a 1593 attack on Margarita Island, in which a group of English privateers fought off three times as many Spaniards, attributed the English success to their sailors' bravery. Conveniently, though, "the Spanyards weapons were broken." Later that year, Governor Villandandro was killed in a fight with either an English or a Dutch ship. Although Margarita Island especially tempted pirates, settlements all along the coast complained of raiding. Recognizing Spanish weakness in Guiana, northern Europeans had a steadily increasing presence there from the 1580s on.[11]

AS EARLY AS 1587, THE SAME YEAR THE "LOST COLONY" SETTLED AT Roanoke, Ralegh might have sent a reconnaissance mission to Guiana. In 1594, he backed an expedition to Trinidad under Jacob Whiddon and arrived there himself in May 1595. He traded with the Spanish and the Indians alike, kidnapped the explorer Berrío to learn more about the region, and formed alliances

---

Domingo de Vera Ybarguen to His Majesty, Giving an Account of the Expedition to Dorado," Oct. 27, 1597, no. 7, both in *British Guiana Boundary: Arbitration with the United States of Venezuela; Appendix to the Case on Behalf of the Government of Her Britannic Majesty*, I, *1593–1723* (London, 1898).

10. Kenneth R. Andrews, ed., *English Privateering Voyages to the West Indies, 1588–1595* . . . , Works Issued by the Hakluyt Society, 2d Ser., no. 111 (Cambridge, 1959), 28–29.

11. Ojer, *La Formacion*, I, 359. Other provinces also repeatedly sought funds to build forts in this period; see "Petición de Caracas para la fábrica de un fuerte," Apr. 20, 1598, Santo Domingo 201, tomo I, n. 33, and "Carta del cabildo de Margarita a S. M.," Apr. 7, 1587, Santo Domingo 182, fol. 16, both in Archivo General de Indias, Seville, Spain; and "A Report of Cumberland's Seventh Voyage," in Andrews, ed., *English Privateering Voyages*, 247.

with local indigenous peoples. Ralegh published an account of his journey, *The Discoverie of the Large, Rich, and Bewtiful Empyre of Guiana*, in 1596. Lawrence Keymis, his second-in-command, likewise wrote an account. These works popularized an image of Guiana as both full of promise and beyond Spanish control. Ralegh's own trip to Guiana centered on the Spanish settlements, which he attacked, but his writing inspired continued interest in the broader region that Hakluyt had advocated a few years before.[12]

Ralegh intended to establish permanent settlements in Guiana. His efforts were curtailed, however, when the newly crowned James I imprisoned him in 1603. But others were better positioned to capitalize on prior English experiences in the region. In 1604, Charles Leigh, a merchant and sea captain, established the first English settlement in South America on the Wiapoco (Oyapock) River. Leigh had previously been to North America, the Caribbean, and Guiana, and he built upon his own experience, as well as that of Ralegh, to establish his settlement. Leigh chose the location for his colony based on his earlier reconnaissance. Once there, he made contact with Natives who had been to England.[13]

Leigh originally sought mines, but he soon turned to renewable commodities. The Dutch already came to the area to trade for flax but paid such high prices that Leigh was unable to buy any himself. Instead, by establishing a settlement, he could procure the commodity more easily. Leigh wrote to his brother Olave, the chief financial backer of the project, that he could "returne a Shippe laden with Flaxe and other commodities the next yeare," and he requested that his brother send weavers to work it. He also asked for gardeners, whom he thought would be among the most helpful laborers to the colony. Leigh's request for skilled weavers and gardeners signaled his intention to make the settlement permanent. His colony failed, however, after he died just before departing for England to resupply. The men he left behind returned to England in 1606, before a group sent to resupply them arrived.[14]

Despite the short tenure of Leigh's colony, his attempt drew renewed atten-

12. Joyce Lorimer, "Ralegh's First Reconnaissance of Guiana? An English Survey of the Orinoco in 1587," *Terrae Incognitae: The Annals of the Society for the History of Discoveries*, IX (1977), 7–22; W[alter] Ralegh, *The Discoverie of the Large, Rich, and Bewtiful Empyre of Guiana* . . . (London, 1596); Lawrence Keymis, *A Relation of the Second Voyage to Guiana, Perfourmed and Written in the Yeare 1596* (London, 1596), A1v. Something of Ralegh's and Keymis's hopes for native alliances is reflected in a poem contained in Keymis's work, which has the line: "Riches with honour, Conquest without Bloud [blood]."

13. John Nicholl, *An Houre Glasse of Indian Newes* . . . (London, 1607); Lorimer, ed., *English and Irish Settlement*, 26. For more on how Leigh capitalized on Ralegh's Native diplomacy, see Alden T. Vaughan, "Sir Walter Ralegh's Indian Interpreters, 1584–1618," *WMQ*, 3d Ser., LIX (2002), 341–376.

14. "Captaine Charles Leighs Letter to Sir Olave Leigh His Brother," July 2, 1604, and "The Relation of Master John Wilson . . . ," in [Samuel Purchas], *Purchas His Pilgrimes, in Five Books* . . . (London, 1625), IV, 1252–1255, 1260–1265 (quotation on 1254); Nicholl, *Houre Glasse*.

tion to Guiana's attractions. In 1609, Robert Harcourt was granted a patent to sail to and settle in Guiana. Harcourt, a gentleman, had connections with previous Guiana explorers as well as the favor of Prince Henry, who had a particular interest in overseas voyages and exploration. He set out for Guiana with about twenty settlers and arrived in May 1609. The group initially settled near Leigh's former colony, but a Native leader intervened to guide them to a healthier location. The new colony eventually consisted of a few settlements dispersed around the Wiapoco. Like Leigh, Harcourt initially came in search of mines but quickly turned to commodities. He left his brother, Michael, in charge and returned to England with news of his success. In 1613, Robert published an account, *A Relation of a Voyage to Guiana,* and in August of that year the king awarded him a patent for exclusive commercial and administrative rights in the region from the Amazon to the Essequibo Rivers. Although Harcourt successfully promoted the colony, he failed to keep it running. Michael Harcourt had died during a 1612 trip to England, and the resulting lack of leadership in the colony contributed to its collapse.[15]

Other groups were also settling in Guiana around this time. In 1612, two men with Virginia connections, expedition leader Matthew Morton and financer Thomas Roe, established a settlement on the Amazon. Roe, a Virginia Company investor and future ambassador to India, had been in the area the year before and had traded for tobacco with the Spanish settlers of San Tomé and San Josef. By the time he returned, the Spanish crown had cracked down on this trade. Roe and others saw establishing Guiana plantations of their own as the surest way to replace lucrative commodity trading.[16]

Nor were the English alone in the region. A group of primarily Irish settlers founded a colony in 1612 near where North's men would settle in 1620. Several

---

15. Joyce Lorimer, "Robert Harcourt, 1574/5–1631," in Goldman, ed., *Oxford Dictionary of National Biography;* "Grant to Robt. Harcourt, Sir Thos. Challoner, and John Rovenson, and to the Heirs of the Said Robert, of All That Part of Guiana or Continent of America between the Rivers Amazon and Dollesquebe," SP 14/141, fol. 126, The National Archives, Kew, U.K. (hereafter cited as TNA); Robert Harcourt, *A Relation of a Voyage to Guiana Describing the Climat, Scituation, Fertilitie, Provisions, and Commodities of That Country* . . . (London, 1613); Harcourt, *Relation,* ed. Harris, 8.

16. Edmund Howes, *The Annales; or, Generall Chronicle of England, Begun First by Maister John Stow* (London, 1615), 946; Sarah Tyacke, "English Charting of the River Amazon, c. 1595–c. 1630," *Imago Mundi,* XXXII (1980), 73–89; Lorimer, "English Contraband Tobacco Trade from Trinidad and Guiana," in Andrews, Canny, and Hair, eds., *Westward Enterprise,* 124–150. For more on Spanish efforts to curtail the illicit tobacco trade, see Marcy Norton and Daviken Studnicki-Gizbert, "The Multinational Commodification of Tobacco, 1492–1650: An Iberian Perspective," in Peter C. Mancall, ed., *The Atlantic World and Virginia, 1550–1624* (Williamsburg, Va., and Chapel Hill, N.C., 2007), 251–273; "Sancho de Alquiça to the King," Feb. 11, 1612, no. 10, "Sancho de Alquiça to the King," June 13, 1612 (extract), no. 11, and "Sancho de Alquiça to the King," June 14, 1612, no. 12, all in *British Guiana Boundary.*

Dutch settlements and trading posts dotted the rivers of Guiana, including the Amazon and its tributaries. In 1616, an Anglo-Dutch colony grew along the Amazon River that was larger than previous efforts, with well over a hundred people, including fourteen families, a sure signal they intended to stay. A Portuguese report on the settlement wrote of alarm at the "many people, women amongst them, making a fort." According to the colonial chronicler John Scott, the group settled with the goodwill of the Natives and the following year loaded a ship with cargo that sold for sixty thousand pounds. The colony initially prospered but was doomed because its settlers got involved "in the Quarrels of the Indians." After a few of the colonists were killed by Natives, the rest departed for home in 1623. Even as they fled, they brought back "Considerable Riches."[17]

This brief history of the Guiana settlements suggests that they had a few things in common with Virginia. There was a long-standing English interest in both the northern coast of South America and the eastern coast of North America. Although this curiosity soon led to attempts to colonize in each area, those first efforts did not lead to permanent colonies. The English became interested in both regions because they were imagined to be adjacent to mineral-laden and commodity-rich Spanish colonies but reasonably beyond Spain's imperial reach.

Yet in several respects Guiana was more attractive than Virginia to the English. The climate was more favorable to European settlers in need of provisions. Guiana is warm year-round and has two growing seasons; Virginia is warm but not tropical. The Powhatans knew seasons of plenty but also of want. The leanest time of all was in late spring and early summer, after the corn reserves were gone and before fruit was ripe. John Smith recorded that food was scarce enough during this period to cause the people to become much thinner. Incidentally, the English first arrived at Jamestown in late April. In northern colonial spaces, needy newcomers drained resources. In Guiana, indigenous groups more easily accommodated hungry colonists. An anonymous Dutch author described Guiana as a place where, when one leaf fell, another sprang forth to take its place. This fanciful description held some truth.[18]

Importantly, Guiana offered the English a greater ability to forge alliances

---

17. "Andres Pereira, 1616: Account of What There Is in the Great and Famous River of the Amazons, Newly Discovered," in Lorimer, ed., *English and Irish Settlement*, 172; Col. John Scott, "An Historical and Geographical Description of the Great River of the Amazons, and of the Several Great Rivers That Pay the Tribute of Their Waters to Her, and of the Several Nations Inhabiting That Famous Country," MS Rawlinson A 175, fols. 356, 370–371, Bodleian Library, Oxford.

18. Helen C. Rountree, *The Powhatan Indians of Virginia: Their Traditional Culture* (Norman, Okla., 1989), 45–46; *Pertinente Beschrijvinge van Guiana Gelegen aen de Vaste Kust van America . . .* (Amsterdam, 1676); Carl O. Sauer, "Cultivated Plants of South and Central America," in Julian H. Steward, ed., *Handbook of South American Indians*, VI, *Physical Anthropology, Linguistics, and Cultural Geography of South American Indians* (Washington, D.C., 1950), 487–543.

with indigenous groups. English colonial promoters often argued that the Natives of the Americas would flock "to the gentle government of the English" because they desired relief from Spanish cruelty. Scholarship on the Black Legend has considered how Protestant northern Europeans deployed an image of Spanish tyranny abroad to protest Spanish power in Europe. The Black Legend was rooted in an anti-Catholic worldview and sometimes worked to obscure the atrocities that all Atlantic empires committed. It is therefore hard for us to take Protestant Europeans' claims of welcoming Natives seriously, but, at least in Guiana, they did indeed find such alliances possible.[19]

The English, beginning with Ralegh, attempted to develop ties with Natives in both Virginia and Guiana. Ralegh adopted the practice of bringing Native people to London. Upon his instruction, the Amadas-Barlowe expedition arrived in England with the first two, the Croatan Island werowance Manteo and the Roanoke Wanchese, in September 1584. In contrast to previous Native visitors to England, they most likely came willingly. In London, they lived at Durham House, Ralegh's residence along the Thames, where they learned English and taught their own languages to Thomas Harriot. Ralegh hoped that, after spending time in England, Manteo and Wanchese would assist the English back in Virginia. The two men returned to their homelands after eight months in England, but their relationships with the English diverged thereafter. Manteo indeed became the loyal ally Ralegh had hoped for. He converted to Christianity, made a return trip to England, and went back to Virginia with the 1587 colonists who settled at Roanoke Island. Wanchese, by contrast, seems to have defied the English. He remained with his people upon his return, offering no assistance to the English. He instead headed up a group hostile to the colonists and perhaps even killed some of them. The results of the first attempt to win over Natives were decidedly mixed. Considered over a longer period, the results are even less encouraging. Despite Manteo's assistance, the Roanoke Colony failed, its fate unknown. When the English returned to Virginia to colonize the Chesapeake in 1607, their alliance with Manteo two decades before and dozens of miles away made no difference.[20]

---

19. "A Pamphlet by Richard Hakluyt the Younger, 1579–80," in Taylor, ed., *Original Writings and Correspondence of the Two Richard Hakluyts*, 142. For more on the Black Legend, see Julián Juderías, *La Leyenda Negra y la verdad histórica* (Madrid, 1914); and Benjamin Keen, "The Black Legend Revisited: Assumptions and Realities," *Hispanic American Historical Review*, XLIX (1969), 703–719. For more on how the Black Legend was deployed by the Dutch and English in this period, see Benjamin Schmidt, *Innocence Abroad: The Dutch Imagination and the New World, 1570–1670* (Cambridge, 2001); and William S. Maltby, *The Black Legend in England: The Development of Anti-Spanish Sentiment, 1558–1660* (Durham, N.C., 1971).

20. Coll Thrush, *Indigenous London: Native Travelers at the Heart of Empire* (New Haven, Conn., 2016), 33–61; Vaughan, "Sir Walter Ralegh's Indian Interpreters," *WMQ*, 3d Ser., LIX (2002), 346–350.

When Ralegh shifted his attention to Guiana in the 1590s, he and others continued the practice of taking Natives to England. Piecing together information from an array of sources, Alden T. Vaughn estimates that "twelve or more natives of Guiana and Trinidad ... made the journey [to London] between 1594 and 1618." Expeditions sponsored by Ralegh took the first Guiana Natives to England. They then accompanied Ralegh on his 1595 voyage, returning home. During this trip, he engineered swaps of people to facilitate future cultural exchanges and to hasten English conquest of Guiana. When Ralegh met with the cacique Topiawari in 1595, he told him that he had made his voyage to deliver Topiawari's people from both the Spanish and their indigenous enemies, the Epuremei. To strengthen their alliance, Ralegh took Topiawari's son, Cayowaroco, to London and left two young Englishmen with the cacique. Later accounts mention several additional Natives who were brought to England, including Leonard Ragapo, John of Trinidad, Martin, and Anthony Canabre.[21]

In Guiana, Ralegh's attempts to build Native alliances met with greater success than in Virginia. In the following decades, both sides continued to remember and respect the alliances Ralegh and the Guiana Natives forged. Other Europeans with imperial aspirations in the region acknowledged it too. The clearest evidence of the success of Ralegh's efforts is that subsequent English colonizers frequently ran into Natives who could speak English and regarded them as potential allies. When Robert Harcourt and his men coasted into the Bay of Wiapoco in 1609, canoes of Indians greeted them and asked where they were from. Then, "understanding that wee were English men[,] boldly came aboard us one of them could speake out language well, and was knowne to some of my company to bee an Indian, that sometime had been in England." Harcourt later wrote that it would be relatively easy to convert the Natives of Guiana because "they love and preferre [the English] before all other stranger whatsoever." In 1598, a Dutch ship that encountered Natives along the Venezuelan coast took advantage of the reputation of the English. As the Natives approached, they asked the men if they were "Anglees," and the Dutch replied, "Si, Si." The Natives came on board the ship to trade with their supposed friends. A Portuguese captain reporting on the affairs of Grão Pará in 1618 or 1619 agreed that the English had a superior reputation even there, far from where any Ralegh expedition had visited. The captain explained that "the Indians of that district do not wish to

21. Vaughn, "Sir Walter Ralegh's Indian Interpreters," *WMQ*, 3d Ser., LIX (2002), esp. 342 (quotation), 367; Alden T. Vaughn, *Transatlantic Encounters: American Indians in Britain, 1500–1776* (Cambridge, 2006); Ralegh, *Discoverie*, ed. Whitehead, 181. One of the men Ralegh left behind was reportedly eaten by a jaguar while the other was captured and taken to Margarita, where he was questioned. For a Spanish account of their fate, see "Carta de Don Roque de Montes á el Rey," Apr. 18, 1596, no. 5, in *British Guiana Boundary*.

come to trade with us at our fort, because as well as the bad things which they [the English and Dutch] tell them about us (and it may be with good cause), they give them what they want more freely and treat them better and with greater honesty, which is what they desire." When Ralegh returned to Guiana after a nearly twenty-year absence, he was nonetheless "fedd and assisted by the Indyans of my ould acquaintance, with a greate deale of love and respect."[22]

These different results raise an important question. Why did the English in Guiana find it easier to win the cooperation of Native groups? English success in building alliances depended on a number of variables. The most immediate factor—distrust of the Spanish—had been precipitated by a complicated chain of events directly preceding Ralegh's arrival. Spanish settlers in the Guianas had become divided into two factions. Those from older settlements, especially Margarita Island, made up the first group. They had established deep ties with local communities, at times trading sons with them. Newer settlers, who had come in search of El Dorado, like Trinidad y Guayana governor Antonio de Berrío, formed the second group. These treasure-seekers offended the older settlers, presuming ownership of possible resources in the interior and upsetting existing alliances. The governor of Margarita Island, Francisco de Vides, attempted to take the governorship of Trinidad by force in 1593, claiming that the island and nearby mainland should be under his jurisdiction. The matter was sent before Philip II, who decided in favor of Berrío. Although Berrío's right to govern Trinidad was upheld for the time being, he realized that, in order to maintain his claim to the interior, he would have to explore it and discover any riches it might contain. To that end, he enlisted the help of a cacique, Morequito, whom he had been assured could take him to the interior of Guiana. Morequito, however, was in alliance with the governors of Margarita Island and Cumaná against Berrío. A misreading of the situation among the Spanish led Morequito and his Native allies to raid a village friendly to Berrío and murder Spanish soldiers and a priest. For this, Morequito was betrayed by his allies and executed. The end result was that Native groups had reason to be wary of both Spanish sides.[23]

Soon after Ralegh arrived in Trinidad in March 1595, two Indians approached

---

22. Harcourt, *Relation*, ed. Harris, 70–71, 128; Vaughan, "Sir Walter Ralegh's Indian Interpreters," *WMQ*, 3d Ser., LIX (2002), 368 (quotation); "Account of a Journey to Guiana and the Island of Trinidad, Performed in the Years 1597 and 1598 . . . ," Feb. 3, 1599, no. 8, in *British Guiana Boundary* (the account goes on to say that they later explained they were actually "Holandees"); "Manoel de Sousa D'Eça: Concerning the Affairs of Grão Pará [1618/9]," in Lorimer, ed., *English and Irish Settlement*, 175. For more on Portuguese policy in Brazil, see John Hemming, *Red Gold: The Conquest of the Brazilian Indians*, rev. ed. (London, 1995), esp. chaps. 9–11.

23. "Don Antonio de Berrío to the King of Spain," Jan. 1, 1593, no. 1, in *British Guiana Boundary*; Ralegh, *Discoverie*, ed. Whitehead, 152.

his ship and came aboard. One of them, a cacique named Cantyman, knew Ralegh's captain, Jacob Whiddon. Cantyman told them how strong the Spaniards were, where their city was, and where they could find Berrío, who was rumored to be dead. Using this intelligence, Ralegh then sailed to San Tomé and kidnapped Berrío. Next, he rallied nearby groups that were enemies of the Spanish, told them he served the cacique Elizabeth, and, "at the instance of the Indians," burned the Spanish settlement at San Tomé.[24]

Ralegh took advantage of the fallout from Morequito's death, but the Natives of Guiana had other, long-standing reasons to be wary of the Spanish. Ralegh's experiences in Guiana were the products of a century of interaction between Europeans and indigenous groups. Neil Whitehead has shown that Ralegh's account, though presented as a discovery, shows indigenous people as "sophisticated actors," well acquainted with "Europeans and their political and economic stratagems." They ably played Europeans' rivalries with one another to their own advantage.[25]

The geopolitical situation in the region, precipitated by the Spanish presence (and to a lesser extent in the south, the Portuguese), made indigenous alliances possible. In the early sixteenth century, when the Spanish began to colonize parts of Venezuela, they allied with the Arawaks, as they had elsewhere. Even though there were no more than a few hundred Spaniards in the area a century later, their presence disrupted existing Native networks of trade and settlement. Arawaks had access to European trade goods and came to occupy an important role in the local economy. Some Arawaks relocated to be nearer to the Spanish settlements and displaced other Native groups, and these dislocations cascaded. In 1604, when Charles Leigh sought to establish his aforementioned colony near the Wiapoco River, he found the area populated by fifteen hundred people: Yaos, Sapaios, and Arawaks, who, "beeing chased from other Rivers, by the Caribes have combined themselves together in this place for their better defense, and are now at deadly warres with the Caribes." Harcourt described roughly the same area: "These Provinces are peopled with divers Nations of severall languages, namely, *Yaios, Arwaccas, Sappaios, Paragotos,* and *Charibes.* The *Charibes* are the ancient inhabitants, and the other Nations are such as have beene chased away from *Trinidado,* and the borders of *Orenoque.*" The situation presented an opportunity for northern European interlopers like the English and Dutch. The Yaos and Sapaios asked Leigh to stay, "that he should ayde and defend

---

24. During Whiddon's previous expedition, Berrío had promised eight of his men could safely come ashore to get water and wood, but they were ambushed and killed. Ralegh sought revenge; see Ralegh, *Discoverie,* ed. Whitehead, 134–135.

25. Neil L. Whitehead, "Introduction," ibid., 3.

them against their enemies the Caribes and others." Non-Iberians who arrived in small numbers could form alliances with indigenous groups whose lives the Spanish had disrupted.[26]

Virginia settlers hoped for similar alliances with indigenous peoples, but geopolitical circumstances prohibited it. Although Ralegh, and by extension the English, won Manteo's loyalty, they were unable to build upon this relationship to win the trust of other tribes. As in Guiana, previous encounters with the Spanish informed the relationship between the English and Native peoples—in this case, the Powhatans. These interactions, however, went quite differently. For much of the sixteenth century, the Chesapeake was a region of interest to the Spanish. Some Spaniards thought a strait ran westward from the bay, dipping south close to Mexico. Keeping the Chesapeake free of foreign influence was therefore vital. It was also strategically important for its proximity to Florida. In 1561, a Spanish ship entered the Chesapeake Bay and arrived at Ajacán, a location likely between the James and York Rivers. They left with a teenaged Powhatan boy, Paquiquineo, whom they hoped would facilitate their future relationships with the people of the Chesapeake. After traveling to Spain and Mexico, Paquiquineo returned a decade later, ostensibly to help establish a mission at Ajacán, with a group of eight missionaries and a boy. Upon his return, however, Paquiquineo rejoined his people and resumed their cultural practices. He rebuffed the Spaniards' pleas for food and for his aid as an interpreter. After a few months of increasingly deteriorating relations, Paquiquineo reportedly led a group that killed the eight men, sparing only the boy, who told the tale.[27]

When they arrived more than forty years later, the English noted that the Powhatans retained a hatred for the Spanish. Their experience, however, had taught them something quite different from what the people of Guiana had learned. The Powhatans compelled the Spanish to leave and not return: resis-

---

26. H. Dieter Heinen and Alvaro García-Castro, "The Multiethnic Network of the Lower Orinoco in Early Colonial Times," *Ethnohistory*, XLVII (2000), 561–579; "Captaine Charles Leigh His Voyage to Guiana and Plantation There," and "Captaine Charles Leighs Letter to Sir Olave Leigh His Brother," July 2, 1604, in [Purchas], *Purchas His Pilgrimes*, IV, 1250–1252 ("with condition" on 1251), 1252–1255 ("being chased" on 1253); Harcourt, *Relation*, ed. Harris, 86. Terms like "Arawak" and "Carib" are useful categories of belonging, but they oversimplify. Although the Arawaks were allies with the Spanish broadly, some groups of Arawaks were displaced by the Spanish and regarded them as enemies.

27. Charlotte M. Gradie, "The Powhatans in the Context of the Spanish Empire," in Helen C. Rountree, ed., *Powhatan Foreign Relations, 1500–1722* (Charlottesville, Va., 1993), 154–172; Camilla Townsend, "Mutual Appraisals: The Shifting Paradigms of the English, Spanish, and Powhatans in Tsenacomoco, 1560–1622," in Douglas Bradburn and John C. Coombs, eds., *Early Modern Virginia: Reconsidering the Old Dominion* (Charlottesville, Va., 2011), 57–89.

tance worked. When the English arrived in late April 1607, no eager English-speaking Natives greeted them. Instead, they immediately drove the English back onto their ships.[28]

Unlike the loosely organized tribes of Guiana, the Powhatans formed a confederation. The lack of interference from the Spanish had left the Powhatans to develop this confederation over the last decades of the sixteenth century. The English had better relations with groups on the fringes of the Powhatan chiefdom, notably the Patawomecks. Such groups wanted European goods and felt less threatened by the English settlement because of their distance from it. They also attempted to use a relationship with the English to obtain greater autonomy within the Powhatan paramount chiefdom. Still, the situation in Virginia was very different from that in Guiana. In Virginia, there was not another European power against which the English might offer themselves as a counter.[29]

As James D. Rice's essay in this volume shows, there were divisions among Chesapeake Natives that created possibilities for alliance, yet the political situation also presented "perils" for the English. In Guiana, too, there were groups that the English could not persuade to aid them. After his successful meeting with Topiawari, Ralegh fought a disastrous battle with the natives of Cumaná on his return home. Ultimately, however, for as long as the English came in small numbers and did not establish a long-standing presence, Guiana Natives seem to have judged them less formidable than the Spanish and Portuguese, and perhaps even other Native enemies. On the whole, Guiana tipped more toward possibilities than perils.

THE ENGLISH SETTLEMENTS IN SOUTH AMERICA ALSO ESTABLISHED different sorts of relationships with the Spanish. After Ralegh's well-publicized trip, English visits were more prosaic. The governor whom Ralegh had captured died a few years later, and his son, Fernando de Berrío, turned away from El Dorado and toward a surer source of income: tobacco cultivation. Spanish settlers who lived on the margins of empire, largely unsupported by the metropole, started growing tobacco to sell to English, Dutch, and French traders who frequented the area.

Those who came to the area for the tobacco trade thus had a complicated relationship with the Spanish settlers. Some hoped to thwart the Spanish in areas of imperial weakness. But they also carried on a trade with the Spanish that kept

---

28. John Smith, *A True Relation of Such Occurrences and Accidents of Note as Hath Hapned in Virginia* ... (London, 1608), 3.

29. Helen C. Rountree, "The Powhatans and the English: A Case of Multiple Conflicting Agendas," in Rountree, ed., *Powhatan Foreign Relations*, 183–184.

the settlements going. The governor of Cumaná wrote in 1607 to Philip III that in Trinidad y Guayana "English and Dutch ships are never lacking." In February 1611, Thomas Roe observed that he had just been to "Port d'espagne in the Island of Trinidad where are 15 sayle of ships freighting Smoke: English, French, Dutch." Roe highlighted Spain's inability to control the area. The Spanish colony, he warned, will "be turned all to Smoke" because the government there "hath more skill in planting Tobacco and selling it, then in erecting Colonyes, or marching of armyes." An English pamphlet published in 1620 admonished these traders who had, the writer argued, kept the settlements from ruin.[30]

Although the settlements in Guiana were connected to the ultimately futile search for El Dorado, they turned to more practical goals sooner than Virginia. Robert Harcourt's experiences most fully convey how the South American colonies offered a model that departed somewhat from Virginia's. When he arrived in 1609, Harcourt was more focused on settlement than on the discovery of great riches. He dispersed his men around the area to receive the best intelligence and worked to make alliances with local leaders. Most strikingly, Harcourt had modest ambitions. At one point, he and his men went on a search for a gold mine. They quickly gave up, and Harcourt, in his 1613 account, admonished his men and himself for "our greedy desire of Gold." Although he hoped that the establishment of a stable, permanent colony would lead to the discovery of mines, he placed greater emphasis on Native commodities: cotton, wool, dyes, gums, feathers, balsam, jasper, porphyry stone, wax, and honey. His account recommended tobacco especially, a crop that "is planted, gathered, seasoned, and made up fit for the Merchant in short time, and with easie labour." "Onely this commodity Tobacco," he predicted, "will bring as great a benefit and profit to the undertakers, as ever the Spaniards gained by the best and richest Silver myne in all their Indies, considering the charge of both." Although Harcourt initially hoped to find gold, he soon became convinced that a surer foundation for a colony was tobacco, or other agricultural resources.[31]

To understand how striking Harcourt's claims were, one need only look to Virginia in this same period. Although John Rolfe had begun planting tobacco in 1612, few looked to it as the colony's ideal economic endeavor. In a 1622 treatise encouraging sericulture and viticulture in Virginia, the personification of Nature asks the settlers why they have forsaken mulberry trees and vines, "all

---

30. "Pedro Suarez Coronel to Philip III," Dec. 18, 1607, Add. MSS 36319, fol. 149, British Library, London; "Sir Thomas Roe to Salisbury," Port d'Espaigne, Trinidad, Feb. 28, 1611, CO 1/1, no. 25, TNA; Edward Bennett, *A Treatise Devided into Three Parts, Touching the Inconveniences That the Importation of Tobacco out of Spaine, Hath Brought into This Land* (London, 1620).

31. Harcourt, *Relation* (1613), 38; Harcourt, *Relation*, ed. Harris, 105.

for a smoakie Witch?" Even when attempts at silk and wine production failed, Virginia Company officials insisted settlers devote less energy to tobacco.[32]

South American colonists, however, turned to tobacco enthusiastically and with little backlash. A 1613 report alleged the English had settled on the mainland near Spanish Margarita Island "with the favour of the Caribs, with the intention of cultivating tobacco." A 1617 letter to Thomas Roe informed him that some of his colonists had returned to England "ryche" because they "brought with them so muche Tobacco." By the 1610s, then, South American and Virginian colonists alike had turned to tobacco. The difference was that in Virginia this transition was contested, whereas in Guiana it was embraced.[33]

THE YEAR 1619 WAS A TURNING POINT FOR ENGLISH COLONIZATION efforts in both Virginia and Guiana. That one colony was quickly aborted while the other was set on the path to prosper had much to do with when the companies in question were chartered and how England's relationship with Spain evolved over the course of James I's reign (1603–1625). The Spanish and English were at war during the reign of Elizabeth I (1558–1603), and America was one theater of that conflict. When James ascended to the throne in 1603, he forged a more conciliatory relationship with Spain. To that end, in 1604 the Spanish and English signed the Treaty of London, an agreement deliberately vague on English activity in the Americas. The Spanish at times pressed James I on his subjects' activities there, but he truthfully admitted that they operated outside his control and at their own risk. James was willing to back colonizing ventures in the 1600s and 1610s, but only if the reward outweighed the danger.[34]

In 1606, James I awarded a patent for the London-based Virginia Company that allowed them "to make Habitation, Plantation, and to deduce a colony of sundry of our People into that part of America commonly called VIRGINIA." Although the Spanish ambassador at the time, Don Pedro de Zúñiga, was aware of the preparations, he was not initially concerned. Virginia, he wrote to Philip III, had little to offer. But Zúñiga soon changed his mind. The English returning from Jamestown thought the area promising, and the Virginia Company prepared to send out more settlers and supplies. Zúñiga quickly sought a meeting

---

32. John Bonoeil, *His Majesties Gracious Letter to the Earle of South-hampton, Treasurer, and to the Councell and Company of Virginia Here: Commanding the Present Setting up of Silke Works, and Planting of Vines in Virginia* ... (London, 1622), 61.

33. "Memorandum on the Condition of the Island of Trinidad and Guayana," 1614, no. 14, in *British Guiana Boundary*; Extracts from a Letter from George Lord Carew to Sir Thomas Roe, in Lorimer, ed., *English and Irish Settlement*, 187.

34. William S. Goldman, "Spain and the Founding of Jamestown," *WMQ*, 3d Ser., LXVIII (2011), 427–450.

with James, who rebuffed his entreaties for months. When he met with James in September 1607 and complained that the Jamestown settlement violated the Treaty of London, the king replied that his hands were tied.[35]

The Spanish worried intensely about Virginia and carefully gathered intelligence to decide how to proceed. They sent two reconnaissance missions to Jamestown in its earliest years, one of which resulted in the Spanish captain's being left onshore and held by the English for several years. Zúñiga's intelligence-gathering operations procured a well-known early map of the area, sent to Philip III in 1607. William Goldman argued that only timing spared the settlement. Philip III was concerned with his overstretched military commitments and excessive spending. In 1607, rejecting the advice of his Council of State, he provided military support to Pope Paul V in a conflict with the Republic of Venice over ecclesiastical rights. The campaign was unsuccessful and expensive, and it perhaps led Philip III to see the folly of overextending Spain's resources in the pursuit of ideological goals. Thus, as he considered whether to try to destroy Jamestown in order to uphold the principle that North America belonged to Spain, Phillip III seems to have taken a more practical approach. He did not intervene, in part because intelligence suggested Jamestown might fail on its own. J. H. Elliott has suggested that Spain and England also desired to keep the peace with one another in the face of an increasingly stronger France. Both scholars posit the timing of the settlement as fortuitous. Whatever the precise reason, the Spanish never attacked Virginia and did not force James to demonstrate his commitment or indifference to the colony.[36]

Although he granted a patent, James, as Andrew Fitzmaurice's essay in this volume demonstrates, grew wary about how the colony might affect England's relationship with Spain. The second (1609) and third (1612) charters distanced the monarch from the colony. By removing himself from participation in Virginia's affairs, James I earned plausible deniability about them. Many of those involved with the Virginia Company did not share James's reluctance to antagonize the Spanish. Yet, they suspected the Spanish might attack. The Virginia Company instructed the colonists at Jamestown to situate their settlement up a river for protection. The English and the Spanish alike imagined Virginia and Guiana to be places adjacent to the Spanish, yet beyond their control: Spanish

---

35. James I, "First Charter of Virginia," Apr. 10, 1606, in *The Avalon Project: Documents in Law, History, and Diplomacy*, Yale Law School, http://avalon.law.yale.edu/17th_century/va01.asp; Goldman, "Spain and the Founding of Jamestown," *WMQ*, 3d Ser., LXVIII (2011), 438.

36. Goldman, "Spain and the Founding of Jamestown," *WMQ*, 3d Ser., LXVIII (2011), 438; J. H. Elliott, "The Iberian Atlantic and Virginia," in Mancall, ed., *The Atlantic World and Virginia*, 541–557.

peripheries. Whether or not the English accepted Spain's right to these places, they at least acknowledged that Spain claimed them. It was not the case that Guiana failed simply because it was more clearly within Spain's orbit than Virginia was.

Far from being enthusiastic about their pacific prince, members of Parliament were worried that he was too friendly with Spain and, perhaps consequently, ambivalent about colonization. A particular point of concern was James's attempt to arrange a marriage between Henry, the Prince of Wales, and the Spanish Infanta, Anne of Austria. After Anne's betrothal to Louis XIII of France and Henry's death in 1612, hopes for a royal union stalled. Negotiations shortly resumed, however, this time between the new Prince of Wales, Charles, and the Infanta Maria Anna. James's hope for a Spanish and Catholic queen of England demonstrated to some detractors both his lukewarm Protestantism and his disdain for counsel.[37]

Zúñiga's successor as ambassador to England, Diego Sarmiento de Acuña, Count Gondomar, was an effective intermediary between Spain and James I. Gondomar was ambassador from 1613 to 1618 and again from 1620 to 1622. It is no coincidence that the charter for the Amazon Company was issued in his absence. He held favor with James, partly for his ability to negotiate a marriage alliance but also because the king genuinely enjoyed his company. Like Zúñiga, who had been concerned about Jamestown in 1607, Gondomar also complained to James about a nascent English colony in the Americas. Gondomar's ambassadorial skill might explain the divergent results he and Zúñiga achieved. The power that Gondomar, and by extension Spain, seemed to exert over James vexed some English nobility and exacerbated fears that he was too sympathetic to Catholics. Thomas Middleton's 1625 play *A Game at Chaess* cast Gondomar as the villain, a hint at the ambassador's notoriety.[38]

Two dramatic incidents in the late 1610s demonstrated the limits of James's commitment to South American colonization. First, in 1617, Walter Ralegh, who had been imprisoned in the Tower since 1603, petitioned the king for release so that he might travel to "Guiana"—the Spanish settlements on Trinidad and along the Orinoco. Nearby, Ralegh promised, he knew of a gold mine that would replenish James's treasury. Ralegh swore that there were no Spaniards near the

---

37. Pauline Croft, *King James* (New York, 2003).
38. Brennan C. Pursell, "James I, Gondomar, and the Dissolution of the Parliament of 1621," *History*, LXXXV (2000), 428–445; Charles H. Carter, "Gondomar: Ambassador to James I," *Historical Journal*, VII (1964), 189–208; Thomas Middleton, *A Game at Chaess as It Was Acted Nine Dayes to Gether at the Globe on the Banks Dide* (London, 1625).

mine, and he was allowed to leave after promising not to attack any settlements. James must have realized that the alleged mine was actually quite close to a Spanish settlement and that, if Ralegh did find it, any attempt to exploit it would bring the English into conflict with Spain. In a pattern that he would later repeat, James was trying to play to both sides. He let Ralegh go under one pretext, figuring that if it failed Ralegh would bear the blame and that if it succeeded and there was a mine James would be willing to support the claim that Guiana belonged to England, not Spain. Importantly, James granted this permission while the able Gondomar was away.[39]

Ralegh's expedition quickly turned disastrous. Many of the men fell ill, including Ralegh, and several died. They made landfall along the Wiapoco in November and sailed along the coast to Trinidad, where a contingent stayed to take on any Spanish reinforcements that might arrive. Ralegh was too sick to travel up the Orinoco to the place the mine was supposed to be. He put his second-in-command, Lawrence Keymis, in charge and sent him out with a group of three hundred men. Soon after they landed near San Tomé, they clashed with Spanish defenders, precisely the kind of action Ralegh had sworn to avoid. There were few deaths, but among them were the Spanish governor and Ralegh's own son. The English captured the town and burned it. They met with Native leaders who encouraged them to stay, and even some who said they knew where gold was, but the English found no mine. Keymis returned to Ralegh in February 1618, reported what had happened, and committed suicide a few days later. Some of the crew quickly returned to England, arriving before Ralegh. Roger North, a captain, was among them, and he related the story of the fiasco. In his statement, North confessed that he thought Ralegh had invented the mine and had anticipated conflict with the Spanish. James had Ralegh executed shortly after his return to England. Although he took part in the voyage, North's accounting of it was later used as evidence that North was more loyal than Ralegh.[40]

North's experience convinced him that Guiana could be profitable if he avoided Ralegh's mistakes. Soon after his return to England, he began planning a new colonial venture for an Amazon company. Perhaps taking a cue from Harcourt, his sometime rival and collaborator, North's prospectus for the company prioritized flora, not just mineral wealth. Guiana was "aboundinge with many rich Commodities, as riche dyes, medicinable drugges, sweete gummes, Cot-

---

39. "King James's Declaration," in V. T. Harlow, *Ralegh's Last Voyage* (London, 1932), 335–356.
40. "The Examination of Captain Roger North, Taken before the Lords at Whitehall," Sept. 17, 1618, in Harlow, *Ralegh's Last Voyage*, 257–259.

ton Woole, sugar Caines, Choice Tobacco, precious Woods, Nuttmegg trees, and other spices, usefull plantes, and pleazant fruites, which the soile naturally bringeth forth." Maybe mindful of Virginia's high mortality rate, he also claimed Guiana was fit "for healthfull habitacion."[41]

North had seen that James only backed such enterprises if they did not encroach upon Spanish settlement or if the reward offset any risk. Potential riches from tobacco, dyes, and sugar might not suffice to persuade the king. Thus, North added that the region was "likewise yelding apparant probabilities of rich Mines, and Minneralls of sundrye sortes." Instead of settling on the area near Spanish Trinidad y Guayana, he proposed colonizing the farthest edge of Guiana—the Amazon River. The claim that this area was "not inhabited by anie Christian Prince" was much more persuasive. James duly chartered the Amazon Company in 1619.[42]

This action demonstrates that James was not willing to cede South America to the Spanish. It is tempting to attribute the failure of early English colonization efforts in South American to their proximity to the Spanish and Portuguese. Northern Europeans, however, continued to contest Iberian claims to Guiana and were ultimately successful. The English, French, and Dutch all established permanent colonies there. Joyce Lorimer has argued that it was not attacks by the Spanish and Portuguese but rather investors' wariness owing to James's lack of support that caused early ventures to fail. In 1619, at least, James lent his backing. Perhaps because Gondomar was again away as the Amazon Company started to form, James was more willing to take risks. Financial pressures also weighed upon the king, as several recent efforts to raise revenue had failed to relieve his debts. Both of these factors might have encouraged him to take another chance on South American settlements.[43]

The projectors of the Amazon Company had to toe a careful line. On the one hand, they had to promise not to make Ralegh's mistakes and encroach upon Spanish claims. On the other hand, the company attracted powerful voices in the anti-Spanish faction at court. Robert Rich, whose attempts to attack Spain from Virginia are explored in Alexander B. Haskell's essay, is one of thirteen subscribers named in the charter. Others included Roger North himself and his brother Dudley, Lord North. Eight of the thirteen were also past or future investors in the Virginia Company. A number of later investors joined these original

---

41. "The Preamble for Subscription to the Amazon Company . . . 6th/16th April 1619," in Lorimer, ed., *English and Irish Settlement*, 192.

42. Ibid., 192–193.

43. Joyce Lorimer, "The Failure of the English Guiana Ventures, 1595–1667, and James I's Foreign Policy," *Journal of Imperial and Commonwealth History*, XXI, no. 1 (1993), 1–30.

subscribers. Gondomar alleged the archbishop of Canterbury and several other prominent men at court were among them.[44]

After his return to England in March 1620, Count Gondomar and other Spanish agents in England loudly protested the Amazon Company. At a packed meeting of the Privy Council on April 14, 1620, the two sides met to discuss the issue. Amazon Company backers argued that the land was "a pagan wilderness where Dutch and Irish and Frenchmen had begun to settle," and thus the company was not an affront to Philip III. Gondomar replied that in fact the area belonged to Philip III "by virtue of discovery, demarcation and possession." It made no difference whether Spaniards did not people the entire land. How would the English nobles like it, he argued, if he went and colonized a vacant corner of their own grand estates?[45]

Ultimately, James and the Privy Council agreed to forbid North to sail, but North disobeyed them in early May. He alleged that friends had told him James wanted him to depart secretly while seeming to keep the peace with Spain. The king revoked the charter when he learned that North had left and imprisoned him on his return. The Amazon Company thus unraveled in England as the first settlers crossed the Atlantic. Left behind in South America, the settlers were "destitute of any supplyes from *England,*" though they had "releefe" from Dutch ships that "gave what they pleased and tooke what they list [desired]." Despite these hardships, many of those left behind had insisted upon staying.[46]

In 1619, Virginia also existed precariously. Only through continued intervention did the colony persevere. Several times during its short history the settlement had survived only by chance. Virginia's high profile in England was its chief advantage. Its settlers were also managed by one company, rather than divided among a motley collection of settlements. By the time the crown took control of the colony, it had only just achieved sufficient population to ensure its survival. It was easier for James to disavow the Amazon Company when the Spanish pressed him. He had granted the charter just a few months before, in a burst of enthusiasm over North's plans. In 1620, the colony was new, with few settlers, and little known. If we believe North's narrative, James wanted him to sail without express permission, and by doing so provide an easy reason for end-

---

44. "The Preamble for Subscription to the Amazon Company . . . 6th/16th April 1619," and "The Count of Gondomar to Philip III, 30th May 1620," in Lorimer, ed., *English and Irish Settlement,* 192, 204; Theodore K. Rabb, *Enterprise and Empire: Merchant and Gentry Investment in the Expansion of England, 1575–1630* (Cambridge, Mass., 1967).
45. "The Count of Gondomar to Philip III," May 30, 1620, in Lorimer, ed., *English and Irish Settlement,* 205.
46. Smith, *True Travels,* 50; *Oxford English Dictionary Online,* s.v. "List," www.oed.com.

ing the colony. When he felt the Amazon Company was becoming a political liability, James simply canceled the charter.

DESPITE THE EVENTS OF 1619 TO 1621, NORTH, HARCOURT, THE REmaining Amazon settlers, and others continued to hold out hope for a renewed interest in colonies to the south. By 1625, Anglo-Spanish relations had soured, and England had a new king, Charles I, whom they hoped would be more amenable to the project. North and Harcourt, former rivals, joined together on a new venture, the Guiana Company. North presented a narrative for the royal councillors, explaining what had gone wrong with the Amazon Company and blaming Gondomar for the demise of an otherwise promising enterprise. Both men also promoted the company to the public. Harcourt published a new edition of his *Relation* in February 1626, and North printed a prospectus for the company the following month. The patent for the Guiana Company, issued in May 1627, granted the two control of a large territory "from the River of Wiapoco Southwarde to the River of Amazons and from thence further Southwards to five degrees of latitude" and stretching "from Sea to Sea."[47]

Once again, Harcourt and North became caught between their visions for the colony and what investors and the new king wanted to hear. Both North and Harcourt had demonstrated a reluctance to pin their hopes on gold mines. Instead, they planned to develop sugar plantations and to rely upon Native commodities. Yet they also knew that, for many Europeans, Guiana meant gold. Ultimately, North's prospectus hedged, offering a measured assessment of other potential riches: "Some peeces of Mettall have beene found worne by the Indians which were mixed with a third part Gold." A few pieces of metal that were one-third gold did not draw in as many investors as anticipated, and the Guiana Company suffered.[48]

Most importantly, the Atlantic world looked very different in 1626 than it had in 1619. In 1619, Virginia had around seven hundred settlers left of thousands sent from England. Just seven years later, there were more than two thousand colonists. By 1629, when the first ship sent out by the Guiana Company finally arrived in South America, English settlers had founded colonies at Plymouth in North America and on the Caribbean islands of Barbados, Bermuda, Nevis, and Saint Christopher. South American settlements now had to compete with a host of other more easily defendable island colonies. Even worse, as the company

---

47. "A Summary Relation concerning the Patent for the River of Amazones and the Countrie and Coast Adjoying [1625]," and "Extract from the Patent of the Guiana Company, Issued 19/29 May 1627," in Lorimer, ed., *English and Irish Settlement*, 276–277, 295 (quotations).
48. "Roger North's Prospectus for the Guiana Company, Issued circa March 1626," ibid., 285.

was being chartered, news spread to England that the Portuguese had ousted several groups of settlers from along the Amazon. This event helped bring the river into "Brazil" and out of "Guiana" in the geographic imagination.

North's own Amazon settlers provided some of that competition. After languishing in the Amazon for a couple of years, Thomas Warner and two others departed "to be free from the disorders that did grow in the *Amazons* for want of Government amongst their Countrey-men." A fellow colonist with some experience in the Americas suggested settling a small Caribbean island to prevent attack and desertion alike. Warner scouted the region to choose the best island and selected Saint Christopher because he deemed the island's leader, Tegreman, friendly. Perhaps, too, he discovered that it had better soil than neighboring islands—indeed its Native name, Liamuga, meant just that. Warner and his two companions stayed there for a year. After returning to England in 1622 to find investors, Warner and a group of fifteen settlers set out on a ship bound for Virginia. They stayed in the colony for a year before proceeding back to Saint Christopher. Warner, his wife and son, and the other colonists arrived on the island in January 1624.[49]

Although the small-scale settlements that had thus far proved most successful were not the future of English imperial expansion, Guiana continued to fascinate. The author of a 1660 work complained that the English have "bestowed much tyme, labour, and cost on Plantations in the Charibdien Eylands, butt have nott beene soo well informed of better progresses to bee made under the best clyme of the firme Land on the Coast of America." Guiana particularly stood as an example of a place where conflict with indigenous peoples had been largely avoided. Reflecting on the progress of English colonization around 1668, John Scott wrote:

> I have also observed the Indians to have a great sense of the Injuries they have sustained from the Europeans, where their countryes have been envaded, and they are strict computers of the wrongs they sustaine from any nation so that unless all power be taken from them, they are apt enough for revenge. You will finde all along the following story that the Christians have ever first injur'd them, and that it hath cost much blood to wrest away those Countries by force where God and nature had given them a propriety; whiles such people as have purchased their lands fairely, or that they have invited to cohabit with them have liv'd in great peace and enjoyed a kind neighbourhood.

49. Smith, *True Travels*, 50; Michael A. LaCombe, "Warner, Sir Thomas (c. 1580–1649)," in Goldman, ed., *Oxford Dictionary of National Biography*.

For Scott, Guiana exemplified such a place. After Ralegh won the affinity of the Natives, local tribes ever after welcomed the English. Because the English showed "great Justice and moderation" to their Indian hosts, they won them over. Guianans allowed settlers to live among them in peace, "which neither the French nor Spaniard could ever do by force of Armes." A 1670 work agreed that the Natives of Guiana not only hated the Spanish but still viewed the English as "their guard against their enemies."[50]

The Guiana colonies—smaller, established where indigenous alliances were feasible and the climate better, and with colonists and investors more amenable to a surer source of income—had advantages in 1619 that Virginia lacked. And yet, even if contemporaries were unaware of their implications, Virginia was developing attributes that would ensure its permanence.

---

50. Balthazar Gerbier Kyt Douvilly, *A Sommary Description, Manifesting That Greater Profits Are to Bee Done in the Hott Then in the Could Parts off the Coast off America* ... (Rotterdam, 1660), A1v; John Scott, "Preface to an Intended History of America," 21, 23, MS Rawlinson A 175, fol. 372, Bodleian Library; John Oxenbridge, *A Seasonable Proposition of Propagating the Gospel by Christian Colonies in the Continent of Guaiana* ... (Cambridge, 1670), 7.

From John Smith to Adam Smith
Virginia and the Founding Conventions of English Long-Distance Settler Colonization

JACK P. GREENE

Just over a decade ago, the quadricentennial of the initial Jamestown settlement, the stunning archaeological discoveries at Jamestown, a burgeoning interest in indigenous American studies, and the broadening scope of early American literary studies combined to produce a formidable body of scholarship on the background, context, and early settlement of Virginia, England's first successful experiment in overseas settler colonization. What is difficult to find in this literature is any systematic consideration of the Virginia colony as the principal site for working out the critical conventions that would structure long-distance settler colonization in the English-speaking world over the next two centuries. This subject had, of course, been of considerable interest to earlier generations of scholars, including Charles McLean Andrews and, most importantly, Wesley Frank Craven, whose pathbreaking studies of the Virginia settlement and its Company leaders remain the essential starting point for any understanding of Virginia's role in the construction of the English overseas empire.[1]

Building upon the foundation supplied by Craven, this essay proposes to revisit this subject from the perspective of two closely interrelated literatures produced since the mid-1980s: state formation studies and the work generated

---

1. James Horn, *A Land as God Made It: Jamestown and the Birth of America* (New York, 2005); Karen Ordahl Kupperman, *The Jamestown Project* (Cambridge, Mass., 2007); William M. Kelso, *Jamestown: The Buried Truth* (Charlottesville, Va., 2006); Frederic W. Gleach, *Powhatan's World and Colonial Virginia: A Conflict of Cultures* (Lincoln, Nebr., 1997); Margaret Holmes Williamson, *Powhatan Lords of Life and Death: Command and Consent in Seventeenth-Century Virginia* (Lincoln, Nebr., 2003); Michael Leroy Oberg, *The Head in Edward Nugent's Hand: Roanoke's Forgotten Indians* (Philadelphia, 2008); James D. Rice, *Nature and History in the Potomac Country: From Hunter-Gatherers to the Age of Jefferson* (Baltimore, 2009); Peter C. Mancall, *Hakluyt's Promise: An Elizabethan's Obsession for an English America* (New Haven, Conn., 2007); Robert Appelbaum and John Wood Sweet, eds., *Envisioning an English Empire: Jamestown and the Making of the North Atlantic World* (Philadelphia, 2005), consisting of twelve essays, an introduction, and a conclusion; Peter C. Mancall, ed., *The Atlantic World and Virginia, 1550–1624* (Williamsburg, Va., and Chapel Hill, N.C., 2007), consisting of eighteen essays and an introduction; Charles M. Andrews, *The Colo-*

by the imperial turn. The objective is not to come up with anything that might have surprised Craven or to challenge any of his remarkable insights. Rather, it is to expand and sharpen those now two-generations-old insights in the light of subsequent understandings of the character of the English / British empire as it developed into the celebrated entity that it became over the next century and a half.

FOR MORE THAN A CENTURY FOLLOWING THE EXPLORATORY VOYAGES of the Cabots in the late 1490s, English interest in overseas activities put settlement colonization, as Kenneth Andrews writes, "well below trade and plunder in their priorities." Almost wholly driven by merchants and mariners, the focus of such activities was principally upon expanding trade to distant eastern markets—Muscovy, the Levant, and India—and "harvesting the seas" and secondarily upon the "predatory drive of armed traders and marauders to win . . . a share of the Atlantic wealth of the Iberian nations" through "maritime warfare, reprisals and piracy." These activities led to the establishment of small commercial factories at trading sites abroad, a fishing base in Newfoundland, and "transient" enclaves "for the management of tobacco planting in early seventeenth-century Guiana," but all of these ventures, as Kenneth Andrews has shown, were nothing more than "artificial creations of merchant syndicates, maintained with labour, capital and everything else necessary for the sole purpose of producing a marketable commodity" or trading for one. By stimulating advances in the nautical sphere and doubling the tonnage of private shipping and by eroding "Spain's control of the outer Caribbean," such activities did indeed raise the possibility of creating English societies "beyond the sea," the most elaborate of which were the Hakluyts' expansive paper constructions for creating an empire of English settlements in the Americas. But, according to Andrews, not even in the failed attempts at Roanoke and Guiana to establish such societies was settlement "the dominant motive." Even in the case of Virginia, which had "from the start" the

---

nial Period of American History, I, *The Settlements* (New Haven, Conn., 1934), 53–213; Wesley Frank Craven, *Dissolution of the Virginia Company: The Failure of a Colonial Experiment* (New York, 1932); Craven, *An Introduction to the History of Bermuda* (Williamsburg, Va., 1938); Craven, *The Southern Colonies in the Seventeenth Century, 1607–1689* (Baton Rouge, La., 1949); Craven, *White, Red, and Black: The Seventeenth-Century Virginian* (Charlottesville, Va., 1971). In their books on Jamestown, James Horn and Karen Kupperman have both thoroughly absorbed Craven's findings. Curiously, however, the Applebaum-Sweet collection finds no place for any of Craven's work in its bibliography, and Craven's name is also missing from that book's index as well as from the index to the Mancall collection. Contrast this neglect with Thad W. Tate's appreciative discussion of Craven's work in "The Seventeenth-Century Chesapeake and Its Modern Historians," in Tate and David L. Ammerman, eds., *The Chesapeake in the Seventeenth Century: Essays on Anglo-American Society* (Williamsburg, Va., and Chapel Hill, N.C., 1979), 5, 7, 14–15, 18, 29, 39–40.

"character of a full-scale settlement," settlement was deeply intertwined with the broader commercial objectives that had driven earlier English overseas involvement.[2]

Of course, contemporary Irish plantation projects gave the English overseas colonizing movement considerable experience with settler colonization in densely populated and recognizably European areas, but Ireland was so profoundly different in terms of its proximity and the character of its indigenous inhabitants that experience there by no means prepared that movement for planting in far-off lands in radically different climes that were inhabited by unfamiliar people with exotic cultures. Nor did it supply the movement with a reliable guide for identifying and solving the many questions posed by long-distance colonization.

As a consequence of the English pattern of overseas activity before the Virginia Company embarked on its colonial project, many of the basic questions about how the English might successfully establish long-distance settlement societies had not been fully anticipated or defined, much less directly confronted and resolved. In making this point, however, I do not mean to endorse in its entirety William Burke's contention—in his remarkable and still insufficiently appreciated two-volume 1757 comparative study of colonialism in the New World entitled *An Account of the European Settlements in America*—that the "settlement of our colonies was never pursued upon any regular plan; but they were formed, grew, and flourished, as accidents, the nature of the climate, or the dispositions of private men happened to operate." "Nothing of an enlarged and legislative spirit," he added, "appears in the planning of our colonies." On the contrary, from the 1580s through the seventeenth century a surfeit of plans surrounded the formation of every new colony that was not merely an offshoot of an existing one, though Burke correctly made the important points that private men, not the state, were usually the authors of them and that colonization by no means followed a grand design emanating from state authorities. My intention, rather, is to underline the salience of a point that David Beers Quinn made a generation and a half ago in specific reference to the Hakluyts' elaborate vision of empire, that such plans when "tested by experience" in America proved "to be largely, if not wholly, impracticable."[3]

---

2. Kenneth R. Andrews, *Trade, Plunder, and Settlement: Maritime Enterprise and the Genesis of the British Empire, 1480–1630* (Cambridge, 1984), 356–357, 362.

3. [William Burke], *An Account of the European Settlements in America: In Six Parts . . .*, 2 vols. (London, 1757), II, 288, 293; David Beers Quinn, *Set Fair for Roanoke: Voyages and Colonies, 1584–1606* (Chapel Hill, N.C., 1985), 414. Although many American scholars, myself included, have often attributed this work to Edmund Burke, no Burke specialist ever has.

On the eve of the Jamestown founding, the English nation, lagging far behind the Iberian nations, had no settlement colony on the western side of the Atlantic, its most substantial effort in that direction at Roanoke in the 1580s having failed for want of supply and attention. By 1623, when Captain John Smith, in his *Generall Historie of Virginia*, vividly and perceptively chronicled the travails and progress of the first surviving English overseas colony, it already had two more: Bermuda and Plymouth. From these modest beginnings, the English empire in America over the next fifteen decades grew with accelerating speed into a formidable collection of prosperous and fully functional polities loosely bound together by a deep attachment to the British state, a common English heritage, and well-established trading connections with the imperial center and with one another. By 1776, when the Scottish philosopher and economist Adam Smith published his remarkable study, *An Inquiry into the Nature and Causes of the Wealth of Nations*, that empire consisted of thirty settlement colonies, seventeen on the North American mainland and thirteen in the West Indies and the western Atlantic, plus the maritime colony of Newfoundland, the recently conquered and formerly French colony of Quebec, and claims to vast territories beyond areas of substantial European settlement on the North American continent.[4]

Impressed by the rapid expansion of settlements and population in North America, the growth and vigor of colonial economies, the burgeoning colonial demand for British goods, the expansion of labor resources throughout the American empire, and the capacity of all but a few colonial polities to cover all the costs of their internal governance, British writers had, for at least two generations before Adam Smith took up the subject, been touting the colonies as an important source of Britain's own expanding domestic wealth, external commerce, internal economic and social development, naval might, maritime superiority, and military capacity. Britain's great victory in the Seven Years' War inspired a surfeit of such works, most of them largely descriptive.[5]

By contrast, Smith, in chapter VII of the *Wealth of Nations*, entitled simply "Of Colonies," set out to provide a capacious and systematic examination of western colonization from antiquity forward, to explain how the American colonizing project had contributed to European wealth, and, more to the point of the discussion that follows, to explore what he called the "Causes of the Prosperity of

---

4. John Smith, *The Generall Historie of Virginia, New-England, and the Summer Isles* ... (1624), in Philip L. Barbour, ed., *The Complete Works of Captain John Smith (1580–1631)*, 3 vols. (Williamsburg, Va., and Chapel Hill, N.C., 1986), II; Adam Smith, *An Inquiry into the Nature and Causes of the Wealth of Nations* (1776), ed. R. H. Campbell and A. S. Skinner, 2 vols. (Indianapolis, Ind., 1976).

5. This literature is discussed in considerable detail in Jack P. Greene, *Evaluating Empire and Confronting Colonialism in Eighteenth-Century Britain* (Cambridge, 2013), 20–49.

new Colonies," an objective that took him deeply into a consideration of the similarities and differences among what we might call *national styles* or *modes of settler colonization*. In this exercise in comparative historical analysis, Smith paid particular attention to the British model, which he regarded as superior to the others, and to identifying how and why British settlement colonies, with neither the mineral resources nor the wealthy and complex indigenous societies encountered by the Iberian powers, had been such a boon to the English-speaking world. Smith was primarily interested in explaining how and why the empire worked. Making no pretense to be writing a history of the settler empire, he showed relatively little concern with exploring the origins and development of the conventions that characterized it and made it work. Thus, in laying out those conventions, Smith made few references to Virginia or to other individual American colonies and no mention at all of either Captain Smith or his *Generall Historie*. Implicitly, however, his analysis draws attention to the questions of where and how those conventions took shape and of the role of England's first successful settler colony in identifying and applying them.[6]

Using Adam Smith's analysis as a retrospective guide to the problems posed by English overseas settler colonization and how those problems were resolved, the remainder of this essay will explore this subject through a framework supplied by nine general questions that he raised in his discussion of colonies. The following discussion will take up each of these questions in turn in a sequence roughly determined by chronology.

1. How Will Settlements Be Established and Administered?

As Adam Smith emphasized, metropolitan governments played but a small role in "projecting" and "effecuatting" settler colonies in America. The Spanish colonies, "carried out with . . . no other publick encouragement, but a general permission to make settlements and conquests in the name of the King of Spain," he wrote, had all been undertaken "at the private risk and expence of the adventurers," and all European colonizing powers, lacking in fiscal resources, followed the Spanish model. State formation studies in the 1980s followed up Smith's insight by showing that the early modern national state was not the highly centralized, tightly integrated, and powerfully coercive entity that emerged in the wake of the French Revolution. With an only recently articulated conception of national sovereignty and as yet quite limited fiscal, administrative, and coercive resources, none of the emerging nation-states of Europe had either the

---

6. Smith, *Wealth of Nations*, ed. Campbell and Skinner, II, 564.

coercive resources to establish hegemony over portions of the New World or the financial wherewithal to pay for them. Hence, during the early stages of colonization, all nation-states had to leave that task to private individuals or groups of adventurers.[7]

England was no exception. Advocates of overseas settlements were well aware that the "limited resources" of the English state—fiscal, administrative, and coercive—would "not permit state sponsored colonization," both the Elizabethan and the Jacobean state having consistently chosen "not to assume the lead in empire building." Instead, using charters or other legal instruments, the English crown authorized influential individuals or joint-stock companies to establish and administer settlements in designated areas of the American territories and let occupation confirm its tenuous claims. With the exception of Jamaica, conquered from the Spanish by a Cromwellian expeditionary force in the mid-1650s, this pattern persisted throughout the seventeenth century and the first three decades of the eighteenth. Only with the founding of Georgia in the early 1730s did the British state partially subsidize the establishment and administration of a colony through an annual parliamentary grant. Overwhelmingly, colony founding in the English-settler American empire was the work of state-authorized but privately directed groups and individuals who, usually initiating their own projects, enjoyed wide scope for action and operated with few and nominal state restraints and little state supervision. In the case of Virginia, provisions in the initial charter for its nominal supervision through a royal council proved unworkable, and the third charter of 1612 eliminated them altogether. From then "until the colony passed under royal rule in 1624," Craven observes, "the central fact in the government of Virginia was the controlling influence of the agencies and conventions of an English commercial company."[8]

2. How Will Settlements Be Financed?

The start-up and maintenance costs for settling a new colony were substantial. Mounting exploratory expeditions; recruiting and supplying settlers and soldiers; erecting fortifications; clearing land; building houses, churches, and public structures; providing tools and domestic animals; supplying trade goods and organizing commercial exchanges with the indigenous population; and

---

7. Ibid., 589–590.
8. Quinn, *Set Fair for Roanoke*, 424; Craven, *Southern Colonies in the Seventeenth Century*, 60–61, 112. For a fuller discussion of this subject, see Jack P. Greene, "Negotiated Authorities: The Problem of Governance in the Extended Polities of the Early Modern Atlantic World," in Greene, *Negotiated Authorities: Essays in Colonial Political and Constitutional History* (Charlottesville, Va., 1994), 1–24.

conducting experiments with a variety of products that might provide economic sustenance for the enterprise and supply the needs of an English market—all required a considerable outlay of capital. In the absence of any funds from the state, the great London overseas merchants involved in the formation and operation of the Virginia Company hoped that a joint-stock enterprise of the kind that had been such an effective instrument in the promotion of English long-distance trade over the half century since 1550 would enable the company to raise the funds necessary to cover these costs by securing private subscriptions and, when that proved insufficient, by conducting lotteries. In the end, however, the company could not muster sufficient resources, and this was especially true once Sir Edward Sandys had undertaken his ambitious program of expansion in 1618, a program that, as Craven observed, was "altogether out of proportion to the financial resources available for its continued support." After 1620, most "emigration to the colony represented an investment by individual or associated groups of adventurers rather than of the company itself." The company's inability to raise funds contributed substantially to its dissolution in 1624.[9]

This dissolution effectively marked the limits of a joint-stock company as a device for colony building. It had worked and for another seventy years would continue to work well in Bermuda, a confined space without indigenous inhabitants, but the financial requirements and complicated interactions in a larger setting on the continent had proven beyond such a company's capacity. Massachusetts, whose charter was captured by settler leaders and emigrants with substantial individual resources and moved to New England, was the last successful colony to be rooted in such a company. But the royalization of Virginia by no means meant that the English state would thenceforth assume responsibility for financing the colony, the crown showing steady reluctance "to part even with the funds necessary for the governor's support, and for relief of the colony's other financial needs," much less to bear "the heavier charges" of maintaining its internal "peace and security." By leaving the colonists with the task of paying for "their own common charges," English colonial administrators contributed to the instantiation and continuance of the principle of private capital financing that, present from the beginnings of the Virginia colony, would become one of the most prominent characteristics of English settlement colonization, as adventurers, merchants, and a growing number of financially independent emigrants who paid their own passages and start-up costs supplied the funds needed to get colonies off the ground and subsequently to become almost wholly self-

---

9. Craven, *Southern Colonies in the Seventeenth Century*, 138–139, 145.

financing for all internal public expenses. For more than a century, a substantial amount of the capital needs of empire construction would come from private sources, not the state.[10]

3. How Will Settlers Interact with Indigenous People?

Writing in broad strokes from the perspective of 1776, Adam Smith did not view indigenous American peoples as an important obstacle to European settlement colonization. In accord with contemporary sensibilities, he pointedly decried "the injustice" of Europeans' "coveting the possession of a country whose harmless natives... had received the first adventurers with every mark of kindness and hospitality" but proceeded to treat settler displacement of indigenous groups as an irresistible process in which scattered and technologically backward indigenous peoples in thinly occupied areas "easily" gave way before rapidly expanding and technologically advanced settler populations.[11]

For the small settler enclaves in the earliest English colonies, however, the problem of working out how settlers would interact with a vastly more numerous and powerful indigenous population was central and one that called for a speedy resolution. The inclusion of so many soldiers in the first expedition and the alacrity with which they fortified Jamestown betrayed a certain wariness about how the indigenes would receive them. Nevertheless, company leaders initially seemed to think of negotiating an arrangement by which they would share the country with the Natives, who would become willing and steady trading partners, the principal source of food for the settlement, and willing converts to Christianity and laborers in English-managed enterprises in an integrated polity acknowledging fealty to the English crown. As it quickly became evident that the Natives had no interest in abandoning their religion or working for and subordinating themselves to the English and seemed, rather, intent on driving the English out, the settlement came to resemble a "military outpost" more than "an infant colony." Company leaders had to lower their expectations, negotiating an arrangement by which the indigenes would tolerate English occupation of space sufficient to produce their own food and to experiment with other agricultural and extractive products that might provide a viable economic base for the colony. This arrangement, which obtained for nearly a decade, brought peace to the colony, led to the development of a profitable staple economy, a major influx of settlers, and an expansion of settlements that seemed to ensure

---

10. Ibid., 150, 158–159.
11. Smith, *Wealth of Nations*, ed. Campbell and Skinner, II, 564, 588.

the colony's future and spawned proposals for the creation of a university and a renewal of interest in evangelizing the Natives.[12]

Alarmed by the growing numbers of settlers and the expansion of settlements, however, indigenous leaders brought this arrangement to an abrupt end with a well-designed and effective surprise attack on white settlements in March 1622, at the very start of the planting season. This attack killed 347 settlers; destroyed buildings, stores, tools, and livestock; and otherwise disorganized settlers' lives, forcing a great number of families to withdraw to safer venues, requiring males to join in defensive measures, and spawning among survivors a high death rate that reduced Virginia's settler population to 1,275 people by 1624. Settlers referred to this attack as a massacre. To "grapple realistically with a situation that threatened their very existence," Virginia settlers after 1622 not only "dropped all thought of missionary effort" and any hopes for subordinating and integrating indigenous people into their societies but also pursued "a settled policy of relentless warfare upon the natives." Not conquest and oversettlement, as in Ireland, nor formal expulsion, the English mode of Indian clearance usually involved settlers crowding, pressuring, or pushing indigenous peoples off territories they wished to expropriate. This approach to the indigenous population, first worked out in the Virginia colony, became a standard feature of the English style of colonizing, even where units of more scrupulous settlers, as in New England and Pennsylvania, formally purchased the lands they wanted for a nominal price. In the construction of an English settlement empire in America, relations with indigenous peoples would be driven by settler demand and settler action and would be limited only by indigenous capacity and inclination to resist.[13]

4. How Will Settlements Be Defended?

Events surrounding and subsequent to the attack of 1622 also provided the answer to the question of how settlement colonies would be defended. An empty treasury prevented the Virginia Company from providing any help to the bloodied colony, its helplessness being an important consideration in the crown's decision to revoke its charter in 1624. Nor after royalization was the crown willing to contribute to the colony's defense. As a consequence, Virginia had no choice but to take responsibility for its own defense, and in 1624 its assembly took the first steps toward the creation of a militia that thenceforth served as the colony's only protection against indigenous attacks and raids, internal uprisings, and

---

12. Craven, *Southern Colonies in the Seventeenth Century*, 75–76, 80, 106.
13. Ibid., 145–146, 172–173.

foreign invasions. In terms of defending Virginia against indigenous attacks, this institution proved to be surprisingly effective. Pursuing "a calculated policy of intimidation against the Indians" and using an "aggressive [military] strategy and harsh tactics" developed in the wake of the 1622 attack, the colony's militia was able to put down a second large-scale surprise attack in 1644 and by the closing decades of the century to establish absolute military supremacy in the tidewater region by either conquering or cowing "all the native peoples within reasonable striking range" of English settlements. No English force appeared in the colony until 1677, when English authorities, alarmed by the prospect of the crown's losing the considerable annual income derived from duties on tobacco entering England, sent a force of more than a thousand troops to put down Bacon's Rebellion, which was over before it arrived, and the commander soon discharged or returned to England all but a hundred men, whom he "retained as a standing guard." Forgotten by London authorities and left without pay or provisions after the first year, this small force was finally "paid off and discharged" in 1682, thus "bringing an end to the brief" English "military presence in seventeenth-century Virginia."[14]

Virginia's experience with defense proved a harbinger for all other settlement colonies founded before 1730. Aside from the conquest of Jamaica from the Spanish in the late 1650s, which Cromwell sponsored during the Interregnum, and the Virginia expedition of 1677, the English state during the seventeenth century contributed little to colonial military expenses and even less when they were incurred in conflicts with indigenous peoples. Everywhere, provincial militias provided the first and usually the only protection against either indigenous attacks or hostile intrusions by agents of rival colonizing powers. Early in the eighteenth century, the British state agreed to support small contingents of troops in New York and South Carolina (later Georgia) at the two points in the continental chain most vulnerable to incursions from the colonies of rival imperial powers as well as larger numbers of soldiers in Jamaica and the Leeward Islands to protect settlers from slave insurrections—troops sent at the request of and largely paid for by settlers. When, from the perspective of 1776, Adam Smith observed that colonial military forces had "never yet been sufficient for their own defence," he was ignoring the fact that before the war with Spain in 1739 the British state had largely left the defense of settler colonies to the settlers themselves, a practice that was so widespread it became a prominent feature in the British mode of imperial construction and constituted a major reason why

---

14. Ibid., 145–146, 150, 158–159, 164; William L. Shea, *The Virginia Militia in the Seventeenth Century* (Baton Rouge, La., 1983), 41, 58–72, 118–119, 136, 138, 140.

the British state had been able to acquire a settlement empire at a "very small" price to the national treasury. Only after 1739 did the state slowly begin to assume the heavy costs in defending, securing, and policing its American colonies.[15]

5. How Will Settlers Be Attracted?

According to Adam Smith, the first and most important cause of the rapid growth of New World colonies was "plenty of good land" that was either vacant or sparsely enough inhabited to invite European expropriation. By "good" land, Smith seems to have meant land that could be used for settlement, European-style agricultural production, and raising livestock. As the company learned through exploration that Virginia was unlikely to offer either precious metals or a water connection to Asia, it quickly became clear that land was to be Virginia's principal natural resource and most attractive lure to coax English people to cross the Atlantic and settle in a distant land already inhabited by indigenous people. Because land in England itself was in short supply, the company's promotional literature early held out the possibility of acquiring land in Virginia. However, although the company after 1612 pursued "a policy of offering economic conditions of settlement that," as Craven characterized them, "were not only in themselves liberal but conceded to the planters a status which naturally carried implications of legal and political advantage," the emphasis on communal responsibility for providing food and experimenting with the production of vendible items militated against the development of a satisfactory arrangement for distributing land among private settlers. In 1614, Sir Thomas Dale began "to enlarge the field of individual endeavor and reward in Virginia by allotment of small farms to the planters there," but not until 1618, with the "greate Charter," did the company provide "a detailed statement of land policies" that effectively operationalized "the principle of using the land to underwrite [and attract] immigration" through the headright system, which made it possible for free settlers to acquire land cheaply, become independent freeholders, and endeavor to build private landed estates. Showing "an increasing disposition to let stand those arrangements of the colony's life that had been shaped by events and by the will of the planters," the crown after 1624 followed the company's lead in the distribution of land, and by 1639 "Virginia's land system ... had been stabilized in accordance with policies and principles" that the company had "first outlined in 1618." Virginia's having led the way, offering freeholds on liberal terms subsequently became a standard feature of English settler empire building in the

---

15. Smith, *Wealth of Nations*, ed. Campbell and Skinner, II, 593, 614–616.

Americas. If, as Adam Smith remarked, on many subsequent occasions (as, for instance, in the cases of Puritan New England and Quaker Pennsylvania) "it was, not the wisdom and policy, but the disorder and injustice of the European governments, which" served as the push factor that "peopled and cultivated America," the pull of land and the prospect of achieving upward social mobility arguably operated as the primary attraction for settlers.[16]

6. How Will Settlers Support Themselves and Sustain and Expand Settlement and Population?

Of course, for English adventurers to profit from their investment, for settlers to achieve independence, or for the English nation to achieve much prestige or advantage from a settlement colony, the colony had to build a viable economy both to sustain itself and to develop commodities that could be exchanged for the trade goods it needed from England. Early on, the unreliability of both the indigenous population and shipments from England as sources of food made it clear that settlement colonies would have to produce their own food through planting, fishing, hunting, and animal husbandry, as the presence on the manifests of the 1609 fleet of land-clearing and agricultural implements and breeding stock revealed. Although Virginia had developed a reasonably profitable trade for furs and skins with Patawomeck Indians and was sending a significant amount of lumber, especially the black walnut prized by English furniture makers, to English markets, five years after the colony's founding it "still lacked a really satisfactory staple that could be procured and marketed in sufficient quantity to" put it on a solid economic footing. However, John Rolfe's experiments with raising and packing tobacco for shipment to England in 1613–1614 were sufficiently successful to give the colony some economic viability and to encourage settlers in the conviction that Virginia had at last found a way to fulfill their economic goals. At the same time, Rolfe's marriage to the Native princess Pocahontas in 1614 sealed a truce with the indigenes that would last into the next decade. During this peace, settlement expanded significantly and the colony achieved self-sufficiency in food. Already by the 1620s the very name of Virginia had become synonymous with tobacco, and, despite many efforts to achieve economic diversification, the combination of subsistence farming, animal husbandry, and the cultivation of tobacco remained the economic mainstay of the colony through the end of the colonial era and beyond.[17]

---

16. Ibid., 572, 589; Craven, *Southern Colonies in the Seventeenth Century*, 89, 119, 127–128, 136–137, 176.
17. Craven, *Southern Colonies in the Seventeenth Century*, 108–109.

Later settler colonies went through a similar process of searching and testing to find ways to develop local economies that would produce marketable goods for exchange and provide settlers a path to economic independence. Not all colonies managed to find such a profitable staple. But, in "improving" the land and establishing their mastery over the landscapes and other resources, settlers in all but the smaller island colonies (except Bermuda) managed to feed and supply themselves and to export surpluses of provisions, grain, fish, lumber, and naval stores to the British Isles and to all the other parts of an expanding Atlantic empire. Enjoying "the most perfect freedom of trade" among themselves, Britain's American colonies all together, Adam Smith noted, made "a great internal market for the produce of one another." In just a few decades, he marveled, they had become a "numerous and thriving" people whose produce and custom were coveted by metropolitan traders, manufacturers, and shopkeepers and who by Smith's time had brought Britain's commercial system to a prominence that commanded the attention of economic analysts and was the envy of rival imperial states.[18]

Impressed by the fecundity of the North American settler populations, Smith had no need to call attention to the importance of gender balance for sustained colonial demographic growth. For the Virginia colony, however, the earliest arrivals had been entirely male, and, even after a decade of settlement, there were just thirty-five women and children in the entire colony. As a later governor would subsequently remark in reviewing the history of the Virginia Company, its failure to identify and resolve this problem deeply contributed to the colony's contingent character, *"populus virorum,"* as he wrote, being "of no long duration any where." Only after the Sandys group took over its leadership in 1618 did the company acknowledge the fundamental importance of women settlers to create, as Karen Ordahl Kupperman has put it, "family structures" that would "give meaning to landownership" and establish "a society of permanent migrants." One of the more important reforms this group undertook in 1619 was a vigorous effort to recruit young women as settlers. Although it took seven or eight more decades before Virginia's settler population actually achieved some semblance of gender balance, this lesson was not lost on subsequent English efforts at settler colonization.[19]

---

18. Smith, *Wealth of Nations,* ed. Campbell and Skinner, I, 375, II, 573–574, 580 (quotations), 614, 626.

19. William Berkeley, *A Discourse and View of Virginia* (London, 1663), 3; Kupperman, *Jamestown Project,* 287.

7. How Will Labor Needs Be Met?

The emergence of tobacco as a profitable export and the spread of settlement in Virginia after 1614 marked the beginnings of an incessant demand for labor that characterized English American settler colonies for the next century and a half. Easy terms for land acquisition, providing every freeholder with more land than he could possibly cultivate on his own, in Adam Smith's view, made him "eager... to collect labourers from all quarters" and fueled a "demand for labourers" that seemed to "increase... faster than" laborers could be found and resulted in a sustained pattern of high wages. As Smith pointed out, with particular reference to Britain's land-rich North American colonies, high wages had two profound effects. First, they proved a great spur to industry and upward mobility among the free population by encouraging people in "the comfortable hope of bettering" their "condition," becoming landlords themselves, and "ending" their "days perhaps in ease and plenty." Second, they stimulated population growth by encouraging marriage, family formation, and child bearing in a situation in which, in contrast to England, "a numerous family of children, instead of being a burthen," was "a source of opulence and prosperity to the parents," the labor of each child being "worth a hundred pounds clear gain to them."[20]

At the same time, the scarcity of free labor encouraged settlers to develop systems of bound labor, especially in sites where increases in production had the prospects of yielding riches sufficient to pay the costs of such labor. By giving settlers grants of land for every head brought into Virginia, the headright system encouraged settlers "to meet the colony's expanding need for labor" by importing indentured servants, who, taking "advantage of an opportunity to work out the cost of their passage through a term of service to some planter," probably constituted as much as three-quarters of the total white immigration to Virginia during the seventeenth century. After the mid-1640s, an increasing supply of Africans, a handful of whom had been sold in the colony in 1619, led to the importation and enslavement of thousands more over the next century and to an ever-deepening commitment to a system of unfree labor that eventually reached into virtually every corner of Britain's settler empire in America. Smith acknowledged that slavery had been a key building block in the creation of that empire. Although he might have minimized the extent to which slavery had spread into Britain's northern continental colonies by the mid-eighteenth century, he was no doubt correct to point out that the "far greater part of the work" in what he called the "corn" colonies was "done by freemen" but that, in

20. Smith, *Wealth of Nations*, ed. Campbell and Skinner, I, 88–89, 98–99, II, 565.

"the sugar colonies, on the contrary, the whole of the work" was "done by slaves" and in "our tobacco colonies a very great part of it," notwithstanding the fact that free labor was more efficient and more dependable than slave. Believing that the preference for slave labor throughout history was rooted, not in rational economic choice, but in human nature, specifically in man's pride and "love to domineer" without condescending to his inferiors, Smith suggested that, "wherever the law allows it, and the nature of the work can afford it," masters had "generally prefer[red] the service of slaves to that of freemen." Although Smith did not dispute the claim that people "born in the temperate climate of Europe" were far less suitable than Africans for labor in "the burning sun of the West Indies" and the more southerly parts of North America, he was by no means an apologist for the institution as it had emerged in the British American colonies; he wrote disparagingly about "the unfortunate law of slavery" in the colonies and was especially critical of the British slave system because, in contrast to those of the French and Spanish, which provided bureaucratic buffers to protect slaves from masters, it placed few restraints upon masters in their relations with slaves.[21]

8. How Will Authority Be Established and Maintained within Settlements?

"By no means the least" of the problems facing the Virginia Company, as it sought to create a settlement colony in Virginia, was the necessity to devise some plan for its internal governance that would provide, as Craven put it, "some vestige of established and recognized authority," *authority* meaning, according to contemporary definition, not simply what was commanded from a distant corporate headquarters in London but also what was acknowledged and obeyed by settlers in the colony. More to the point, Governor Sir Thomas Dale's experiments with martial law raised the questions of whether and how settlers in distant polities might enjoy the traditional English rights guaranteed to them by royal charter, particularly their rights to consensual governance and rule of law that English Whig lawyers were then championing as the hallmarks of English national identity. The company reforms of 1618 addressed these concerns directly and sought to stimulate immigration by providing for an annual assembly of elected freeholders, the consent of whom to all legislation and taxes would be required, thus providing settlers with the promise of living under a government

---

21. Craven, *Southern Colonies in the Seventeenth Century*, 128, 177; Smith, *Wealth of Nations*, ed. Campbell and Skinner, I, 98–99, 388–389, II, 586–587.

that would guarantee them "the full rights of Englishmen." As Craven noted, along with the headright system for distributing land, this system of colonial representative government, implemented in 1619, turned out to be "of more than momentary or local significance, for they fixed a pattern of fundamental guarantees which Englishmen thereafter, and wherever they went, were disposed to regard as proper and necessary."[22]

Two caveats need to be entered to this judgment, the first of which Craven himself fully acknowledged. For fifteen years after the crown assumed responsibility for Virginia, it was uncertain "whether the Assembly would be permitted to survive the company." It had no place in the commission to Governor Sir Francis Wyatt in 1624 and did not meet again to exercise full legislative powers until 1628. Focused during these years on domestic and foreign issues that rendered issues of colonial governance "relatively unimportant," the king's ministers failed "to maintain the same alert oversight of its [provincial governance] as had the company" and left the colony "dependent upon year to year decisions regarding the management of its affairs." "In many ways," Craven reported, Virginia "was . . . a backwater, outside the main currents of England's maritime expansion." Under these conditions, assemblies met annually after 1630 and, with the cooperation of the royal governor and council, "proceeded to take the fullest possible advantage of the situation." Exhibiting a "strong will to self-government" and fully exercising the inherited English right to consensual governance, the assembly played a major role in providing the funds and shaping the legislation required to turn Virginia into a functional polity by organizing and extending the benefits of local self-government to an expanding agglomeration of settlements and adapting English legal inheritances, social practices, and cultural preferences to fit conditions they found and created in Virginia. In the end, the crown, showing "an increasing disposition to let stand those arrangements of the colony's life that had been shaped by events and by the will of the planters," decided "simply to let stand what had been established by custom and usage" and conceded "the right of taxation, along with the older privileges of petition and legislation . . . to the Virginia Assembly." But, by 1639, when Governor Wyatt sailed for his post with instructions that the assembly should be held annually, the colony's "political structure" had already "been stabilized in accordance with policies and principles first outlined in 1618" by the company and then put into effect by "the Virginians themselves" in "meeting realistically through their Assembly the problems of a growing community."[23]

22. Craven, *Southern Colonies in the Seventeenth Century,* 63, 133, 137.
23. Ibid., 135, 150, 153–155, 158–160, 163–165, 176–177, 183.

The second caveat derives from Thomas Yunlong Man's probing study of the first half century of development of provincial political institutions in England's five most successful colonies. Man finds that in every English settlement colony the demand for representative government was an almost spontaneous development arising out of settler determination to exert and enjoy English liberties in their new abodes and to provide authoritative legal and political institutions that would protect their lives, liberties, and properties. Between roughly 1620 and 1660, every American colony with a substantial body of settlers adopted some form of elected assembly to pass laws for the polities they were creating, and by 1660 all thirteen settled English colonies in the Americas had functioning representative assemblies. From New England to Barbados, colonial English America proved to be an extraordinarily fertile ground for parliamentary governance.[24]

Even in situations in which company officials or proprietors took the initiative in establishing these early law-making institutions, as was the case with Virginia, Bermuda, and Maryland, the representative bodies acted, not as the "passive servants and petitioners of the prerogative," as had been the case with the medieval House of Commons, but as the aggressive spokesmen for the proliferating settlements within the colonies. Claiming their constituents' rights to the traditional English principles of consensual governance, they early insisted that no laws or taxes could go into effect without their assent, demanded the initiative in legislation, turned themselves into high courts of appeal and original jurisdiction in the manner of the medieval House of Commons, and rarely shrank from controversy with "local executives, proprietors, or the Crown."[25]

It took about twenty years for these bodies "to materialize, stabilize, and take permanent form in each colony." During the early years, they usually did not sit as a separate body but met together with the governor's council or even with the governor himself to hear cases and pass laws. But they early set course toward achieving their independence from the executive, and by the 1640s the larger colonies, each of them on its own initiative, had moved toward a bicameral legislature, with the lower house sitting separately from the governor and council. According to Man, local exigencies, not emulation, drove this development. In every case, the specific shape of a provincial polity was the product of what Man calls an "indigenous development." Some popular provincial governors, such as Sir William Berkeley in Virginia and Philip Bell in Barbados, fostered these developments, but in so doing they were invariably merely consolidat-

---

24. Thomas Y. Man, *English Colonization and the Formation of Anglo-American Polities, 1606–1664* (Beijing, China, 2015), 16–50, 371. See Michael Kammen, *Deputyes and Libertyes: The Origins of Representative Government in Colonial America* (New York, 1969), 11–12.

25. Kammen, *Deputyes and Libertyes*, 7, 9, 62, 67.

ing the political frameworks earlier worked out by emerging local leaders and acknowledging that the capacity to govern, in Man's formulation, "compelled [crown, company, or proprietary] recognition of indigenous colonial government that emerged out of colonial conditions."[26]

At the same time, Man reports, English authorities neither anticipated the development of colonial demands for representative government nor "devised, or even conceived of," an arrangement by which colonial governance would have a legislative branch or be modeled on "the national government of England." Instead, they remained suspicious of representative government even after officially acknowledging the permanence of the Virginia Assembly in 1639, preferring instead a conciliar form of the kind specified in the Virginia Company charters. This form consisted of an appointed governor and councillors and included no formal devices for consulting the broader settler population, and English authorities continued for several decades to think of this conciliar form as the norm for English colonial governance.[27]

By the end of the second quarter of the seventeenth century, however, the tradition of consensual governance was "firmly rooted" in colonial English America. Moreover, once their governments had acquired a bicameral form, provincial magnates had no difficulty in noting "the remarkable resemblance" between colonial polities and the traditional form of metropolitan English governance, and they began, as did the Barbadian government in 1651, to defend the polities they had created on the grounds that they represented "the nearest model of conformity to that under which our predecessors of the English nation have lived and flourished for above a thousand years." English officials were similarly impressed by the structural similarities between the colonial polities and the metropolitan government, and the Stuart monarchy provided "official sanction" for this "conceptual transformation" in 1661 when it "introduced just such a government into Jamaica," recently captured from the Spanish and only the second English colony to come under royal control, instructing its new governor "to proceed 'according to such good, just and reasonable customs and constitutions as are exercised and settled in our colonies and plantations.'"[28]

Although this action with regard to Jamaica did not completely settle the issue of the structure of English colonial governance, most of the new proprietary colonies created during the Restoration—Carolina, the Jerseys, and Pennsylvania—and the new royal colony of New Hampshire, separated from Mas-

---

26. Ibid., 11. Man, *English Colonization*, 191–249, traces these developments in detail (quotations on 339, 371).

27. Man, *English Colonization*, 16–50, 371.

28. Kammen, *Deputyes and Liberties*, 61; Man, *English Colonization*, 12–13, 319.

sachusetts in 1679, quickly moved to institute the sort of tripartite polities that had developed in the older colonies. But the duke of York, the future James II and the proprietor of the colony of New York, captured from the Dutch in the mid-1660s, resisted the creation of an assembly for nearly twenty years until 1683 and immediately reversed this concession when he became king. Moreover, James II's attempt to consolidate the New England colonies into a single polity, the Dominion of New England, without representative institutions, deeply threatened the long-established tradition of representative government in those colonies. Although the constitutional status of the assemblies remained a subject of dispute up to and after the American Revolution, the Glorious Revolution effectively ended any efforts to deny representative government to English colonies.[29]

These findings effectively confirm Adam Smith's subsequent observations on the role of settlers in creating their own polities. Carrying "out with them ... the habit of subordination, some notion of the regular government which takes place in their own country, of the system of laws which support it, and of a regular administration of justice," he wrote, settlers "naturally" took advantage of the considerable leeway they enjoyed to construct their own polities to "establish something of the same kind in" each "new settlement."[30]

Indeed, for Smith, representative government was the defining characteristic of the British style of settler colonization. Rating "liberty to manage their own affairs their own way" as one of "two great causes of the prosperity of all new colonies," Smith asserted that, "in every thing, except their foreign trade, the liberty of the English colonists" was "complete" and "in every respect equal to that of their fellow-citizens at home" and was "secured in the same manner, by an assembly of the representatives of the people, who claim the sole right of imposing taxes for the support of the colony government." With full control over all public funds, these assemblies had the "authority" to overawe "the executive power," which, in contrast to the situation in Britain, had "not the means to corrupt them" and enjoyed "not only the legislative, but a part of the executive power," appointing "the revenue officers who collected the taxes imposed by those respective assemblies, to whom those officers were immediately responsible." In three of the New England colonies, the assemblies also elected the councils, "which, in the colony legislatures, correspond[ed] to the House of Lords in Great Britain," and in both Rhode Island and Connecticut

29. This subject is discussed more fully in Jack P. Greene, *Peripheries and Center: Constitutional Development in the Extended Polities of the British Empire and the United States, 1607–1788* (Athens, Ga., 1986), 12–18. See also David S. Lovejoy, *The Glorious Revolution in America* (New York, 1972).
30. Smith, *Wealth of Nations*, ed. Campbell and Skinner, II, 564–565.

also elected the governor. Having a more "equal representation of the people" than the British House of Commons and being "perhaps in general more influenced by the inclinations of their constituents," the assemblies, Smith noted, were filled with "the leading men" of every colony who, desirous of having "some share in the management of publick affairs chiefly on account of the importance which it gives them," constituted "the natural aristocracy of every" colony. With no "hereditary nobility" in any colony and no legally privileged group by which any individual could, in Smith's words, "be troublesome to his neighbours," the "manners" of American settlers, Smith claimed, had become ever "more republican, and their governments, those of three of the provinces of New England in particular, have hitherto been more republican too."[31]

In the colonies of no other contemporary European state, Smith argued, had the "political institutions... been more favourable to the improvement and cultivation" of so much land. Settlers were able to preside over their own internal affairs and to develop polities that, by keeping government small and voluntary and taxes low, encouraged industry and population and permitted settlers, few of whom had a landlord to whom he owed rents, to retain a greater percentage of their earnings, which they could "store up and employ in putting into motion a still greater quantity of labour" or otherwise use for expansion. The system of government English settlers had created in America, Smith thought, was a standing example of how an expanding population could "not only be governed, but well governed." This system, he was persuaded, was "perhaps the only one which, since the world began, could give perfect security to the inhabitants of" a set of provinces "so very distant."[32]

9. What Kind of Relationship Will Settlement Colonies Have with the Parent State?

When the English crown authorized private projectors to establish settler colonies in territories over which it had no more than what Adam Smith accurately characterized as "fictitious possession," contributing no financial support to such undertakings, it assumed that the continuing allegiance of distant settlers would be unproblematic and would somehow involve the ongoing subordination—the dependency—upon the crown and the parent state of whatever polities resulted. Expropriating the Hakluyts' aspirations for the creation of an English New World settlement empire that would rival that of the Spanish, the Virginia

---

31. Ibid., 572, 583–586, 621–622.
32. Ibid., 564–565, 572–574, 586.

Company, through the publicity and promotional literature it generated, certainly succeeded, as Craven emphasized, in defining Virginia "as an instrument for the achievement of national ends," thereby turning a non-state-supported settlement into a national undertaking and establishing a tradition that, in large measure, applied to imperial conceptions of all subsequent settler colonies.[33]

But this achievement raised the serious questions of how, precisely, American settler colonies could be subordinated to the parent state and what the exact role of the state should be in shaping the wider empire. As we have seen, the crown's passive approach to colonial governance in the wake of the royalization of Virginia essentially left the principal agency in shaping the metropolitan-colonial relationship in the hands of the settlers themselves. If, however, as Adam Smith remarked, the English colonies "were for a long time in a great measure neglected" by the parent state, he did not think that the English empire in America was "the worse in consequence of this neglect." Encouraged by the ease of land acquisition and the fertility of the soil, large numbers of immigrants flowed into Virginia and new West Indian colonies after 1625 and into New England throughout the 1630s. Lightly monitored, settlers everywhere created functional societies that "for some time" constituted virtually free trade zones with the "liberty to sell their produce where[ver] they pleased," and, as Smith reported, "became in the course of little more than thirty or forty years (between 1620 and 1660) so numerous and thriving a people, that the shopkeepers and other traders of England wished to secure to themselves the monopoly of their custom" and to persuade the English state that such valuable entities should be put under tighter supervision.[34]

In pursuit of these two objectives, English commercial interests enjoyed the most success. As Smith stressed, England was already "a great trading country" before the colonial trade was very considerable and before the "commercial revolution" that would over the last four decades of the seventeenth century turn "London into a great international entrepôt" and England into a formidable naval power had been fully accomplished. Nevertheless, mercantile interests were already sufficiently influential to persuade the king's ministers "to devise and carry out a more coherent colonial policy" that, following the example of other European states with American empires, included systematic restrictions upon many English colonial trades with rival countries. "Without pretending... that they had paid any part, either of the original purchase-money, or of the subsequent expence of improvement" for any of the colonies, English merchants,

33. Ibid., 614; Craven, *Southern Colonies in the Seventeenth Century*, 60–62.
34. Smith, *Wealth of Nations*, ed. Campbell and Skinner, II, 568, 614.

Smith sardonically observed, successfully "petitioned the parliament that the cultivators of America might for the future be confined to their shop."[35]

Until the end of the Seven Years' War a century later, England's limited bureaucratic and naval resources prevented the wholesale enforcement of the resulting Navigation Acts in the face of significant colonial opposition and evasion. However, as after 1690 more and more settlers found ways to work profitably within the British mercantile system, usually violating it only when it was patently against their immediate economic interests, and as the British Parliament enacted measures of immediate economic benefit to the colonies, such as subsidies for the production of various items or relaxation of trade restrictions for the benefit of specific colonial staples, colonial opposition to the navigation system declined. By the middle of the eighteenth century, the vast majority of colonial traders were operating within that system, albeit, as Smith emphasized, British merchants had either initiated or endorsed all such beneficial changes. Always the "principal advisers" on all matters involving the Navigation Acts, merchants, he said, had so much influence with the government that the "maintenance of this monopoly" had "hitherto been the principal, or more properly perhaps the sole end and purpose of the dominion which Great Britain assumes over the colonies." This monopoly, he insisted, had been "the principal badge" of the colonists' "dependency" and was "the sole fruit which has hitherto been gathered from that dependency." "Whatever expence Great Britain has hitherto laid out in maintaining" the economic subordination of the colonies, he charged, ignoring important strategic objectives that emerged during the 1730s, "has really been laid out in order to support this monopoly."[36]

The English state's efforts to bring settler colonies under closer political supervision were less effective. The fragmented and loose character of the many transatlantic polities established in and across the Atlantic would never fully conform to metropolitan visions of imperial organization as they took shape after 1660, and the resulting disparity between structure and theory stimulated over the following century periodic demands on the part of metropolitan agents and exponents for the redefinition and reconstruction of empire. The recurrence of such demands registered a deep and abiding unease about the long-range consequences of the failure of metropolitan efforts at centralization and betrayed a mounting conviction that the continuing viability of empire required tighter metropolitan oversight. Even after the creation in 1696 of the Board of Trade to collect better information about the colonies and to provide direc-

---

35. Ibid., 597, 614; Andrews, *Trade, Plunder, and Settlement*, 360–362.
36. Smith, *Wealth of Nations*, ed. Campbell and Skinner, II, 582, 584, 614–615.

tion to the Privy Council and colonial governors, distance and the small size and inattention of the imperial bureaucracy made it very difficult to persuade, much less compel, settler leaders to change their ways. In contrast to the Roman colonies or even Ireland, Smith noted, the "great distance" of the American colonies "from Europe has in all of them alleviated more or less the effects of" their "dependency." "Their situation has placed them less in the view and less in the power of their mother country. In pursuing their interest their own way, their conduct has, upon many occasions, been over-looked, either because not known or not understood in Europe; and upon some occasions it has been fairly suffered and submitted to, because their distance rendered it difficult to restrain it."[37]

As was the case with their internal governance and use of their English inheritance to structure the social and legal regimes in their respective polities, settlers had a powerful role in determining how those polities would be attached to the empire and how the boundaries between metropolitan and overseas provincial authority would be negotiated. Throughout the early history of the English / British empire, the American settler colonies had been bound to the parent state, not by coercion, nor by the relatively rare exertions of metropolitan military or naval might, but by the settlers' voluntary attachment, an attachment that was deeply rooted in a shared cultural, legal, political, and religious inheritance and continually reinforced by a long history of mutually beneficial commercial interactions and that facilitated a remarkable degree of colonial allegiance to the parent state.

IN ADAM SMITH'S VIEW, THE ENGLISH GOVERNMENT HAD ACQUIRED a settler empire on the cheap. "For some of her subjects, who found themselves uneasy at home," he wrote, "England purchased . . . a great estate in a distant country" for a "very small" price, amounting "to little more than the expence of the different equipments which made the first discovery, reconnoitred the coast, and took a fictitious possession of the country." Not until the decades after 1730, when the importance of the colonial trades to Britain's domestic economy and naval might was becoming ever more obvious, the competition for American empire with Spain and France more intense, and the colonies were well on the road to being what Smith called the "splendid and showy equipage of the empire," did the British state invest heavily in expanding and preserving its settlement empire in America, spending large sums to establish buffer colonies in Georgia (1734) and Nova Scotia (1749) and fighting a series of intercolonial

37. Ibid., 567.

wars. With very few exceptions after 1734, Saint John (Prince Edward Island) being one, the British state, not authorized private agents, took the lead in establishing new settlement colonies. During the previous century, however, the English state like all "the European governments" of countries having settlement colonies in the Americas, Smith contended, took little role in and deserved little credit for either "the original establishment, or, so far as concerns their internal government," for "the subsequent prosperity of" its American colonies.[38]

Limited fiscal resources precluded any possibility of the state's contributing to the costs of settler colonization and along with limited administrative resources prevented it from providing close oversight over distant colonies even after it had assumed responsibility for administering them. Crown-authorized private adventurers—commercial companies or landed proprietors—performed many valuable roles. Promoting non-state-sponsored settlement as a national undertaking that would enhance the glory of the English nation, the Virginia Company first encountered and at least partially resolved many of the problems that confronted every attempt at settler colonization. It provided a substantial proportion of the start-up costs, subsidized economic experiments to find products that would provide the necessary economic foundations for a successful colony, and devised the land-distribution policies and form of consensual governance that would attract English settlers.

Ultimately, however, it was the settlers themselves upon whom devolved the primary responsibility for resolving the many problems that they faced. Along with whatever labor they could acquire, they took possession of the land, cleared it, farmed it, tended to the domestic animals, and provided the food necessary to feed themselves, and they developed and produced the commodities to exchange for the trade goods they needed from England and to turn a profit for themselves. By means of savings, borrowings, and their own industry, they provided most of the capital needed to build and sustain a settlement colony. They paid for their own internal governance and their own defense. They devised the policies and provided the force necessary to rid the territories they coveted of indigenous peoples. They constructed and refined the bound labor systems they used to pursue their economic goals and thereby stimulated the servant and African slave trades that provided much of the labor that accounted for their rapid expansion and that was so profitable to English traders. Exercising their inherited rights as English people, they modeled their systems of representative government and law to enable them to protect the property they were creating, to pass that property along with their estates to their descendants, to regulate

---

38. Ibid., 588–589, 614, 946.

social and political relations within the localities, and otherwise to adapt English legal, religious, and social norms and other aspects of their cultural inheritance to meet the radically different physical conditions they found in their respective areas of settlement. From the 1660s on, they successfully resisted metropolitan efforts to weaken the institutions and traditions of provincial self-governance that they had created during their early decades and in the process devised a credible constitutional defense for so doing.

Using the ease of land acquisition and the freedom of action that flowed from landownership, settlers pursued an energetic course of expansion, rustication, wealth accumulation, demographic growth, and civic empowerment that would have been impossible for most of them had they remained on the eastern side of the Atlantic. They created societies that were English to the core but in many respects differed fundamentally from those anywhere in the British Isles. Nowhere in the home islands was landownership so widely distributed, did marriage routinely occur at such an early age, was the birth rate and population growth so high, was there "No oppressive aristocracy," was civic participation "so nearly democratical," were legislative representatives and magistrates so influenced by their constituents, and were "manners ... more republican." Such societies, as Craven has remarked, "would exert an increasingly strong attraction on the men of Europe."[39]

If for so many free and mostly white settlers the overseas colonies that they created had fulfilled their expectations, the English settlement colonies in America, beginning with Virginia, had also turned out to be enormously beneficial for the English state, contributing to its ascendence to the first power in Europe by the end of the Seven Years' War. For the "merchants and manufacturers of the mother country," expanding colonial trades through the century from 1660 to 1760 had been a major element in raising, in Adam Smith's words, "the mercantile system to a degree of splendor and glory which it could never otherwise have attained" and, along with the African and Asian trades, in making the "commercial towns of" not just Great Britain but all of Europe "the manufacturers for the numerous and thriving cultivators of America, and the carriers, and in some respects the manufacturers too, for almost all the different nations of Asia, Africa, and America."[40]

But Smith was also deeply aware that settler colonization had exacted a high price from the indigenous peoples caught up in it. "To the natives ... both of the East and West Indies, all the commercial benefits which can have resulted

---

39. Ibid., 585, 645, 944–945; Craven, *Southern Colonies in the Seventeenth Century*, 136.
40. Smith, *Wealth of Nations*, ed. Campbell and Skinner, II, 532.

from" European expansion into their territories had "been sunk and lost in the dreadful misfortunes which they have occasioned." When settler colonization got under way, he wrote, "the superiority of force happened to be so great on the side of the Europeans, that they were enabled to commit with impunity every sort of injustice in those remote countries." Curiously, in condemning slave labor as less productive than free, he showed in the *Wealth of Nations* no such concern for the injustices inflicted on the millions of Africans that Europeans bought in Africa and transported to America, where settlers subjected them to the most brutal and dehumanizing forms of enslavement.[41]

Whatever its mixed and differential results for those who participated in it, the emergence and development of the English settler American empire analyzed by Adam Smith seventeen decades after 1607 was a major development in the history of the western hemisphere and the Atlantic world. By identifying the salient features of the English style of settler colonization as they had taken shape over those decades, Smith called attention to the several problems that had confronted the colonizing movement from the very start and to the agents responsible for working out the solutions that shaped and defined the character of the settler empire that they created.

The central argument of this essay has been that the Virginia colony, as England's first sustained experience with long-distance settler colonization, played a foundational role as a testing ground or learning laboratory, identifying, confronting, and working out solutions to the many problems that settler colonizers throughout the Anglo-American world encountered as they created new societies. Not all colonies, as Man has shown in his examination of their political institutions, were directly influenced by Virginia precedents, of course. In grappling with the common problems of settlement colonization, each colony worked out solutions specific to its own situation, creating provincial distinctions to which later generations proudly and tenaciously clung. However, because each new colony responded to the same problems in similar ways, these distinctions were functionally similar from one colony to another and faded into the general style of English colonizing limned by Smith and outlined above. This style, first exhibited in Virginia, produced the powerful and highly successful settler empire that observers such as Smith would subsequently find so astonishing and in which they would take such pride. In the history of the English / British empire and in the histories of the American Republic, Canada, Australia, New Zealand, South Africa, and other nations emerging out of that empire and deeply informed by it, this achievement must be the most important feature of the legacy of 1619.

41. Ibid., 626.

Notes on the Contributors

NICHOLAS CANNY is Established Professor of History, Emeritus, at the National University of Ireland, Galway. He edited the first volume of *The Oxford History of the British Empire* (Oxford, 1998) and, with Philip D. Morgan, *The Oxford Handbook of the Atlantic World, c.1450–c.1850* (Oxford, 2011). His major monograph is *Making Ireland British, 1580–1650* (Oxford, 2001). The book he is currently writing, also for Oxford, is *Imagining Ireland's Pasts: Early Modern Ireland through the Centuries*.

MISHA EWEN is research fellow in political economy, University of Manchester. She completed her Ph.D. at University College London and has also worked at the University of Kent. Her research focuses on colonization in the Atlantic world and its impact on society in early modern England. Her current project investigates the role of women in English overseas expansion between 1550 and 1650.

ANDREW FITZMAURICE is professor of history at the University of Sydney. He will be Professor of the History of Political Thought at Queen Mary University of London from 2020. He is the author, most recently, of *Sovereignty, Property, and Empire, 1500–2000* (Cambridge, 2014).

JACK P. GREENE is Andrew W. Mellon Professor in the Humanities, Emeritus, Johns Hopkins University.

PAUL D. HALLIDAY is Julian Bishko Professor of History and Professor of Law at the University of Virginia.

ALEXANDER B. HASKELL is associate professor of history at the University of California, Riverside. He is the author of *For God, King, and People: Forging Commonwealth Bonds in Renaissance Virginia* (Williamsburg, Va., and Chapel Hill, N.C., 2017). His current research focuses on changing patterns of governance in seventeenth-century English America.

JAMES HORN is president of the Jamestown Rediscovery Foundation (Preservation Virginia) at Historic Jamestowne. He is the author and editor of seven books, including, most recently, *1619: Jamestown and the Forging of American Democracy* (New York, 2018).

MICHAEL J. JARVIS is associate professor of Atlantic and digital history and director of a Digital Media Studies program at the University of Rochester. He runs two historical archaeology field schools based in Bermuda and Ghana that focus on material maritime circum-Atlantic exchange and connections, circa 1482–1835. His forthcoming *Atlantic Crucible: Bermuda and the Beginnings of English America, 1609–1684* (Johns Hopkins Press) provides more-detailed coverage of race, settlement, and intercolonial linkages in seventeenth-century Bermuda.

PETER C. MANCALL, Andrew W. Mellon Professor of the Humanities at the University of Southern California, is the author of six books, including *Hakluyt's Promise: An Elizabethan's Obsession for an English America* (New Haven, Conn., 2007), *Fatal Journey: The Final Expedition of Henry Hudson—A Tale of Mutiny and Murder in the Arctic* (New York, 2009), and *Nature and Culture in the Early Modern Atlantic* (Philadelphia, 2018).

PHILIP D. MORGAN is Harry C. Black Professor of History at Johns Hopkins University. He is presently working on a history of the early Caribbean.

MELISSA N. MORRIS is assistant professor of history at the University of Wyoming. She is working on a book about the early tobacco trade in the Atlantic world and its relationship to the nascent English, French, and Dutch empires.

PAUL MUSSELWHITE is assistant professor of history at Dartmouth College. His research focuses on the political and economic thought that lay behind the emergence of the plantation system. He is the author of *Urban Dreams, Rural Commonwealth: The Rise of Plantation Society in the Chesapeake* (Chicago, 2019) and co-editor of *Empire of the Senses: Sensory Practices of Colonialism in Early America* (Boston, 2018).

JAMES D. RICE is the Walter S. Dickson Professor of History at Tufts University. His publications include *Nature and History in the Potomac Country: From Hunter-Gatherers to the Age of Jefferson* (Baltimore, 2009) and *Tales from a Revolution: Bacon's Rebellion and the Transformation of Early America* (New York, 2012).

LAUREN WORKING is a historian on "Travel, Transculturality, and Identity in England, 1550–1700," a project funded by the European Research Council at the University of Liverpool. Her interest in Anglo-Algonquian history and heritage have led to fellowships at the Jamestown archaeological site and the Royal Anthropological Institute at the British Museum, London.

Index

Page numbers in italics refer to illustrations.

Abenakis, 34
Accomacs, 216, *218*, 219–222, 231–233
Acuña, Diego Sarmiento de. *See* Gondomar, Count
Admiralty law, 36, 237, 244, 254
Adventurers, private: as investors, 46–47, 154, 170, 187, 203, 210; concerns about, 176–177, 179–181, 196–199, 202; and state formation, 286–288, 304–305
Africa: West Central, 14–15, 101–105 (*see also* Angola); Gold Coast, 102–103
Africans, 16, 90, 97–98, 100–106, 131. *See also* Slave trade
African-Virginians, 97, 104–105, 253–254; charter generation of, 3, 11, 14, 16, 85–86, 97, 101, 108, 122, 236–237
Agriculture, commercial, 11, 95, 150, 152–153, 157–158, 166, 171–172. *See also* Tobacco
Ajacán, 38, 270
Algonquians, 38, 40, 217, 220, 222; and English political culture, 42–45, 47–49, 51–56, 58–59. *See also individual peoples*
Amadas, Philip, 32, 260, 266
Amazon Company, 20, 256, 258, 275–279
Amazon River, 256, 257, 265, 277, 280
Ambergris, 110
Andrews, Charles McLean, 282
Andrews, Kenneth, 283–284
Anglo-America, black, 85, 108
Anglo-Indian relations, 4, 58, 220, 225, 235, 271, 280–281, 289–290; through trade, 11, 39–40, 70, 78, 84, 112, 217–220, 227, 258, 263; and scarcity, 265–266. *See also* Anglo-Powhatan wars; *individual peoples*
Anglo-Powhatan wars: First (1609), 1, 40, 216, 221, 222; Second (1622), 14, 52–55,
73, 79–81, 93, 166–167, 171, 232–234, 290; Third (1644), 79, 234–235
Angola, 11, 14, 85, 101–104, 122, 126–127
Arawaks, 257, 269–270
Argall, Samuel, 1, 10–11, 18, 176, 189–191, 217; manorial system of, 152, 159–163, 165–168, 171; and Algonquians, 221, 223, 225–227
Argall Town, *8*, 161–162
Artisans: recruitment of, 3, 62, 71, 74, 111, 114, 118, 136–137, 263
Asiento, 102
Atlantic world: Virginia's impact on, 12, 21, 87, 150, 307; and Guiana colonization, 279–280

Bacon, Francis, 51, 71, 166–167
Bailyn, Bernard, 31, 68
Barbados, 63, 94–95, 117n, 245n, 298–299
Barbour, Philip, 201
Bargrave, John, 156, 167–168, 206–207
Barlowe, Arthur, 32, 260, 266
Berkeley Town and Hundred, *8*, 137, 165, 169, 250
Bermuda (Somers Islands), 6, 10, 12, 15–16, 108–132, 188–190, 288, 294; and slave labor, 87, 93, 96, 115; comparison of, with Virginia, 109–111, 113, 118, 130–132. *See also* Bermudians, black
Bermuda City, *8*, 159–160, 162
Bermuda Company (Somers Islands Company), 111–116, 120, 122–123, 125–130, 160, 163, 208, 213
Bermuda Nether Hundred, 3, *8*
Bermudians, black, 108, 114–120, 130–132, 253; ambiguous status of, 123–129
Berrío, Antonio de, 261–262, 268–269, 271
Bight of Benin, 102–103

Bight of Biafra, 102–103
Black James (African), 117, 127–128
Black Legend, 266
Bodin, Jean, 177, 180–181, 192
Body politic, 146, 148; corporations as, 18, 193–195, 197, 199; Virginia Company as, 175n, 201–206, 212–214
Boroughs, corporate: in England, 151, 157, 159, 164, 167; in Virginia (*see* Corporate plan)
Botero, Giovanni, 177–178, 198–199
Bound labor, 87, 94–95, 129, 169, 295, 305; as essential to commonwealth, 135, 137, 148–149. *See also* Indentured servants; Slavery
Boyse, John, 173, 174n, 186
Bradford, William, 260
Brandon Plantation. *See* Martin's Brandon
Brase, 236–238, 246–247, 252–255
Brazil, 99–100, 102, 256, 259, 280
Brewster, Edward, 190
Bridewell house of correction, 133–134, 137, 140–142, 144–145
Brooke, Christopher, 55–56
Brownists, 206–207
Burke, William, 284
Butler, Nathaniel, 87, 122–126, 166

Cabot, John and Sebastian, 27, 29, 283
Cannibalism, 29, 37, 261
Caribbean: raiding in, 7, 15–16, 116–117, 122–123, 189, 236, 262; British colonies in, 62, 87, 100, 279–280, 285, 296, 306–307; slavery in, 94–99, 101, 123; Spanish presence in, 96, 102, 108, 123, 283
"Caribes," 259, 269–270, 273
Carleton, Dudley, 55, 58, 148
Cartier, Jacques, 28, 30
Catholicism, 48, 60, 76–79, 83, 151, 275; English antagonism toward, 58, 176, 178, 189–190, 266. *See also* Spain
Cattle, 3, 97, 114, 117, 161, 175, 228; in public resources, 18, 175, 189–191
Cavendish, William, 16–17, 204, 207–213
Cecil, Robert. *See* Salisbury, first earl of
Challons, Henry, 34–35
Chamberlain, John, 4, 6, 46–47, 51, 54–55
Charles I, 56–57, 79, 279

Chartered companies, 18, 45, 140, 149, 258, 273, 287; and political discourse, 193–195, 197, 212–214
Chichester, Arthur, 13, 45–46
Chickahominies, 52, 68, 217, 218, 219, 222, 225, 231–232
Children: pauper, as labor, 17, 133–137, 139–144, 148; Indian, 19, 43, 51, 93, 146, 234; African, 86, 119, 127
Christianity, 91–92; converts to, 1, 5, 6, 80, 130, 239, 266. *See also* Catholicism; Protestantism
Churches, colonial, 5, 50, 111–112, 121–122, 130
Citizens, corporate, 160, 163, 166, 195, 203, 209–210, 213
Civility, 4, 57; and indigenous savagery, 14, 47–52, 80–82
Climate, 37, 112, 296; and Guiana colonization, 258, 265, 281, 284
Coke, Edward, 239–240
Colombia, 261–262
Colonization, English, 11, 77; and indigenous conversion, 4–6, 13, 17, 19, 31–32, 39, 42–43, 49–50; Virginia as prototype for, 21, 57–58, 284, 287–289; failures of, 26–27, 33, 35, 40, 258–259, 263–265; social benefits of, 31–32, 134, 149; and indigenous subordination, 39, 44–45, 48, 57, 63; visions of, 175–183, 187, 197, 280–281. *See also* Guiana
Columbus, Christopher, 27, 261
Commerce: and colonial purpose, 14, 112, 183, 186–187, 287; regulation of, 150–153, 165–167, 171 (*see also* Profit)
Commission for the Remedy of Defective Titles, 66, 69
Commodities, 23, 34, 77, 272, 276–277, 293. *See also* Flax; Gold; Pearls; Tobacco
Common Council, Court of, 134, 141–143, 148
Common good, 139, 147, 156, 213; and profit, 150, 152, 157–158, 165; versus private interests, 159, 172, 194, 199, 206, 208. *See also* Public resources
Common law: in Virginia, 50, 52, 58, 67; in Ireland, 66; in Bermuda, 128–129; and General Court decisions, 238–239, 241, 243–244, 247–248

Commonwealth, 9, 11–12, 16–18, 58; Christian, 6, 110, 112, 122, 181; dependence of, on migration, 134, 136–139, 147–149; and public resources, 152–153, 157, 172; as "the public," 175, 177, 180, 188, 192, 205; Virginia Company as microcosm of, 182–183, 185, 199, 201–204, 206, 214; as corporation, 194–195, 197; moral philosophy of, 196–199, 208, 211, 213
Conquest, 39, 43, 49, 53, 57, 176, 197, 200; of Ireland, 62, 66–67, 81–82, 291; by Portugal, 102, 104
Constitutions, 110, 202, 208, 212–213, 241, 299–300
Contempt: prosecution of, 246, 248–250
Coombs, John, 85, 105–106
Corn, 3, 110, 127, 143, 158, 225, 228, 295; in public resources, 125, 175, 189–191; in Anglo-Indian relations, 216–217, 219, 221, 223, 229–230
Corporate plan, 10, 17, 158–160, 162–172. *See also* Sandys, Edwin
Corporations. *See* Body politic; Corporate plan
Corruption, 206; avoidance of, 192, 199, 204–205, 213
Cosmographies, 25, 28
Council for New England, 140
Council of State, 53, 192, 203, 241. *See also* General Assembly
Court of King's Bench, 66, 212, 243–245, 255n
Courts, county, 239, 241–242
Craftsmen. *See* Artisans
Cranfield, Lionel, 187, 189
Craven, Wesley Frank, 107, 174, 282–283, 287–288, 292, 296–297, 302, 306
Cromwellian era, 62–63, 83, 287, 291
Cumaná, 259, 262, 268, 271–272
Custom, 40, 45, 49, 97, 244, 299. *See also* Customary law
Customary law, 19, 237, 239–241, 246–255
Customs revenue, 11, 180, 182, 187

Dale, Thomas, 1–4, 55, 68, 113, 158–160, 162, 205, 292, 296; *Lawes Divine, Morall, and Martiall*, 242–243
Dalton, Michael, 245
Danvers, John, 139, 147–148

Davies, John, 48, 60, 65–67, 71, 73, 81–82
Davis, John, 33–34, 36
De Bry, Theodor, 32, 33, 260
De La Warr, third Baron (Thomas West), 5, 160, 190
Democracy, 207, 209–214
Devereux, Robert. *See* Essex, second earl of
Digges, Dudley, 204
"Discourse of the Old Company" (1625), 56
Discourses, 18, 31, 44, 80, 175n, 193–194, 198–202, 204–207, 209–212. *See also* Savage: in English political discourse
Disease: among indigenous peoples, 39–40, 93, 100; among colonists, 40, 46, 136, 140, 166
Donne, John, 134n, 146, 185
Downing, Abigail, 138
Drake, Francis, 97–98, 112
Duty Boys, 137

Eastern Shore, 97, 216, 219–222, 226–229, 232–234
East India Company: English, 45, 118, 184, 194–195, 213; Dutch, 194, 197–198
Eburne, Richard, 147
Economic diversification, 2, 161, 167, 191, 204, 227–228; in Bermuda, 112, 114–115
Education: of Indian youth, 4, 146, 228; through pauper apprenticeships, 143, 144
El Dorado, 268, 271–272
Elfrith, Daniel, 85–86, 116, 122, 126, 128, 189
Elizabeth I, 27, 30, 71, 179–180, 273
Elizabeth City, 51, 162
Elliott, J. H., 274
Eltis, David, 91, 94
Empire, English / British: Virginia legacies for, 12, 20, 44n, 149, 150, 238, 254–255; character of, 282–286, 289–290, 292, 295, 301–307
Enclosure, 156–157, 171
England: political culture of, 42–44, 55–58; and early slaving practices, 102–103, 126; relations of, with Spain, 111, 116, 189, 194, 202, 258, 273–274, 279; poverty and vagrancy in, 140–141, 144–145, 148; agricultural changes in, 151, 156–157, 172;

legal practices in, 238–239, 243–245, 251. *See also* London
Essex, second earl of (Robert Devereux), 179, 188
Establishmentarianism, 178, 188–189
Exclusion of Irish, 14, 75–76, 78, 81–84

Fabian, Robert, 27, 29
Famine: in Ireland, 63, 82; in Virginia, 154, 171, 265
Farrell, Gerard, 72, 75
Fausz, J. Frederick, 226
Ferrar, John, 16, 46, 129–130, 175, 208
Ferrar, Nicholas, 16, 46, 190n
"Firsts," 3n, 9, 44, 110, 113, 154, 171n, 237, 263; and slavery, 85, 93–94, 106, 108, 128, 130
Flax, 77, 228, 263
Flight of the earls, 45, 70–71
France: and imperial competition, 25, 30, 33, 274, 304; as Catholic monarchy, 73, 275; in South America, 256, 262, 271–272, 277–278, 281
Francisco (African), 117–118, 127–128
Freedom dues, 135, 143
Freeholders: in Ireland, 69, 71; in Virginia, 158, 163, 169, 172, 292–293, 296
Free trade, 164, 169–170, 302
Frobisher, Martin, 29, 33, 34
Fur trade, 30, 32, 227–229, 231

Gates, Thomas, 109, 153, 167, 205, 245–246
General Assembly, 148, 152, 203, 296–297, 299; context of, 18, 162, 168–169, 173–176, 184, 188, 190–191, 201; first meeting of, 42, 135, 192, 215–216, 235, 241; House of Burgesses in, 50, 192, 224; and indigenous trade, 216, 221–222, 228–229
General Court, 19–20, 186; jurisdiction of, 241–250. *See also* Judges, General Court; Law making
Gilbert, Humphrey, 26, 29, 33, 35, 37, 176, 196, 260
Gold, 90, 100, 153, 272; reports of, 6, 11, 37, 153, 259–261, 275–276, 279
Goldman, William, 274
Gondomar, Count (Diego Sarmiento de Acuña), 258, 275–279
Gorges, Ferdinando, 34–35

Gray, Robert, 43, 47, 49, 146
"Greate Charter," 162, 215, 241, 248n, 292; reforms of, 164–165, 174, 184–185, 245–246, 250, 296. *See also* Yeardley, George: 1618 instructions for
Grotius, Hugo, 26, 197–198, 200
Guesthouses, 163, 168
Guiana, 6, 11, 13, 20, 45, 96, 256, 257, 258–281, 283; comparison of, with Virginia colony, 258, 265–268, 270–273, 281
Guiana Company, 279–280

Hakluyt, Richard, 12–13, 22–34, 37–38, 41, 103, 178, 284, 301; "Discourse of Western Planting," 27, 29–30, 38, 259–260
Hakluyt, Richard (the elder), 31–32
Hall, Thomas / Thomasine, 249
Hamor, Ralph, 2, 155, 158–159, 249
Harcourt, Robert, 264, 267, 269, 272, 276, 279
Harriot, Thomas, 22, 32, 38, 47–48, 260, 266
Harrison, James, 219, 222
Harwood, William, 171
Hawkins, John, 102–103, 262
Hayes, Edward and Thomas, 196–201
Headright system, 135, 169–170, 226, 292, 295, 297
Henrico, 8, 158, 159, 162
Henry, Prince of Wales, 47, 264, 275
Henry VIII, 65, 66
Heywood, Linda M., 15, 104
Hispaniola, 96, 99, 106, 117
Hobbes, Thomas, 194, 207n, 208, 211
Hooker, Richard, 178
Horning, Audrey, 74–75, 77
House of Burgesses. *See* General Assembly
Hudson, Henry, 36
Humanism, 138, 192, 198; civic, 157

Imbangala, 15, 102
Imperium, 44, 49, 56, 58–59, 176
Impositions, royal, 180–181
"Improvement," agricultural, 151, 156–157, 161, 163, 165, 168, 172, 294
Incorporation: of indigenous peoples, 5–6, 19, 42–43, 48, 59, 93, 289–290; of indigenous Irish, 60, 74–76, 78, 81–84; of English, 93, 220; of Africans in Virginia, 104–105. *See also* Intermarriage

Indebtedness, 72, 89, 92, 137, 161, 251
Indentured servants, 12, 17, 87, 128, 169–170, 249, 295, 305; replacement of, by slaves, 87, 92, 94–95; in Bermuda, 112–113, 125, 128; children and prisoners as, 133–140, 143, 147–149
Indentures, 129–130, 134–135, 143, 240n; assignability of, 250–253
Indigenous Irish: English perceptions of, 48, 62–63, 82–84. See also Exclusion of Irish
Indigenous peoples, 92–94; in Europe, 1, 4, 6, 27–29, 34, 43–44, 225, 263, 266–267, 270; internal politics of, 19, 216–217, 222, 229–235; early English encounters with, 27, 32–36, 47; and disease, 39–40, 93, 100; disinterest of, in assimilation, 68, 70, 77–78, 80, 84, 93; outrages against, 216–219, 222, 233, 234; in Guiana, 262–263, 265–272, 276, 280–281. See also Accomacs; Algonquians; Anglo-Indian relations; Chickahominies; Pamunkeys; Powhatans
Information, circulation of: on Western Hemisphere, 23, 26–30, 32–33, 37, 41, 264; on Virginia, 55–59; about enslaved Africans, 95–96; between Bermuda and Virginia, 131; about transportation of poor, 134, 140, 146–148. See also Promotional literature
Intermarriage, 1, 2, 4, 68, 74–75, 82–84
Inuit, 29, 34, 36
Iopassus (Patawomeck), 223, 229–231, 233–234
Ireland, 45–46, 64, 159, 264; and Old English, 48, 60, 151; comparison of, with Virginia plantation, 60–61, 67–70, 73–75, 77–79, 81–82, 84; flight from, 70–71, 73, 76, 78, 136. See also Protestantism: in Ireland
Irish insurrection, 61, 73–74, 76; comparison of, with Second Anglo-Powhatan war, 14, 79–81
Itoyatin (Powhatan), 8n, 19, 217–220, 223, 225–226, 229–235

Jamaica, 245n, 255, 287, 291, 299
James I, 57, 140, 166–167, 182n, 204, 213, 273–276; on Powhatan conversion, 5, 13, 49–50; and the Virginia Company, 51, 54–55, 175–176, 187, 191, 201–202, 206, 209, 212; and relations with Spain, 273–276
James River, 3, 38, 52, 59, 70, 73, 152, 219–220, 270
Jamestown, 9, 42–44, 50, 55, 192, 215, 218, 274, 282; conditions in, 46, 109, 135–138, 154, 160, 227–228, 265; Africans in, 85, 101 (see also African-Virginians); and Bermuda connection, 109, 111–112; and indigenous diplomacy, 216–217, 220–226, 230, 233–235, 289
Jamestown Rediscovery Team, 74
Jesuits (Society of Jesus), 35, 38, 49
Johnson, Robert, 161, 166, 178–179, 184–185, 206–208, 213; Nova Britannia, 146, 155
Joint-stock companies, 56–57, 111–112, 140, 194–195, 197, 199, 287–288; debate over, 152–155, 182–183. See also Virginia Company of London
Jones, Nathaniel, 236–238, 254
Jope, John Colyn, 85, 122
Jordan, Winthrop, 88, 92, 95–96, 105–108
Judges, General Court, 239, 242–243; and abuse of discretion, 19–20, 245–248, 251–253, 255; and conflicts of interest, 238, 247–249, 251, 254
Juries, 72, 247
Justices of the peace: in England, 141, 243–245

Kendall, Miles, 122–123, 125–126
Keymis, Lawrence, 263, 276
Kupperman, Karen Ordahl, 94, 294

Labor: demand for, 3, 11–12, 86–87, 106, 135, 148–149, 168, 295–296; incentives for, 77–78, 154–155, 158; authority over, 125, 238; specialized knowledge of (see Artisans; Bermudians, black). See also Servants; Slavery; Tenancy
Landownership
—in Bermuda, 10, 111, 120, 160, 163
—in Virginia: mixed public and private, 10, 162–165; competing visions for, 17, 150, 152, 156–160, 169–172, 204–205; and resource use, 77, 200; and deed

registration, 247–248; as pattern for settlement colonies, 292–293, 306
—in Ireland, 66–67, 69–70, 72, 151, 157
Larratt, William, 133–134, 144–145
Law making: as General Court innovation, 236–237, 241, 246–253; official instructions concerning, 241, 243–246, 248n, 250
Law of nations, 197–198, 200
Leigh, Charles, 260, 263–264, 269–270
Levant Company, 45, 195, 283
Livestock, 63, 70, 77, 125, 128, 219, 292. See also Cattle
Locke, John, 200
London (England), 194, 302; natives in, 1, 4, 6, 29, 34, 43–44, 225, 266–267; culture of civility in, 4–5, 47, 49, 52–53, 55, 57, 59; and the poor, 17, 133, 140–143, 146–147; consumption in, 116, 118
Lorimer, Joyce, 277
Luanda, 15, 85, 100, 104, 122

Macarnesse, Thomas, 43–44
Mac Cuarta, Brian, 77
Machiavelli, Niccolò, 193, 198
Magazine, 156, 161, 164, 166–167, 185–186, 191, 206, 208
Man, Thomas Yunlong, 298–299, 307
Manorial estates, 17, 152, 160–161, 163, 167–169, 171–172. See also Argall, Samuel
Manteo (Croatan Island), 266, 270
Maps, 30, 74–75, 220, 274
Margarita Island, 115, 262, 268, 273
Maroons, 97–98, 115n
Martial law, 239, 243–244, 249; imposition of, by Thomas Dale, 2, 154, 158–159, 242, 296; revocation of, 50, 135; in Ireland, 66, 69; in Bermuda, 113
Martin, John, 11, 159–161, 167–169, 215–222, 228, 234–235
Martin's Brandon, 8, 161, 167, 169, 215–217, 218
Martin's Hundred, 8, 171, 173
Mayflower Compact, 110
Menard, Russell, 95
Mercantilism, 302–303
Merchant Adventurers of London, 187
Merchants: and Atlantic investment, 11, 20, 95, 111, 131, 153–154, 283; in Virginia Company leadership, 50, 164, 166 (see also Smythe, Thomas); mistrust of, 155–156, 180–185
"Mere" Irish. See Indigenous Irish
Migration: to Chesapeake, 62, 292–293, 302; forced, 63, 134–136, 139–140, 142–145, 148–149, 252; to Bermuda, 111, 118, 123
Miller, Joseph, 104
Mines: search for, 3, 32, 37, 47, 263–264, 274, 277, 279
Monopoly, 16, 197, 303. See also Magazine
Moore, Richard, 110–113, 115
Morgan, Edmund, 98, 193
Muscovy Company, 45, 195, 283

Naming: of towns, 51, 58; and personhood, 253
Natural histories, 22–23, 28, 41
Natural resources: and abundance, 30, 32, 34, 37, 260–261, 265, 276–277; neglect of, as argument for dispossession, 62, 71, 77, 80–81. See also Commodities
Navigation Acts, 303
Netherlands, 100, 102, 194, 197–198; in South America, 256, 262–265, 267–269, 271–272, 277–278
Newce, Christopher, 170
New England, 34–35, 46, 57, 94, 140, 206, 288, 300–301
Newfoundland, 6, 30, 33, 40, 57, 196, 283
Newport, Christopher, 67–68
Nobility: proposals for, 52, 61, 65
Nonconformity: fears of, 42, 50, 178, 191, 206–207
North, Roger, 258, 276–279
Northeast Passage, 36
Northwest Passage, 29, 32–33, 35–36, 46, 153
Norwood, Richard, 120, 121

Occohannocks, 218, 219–220
O'Malley, Gregory E., 103, 105
Opechancanough (Powhatan), 1, 6, 79, 217, 219, 221–227, 229–235; and Second Anglo-Powhatan war (1622), 226, 231–233
Oral testimony, 247, 251–252

Origins debate, 9. *See also* Jordan, Winthrop
Orinoco River, 34, 96, 257, 259, 261, 275–276
"Othering," 4, 45, 83, 90, 238–239
Ottoman Empire, 89–90

Pamunkey (town), 224, 226
Pamunkey River, 58, 224
Pamunkeys, 52, *218*, 226–227, 232
Paquiquineo (Algonquian), 38, 270
Parishes, Anglican: and forced migration, 135, 140–147
Patawomecks, 216, *218*, 223, 229–231, 233–234, 271, 293
Patent, 69, 171, 215, 247, 260–261, 264, 279; letters, for Virginia Company, 54–55, 182, 187–188, 209, 212, 273–274
Pauper apprenticeship, 17, 134, 139–145, 149
Pearls, 26, 37, 58, 114–116, 260–262
Pernambuco, 100
Philip II, 268
Philip III, 272–274, 278
Piersey, Abraham, 86, 242, 252n
Pirates, 7, 27, 103, 105, 262; on Bermuda, 16, 116, 122–124
"Plantation": meaning of, 150, 152, 171–172
Plantations, particular, 17, 150–152, 163–166, 169, 171–172, 205
Plymouth colony, 20, 110, 206, 260, 279, 285
Pocahontas (Matoaka, Amonute), 1–2, 4–6, 40, 84, 217n, 221n, 223, 225, 293
Poole, Robert, 222–229, 234–235
Poor relief: in England, 140–141, 145
Popular government: discourses of, 18, 193, 201, 206–207, 209–212
Portugal, 27, 140; influence of, on slavery, 12, 88–90, 95–98; and slave trade, 14–16, 99–100, 103, 122, 198; and colonization of Africa, 15, 85, 102, 104; in South America, 256, 259, 265, 267–269, 271, 277, 280
Pory, John, 42, 58, 148–149, 166, 215–216, 227–229, 241; on indigenous relations, 219, 224, 226, 231–233
Potomac River, 216, 219, 222–223, 226, 229–230, 234
Powell, John, 116–117, 121, 123, 125, 237
Powhatan. *See* Wahunsonacock

Powhatan "massacre." *See* Anglo-Powhatan wars: Second; Opechancanough
Powhatans, 1, 4–6, 44, 58, 200, *218*, 265; and perception of Europeans, 6, 39–40, 220–221, 270–271; indigenous politics of, 220–226, 229, 231–235. *See also* Anglo-Powhatan wars; Itoyatin; Opechancanough; Pocahontas; Wahunsonacock
Prerogative, 125n, 201, 244, 298
Prisoners: as forced labor, 91, 94, 134, 149
Privateers, English, 236, 262; and stealing Africans, 14–16, 19, 85, 103–105, 125, 127; Bermuda as base for, 115, 122–123. *See also Sea Venture; Treasurer; White Lion*
Private land: in England, 151; in Bermuda, 120, *121*, 160; in Virginia (*see* Landownership)
Privy Council, 54, 57, 89, 142–143, 187, 212, 244, 278, 304
Profit, 2, 20, 109, 153–154, 174–175, 206; and common good, 61, 139, 152, 163, 185–186
Promotional literature: on colonization, 12–13, 28–30, 37; on transportation of the poor, 134, 140, 146–148; of Virginia Company, 153–155, 164, 183, 292, 302; on Guiana, 259–260, 263–264, 266, 279–281
Protestantism: and English colonization, 13–15, 19, 31–32, 39, 53; Nonconformity, 42, 50, 178, 191, 206–207; in Ireland, 60, 63, 69, 81, 83–84 (*see also* Ulster plantation); establishmentarianism, 178, 188–189; militant Puritanism, 188–190
Protestant Reformation, 30, 194
Providence Island, 93–94
Public good. *See* Common good
"Publick." *See* Public resources
Public resources, 18, 160, 173–175, 184–186; in Bermuda, 122–123, 125; from public lands, 162–164, 168, 192, 204–205; Warwick's raid on, 175–176, 188–191; role of, in colonization ideology, 176–183, 197–199
Public works: in Bermuda, 111, 114, 120; for infrastructure, 157, 163, 166, 168, 185
Punishments, colonial, 113, 120, 123–124, 130n, 190, 224, 242n, 248–249
Purchas, Samuel, 4, 25, 57

Quinn, David Beers, 26, 196
Quo warranto writ, 173, 174n, 212

Race, 105, 114, 131; conflation of, with slavery, 14, 88, 90, 97, 124–125; and indigenous difference, 82–84; in law, 93, 128, 239, 242n, 254–255
Ralegh, Walter, 34, 45, 47, 176, 179–180; in Guiana, 258, 260, 262–263, 275–277; and relations with natives, 266–269, 270–271, 281
Ramusio, Giovanni Battista, 28
Reason of state discourse, 18, 193–194, 198–200, 202, 204–205, 209–210, 214
"Reasons to Move the High Court of Parliament" (circa 1605–1606), 177, 180–183, 195–201
Reforms of 1618–1619. *See* "Greate Charter"
Representative government, 297–301, 305. *See also* General Assembly
Republics, 197, 201, 206–207, 210–212, 301, 306
Rich, Nathaniel, 53, 127, 130, 206
Rich, Robert (agent), 117, 120, 126
Rich, Robert. *See* Warwick, second earl of
Roanoke colony, 33, 47, 109, 180, 220, 260, 266, 285
Roe, Thomas, 264, 272–273
Rolfe, John, 85, 162n, 168, 185–186, 217, 222, 224–225, 230; "A True Relation of the State of Virginia," 1, 3, 6–7, 16, 159; and Pocahontas, 2, 4, 5, 21, 40, 84; and tobacco, 115, 157, 272, 293
Rolfe, Rebecca. *See* Pocahontas
Roman precedents, 48, 66, 194–195, 198, 200
Russia, 89, 91, 95

Sackville, Edward, 206
Sagadahoc, 35
Saint Christopher, 279–280
Saint George's, 111, 113–115, 117, 120–121, 125–126, 128–131
Salisbury, first earl of (Robert Cecil), 183–185, 188–189, 196; on Virginia colonization, 175–182
Saltworks, 3, 221, 227, 228
Sandys, Edwin, 11, 13, 16–18, 55, 183, 213, 288, 294; as Virginia Company leader, 7, 50, 54, 166–169, 174n, 206–208; corporate plan of, 10–11, 152, 161–165, 169–170; on Bermuda, 16, 112, 125, 126n; and forced labor, 135, 142, 145; as member of Parliament, 167, 178, 204; commonwealth vision of, 175–176; and defense of public resources, 184–189, 192, 205
San Tomé, 257, 261, 264, 269, 276
Savage: as "Indian," 6, 13, 35, 43, 53–54; as "other," 33, 44, 47–48, 90, 224; in English political discourse, 45, 48–50, 53–55
Savage, Thomas, 222–223, 226, 232, 234
Scotland, 27; and Ulster plantation, 45, 61–62, 70, 72, 75–76, 78–79; life bondage in, 89
Scott, John, 265, 280–281
Scottish Covenanters, 74, 79
Sea Venture (ship), 109, 110, 112, 115
Senegambia, 101–103
Separatists, 178, 207
Servants: black, 14, 18, 94, 126–128, 237, 242, 253; laws concerning, 20, 125, 128–129, 242–243, 246, 249–255; Irish, 63, 76, 83–84; white, 92, 94, 105, 189–191; in Bermuda, 105, 120–121, 126–127, 130
Seven Years' War, 285, 303, 306
Silk industry, 2, 37, 48, 51, 114, 136, 191, 227–228, 272–273
1619: signal events of, 9, 85, 216, 235–237, 258–259, 273; in longer perspective, 106, 108, 149, 307
Slavery: and language, 4, 88–89, 92, 97, 123–124; in law, 20, 93, 103, 238, 241–242, 246, 254–255; white, 85, 91–92, 124; early commitment to, in Virginia, 85–86, 100, 103, 105–107; in law, as chattel, 86, 92, 94, 125, 127, 149; and Iberian influences in Virginia, 88, 95–98, 106, 115; early modern, 89–91, 95, 124; in Barbados, 94–95; transition to, in Bermuda, 123–129
Slaves: status of, 86, 98, 123–124; skills of, 98, 115–119, 127–128, 130–132; African origins of, 101–105
Slave trade: Atlantic, 14, 87, 99–104; intercolonial, 104–105; as plunder, 108, 114–117, 122–124

Smith, Adam, 20, 285–286, 289, 291–296, 300–307
Smith, John, 6, 35–36, 43, 59, 164–165, 265, 285; and adoption ritual, 220–221; in Amazonia, 256, 260
Smith, Thomas (diplomat), 13–14
Smith, Thomas (merchant). *See* Smythe, Thomas
Smythe, Thomas, 2, 7, 161, 184–186, 204, 206, 208; and Bermuda, 16, 112, 115
Solow, Barbara, 106
Somers Islands. *See* Bermuda
Somers Islands Company. *See* Bermuda Company
South America: European interest in, 47, 258, 262–263, 271–272, 279–280. *See also* Guiana
Southampton, third earl of (Henry Wriothesley), 1–2, 50–51, 54, 175, 204, 206–207
Sovereignty: ideas of, 44, 56, 154, 176–177, 181, 194, 201, 286
Spain, 99–100, 108, 254, 286; in Chesapeake, 38–39, 270, 274; as refuge for Irish Catholics, 67, 71, 73–74, 76, 78; role of, in Atlantic slave trade, 87–88, 99–100; influence of, on slavery, 88, 95–98, 106, 115, 124–125; and diplomatic relations with England, 111, 116, 189, 194, 202, 258, 273–274, 279; claim of, to Americas, 199, 274–275, 278; and colonization of Guiana, 256, 259, 262–264, 271–272, 276–278; relations of, with indigenous peoples, 266–271, 281
Sparke, Michael, 140, 146
Spelman, Henry, 222–226, 229, 232, 234–235
State formation: and Virginia colonization, 44, 184, 187–188, 191, 282–283, 286; discourses of, 175n, 193–194, 198–200; divine sanction for, 177–178, 180–181, 183; and the Virginia Company, 203–205, 209–210
Strachey, William, 68, 184–185
Sugar cultivation, 99, 100, 102, 296; in Bermuda, 114, 121, 125; in Guiana, 277, 279
"Surrender and re-grant" system, 65, 68, 83
Symonds, William, 178

Taxation, 173–174, 180–181, 187, 192, 203, 296–301
Temple, John, 79–81, 83
Tenancy, 70, 137, 143, 157, 172, 190, 250; in Ireland, 62, 71, 73, 75–76, 78–79, 83–84; in Bermuda, 120, 126–130; in manorial model, 160–163, 166, 168–170
Thevet, André, 25, 28
Thirty Years' War, 91, 194–195, 204, 213
Thornton, John, 15, 104
Thorpe, George, 55, 140
Tobacco, 2, 3n, 9, 16, 40–41, 47, 96, 105, 293; labor needs for, 11, 84, 124, 136, 148, 295–296; in Guiana, 20, 96, 271–273; in Bermuda, 93, 110–112, 114–120, 129–130; as currency, 119, 127–128, 237, 240; implications of, for Virginia Company, 152–153, 155–158, 185, 208–209, 227; efforts to limit production of, 161, 163–164, 173, 191, 205
Topiawari, 267, 271
Topsell, Edward, 22–23, 24, 26, 41
Towhee, 23, 24, 26, 41
Towns, 145, 244; civilizing function of, 14, 51, 62; of Algonquians, 74, 167, 230, 232; incorporated (*see* Corporate plan)
Trading companies, 56, 156, 182–183, 187, 195, 211
Transportation. *See* Migration: forced
Travel narratives, 28–30. *See also* Promotional literature
Treasurer (ship), 1, 4, 11, 16, 85–86, 103, 122–123, 126, 189–190
Treaty of London, 273–274
Tribute, 25, 90, 190, 221, 225
Trinidad, 96, 259, 261–262, 267–269, 272, 275–276
Trinidad y Guayana, 259, 261, 268, 272, 277
Tsenacommacah, 38, 217, 218, 220, 227, 230–231, 233, 235
Tucker, Daniel, 112–114, 117, 120–125, 167
"20. and odd Negroes." *See* African-Virginians: charter generation of

Ulster plantation, 13–14, 60–61, 64, 70–78, 81–83, 284
Upper Guinea, 100–101
Uttamatomakkin (Powhatan), 1, 6, 225

"Vacant" land, 39, 63, 150, 168, 278, 292
Vagrancy: and forced migration, 42, 133–134, 140–142, 145–147
Vansina, Jan, 104
Vassalage, 65, 68
Vaughn, Alden T., 267
Venezuela, 34, 115–117, 256, 259, 261, 267, 269
Vereenigde Oost-Indische Compagnie (VOC). *See* East India Company: Dutch
Virginia: survival of, 4, 6–7, 21, 235, 274; area of, 8, 23, 31, 38 (*see also* Tsenacommacah); historical perspectives on, 9–10, 44n, 150, 171–172, 174, 241–242, 282; as improvement on English society, 12, 17, 20–21, 42, 57; early social conditions of, 42, 53, 105, 168, 203–204, 227, 265; as royal colony, 55, 287–288, 290, 302
Virginia, Council of, 46, 50, 182, 201–203, 243
Virginia Company of London, 2, 7, 39, 46, 187, 277–278, 301–302; as corporate commonwealth, 18, 154, 175, 182–183, 187, 193, 195, 199, 202–204, 214; charters of, 21, 54–56, 201–203, 206, 274, 288, 299; *True Declaration of the Estate of the Colonie in Virginia*, 36–37, 39, 145; and Bermuda charter, 109–111, 131; and promotion of migration, 134–135, 138–140, 142–145; and indigenous diplomacy, 225–227, 229, 231; factions in (*see* Argall, Samuel; Sandys, Edwin; Smythe, Thomas; Warwick, second earl of)
Virtue: in governance, 193, 195–196, 198, 200, 210, 213

Wahunsonacock (Powhatan), 19, 39–40, 44, 67–68, 217, 220–225, 231, 233; family of, 1, 4, 6. *See also* Opechancanough; Powhatans
Wales, 27, 61–62, 136, 203
Wanchese (Roanoke), 266
Warner, Thomas, 280
Warwick, second earl of (Robert Rich), 7, 10–11, 50, 160, 166, 170n, 206, 277; in Bermuda, 15–16, 96, 112, 116, 120, 122–123, 126–127, 131; raid of, on company resources, 18, 174n, 188–189, 190n, 191; Puritanism of, 176, 188–189. *See also* Argall, Samuel
Waterhouse, Edward, 52–53, 79–81, 92–93
Werowance, 57, 217, 220–223, 231–233, 266
West, Thomas. *See* De La Warr, third Baron
Western Hemisphere, 106, 307; title to, 27, 30, 52, 67–68, 200, 274, 278. *See also* Information, circulation of
West Indies. *See* Caribbean
Wheat, David, 15, 98, 102
Whiddon, Jacob, 262, 269
White, John, 23, 25, 26, 32–33, 260
Whitehead, Neil, 269
White Lion (ship), 1, 11, 16, 85–86, 94, 103–104, 122
Wiapoco (Oyapock) River, 263–264, 269, 276, 279
Wine making: project for, 227, 272–273
Withington, Phil, 139
Women, 86, 89, 95, 109, 265; indigenous, 1, 29, 68, 74, 84, 234 (*see also* Pocahontas); recruitment of, as essential to commonwealth, 9, 17, 136–139, 149, 166, 168, 294; Irish, 73, 83; among black Bermudians, 117, 119n, 123, 125–127
Wood, Andy, 240
Wriothesley, Henry. *See* Southampton, third earl of
Wyatt, Francis, 52–53, 55, 58, 237, 242, 246, 250, 254–255, 297

Yeardley, George, 54, 159, 215, 247, 249–250; 1618 instructions for, 10, 162–164, 188, 190–191, 203–204, 241, 250 (*see also* "Greate Charter"); and indigenous relations, 19, 58, 216–217, 221–224, 226–227, 230, 235; meeting of, with James I, 49–51, 191; and laborers, 86, 168, 237, 249n, 252, 255
York River, 38, 219, 220, 270

Zúñiga, Pedro de, 273–274